Letters of
William Wordsworth

Letters of
William Wordsworth

A New Selection

EDITED BY

ALAN G. HILL

Oxford   New York

OXFORD UNIVERSITY PRESS

1984

Oxford University Press, Walton Street, Oxford OX2 6DP

London Glasgow New York Toronto
Delhi Bombay Calcutta Madras Karachi
Kuala Lumpur Singapore Hong Kong Tokyo
Nairobi Dar es Salaam Cape Town
Melbourne Auckland

and associated companies in
Beirut Berlin Ibadan Mexico City Nicosia

Oxford is a trade mark of Oxford University Press

The text of the letters is taken from the six published volumes of The
Letters of William and Dorothy Wordsworth, second edition,
general editor Alan G. Hill, © Oxford University Press 1967, 1969,
1970, 1978, 1979, and 1982, and from the two forthcoming volumes

British Library Cataloguing in Publication Data

Wordsworth, William, 1770–1850
The letters of William Wordsworth.—(Oxford paperbacks)
1. Wordsworth, William, 1770–1850—Biography
2. Poets, English—19th century—Correspondence
I. Title   II. Hill, Alan G.
821'.7   PR5881
ISBN 0–19–281372–2

Library of Congress Cataloging in Publication Data

Wordsworth, William, 1770–1850.
The letters of William Wordsworth.
Bibliography: p.   Includes index.
1. Wordsworth, William, 1770–1850—Correspondence.
2. Poets, English—19th century—Correspondence.
I. Hill, Alan G. II. Title.
PR5881.A4 1984   821'.7 [B]   83–17309
ISBN 0–19–281372–2 (pbk.)

Set by Wyvern Typesetting Ltd.
Printed in Great Britain by
Richard Clay (The Chaucer Press) Ltd.
Bungay, Suffolk

Contents

*

List of Letters

*

Acknowledgements

*

ACKNOWLEDGEMENT is due to the following holders of the originals of manuscript letters: the Berg Collection, New York Public Library (nos. 60, 133), the Bodleian Library (nos. 73, 93), the British Library (nos. 2–6, 8, 10, 12, 48, 69, 81, 122–3, 141, 151, 155), the Broadley Collection, Westminster Public Libraries (no. 136), Clifton College (no. 72), Cornell University Library (nos. 35, 68, 76, 96, 106, 108, 127, 135, 146, 160, 162), University Library, Davis, California (no. 44), Dr Williams's Library (nos. 79, 99, 139, 153), Harvard University Library (nos. 18, 59, 105, 129–30), the Henry E. Huntington Library (nos. 7, 17, 27, 43, 46, 53, 119, 126, 154), the Hyde Collection (no. 71), the Lilly Library, Indiana University (no. 150), the Miriam Lutcher Stark Library, University of Texas (no. 121), the National Library of Scotland (nos. 26, 40, 42, 65, 116), the Pierpont Morgan Library (nos. 36, 38–9, 41, 89, 97, 143), the Record Office, Carlisle (nos. 22, 56, 63, 83–4, 86, 88, 95, 102), the Robert H. Taylor Collection, Princeton, NJ (no. 145), the Sharpe Collection, University College, London (nos. 45, 104, 111), Trinity College, Cambridge (no. 120), the Victoria and Albert Museum (nos. 9, 14, 90, 94, 118), the University of Virginia Library (no. 98), the Wedgwood Museum (no. 13), and the Wordsworth Library, Grasmere (nos. 1, 15–16, 19, 20, 25, 29–30, 32–4, 37, 47, 49–52, 54–5, 58, 61–2, 64, 66–7, 70, 80, 85, 91, 107, 112–13, 125, 128, 131–2, 134, 140, 142, 148, 152, 156–7, 159); and to the following individual owners of letters: Mr R. L. Bayne-Powell (no. 137), Mr Gregory Stevens Cox (nos. 24, 28), Dr M. J. Liversidge (no. 158), Mr W. Hugh Peal (nos. 100, 124), and Mr Jonathan Wordsworth (nos. 74, 110).

Abbreviations

*

W. W.	William Wordsworth
D. W.	Dorothy Wordsworth
M. W.	Mary Wordsworth
C. W.	Christopher Wordsworth
S. H.	Sara Hutchinson
S. T. C.	Samuel Taylor Coleridge
H. C. R.	Henry Crabb Robinson
E. Q.	Edward Quillinan
I. F.	Isabella Fenwick

Biographical Summary

*

1770	7 April. W. W. born at Cockermouth, the second of five children and brother of Richard, Dorothy, John, and Christopher.
1779–87	At Hawkshead Grammar School.
1787–91	At St. John's College, Cambridge.
1790	Summer walking tour through France and Switzerland with Robert Jones: witnesses early phase of French Revolution.
1791–2	December, in France: becomes politically identified with the Revolution. Love affair with Annette Vallon: their child Caroline born at Orléans.
1793–5	In London, Wales, and Cumberland. Publishes *An Evening Walk* and *Descriptive Sketches* (1793). Reunited with D. W. (1794), after his withdrawal from the French Revolution. Moves with her to Racedown, Dorset (Sept. 1795): meets S. T. C. and Southey.
1795–7	At Racedown with D. W. Writes *The Borderers* and early version of *The Ruined Cottage*. They move to Alfoxden, nr. Nether Stowey, Somerset, to be near S. T. C. (July 1797). (Charles Lamb visits Nether Stowey.)
1798	At Alfoxden. *Lyrical Ballads* written jointly with S. T. C. Visit of Hazlitt (June). July, August, tours of the Wye. September, they leave for Germany with S. T. C.: *Lyrical Ballads* published at Bristol. October, arrival at Goslar: *The Prelude* begun over the ensuing winter.
1799	May, return to England. At Sockburn-on-Tees with the Hutchinsons. 20 December, arrival at Grasmere.
1800	January, W. W. settles with D. W. at Dove Cottage: S. T. C. at Keswick. May, D. W. begins *Grasmere Journal*. *Lyrical Ballads* enlarged and reissued with Preface.
1802	August, at Calais with D. W. to visit Annette Vallon and Caroline. 4 October, W. W. marries Mary Hutchinson at Brompton, Yorks. (1803–10, five children born to them at Grasmere: John, Dorothy or 'Dora', Thomas, Catharine, and William.)

1803	August–September, Scottish tour with D. W. and S. T. C. Meeting with Scott. (Southey settles at Keswick.)
1805	5 February, death by shipwreck of W. W.'s and D. W.'s brother John. W. W. completes *The Prelude*.
1806–7	Winter at Coleorton, Leics. S. T. C. returns from Malta. *Poems in Two Volumes* published.
1808–11	At Allan Bank, Grasmere. W. W. works on *The Excursion*. (S. T. C. lives there intermittently, 1808–10, producing *The Friend*; De Quincey helps W. W. with the *Cintra* pamphlet.) Rift with S. T. C. The Wordsworths move to the old vicarage, Grasmere.
1812	Deaths of Catharine and Thomas.
1813	May, the Wordsworths leave Grasmere for Rydal Mount. W. W. appointed a Distributor of Stamps.
1814–15	July, tour of Scotland with M. W. and S. H.; W. W. publishes *The Excursion*, and first collected edition of his shorter poems.
1817	December, meets Keats at Haydon's during visit to London.
1818	Writes *Two Addresses to the Freeholders of Westmorland* in support of the (Tory) Lowther cause in the Westmorland election.
1820–2	July–October, Continental tour with M. W., D. W., and H. C. R. Publishes the sonnet series *The River Duddon*, and (1822) *Ecclesiastical Sketches*.
1823–33	Tours of Holland (with M. W.), Wales (with M. W. and Dora W.), the Rhineland (with Dora W. and S. T. C.), Ireland (with John Marshall), Abbotsford and the Borders (with Dora W.), and the Isle of Man and the Western Isles (with H. C. R.).
1830	November, meets Tennyson, during visit to Cambridge. (1830–5, progressive decline in D. W.'s health.)
1835	Publishes *Yarrow Revisited* volume and the enlarged *Guide to the Lakes*. July, death of S. H.
1836	Campaigns for new church at Cockermouth. May–July, lionised in London society: meets Browning.
1837	March–August, Italian tour with H. C. R. Copyright campaign opens.
1839	June, receives honorary degree at Oxford, to universal acclaim.
1841	May, marriage of Dora W. to Edward Quillinan at Bath.
1842	Publishes *Poems, Chiefly of Early and Late Years*.
1843	Succeeds Southey as Poet Laureate.

1845   Opposes the Kendal and Windermere Railway.

1847   July, death of Dora Quillinan.

1850   23 April. W. W. dies at Rydal Mount. Publication of *The Prelude*. (D. W. dies in 1855, M. W. in 1859.)

Introduction

*

THE reader who comes to Wordsworth's letters for the first time would do well to put on one side the popular stereotypes of Wordsworth the poet. These are not the letters of a 'Romantic' dreamer, a rustic moralist, or a 'lost leader' in retreat from the world; nor do they give the impression of a self-absorbed genius preoccupied with his own powers. The letters of a poet they certainly are, one who never hesitated in his lifelong commitment to his art—but one for whom the life of the imagination was intimately bound up with the 'common things that round us lie', a Cumbrian whose feet were firmly planted on the ground of his native region, and whose shrewd common sense and broad human sympathies are reflected in everything he wrote. All his letters have a natural and serious purpose. They are all surprisingly matter-of-fact, direct, and suited to the recipient and occasion. He never wrote to impress or flatter his correspondents, or with half an eye to amusing a wider audience later on. Taken together, they build up a memorable picture of his personality—his robust independence of mind and largeness of outlook, his equable good humour, and the unaffected eloquence and earnestness to which he could rise when his vital concerns as a poet were at stake.

Personal and business affairs apart, the subject-matter of the letters is as varied as Wordsworth's own interests and occupations; but every letter is recognisably a product of the same mind and sensibility, as the reader may easily discover for himself by comparing the letters with each other and with the poet's other writings. Poetry, taste in literature and art, landscape, history, religion, education, politics, and the progress of society—his views on all these matters are interrelated: indeed they spring naturally and inevitably from his central preoccupations as the poet of Man, Nature and Society. So that he never adopts a superior tone, but writes (in his own words) as 'a man speaking to men' about what should concern everyone who has the interests of his fellows at heart. The letters offer a portrait of the poet, his family and his wider circle which is refreshingly direct and uncomplicated by the speculations of later critics and biographers. They also quicken and enlarge the reader's understanding of Wordsworth's priorities as man and poet, and bring home their continuing relevance today.

Wordsworth made an extraordinary impact on everyone he met, long before he became a celebrity. Hazlitt's recollections, in *My First Acquaintance with Poets*, of their first meeting in 1798 create a complex and arresting impression of genius which is quite unlike the conventional notion:

The next day Wordsworth arrived from Bristol at Coleridge's cottage . . . He answered in some degree to his friend's description of him, but was more gaunt and Don Quixote-like. He was quaintly dressed (according to the *costume* of that unconstrained period) in a brown fustian jacket and striped pantaloons. There was something of a roll, a lounge in his gait, not unlike his own Peter Bell. There was a severe, worn pressure of thought about his temples, a fire in his eye (as if he saw something in objects more than the outward appearance), an intense high narrow forehead, a Roman nose, cheeks furrowed by strong purpose and feeling, and a convulsive inclination to laughter about the mouth, a good deal at variance with the solemn, stately expression of the rest of his face . . . Haydon's head of him, introduced into *The Entry of Christ into Jerusalem* is the most like his drooping weight of thought and expression.

If Wordsworth projected such an image of intellectual and imaginative power, it is hardly surprising that his contemporaries detected the same quality in his letters and preserved them with care. He mellowed over the years, but John Stuart Mill painted a not dissimilar picture of the poet's 'extreme comprehensiveness and philosophic spirit' over thirty years later, after his visit to Rydal Mount and its now famous occupant.

None of Wordsworth's letters from his schooldays at Hawkshead has survived, though the Wordsworth children were driven closer together by the early death of their parents and must have corresponded during their frequent separations. The earliest letters now extant take the reader straight into the heady days of the Revolution, with France (in the words of *The Prelude*)

standing on the top of golden hours,
And human nature seeming born again.

The letters from the earlier 1790s, the years of Wordsworth's revolutionary fervour, help to chart the course of his progressive disenchantment with the radical cause, and the flowering of his poetic powers in retirement with his sister Dorothy at Racedown and Alfoxden, culminating in the wonderful year of 1798, his literary partnership with Coleridge, and the publication of *Lyrical Ballads*. Many more letters belong to his years at Grasmere, after he had returned permanently to the Lakes with Dorothy and become a focal point for a much wider circle of friends and literary associates, Southey and De Quincey included. Much of Wordsworth's greatest lyrical and meditative poetry, including the *Immortality Ode* and *The Prelude*, the poem on the growth of his own mind, dates from these years. It is also the period of his crusade, in the *Poems Dedicated to National Independence and Liberty*, against Napoleon's European ambitions, and of the composition of *The Excursion*, the only part to be completed of his long philosophical poem on Man, Nature, and Society. The letters illuminate these years of supreme creative activity, and the almost overwhelming family tragedies which overshadowed them, and demonstrate that the loftiest visionary power can coexist with 'plain living and high thinking' and the values Wordsworth commended to his countrymen in time of war. Later still, when he had finally triumphed over his critics and was universally accepted as the leading poet of the age, he was revered as the last of the great Romantics, one who had outlived his contemporaries and carried over the ideals of a previous era into the harsher climate of early Victorian England. In his later letters he found a new role as the first of the Victorian sages, upholding the higher vision and humanitarian hopes of the poet against the 'march of mind' and the gospel of Utility, as the human spirit seemed increasingly at the mercy of science and technology, and railways and factories spread across the face of the English landscape he had so faithfully celebrated.

Wordsworth himself was uneasy about the indiscriminate publication of the correspondence of literary men. He was old-fashioned enough to believe that their private affairs could be of no possible concern to the public at large. Burns's letters, and later Coleridge's, were (he believed) misused by their early biographers, and he feared that Lamb's and Southey's might meet the same fate. That was one reason why he measured his own words so carefully when he put pen to paper. He could hardly have anticipated the recent publication of a group of his private letters to his wife Mary, which strike a note of passion unique in his whole correspondence. On the other hand, he recognised that many of his letters were more like little essays on matters of general concern than private communications, and he kept copies of them himself, probably for a projected volume of his prose which never appeared. Perhaps he thought they offered a key to the development of his mind and the consistency of his principles. And so he gave his nephew Christopher permission to use letters in his *Memoirs of William Wordsworth*, published the year after the poet's death, and it was in this form that the wider reading public had their first taste of Wordsworth as a letter-writer, and of 'the large and temperate judgment, the instinct of just taste, the simple dignity of conscious power, and the benevolence of heart', which Gladstone found in all his productions. Thereafter the letters continued to appear piecemeal, as interest gradually shifted from the later to the earlier phases of the poet's career. The next major collection was William Knight's *Letters of the Wordsworth Family* (3 vols., 1907), and this was replaced in due course by Ernest de Selincourt's much larger and more accurate *Letters of William and Dorothy Wordsworth* (6 vols., 1935–9), which is now in turn being extended and re-edited as new letters come to light. It is on this new edition that the present selection is based.

The bulk of Wordsworth's surviving correspondence is surprisingly large when one recalls that he had great difficulty in writing legibly and was forced by eye trouble in later life to employ an amanuensis, usually his wife. On what principles should a new selection be made? Many letters select themselves and make an immediate appeal. No reader could fail to be impressed by his discussions of poetry—especially his own—his views on art and artists, and his acute analysis of European politics and the future of nationalism. His accounts of travel at home and abroad make equally fascinating reading. Yet, inevitably, many of the letters, though valuable to a specialist, are uneven in quality and interest for the general reader; and often bread-and-butter matters mingle disconcertingly with exalted themes within the same letter. In these circumstances it might seem better to present extracts rather than whole texts, and previous selections have been formed on this assumption. But to do so would be to destroy the authentic shape and flavour of each letter, the 'occasional' quality which each has, and this procedure has been unhesitatingly rejected in the present volume. Apart from a few fragments of letters which have not survived in their entirety, this selection consists of complete letters, reproduced as nearly as possible as they were written, and chosen to provide a portrait of the poet and his milieu which can be read as a continuous narrative with the minimum of editorial commentary. Eight items (Letters 62, 64, 73, 80, 150, 152, 155, and 162) have not appeared in print before.

What can the reader today expect to learn from these pages, as he follows the poet's progress through a critical phase in our history, from the first flush of his republican enthusiasm at Cambridge in 1790 to a dignified old age at Rydal Mount half a century later as Queen Victoria's Poet Laureate? There have always been mysteries and uncertainties in Wordsworth's life, and the surviving letters do not resolve them all. The early love affair with Annette Vallon, like his other activities in revolutionary France, remains a shadowy episode; and while the love letters to Mary have modified the traditional view of Wordsworth's marriage, his whole relationship with Dorothy and her influence on his poetic development remain an enigma—and one which is perhaps best left as the poet himself described it:

> She gave me eyes, she gave me ears;
> And humble cares, and delicate fears;
> A heart, the fountain of sweet tears,
> And love, and thought, and joy.

The letters—like Dorothy's—offer few intimate revelations: but perhaps they are not to be expected from one who was seldom parted from his loved ones long enough to make correspondence necessary.

On other debatable issues there is more material available but little more agreement. Opinions will no doubt continue to differ about Wordsworth's later poetry, his emergence as a Tory supporter and opponent of Reform, and his adherence to the Established Church as a focus for time-honoured loyalties and values which seemed to be slipping away from the society around him. For many, Wordsworth's hopes for the Revolution are sacrosanct, a rallying-cry for the youth and young at heart in every generation, and he cannot easily be forgiven for applying his principles anew to changing circumstances. Others, while allowing that he feared change too much in his later years, will note that in seeking a common ground for social and religious renewal he anticipated the secret of Victorian stability which was to keep Britain, unlike her Continental neighbours, free from sectarian strife for over half a century. As far as they go, the letters suggest that many of his later attitudes are genuine developments from earlier positions rather than reactions against them. They also suggest that conventional party labels do not apply to one whose broad humanitarian and patriotic aims so obviously transcend them. But these larger problems of interpretation cannot be settled from the letters alone.

What the correspondence does convey openly and unforgettably is Wordsworth's faith in his own genius and in the permanent value of what he was doing for English poetry. 'Trouble not yourself upon their present reception,' he wrote to Lady Beaumont about the *Poems* of 1807:

Of what moment is that compared with what I trust is their destiny, to console the afflicted, to add sunshine to daylight by making the happy happier, to teach the young and the gracious of every age, to see, to think and feel, and therefore to become more actively and securely virtuous; this is their office, which I trust they will faithfully perform long after we (that is, all that is mortal of us) are mouldered in our graves.

And yet, unwavering though he was in his sense of his own greatness, Wordsworth was not buried away in his own concerns to the exclusion of others. The letters illustrate his deep and discriminating knowledge of the poets of the past—and not only those in English; his judgements on his contemporaries, which were sometimes more generous than is supposed; his taste and expertise as a literary scholar; and his concern for the well-being of literature as a whole, particularly during the Copyright struggle which preoccupied him in old age. A shrewd campaigner who carried his learning so lightly was a formidable opponent in any controversy.

For Wordsworth, literature was not divorced from the workaday world. The new poetry grew out of a new life-style, a sense of fresh priorities. The reader can share the excitement with which the poet and his sister set out on their quest to secure, 'home at Grasmere',

> A portion of the blessedness, which love
> and knowledge, will, we trust, hereafter give
> To all the vales of earth and all mankind.

Composition was a natural response to circumstances and surroundings, as Dorothy's *Journals* bear out; and often, verse drafts jostle with family news in the same letter. So that Wordsworth could claim quite literally to be celebrating the 'Truth that cherishes our daily life'. The simple, almost frugal life-style, 'the seemly plainness' which had been so lacking in the Cambridge of his youth, remained largely unchanged even after the Wordsworths had moved to Rydal Mount and a place among the gentry. The supreme satisfactions were always the same—the passing seasons, the changing moods of lake and mountain, rural society, family and friends, walks, books:

> Wisdom doth live with children round her knees:
> Books, leisure, perfect freedom, and the talk
> Man holds with week-day man in the hourly walk
> Of the mind's business: these are the degrees
> By which true Sway doth mount; this is the stalk
> True Power doth grow on; and her rights are these.

There was a remarkable integrity and consistency in the way Wordsworth 'lived out' his principles in the region which had nourished his poetic vision, accepting the drudgery of a Distributor of Stamps among his beloved Lakes rather than the more lucrative employment he was offered elsewhere. It showed more than a touch of heroism, as Thoreau noted. Wordsworth never broke faith with Nature. Near the end of his life, in the year of revolutions all over Europe, his thoughts turned to the preservation and improvement of his little estate at Applethwaite, hallowed by memories of Sir George Beaumont, who had presented it to him nearly half a century before. The letters, taken in sequence, will tell the reader much of what Wordsworth meant in one of his best-known poems by 'natural piety'. It was indeed exemplified in all his dealings, as brother, husband, father, and friend, and in the whole tenor of his days.

The correspondence paints a memorable picture of Wordsworth's strong, almost stoical, sense of duty, as he struggled to bring his own wishes into line with circumstances, and what he called 'the constitution of things'. This was what living in communion with Nature meant. Over a long life he had more than his fair share of sorrow and disappointment. His days were punctuated by a series of shattering losses—his own parents in childhood, his brother John by shipwreck, his young children Catharine and Thomas, Mary's sister Sara, and finally his daughter Dora, after her years of illness and a marriage that deeply distressed him. He had also to come to terms with Dorothy's irreversible decline into a shadow of her former 'exquisite' self, and the death of many of his closest literary friends. There is a certain grandeur about his attempts to bend a strong-willed and passionate nature to the discipline of circumstances, and to do his duty by all those who depended on him, within his family circle and beyond it.

> We will grieve not, rather find
> Strength in what remains behind

Life was the best school of all, as he maintained in his letters on the philosophy of education, but its lessons were bitter indeed and hard to accept.

But there was always the encouragement of friends whose paths crossed his own, or with whom he forged deeper sympathies in the course of time. Wordsworth's letters show how important his friends were to him. He was not one to wear his heart on his sleeve: 'A sound and healthy friendship is the growth of time and circumstance,' he warned De Quincey, 'it will spring and thrive like a wildflower when these favour, and when they do not, it is in vain to look for it.' But once established, Wordsworth's friendships enriched his life, and helped him to find his true self. The letters recapture the ups and downs of his relationship with Coleridge, the exhilaration and then anxiety, as Coleridge's pathetic love for Sara Hutchinson and his opium addiction threatened to destroy him. Wordsworth's solicitude, when these weaknesses were only too clear, went right beyond the call of duty, and even extended to Coleridge's children, whose well-being he watched over like a parent. Some of Wordsworth's most moving letters were addressed to Sir George and Lady Beaumont, who offered him so much encouragement when he stood most in need of it. Many happy days were spent at their estate at Coleorton, where he laid out the winter garden. Another friend with whom he found unexpected affinities was Charles Lamb, 'the frolic and the gentle', whose care for his sister was a mirror image of Wordsworth's own, and who was able to bring out the latent humour in Wordsworth's disposition. Lamb's whole life—like Southey's—was an object-lesson in independence and devotion to duty, which won the poet's admiration. With Scott and Rogers too, Wordsworth was able to see beyond literary differences to deeper bonds of sympathy. He kept his early Cambridge friends to the end, and he made many new friends in middle age—from local visitors like the Arnolds of Rugby, from the younger writers, artists, and politicians who lionised him in London, and from the scientists and churchmen in his brother Christopher's circle at Cambridge. Most loyal of all were Henry Crabb Robinson and Isabella Fenwick, who became mainstays of his old age. The poet also developed close ties with one correspondent whom he was destined never to meet, his American editor Henry Reed. They were bound together by peculiar bonds of sympathy—Reed's instinctive understanding of the Wordsworthian ethos, and the poet's hopes for the English-speaking peoples of America and their literature. As so often with Wordsworth, friendship did not offer a refuge from the real world, but a chance of opening up a dialogue about the future.

Perhaps the most lasting impression given by these letters is of the human face of true genius. They reveal the originality and power of Wordsworth's personality as it would strike those who knew him best in the ordinary transactions of life. In his poems Wordsworth sometimes seems withdrawn, brooding, absorbed in self-contemplation, as if indeed the mind of man was the main region of his song, and as if he was not vitally concerned with very much else. In portraits by contemporary artists too, he is sometimes over-sentimentalised and made to seem effete and remote. The letters are indispensable to the modern reader who seeks to understand the poet because they show him in all his dealings with his fellow men, confronting the ultimate questions of life not by defying the world (like Byron), but by immersing himself in it. The world of Nature to which he retired was a springboard from which he could recapture Man's true source of happiness, his sense of sharing in the total harmony of things. Never before had such a range of mind, intensity of feeling, and moral aspiration been turned to such homely purposes.

> Paradise, and groves
> Elysian, Fortunate Fields—like those of old
> Sought in the Atlantic Main—why should they be
> A history only of departed things,
> Or a mere fiction of what never was?
> For the discerning intellect of Man,
> When wedded to this goodly universe
> In love and holy passion, shall find these
> A simple produce of the common day.

ALAN G. HILL

List of Correspondents

*

ALFORD, the Revd Henry (1810–71), poet and hymn writer: later Dean of Canterbury.

ANDERSON, Dr Robert (1750–1830), author of *A Complete Edition of the Poets of Great Britain*, 1792–5

BARTON, Bernard (1784–1849), poet and Quaker.

BEAUMONT, Sir George, 7th Bt. (1753–1827), of Coleorton Hall, Leics.: amateur painter, patron of the arts, and W. W.'s benefactor.

BEAUMONT, Lady (1756–1829).

BOWLES, the Revd William Lisle (1762–1850), poet: author of *Fourteen Sonnets*, 1789.

BOXALL, William, later Sir William, RA (1800–79), painter: later Director of the National Gallery.

CLARKSON, Catherine (1772–1856), wife of Thomas Clarkson, the abolitionist.

COLERIDGE, Henry Nelson (1798–1843), S. T. C.'s nephew and editor.

COLERIDGE, Samuel Taylor (1772–1834), poet and philosopher.

COLERIDGE, Sara (1802–52), S. T. C.'s daughter, author of *Phantasmion*: married to her cousin H. N. Coleridge.

COLLIER, John Payne (1789–1883), antiquarian and editor of Shakespeare.

COTTLE, Joseph (1770–1853), of Bristol, publisher of *Lyrical Ballads*.

CUNNINGHAM, Allan (1784–1842), Scottish poet, and assistant to Sir Francis Chantrey.

DE QUINCEY, Thomas (1785–1859), essayist, author of *Confessions of an English Opium Eater*.

DYCE, the Revd Alexander (1798–1869), literary scholar and editor.

FENWICK, Isabella (1783–1856), the devoted friend of W. W.'s later years.

FIELD, Barron (1786–1846), lawyer and student of W. W.'s poetry.

FLETCHER, Jacob (1790–1863), a Liverpool merchant.

FOX, Charles James (1749–1806), Whig statesman.

GARDNER, Dr John (1804–80), medical writer.

GILLIES, Robert Pearce (1788–1858), poet and journalist.

GLADSTONE, William Ewart (1809–98), statesman and churchman.

GODWIN, William (1756–1836), philosopher: author of *Political Justice*, 1793.

GORDON, George Huntly (1796–1868), of the Stationery Office: protégé of Sir Walter Scott.

HALL, Samuel Carter (1800–89), editor of *The Amulet* and (later) the *Art Journal*.

HAMILTON, Sir William Rowan (1805–65), mathematician and Professor of Astronomy at Trinity College, Dublin.

HARE, the Revd Julius Charles (1795–1855), German scholar, broad-churchman, and disciple of Coleridge.

HAYDON, Benjamin Robert (1786–1846), painter.

HUTCHINSON, Sara (1775–1835), W. W.'s sister-in-law.

JONES, the Revd Robert (1769–1835), Welsh clergyman and college friend of W. W.'s.

KENYON, John (1784–1856), patron of poets.

LAMB, Charles (1775–1834), the essayist.

LANDOR, Walter Savage (1775–1864), poet and author of the *Imaginary Conversations*.

LEITCH, David (1809–81), physician at Keswick.

LOSH, James (1763–1833), W. W.'s early radical friend: later Recorder of Newcastle.

LOWTHER, Sir William, Bt., Viscount Lowther, later 1st Earl of Lonsdale (1757–1844), W. W.'s patron.

LOWTHER, William, Viscount Lowther (1787–1872), MP for Westmorland: later 2nd Earl of Lonsdale.

MARSHALL, Jane, née Pollard, D. W.'s friend: later, wife of John Marshall, MP, of Hallsteads, on Ullswater.

MATHEWS, William (1769–1801), W. W.'s Cambridge friend, later a victim of yellow fever in the West Indies.

MILLER, the Revd John (1787–1858), friend of De Quincey's: later a clergyman in Worcestershire.

MITCHELL, John Forbes (1786–1822), Scottish landowner in Aberdeenshire.

MONKHOUSE, Elizabeth (1750–1828), M. W.'s aunt.

MONTAGU, Basil (1770–1851), natural son of 4th Earl of Sandwich: lawyer and author.

MOXON, Edward (1801–58), publisher, married to Lamb's adopted daughter.

NICHOL, John Pringle (1804–59), Regius Professor of Astronomy at Glasgow.

PASLEY, Capt. Charles William, later Sir Charles (1780–1861), Director of the Royal Engineers Establishment at Chatham.

PEACE, John (1785–1861), City Librarian at Bristol, and W. W.'s 'devoted admirer'.

PEEL, Sir Robert (1788–1850), Prime Minister.

POOLE, Thomas (1765–1837), tanner, of Nether Stowey, Somerset.

POWELL, Thomas (1809–87), miscellaneous writer and literary forger.

QUILLINAN, Edward (1791–1851), half-pay officer and occasional writer: married W. W.'s daughter Dora as his second wife in 1841.

REED, Henry (1808–54), Professor of English Literature in the University of Pennsylvania: W. W.'s American editor.

ROBINSON, Henry Crabb (1775–1867), barrister and diarist.

ROGERS, Samuel (1763–1855), banker, poet, and patron of the arts.

SCOTT, John (1783–1821), editor of the *Champion* and of the *London Magazine*.

SCOTT, Sir Walter (1771–1832), poet and novelist.

SEDGWICK, the Revd Adam (1785–1873), Fellow of Trinity and Professor of Geology at Cambridge.

SHARP, Richard (1759–1835), 'Conversation Sharp', business man and MP.

SOUTHEY, Robert (1774–1843), W. W.'s predecessor as Poet Laureate.

STANGER, James (1796–1866), of Keswick, Evangelical churchman and philanthropist.

STODDART, John, later Sir John (1773–1856), lawyer and author, King's Advocate at Malta.

STUART, Daniel (1766–1846), editor of the *Courier*.

TALFOURD, Thomas Noon, later Sir Thomas (1795–1854), MP, proponent of Copyright reform, and judge.

TAYLOR, Anne, sister of John Taylor, editor of the *Sun*.

TAYLOR, Henry, later Sir Henry (1800–86), of the Colonial Office: dramatist.

TREMENHEERE, Hugh Seymour (1804–93), Inspector of Schools, and Commissioner investigating the state of the poor and child labour.

VERE, Aubrey de (1814–1902), Irish poet.

WATTS, Alaric (1797–1864), journalist and editor of the *Literary Souvenir*.

WEDGWOOD, Josiah (1769–1843), of the Staffs. pottery family, later MP for Stoke-on-Trent: with his brother Thomas (1771–1805), the early friend and benefactor of S. T. C. and W. W.

WHEWELL, the Revd William (1794–1866), scientist and philosopher: C. W.'s successor as Master of Trinity.

WILBERFORCE, William (1759–1833), politician and abolitionist.

WILSON, John (1785–1854), 'Christopher North' of *Blackwood*'s, later Professor of Moral Philosophy at Edinburgh: lived for a time at Elleray on Windermere.

WORDSWORTH, Charles (1806–92), W. W.'s nephew: schoolmaster, and later Bishop of St. Andrews.

WORDSWORTH, Christopher (1774–1846), W. W.'s youngest brother, Master of Trinity College, Cambridge, from 1820.

WORDSWORTH, Christopher, jnr. (1807–85), W. W.'s nephew: Master of Harrow and later Bishop of Lincoln.

WORDSWORTH, Dora (1804–47), W. W.'s daughter, later married to Edward Quillinan.

WORDSWORTH, Dorothy (1771–1855), W. W.'s sister.

WORDSWORTH, Mary, née Hutchinson (1770–1859), W. W.'s wife.

WORDSWORTH, Richard (1768–1816), W. W.'s eldest brother, solicitor in Staple Inn.

WRANGHAM, the Revd Francis (1769–1842), scholar, clergyman, and poet: later Archdeacon of the East Riding.

Letters of
William Wordsworth

*

1. *To* Dorothy Wordsworth

Sept. 6th [and 12, 1790] Keswi (a small
village on the lake of Constance)

My dear Sister

My last letter was addressed to you from St Valier and the
Grande Chartreuse. I have since that period gone over a very
considerable tract of country and I will give you a sketch of my
route, as far as relates to mentioning the places where I have been,
after I have assured you that I am in excellent Health and Spirits,
and have had no reason to complain of the contrary during our
whole tour. My Spirits have been kept in a perpetual hurry of
delight by the almost uninterrupted succession of sublime and
beautiful objects which have passed before my eyes during the
course of the last month, and you will be surprized when I assure
you that our united expenses since we quitted Calais which was on
the evening of the 14th of July have not amounted to more than
twelve pounds. Never was there a more excellent school for
frugality than that in which we are receiving instructions at
present. I am half afraid of getting a slight touch of avarice from it.
It is the end of travelling by communicating Ideas to enlarge the
mind; God forbid that I should stamp upon mine the strongest
proof of a contracted spirit. But I will resume the intent of this
letter by endeavouring to give you some Idea of our route; it will be
utterly impossible for me to dwell upon particular scenes, as my
paper would be exhausted before I had done with the journey of
two or three days. On quitting the Grande Chartreuse where we
remained two days contemplating, with encreased pleasure its
wonderful scenery, we passed thro' Savoy to Geneva, and thence,
along the Pays de Vaud side of the lake, to Ville-neuve a small

town seated at its head. The lower part of the lake did not afford us a pleasure equal to what might have been expected from its celebrity. This was owing partly to its width, and partly to the weather, which was one of those hot glaring days in which all distant objects are veiled in a species of bright obscurity. But the higher part of the lake made us ample amends, 'tis true we had the same disagreeable weather but the banks of the water are infinitely more picturesque, and as it is much narrower, the landscape suffered proportionally less from that pale steam which before almost entirely hid the opposite shore. From Villeneuve we proceeded up the Rhone to Martigny where we left our bundles and struck over the mountains to Chamouny to visit the glaciers of Savoy. You have undoubtedly heard of these celebrated scenes, but if you have not read of them any description which I have here room to give you must be altogether inadequate. After passing two days in the environs of Chamouny we returned to Martigny, and pursued our Route up the Valais along the Rhone to Brig. At Brig we quitted the Valais and passed the Alps at the Semplon in order to visit part of Italy. The impressions of three hours of our walk among the Alps will never be effaced.[1] From Duomo d'Ossola a town of Italy which lay in our Route we proceeded to the lake of Locarno, to visit the Boromaean Islands there, and thence to Como. A more charming path was scarce ever travelled than we had along the lake of Como. The banks of many of the Italian and Swiss lakes are so steep and rocky as not to admit of roads; that of Como is partly of this character. A small footpath is all the communication by land between one village and another on the side along which we passed for upwards of thirty miles. We entered upon this path about noon, and owing to the steepness of the banks, were soon unmolested by the sun, which illuminated the woods rocks and villages of the opposite shore. The lake is narrow and the shadows of the mountains were early thrown across it. It was beautiful to watch them travelling up the sides of the hills for several hours, to remark one half of a village covered with shade, and the other bright with the strongest sunshine. It was with regret that we passed every turn of this charming path, where every new picture was purchased by the loss of another which we would never have been tired of gazing at. The shores of the lake consist of steeps

[1] See *Prelude*, Bk. vi.

covered with large sweeping woods of chestnut spotted with villages, some clinging from the summits of the advancing rocks, and others hiding themselves within their recesses. Nor was the surface of the lake less interesting than its shores; part of it glowing with the richest green and gold the reflexion of the illuminated woods and part shaded with a soft blue tint. The picture was still further diversified by the number of sails which stole lazily by us, as we paused in the woods above them. After all this we had the moon. It was impossible not to contrast that repose that complacency of Spirit, produced by these lovely scenes, with the sensations I had experienced two or three days before, in passing the Alps. At the lake of Como my mind ran thro a thousand dreams of happiness which might be enjoyed upon its banks, if heightened by conversation and the exercise of the social affections. Among the more awful scenes of the Alps, I had not a thought of man, or a single created being; my whole soul was turned to him who produced the terrible majesty before me. But I am too particular for the limits of my paper. We followed the lake of Como to its head, and thence proceeded to Chiavenna, where we began to pass a range of the Alps, which brought us into the Country of the Grisons at Sovaza. From Sovaza we pursued the valley of Missox[1] in which it is situated to its head, passed Mount Adel to Hinter Rhine a small village near one of the sources of the Rhine. We pursued this branch of the Rhine downwards thro' the Grisons to Richene, where we turned up the other Branch of the same River, and followed it to Cimut a small village near its source. Here we quitted the Grisons and entered Switzerland at the valley of Urseren, and pursued the course of the Russ down to Altorf. Thence we proceede[d,] partly upon the lake, and partly behind the mountains on its banks, to Lucerne, and thence to Zurich. From Zurich along the banks of the lake we continued our route to Richlesweel. Here we left the lake to visit the famous church and convent of Enseilden, and thence to Glarus. But this Catalogue must be shockingly tedious. Suffice it to say that after passing a day in visiting the romantic valley of Glarus, we proceeded by the lake of Wallestadt and the Canton of Appenzell to the lake of Constance

---

[1] Mesocco. Richene is Reichenau; Cimut, Tschamut; Russ, Reuss; Richlesweel, Richterswil; Enseilden, Einsiedeln; Wallestadt, Walenstadt; and Schaffhouse, Schaffhausen.

where this letter was begun nine days ago. From Constance we proceeded along the banks of the Rhine to Schaffhouse to view the fall of the Rhine there. Magnificent as this fall certainly is I must confess I was disappointed in it. I had raised my ideas too high. We followed the Rhine downwards about eight leagues from Shaffouze, where we crossed it and proceeded by Baden to Lucerne. I am at this present moment (14th of Septbr) writing at a small village in the road from Grindelwald to Lauterbrunnen. By consulting your maps, you will find these villages in the southeast part of the Canton of Berne not far from the lakes of Thun and Brientz. After viewing the valley of Lauterbrunnen we shall have concluded our tour of the more Alpine parts of Swisserland. We proceed thence to Berne, and propose after making two or three small excursions about the lake of Neuchatel to go to Basle a town of Swisserland, upon the Rhine, whence we shall if we find we can afford it take advantage of the River down to Cologn, and so cross to Ostend, where we shall take the pacquet for Margate. Today is the 14th of Septbr and I hope we shall be in England by the 10th of Ocbr. I have had during the course of this delightful tour a great deal of uneasiness from an apprehension of your anxiety on my account. I have thought of you perpetually and never have my eyes burst upon a scene of particular loveliness but I have almost instantly wished that you could for a moment be transported to the place where I stood to enjoy it. I have been more particularly induced to form those wishes because the scenes of Swisserland have no resemblance to any I have found in England, and consequently it may probably never be in your power to form any idea of them. We are now as I observed above upon the point of quitting the most sublime and beautiful parts and you cannot imagine the melancholy regret which I feel at the Idea. I am a perfect Enthusiast in my admiration of Nature in all her various forms; and I have looked upon and as it were conversed with the objects which this country has presented to my view so long, and with such encreasing pleasure, that the idea of parting from them oppresses me with a sadness similar to what I have always felt in quitting a beloved friend. There is no reason to be surprized at the strong attachment which the Swiss have always shewn to their native country. Much of it must undoubtedly have been owing to those charms which have already produced so powerful an effect upon me, and to which the rudest minds cannot possibly be indifferent. Ten thousand times in the course of this tour have I regretted the inability of my memory to retain a more strong impression of the beautiful forms before me, and again and again in quitting a fortunate station have I returned to it with the most eager avidity, with the hope of bearing away a more lively picture. At this moment when many of these landscapes are floating before my mind, I feel a high [enjoyment] in reflecting that perhaps scarce a day of my life will pass [in] which I shall not derive some happiness from these images. With regard to the manners of the inhabitants of this singular country, the impression which we have had often occasion to receive has been unfavourable. But it must be remembered that we have had little to do but with innkeepers and those corrupted by perpetual intercourse with strangers. Had we been able to speak the language, which is German, and had time to insinuate ourselves into their cottages, we should probably have had as much occasion to admire the simplicity of their lives as the beauties of their country. My partiality to Swisserland excited by its natural charms induces me to hope that the manners of its inhabitants are aimiable, but at the same time I cannot help frequently contrasting them with those of the French, and as far as I have had opportunity to observe they lose very much by the comparison. We not only found the French a much less imposing people, but that politeness diffused thro the lowest ranks had an air so engaging, that you could scarce attribute it to any other cause than real benevolence. During the time which was near a month which we were in France, we had not once to complain of the smallest deficiency in civility in any person, much less of any positive rudeness. We had also perpetual occasion to observe that chearfulness and sprightliness for which the French have always been remarkable. But I must remind you that we crossed it at the time when the whole nation was mad with joy, in consequence of the revolution. It was a most interesting period to be in France, and we had many delightful scenes where the interest of the picture was owing solely to this cause. I was also much pleased with what I saw of the Italians during the short time we were amongst them. We had several times occasion to observe a softness and elegance which contrasted strongly with the severity and austereness of their neighbours on the other side of the Alps. It was with pleasure

5

I observed at a small Inn on the lake of Como, the master of it playing upon his harpsicord, with a large collection of Italian music about him. The outside of the instrument was such that it would not have much graced an English drawingroom, but the tones that he drew from it were by no means contemptible.

But it is time to talk a little about England. When you write to my Brothers, I must beg of you to give my love, and tell them I am sorry it has not been in my power to write to them. Kit will be surprized he has not heard from me, as we were almost upon terms of regular correspondence. I had not heard from Richard for some time before I set out; I did not call on him when I was in London; not so much because we were determined to hurry through London, but because he, as many of our friends at Cambridge did, would look upon our scheme as mad and impracticable. I expect great pleasure on my return to Cambridge, in exulting over those of my friends who threathned us with such an accumulation of difficulties as must undoubtedly render it impossible for us to perform the tour. Every thing however has succeeded with us far beyond my most sanguine expectation. We have it is true met with little disasters occasionally, but far from depressing us they rather gave us additional resolution and Spirits. We have both enjoyed most excellent health, and we have been this some time so inured to walking, that we are become almost insensible of fatigue. We have several times performed a journey of thirteen leagues over the most mountainous parts of Swisserland, without any more weariness, than if we had been walking an hour in the groves of Cambridge. Our appearance is singular, and we have often observed that, in passing thro' a village, we have excited a general smile. Our coats which we had made light on purpose for our journey are of the same piece; and our manner of bearing our bundles, which is upon our heads, with each an oak stick in our hands, contributes not a little to that general curiosity which we seem to excite. But I find I have again relapsed into Egotism, and must here entreat y[ou, not only] to pardon this fault, but also to make allowance for [the] illegible hand and desultory stile of this Letter. It has been written as you will see by its different shades at many sittings and is in fact the produce of most of the leisure which I have had since it was begun and is now *finally drawing to a conclusion*, Berne on *the 16th of* Septbr. I flatter myself still with the hopes of seeing you for a fortnight or three weeks, if it be agreeable to My Uncle,[1] as there will be no necessity for me to be in Cambridge before the 10th of Novbr, but I shall be better able to judge whether I am likely to enjoy this pleasure in about three weeks. I shall probably write to you again before I quit France, if not most certainly, immediately on my landing in England. You will remember me affectionately to my Uncle and Aunt—as he was acquainted with my having given up all thoughts of a fellowship, he may perhaps not be so much displeased at this journey. I should be sorry if I have offended him by it. I hope my little cousin is well. I must now bid you adieu, with assuring you that you are perpetually in my thoughts, and that I remain, Most affectionately yours,

W. Wordsworth

Septb 12th

Upon looking over this letter, I am afraid you will not be able to [read] half of it I must again beg you would excuse me.

2. *To* William Mathews

Brighton Novbr. 23d [1791]

Dear Mathews,

I have been prevented from replying to your Letter, by an uncertainty respecting the manner in which I should dispose of myself for the winter, and which I have expected to be terminated every day this month past. I am now on my way to Orleans, where I purpose to pass the Winter, and am detained here by adverse winds. I was very happy to hear, that you had given up your travelling scheme, that your father had consented to your changing your situation, and that in consequence your mind was much easier. I approve much of your resolution to stay where you are, till you meet with a more eligible engagement, provided your health does not materially suffer by it. It argues a manly spirit which you

---

[1] Dr William Cookson, rector of Forncett, Norfolk, in whose household D. W. was living at this period.

will undoubtedly be careful to preserve. I am happy to find that my Letter afforded you some consolation. There are few reflexions more pleasing than the consciousness, that one has contributed in the smallest degree to diminish the anxiety of one's friends. I wrote to Terrot[1] a week ago, requesting that he would not fail to give me a letter at Orleans as soon as possible. I never have heard from him in answer to the Letter I addressed to him from Wales. This I am extremely sorry for. I know not that you may be informed he has lost his second Brother in the East Indies. He was shot, tho' I was told not in an engagement; but I do not know the circumstances. This King[2] informed me of who had been staying with Terrot during the summer.

I expect I assure you considerable pleasure from my sojourn on the other side of the water, and some little improvement, which God knows I stand in sufficient need of.

I am doomed to be an idler thro[ughou]t my whole life. I have read nothing this age, nor indeed did I ever. Yet with all this I am tolerable happy; do you think this ought to be a matter of congratulation to me, or no? For my own part I think certainly not. My Uncle the clergyman proposed to me a short time ago to begin a course of Oriental Literature, thinking that that was the best field for a person to distinguish himself in as a man of Letters. To oblige him I consented to pursue the plan upon my return from the continent. But what must I do amongst that immense wilderness, who have no resolution, and who have not prepared myself for the enterprise by any sort of discipline amongst the Western languages? who know little of Latin, and scarce anything of Greek. A pretty confession for a young gentleman whose whole life ought to have been devoted to study. And thus the world wags. But away with this outrageous Egotism. Tell me what you are doing, and what you read. What authors are your favourites, and what number of that venerable body, you wish in the red sea? I shall be happy to hear from you immediately. My address a Mon. Mons? W. Wordsworth, Les Trois Empereurs a Orléans. I am no Frenchman, but I believe that is the way, that a Letter is addressed in France. I should have deferred this epistle till I had crossed the water, when I might have had an opportunity of giving you something new, had I not imagined you would be surprized at not

---

[1] A Cambridge friend.   [2] Another friend.

hearing from me, and had I not had more time on my hands at present than I am likely to have for some time. Adieu.

　　　　　　　　　　　　　Yours most affly and sincerely,

　　　　　　　　　　　　　　　　　W. Wordsworth

3. *To* William Mathews

　　　　　　　　　　　　　　Blois, May 19th [1792]

Dear Mathews,

　When I look back on the length of time elapsed since my receipt of your last letter I am overwhelmed by a sense of shame which would deprive me of the courage requisite to finish this sheet did I not build upon that indulgence which always accompanies warm and sincere friendship. Your last reached me just at the moment when I was busy in preparing to quit Orleans, or certainly the sentiments which it breathes had forced from me an immediate answer. Since my arrival day after day and week after week has stole insensibly over my head with inconceivable rapidity. I am much distressed that you have been so egregiously deceived by Mrs. D.[1] and still more so that those infamous calumnies prevent you from taking upon you an office you are so well qualified to discharge. It gives me still more heartfelt concern to find that this slander has sunk so deep upon your spirits. Even supposing, which is not at all probable that it should exclude you from the clerical office entirely, you certainly are furnished with talents and acquirements which if properly made use of will enable you to get your bread unshackled by the necessity of professing a particular system of opinions. You have still the hope that we may be connected in some method of obtaining an Independence. I assure you I wish it as much as yourself. Nothing but resolution is necessary. The field of Letters is very extensive, and it is astonishing if we cannot find some little corner, which with a little tillage will produce us enough for the necessities, nay even the comforts, of life. Your residence in London gives you if you look abroad an excellent opportunity of starting some thing or other. Pray be particular in your answer upon this subject. It is at present

[1] Apparently wife of the schoolmaster for whom Mathews was working.

my intention to take orders in the approaching winter or spring. My Uncle the Clergyman will furnish me with a title. Had it been in my power I certainly should have wished to defer the moment. But tho' I may not be resident in London, I need not therefore be prevented from engaging in any literary plan, which may have the appearance of producing a decent harvest. I assure you again and again that nothing but confidence and resolution is necessary. Fluency in writing will tread fast upon the heels of practice, and elegance and strength will not be far behind. I hope you will have the goodness to write to me soon, when you will enlarge upon this head. You say you have many schemes. Submit at least a few of them to my examination. Would it not be possible for you to form an acquaintance with some of the publishing booksellers of London, from whom you might get some hints of what sort of works would be the most likely to answer?

Till within a few days I nourished the pleasing expectation of seeing Jones[1] upon the Banks of Loire. But he informs me that at the earnest request of the Bishop of Bangor he has till Michaelmas taken upon [him] the office of Usher in a school which the Bishop has just built. You know well that the Welsh Bishops are the sole patrons. This circumstance will connect him with D. Warren,[2] and I hope prepare the way for a snug little Welsh living, of which our friend is certainly well deserving. Terot sometime ago addressed a letter to me at Orleans, promising me that it should soon be followed by another, in which he represented himself as stickling for preferment not in the church or the army, but in the custom-house. 'Tis all well. I wish heartily he may succeed. Let me entreat you most earnestly to guard against that melancholy, which appears to be making daily inroads upon your happiness. Educated as you have been, you ought to be above despair. You have the happiness of being born in a free country, where every road is open, where talents and industry are more liberally rewarded than amongst any other nation of the Universe. You will naturally expect that writing from a country agitated by the storms of a revolution, my Letter should not be confined merely to us and our friends. But the truth is that in London you have perhaps a better opportunity of being informed of the general concerns of france, than in a petty provincial town in the heart of the

[1] Robert Jones (see List of Correspondents).   [2] The Bishop.

kingd[om] itself. The annals of the department are all with which I have a better opportunity of being acquainted than you, provided you feel sufficient interest in informing yourself. The horrors excited by the relation of the events consequent upon the commencement of hostilities, is general. Not but that there are men who felt a gloomy satisfaction from a measure which seemed to put the patriot army out of a possibility of success. An ignominious flight,[1] the massacre of their general, a dance performed with savage joy round his burning body, the murder of six prisoners, are events which would have arrested the attention, of the reader of the annals of Morocco, or of the most barbarous of savages. The approaching summer will undoubtedly decide the fate of france. It is almost evident that the patriot army, however numerous, will be unable [to] withstand the superior discipline of their enemies. But suppose that the German army is at the gates of Paris, what will be the consequence? It will be impossible to make any material alteration in the constitution, impossible to reinstate the clergy in its antient guilty splendor, impossible to give an existence to the *noblesse* similar to that it before enjoyed, impossible to add much to the authority of the King: Yet there are in France some [?millions]—I speak without exaggeration—who expect that this will take place. I shall expect your Letter with impatience, tho', I little deserve, from my general remissness, this attention on your part. I shall return to England in the autumn or the beginning of Winter. I am not without the expectation of meeting you a circumstance which be assured would give me the greatest pleasure, as we might then more advantageously than by Letter consult upon some literary scheme, a project which I have much at heart. Adieu. I remain my dear Mathews, Your most afft friend,

W. Wordsworth

4. *To* William Mathews

Whitehaven, Friday May 23 [1794]

Dear Mathews,

I am sorry I did not receive your's of the 11th till yesterday, as I certainly should have answered it sooner. I am very happy to find

---

[1] The French had been routed by the Austrians near Lille.

that your regard for me continues unimpaired and that you wish so ardently to see me. I assure you it would give me great pleasure to cultivate your friendship in person, but I really cannot on any account venture to London unless upon the certainty of a regular income.

Living in London must always be expensive however frugal you may be. As to the article of eating that is not much; but dress, and lodging, are *extremely* expensive. But I must do something to maintain myself even in this country. You mention the possibility of setting on foot a monthly miscellany from which some emolument might be drawn. I wish I assure you most heartily to be engaged in something of that kind, and if you could depend on the talents, and above all the industry of the young man you speak of, I think we three would be quite sufficient with our best exertions to keep alive such a publication. But, as you say, how to set it afloat!

I am so poor that I could not advance any thing, and I am afraid you are equally unable to contribute in that way! Perhaps however this might be got over if we could be sure of the patronage of the public. I do not see that my being in the country would have any tendency to diminish the number or deduct from the value of my communications. It would only prevent me from officiating as an editor, and, as you are I suppose both resident in Town that circumstance would not be of much consequence. I wish much to hear further from you on this head, as I think if we could once raise a work of this kind into any reputation it would really be of consequence to us both. But much is to be attended to before we enter the field. What class of readers ought we to aim at procuring; in what do we, each of us, suppose ourselves the most able either to entertain or instruct?

Of each others political sentiments we ought not to be ignorant; and here at the very threshold I solemnly affirm that in no writings of mine will I ever admit of any sentiment which can have the least tendency to induce my readers to suppose that the doctrines which are now enforced by banishment, imprisonment, etc, etc, are other than pregnant with every species of misery. You know perhaps already that I am of that odious class of men called democrats, and of that class I shall for ever continue. In a work like that of which we are speaking, it will be impossible (and indeed it would render our publication worthless were we to attempt it,) not to inculcate principles of government and forms of social order of one kind or another. I have therefore thought it proper to say this much in order that if your sentiments or those of our coadjutor are dissimilar to mine, we may drop the scheme at once. Besides essays on morals and politics I think I could communicate critical remarks upon poetry, etc, etc, upon the arts of painting, gardening, and other subjects of amusement. But I should principally wish our attention to be fixed upon life and manners, and to make our publication a vehicle of sound and exalted Morality. All the periodical miscellanies that I am acquainted with, except one or two of the reviews, appear to be written to maintain the existence of prejudice and to disseminate error. To such purposes I have already said I will not prostitute my pen. Besides were we ignorant or wicked enough to be so employed, in our views of pecuniary advantage (from the public at least) we should be disappointed. But on the subject of this scheme I shall be happy to give my ideas at large, as soon as I have received yours and those of your friend. I repeat it, I think if we are determined to be industrious, we are a sufficient number for any purpose of that kind. I beg therefore I may hear from you immediately, and at great length, explaining your ideas upon our plan. I should also be happy to hear from your friend on the same subject. I am at present nearly quite at leisure, so that with industry I think I can perform my share. I say nearly at leisure, for I am not quite so as I am correcting and considerably adding to those poems which I published in your absence.[1] It was with great reluctance I huddled up those two little works and sent them into the world in so imperfect a state. But as I had done nothing by which to distinguish myself at the university, I thought these little things might shew that I could do something. They have been treated with unmerited contempt by some of the periodical publications, and others have spoken in higher terms of them than they deserve. I have another poem[2] written last summer ready for the press, though I certainly should not publish it unless I hoped to derive from it some pecuniary recompence. As I am speaking on this subject, pray let me request you to have the goodness to call on Johnson my publisher, and ask him if he ever sells any of those poems and what number he things are yet on his

[1] *An Evening Walk* and *Descriptive Sketches*.
[2] The Salisbury Plain poem that eventually became *Guilt and Sorrow* (publ. 1842).

hands. This will be doing me a great favor. I ought to have thanked you long since for your account of your plans. I wish you most heartily all the success which you deserve. Pray, in what print are you engaged? I am yours most affectionately.

W. Wordsworth

Do write as soon as possible. My address, R. Wordsworth's,[1] Esq, Whitehaven. This pen and ink are so bad, I can scarce write with them at all.

5. *To* William Mathews

Whitehaven, Sunday, [8] June [1794]

Dear Mathews,

Your packet of letters received yesterday night relieved me from great anxiety. I began to be apprehensive that our intended scheme was falling to the ground, my fears, however, are now done away. This letter I address to you and your friend to whom the satisfaction I have already expressed, will, I have no doubt be sufficient thanks for his ready compliance with my request. I read the explicit avowal of your political sentiments with great pleasure; any comments which I have to make upon it will be expressed in the best manner by a similar declaration of my own opinions. I disapprove of monarchical and aristocratical governments, however modified. Hereditary distinctions and privileged orders of every species I think must necessarily counteract the progress of human improvement: hence it follows that I am not amongst the admirers of the British constitution. Now, there are two causes which appear to me to be accomplishing the subversion of this constitution; first, the infatuation profligacy and extravagance of men in power, and secondly, the changes of opinion respecting matters of Government which within these few years have rapidly taken place in the minds of speculative men. The operation of the former of these causes I would spare no exertion to diminish, to the latter I would give every additional energy in my power. I conceive that a more excellent system of civil policy might be established

[1] W. W.'s uncle Richard.

amongst us yet in my ardour to attain the goal, I do not forget the nature of the ground where the race is to be run. The destruction of these institutions which I condemn appears to me to be hastening on too rapidly. I recoil from the bare idea of a revolution; yet, if our conduct with reference both to foreign and domestic policy continues such as it has been for the last two years how is that dreadful event to be averted? Aware of the difficulty of this it seems to me that a writer who has the welfare of mankind at heart should call forth his best exertions to convince the people that they can only be preserved from a convulsion by oeconomy in the administration of the public purse and a gradual and constant reform of those abuses which, if left to themselves, may grow to such a height as to render, even a revolution desirable. There is a further duty incumbent upon every enlightened friend of mankind; he should let slip no opportunity of explaining and enforcing those general principles of the social order which are applicable to all times and to all places; he should diffuse by every method a knowledge of those rules of political justice,[1] from which the farther any government deviates the more effectually must it defeat the object for which government was ordained. A knowledge of these rules cannot but lead to good; they include an entire preservative from despotism, they will guide the hand of reform, and if a revolution must afflict us, they alone can mitigate its horrors and establish freedom with tranquillity. After this need I add that I am a determined enemy to every species of violence? I see no connection, but what the obstinacy of pride and ignorance renders necessary, between justice and the sword, between reason and bonds. I deplore the miserable situation of the French;[2] and think we can only be guarded from the same scourge by the undaunted efforts of good men in propagating with unremitting activity those doctrines which long and severe meditation has taught them are essential to the welfare of mankind. Freedom of inquiry is all that I wish for; let nothing be deemed too sacred for investigation; rather than restrain the liberty of the press I would suffer the most atrocious doctrines to be recommended: let the field be open and

---

[1] *Political Justice*, by William Godwin (see List of Correspondents), had appeared the previous year.

[2] During the recent Reign of Terror. W. W. may have returned briefly to France the previous autumn.

unencumbered, and truth must be victorious. On this subject I think I have said enough, if it be not necessary to add that, when I observe the people should be enlightened upon the subject of politics, I severely condemn all inflammatory addresses to the passions of men, even when it is intended to direct those passions to a good purpose. I know that the multitude walk in darkness. I would put into each man's hand a lantern to guide him and not have him to set out upon his journey depending for illumination on abortive flashes of lightning, or the coruscations of transitory meteors. To come now to particulars. I cannot say that the title you have chosen pleases me. It seems too common to attract attention. Do you think any objection can be made to the following *"The Philanthropist a monthly Miscellany"*. This title I think would be noticed; it includes everything that can instruct and amuse mankind, and, if we exert ourselves, I doubt not that we shall be able to satisfy the expectations it will raise. Here let me observe that whatever plans I approve or disapprove I neither wish to be adopted or rejected on the strength of my opinion. As to the choice of matter and its distribution I see nothing to object to what you have said upon that subject. I think as you, that each number should open with the topic of general politics; here it will be proper to give a perspicuous statement of the most important occurrences, not over-burthened with trite reflections yet accompanied with such remarks as may forcibly illustrate the tendency of particular doctrines of government; next should follow essays upon morals and manners, and institutions whether social or political. These several departments entirely for such as read for instruction; next should come essays partly for instruction and partly for amusement, such as biographical papers exhibiting the characters and opinions of eminent men, particularly those distinguished for their exertions in the cause of liberty, as Turgot,[1] as Milton, Sydney,[2] Machiavel,[3] Beccaria,[4] etc. etc. etc. It would perhaps be advisable that these should, as much as possible form a series exhibiting the advancement of the human mind in moral knowledge, in this department will be included essays of taste and criticism, and

[1] The French economist.
[2] Algernon Sydney (1622–82), English republican.
[3] Machiavelli, author of *The Prince*.
[4] Cesare Beccaria (1738–94), penal reformer.

works of imagination and fiction. Next should come a review of those publications which are particularly characterized for inculcating recommendations of benevolence and philanthropy. Some poetry we should have. For this part of our plan we ought to have no dependence on original communications, the trash which infests the magazines strongly impresses the justice of this remark; from *new* poetical publications of merit and such *old* ones as are not generally known the pages allotted to verse may generally be filled. Next come parliamentary debates, detailed as you have specified, and such state papers as are of importance. As to our readers you think that we should endeavour to obtain as great a variety as possible, you cannot, however, be ignorant that amongst the partizans of this war, and of the suspension of the *habeas corpus* act amongst the mighty class of selfish alarmists we cannot obtain a single friend. We must then look for protection entirely amongst the dispassionate advocates of liberty and discussion; these whether male or female, we must either amuse or instruct nor will our end be fully obtained unless we do both. The clergy of the church of England are a body from which periodical publications derive great patronage: they however will turn from us. At the Universities of Oxford and Cambridge, amongst the young men, we shall not look in vain for encouragement. The dissenters, in general are not rich but in every town of any size there are some who would receive a work like ours with pleasure. I entirely approve of what you say on the subject of Ireland, and think it very proper that an agent should be appointed in Dublin to disseminate the impression. It would be well if either of you have any friends there, to whom you could write soliciting their recommendation. Indeed it would be very desirable to endeavour to have, in each considerable town of Great Britain and Ireland, a person to introduce the publication into notice. To this purpose, when it is farther advanced, I shall exert myself amongst all my friends. As to coming to town this step I must at present decline. I have a friend in the country[1] who has offered me a share of his income. It would be using him very ill to run the risque of destroying my usefulness by precipitating myself into distress and poverty at the time when he is so ready to support me in a situation wherein I feel I can be of

---

[1] Raisley Calvert (1773–95), whose timely legacy to W. W. enabled him to be a poet instead of entering the Church.

some little service to my fellowmen, hereafter, if our exertions are sufficient to support us by residing in London, perhaps I may be enabled to prosecute my share of the exertions with greater vigour. While I continue in the country, it will not be easy for me to be of much use, either in the first or last province of the work. In every other I promise my best exertions. I have not been much used to composition of any kind particularly in prose, my style therefore may frequently want fluency and sometimes perhaps perspicuity but these defects will gradually wear off; an ardent wish to promote the welfare of mankind will preserve me from sinking under them. Both of you appear much engaged. Will it not be necessary to free yourselves from some of those occupations to which your time is at present devoted? Here you will be the sole judges. As to money I have not a single sixpence of my own to advance but I have several friends who though not rich, I daresay would be willing to lend me assistance. The first thing now to be done is, I think (after establishing a cover correspondence[1]) to communicate to each other a sufficient portion of matter to compose at least two numbers—I mean of general not temporary matter as that must depend upon circumstances as they occur. I mention this, both because each would be a better judge of his strength and because such papers may be circulated in manuscript amongst my friends in this part of the world as specimens of the intended work. After this is done, we should then see how much money each of us can raise, what will be the expense of advertizing and printing a certain number of copies and the sale of what number of copies would indemnify us. You have probably both had more experience amongst booksellers than myself and may be better able to judge how far our publisher may be induced to circulate the work with additional spirit if he himself participates in the profits. For my part I should wish that if possible it were printed entirely at our own risk and for our own emolument. But the final decision on all these matters I leave to you. We should by no means *promise* any embellishments, and as our work will relate rather to moral than natural knowledge, there will not often be occasion for them. I am far from thinking that we should not vary it by occasionally introducing topics of physical science. They should however be as popular and as generally interesting as we can collect. We should

[1] i.e. for free transmission by post.

print in the review form. If you think that by going over to Dublin I could transact any business relative to the publication in a better manner than it could be done by Letter, though I have no friends there I would willingly undertake the voyage, which may be done at any time from this place. Probably I have omitted many things which I ought to have adverted to, you will therefore excuse the little method pursued in the few following remarks which I shall set down as they arise lest in attempting to arrange them they should slip from my memory. I think it essential that we should not have the least reliance on any accidental assistance; at the same time we should by no means neglect to stir up our friends to favour us with any papers which a wish to add to the stock of general knowledge may induce them to write. Would it not be advisable that each of us should draw up a prospectus of our object and plan and from the whole may be composed one which we should not delay to submit to the public? Of this prospectus when finished the style should be particularly polished and perspicuous. It would contribute much to render our work interesting could we have any foreign correspondence informing us of the progress of knowledge in the different metropolises of Europe, and of those new publications which either attract or merit attention. These writings our knowledge of languages would enable us to peruse and it would be well to extract from them the parts distinguished by particular excellence. It would be well also if you could procure a perusal of the french monitor,[1] for while we expressed our detestation of the execrable measures pursued in France we should belie our title if we did not hold up to the approbation of the world such of their regulations and decrees as are dictated by the spirit of Philosophy. We should give also an accurate account of the Polish revolution, and purify it from those infamous representations which ministerial hirelings have thrown over it.[2] I am not acquainted with the German language a circumstance which I greatly regret, as the vast tract of Country where that tongue is spoken cannot but produce daily performances which ought to be known amongst us. I wish you would answer this letter, as soon as possible; and at

[1] The official newspaper of the French National Convention.
[2] Following the declaration of war on France in Feb. 1793, Pitt's Government was now seeking an alliance with Prussia and Russia, the two powers which had invaded Poland after the revolution there (1791).

great length. I hope you will be able to procure covers, as in this remote part I cannot at present. You would do well to enclose me one for yourselves fixing the date two or three days after the time when I shall have received yours. I am, with great respect and esteem your fellow labourer and friend,

W. Wordsworth

6. *To* William Mathews

Keswick, November 7th, 1794

Dear Mathews,

The more nearly we approached the time fixed for action, the more strongly was I persuaded that we should decline the field. I was not therefore either much surprized or mortified at the contents of your Letter. It is true my distance from town unless we were once set forward could not but be a great obstacle in our way; and at present it is absolutely out of my power to leave this place. My friend,[1] of whom I have spoken to you, has every symptom of a confirmed consumption of the lungs, and I cannot think of quitting him in his present debilitated state. If he should not recover, indeed whatever turn his complaint takes, I am so emboldened by your encouragement that I am determined to throw myself into that mightly gulph which has swallowed up so many, of talents and attainments infinitely superior to my own. One thing however I can boast and on that one thing I rely, extreme frugality. This must be my main support, my chief *vectigal*. Pray let me have accurate information from you on the subject of your newspaper connection. What is the nature of the service performed by you, and how much of your time does it engross? etc etc. You say a newspaper would be glad of me; do you think you could ensure me employment in that way on terms similar to your own? I mean also in an opposition paper, for really I cannot in conscience and in principle, abet in the smallest degree the measures pursued by the present ministry. They are already so deeply advanced in iniquity that like Macbeth they cannot retreat. When I express myself in this manner I am far from reprobating those whose sentiments on

---

[1] Raisley Calvert (see previous letter).

this point differ from my own; I know that many good men were persuaded of the expediency of the present war, and I know also that many persons may think it their duty to support the acting ministry from an idea of thereby supporting the government, even when they disapprove of most of the present measures.

You will return my best thanks to Burleigh[1] for his obliging Letter, and give him to understand, I regret no less than himself my inability to bring about an interview; and that I look forward with eagerness to the time when I may enjoy the pleasures of his conversation. You speak both of Jones and Myers,[2] the former I have used ill and want resolution to make an apology. Myers I hope continues a patriot of unabated energy. You would probably see that my Brother has been honoured with two college declamation prizes;[3] the second english, and the sole latin one given. *Ça va*, I mean towards a fellowship, which I hope he will obtain, and I am sure he will merit. He is a lad of talents, and industrious withal. This same industry is a good old Roman quality, and nothing is to be done without it. In colleges this truth is not, at least among the younger part, very generally received. I begin to wish much to be in town; cataracts and mountains, are good occasional society, but they will not do for constant companions; besides I have not even much of their conversation, and still less of that of my books as I am so much with my sick friend, and he cannot bear the fatigue of being read to. Nothing indeed but a sense of duty could detain me here under the present circumstances. This is a country for poetry it is true; but the muse is not to be won but by the sacrifice of time, and time I have not to spare. You inquired after the name of one of my poetical bantlings, children of this species ought to be named after their characters, and here I am at a loss, as my offspring seems to have no character at all. I have however christened it by the apellation of Salisbury Plain, though, A night on Salisbury plain, were it not so insufferably awkward would better suit the thing itself. Pray let me hear from you as soon as possible, giving me a just representation of your own employment, not concealing from me any of its disadvantages, and letting me know also what prospect there is of

---

[1] Probably the friend mentioned in the last two letters.
[2] W. W.'s cousin John Myers, a contemporary at St. John's.
[3] C. W. had entered Trinity in 1792.

my procuring a similar occupation. I shall wait for your letter in patience.

Believe [me,] dear Mathews, your very affectionate friend,

W. Wordsworth

7. *To* Francis Wrangham

Racedown. March 7 [1796]

My dear Wrangham,

Your Letter had long been looked for. The agreeable intelligence it contained respecting your good fortune (I believe among the antients good fortune was reckoned among the first of a man's merits; as being a proof, perhaps, of his being under the special care of the gods, and therefore the expression is not to be objected to,) the intelligence then of your good fortune made me quite forget that there was any occasion to apologize for your *inveterate* silence. I sincerely congratulate you on your late induction,[1] as it must set you entirely above the necessity of engaging in any employment unsuited to your taste and pleasures. I am glad to hear of your projected Volume;[2] and hope you will not suffer your *promotion* to interfere with the advancement of your Literary reputation, or to rob your friends and the public of the pleasure to be derived from the pieces you are possessed of. I shall be happy to communicate any observations which may suggest themselves to me on perusal of your Mss. I assure you I do not mean to drop the Juvenal scheme,[3] on the contrary I am determined to bring it to a speedy conclusion. With this view I have this morning sketched out ideas to run parallel with the last forty lines beginning at Quis Catilina tuis natalibus, and mean to compose them forthwith. We have had the two Pinneys[4] with us, John for a month: they left us yesterday, and as I now feel a return of literary appetite I mean to take a snack of satire by way of Sandwich.[5] My next Letter then will probably contain the passage, for your strictures. If you could find leisure

[1] To the living of Hunmanby, Yorks.
[2] Of poems. [3] W. W.'s imitation of Juvenal, *Satire* viii.
[4] John and Azariah Pinney, sons of the owner of Racedown Lodge.
[5] A reference to the parentage of Basil Montagu (see List of Correspondents).

you would oblige me by employing an hour on some part of the work as there is more of it than I wish to execute. I am afraid you have neglected to make application for the newspapers; they would be a great amusement to us in the depth of our present solitude. I have been engaged an hour and a half this morning in hewing wood and rooting up hedges, and I think it no bad employment to feel "the penalty of Adam" in this way; some of our friends have not been so lucky; witness poor Montague. You are now a rich man and of course, like every sensible rich man, will occasionally turn your thoughts towards travel, foreign, or domestic. Devonshire and Cornwall have many attractions if they should be powerful enough to lead you this way you will not pass us by. I have some thoughts of exploring the country westward of us, in the course of next summer, but in an humble evangelical way; to wit à pied. As there are no large cities that road, I shall not have much occasion to shake the dust of[f] my feet in sign of indignation or abhorrence, on other accounts however it will be necessary to perform that operation. I mean to publish volume-wise; could you engage to get rid for me of a dozen copies or more among your numerous acquaintance. *The damages* to use a Lancashire phrase will be four or five shillings per copy. I do not mean to put forth a[ny] formal subscription; but could wish upon my acquaintances and *their* acquaintances to quarter so many as would ensure me from positive loss; further this adventurer wisheth not[1] Adieu—your affectionate friend,

W. Wordsworth

Basil[2] is quite well quant au physique mais pour le moral il-y-a bien à craindre. Among other things he lies like a little devil. adieu

8. *To* William Mathews

Racedown near Crewkern,
March 21st, [1796]

Dear Mathews,

I could wish our correspondence were more frequent. I fully expected to hear from you by Azor Pinney, and was not a little

[1] An echo of the dedication of Shakespeare's *Sonnets.*
[2] Montagu's son, who was living with W. W. and D. W.

surprized you omitted so good an opportunity of sending me the
Vol: of fugitive poetry. Pray write to me at length and give me an
account of your proceedings in the society or any other information
likely to interest me. Are your members much encreased? and what
is of more consequence have you improved I do not ask in the [art]
of speaking, but in the more important one of thinking? I believe I
put these questions to you once before, but they were never
answered. You were right about Southey,[1] he is certainly a
coxcomb, and has proved it completely by the preface to *his Joan of
Arc*, an *epic* poem which he has just published. This preface is
indeed a very conceited performance and the poem though in some
passages of first-rate excellence is on the whole of very inferior
execution. Our present life is utterly barren of such events as merit
even the short-lived chronicle of an accidental letter. We plant
cabbages, and if retirement, in its full perfection, be as powerful in
working transformations as one of Ovid's Gods, you may perhaps
suspect that into cabbages we shall be transformed. Indeed I learn
that such has been the prophecy of one of our London friends. In
spite of all this I was toleraby industrious in reading, if reading can
ever deserve the name of industry, till our good friends the Pinneys
came amongst us; and I have since *returned* to my books. As to
writing it is out of the question. Not however entirely to forget the
world, I season my recollection of some of its objects with a little
ill-nature, I attempt to write satires! and in all satires whatever the
authors may say there will be found a spice of malignity. Neither
Juvenal or Horace were without it, and what shall we say of
Boileau and Pope or the more redoubted Peter.[2] These are great
names, but to myself I shall apply the passage of Horace, changing
the bee into a wasp to suit the subject.

> Ego apis matinae
> More modoque, etc, etc.[3]

I hope you have preserved the catalogue of my books left at
Montagu's. You would oblige me much by calling there; and
desiring Jones[4] to procure a box sufficient to contain them. See that

---

[1] See List of Correspondents.
[2] John Wolcot, 'Peter Pindar' (1738–1819).
[3] Horace, *Odes*, IV. ii. 27.
[4] Wrangham's pupil, now living with Montagu.

they are nailed up in it. Gilpin's tour into Scotland, and his northern tour, each 2 vol.,[1] ought to be amongst the number. Montagu either did lend, or talked of lending, one of these to Miss Raby.[2] Pray request that he would take care to have it returned immediately. I am the more solicitous on this account as the books, being very expensive, they are the *less likely* to be returned. Pray give my best compts to Myers, and say I mean to write to him very soon. How are you now employed? and what do you do for money? If you could muster the cash to come down, we should be glad to see you during the course of this summer. If the outside of a coach should not disagree with you you might come for a trifle, the fare being only 14 shillings. Pray write soon. Adieu. Your affectionate friend,

W. Wordsworth

My Sister would be very glad of your assistance in her Italian studies. She has already gone through half of Davila,[3] and yesterday we began Ariosto. I have received from Montagu, Godwyn's second edition.[4] I expect to find the work much improved. I cannot say that I have been encouraged in this hope by the perusal of the second preface, which is all I have yet looked into. Such a piece of barbarous writing I have not often seen. It contains scarce one sentence decently written. I am surprized to find such gross faults in a writer who has had so much practise in composition. Give me some news about the theatre. I have attempted to read Holcroft's *Man of Ten Thousand*,[5] but such stuff! Demme hey, humph.

9. *To* Joseph Cottle

[Alfoxden],
13th September, [1797]

My dear Cottle

I ought to have answered your last kind Letter immediately. I have nothing that can be urged in my excuse so that I must throw

---

[1] Works by William Gilpin (1724–1804), writer on the picturesque.

[2] A friend of Montagu and Wrangham.

[3] Author of *Historia delle Guerre Civili di Francia*, 1630.

[4] Of *Political Justice*.   [5] The comedy by Thomas Holcroft (1745–1890).

myself entirely upon your friendship. Your offers of pecuniary accomodation were in a very small degree indeed less acceptable than if I had really had occasion to avail myself of them. This is not the case at present—if it should happen to be so you may be assured I will not fail to betake myself to you. I propose to be in Bristol ere three weeks are past, when I shall have the pleasure of talking to you on books, etc. If you can manage to come over to Allfoxden before, we shall be *very glad* to see you. We hope your health is by this time completely reestablished. My sister joins in affectionate Remembrances.

Your sincere friend,

W. Wordsworth

Coleridge is gone over to Bowles with his tragedy,[1] which he had finished to the middle of the 5th act; he set off a week ago.

10. *To* James Losh

Allfoxden, near Stowey, Bridgwater, Somersetshire

March 11th, [1798]

My dear Losh,

I have wished much to hear from you. I suppose that your marriage has not yet taken place or I should certainly have been apprized of it. I have had some fears about your health, but I have constantly banished them as soon as they came into my mind. Perhaps you have heard of the unexampled liberality of the Wedgwoods[2] towards Coleridge; they have settled an annuity of 150£ upon him, for life. We are obliged to quit this place at Midsummer. I have already spoken to you of its enchanting beauty. Do contrive to come and see us before we go away. Coleridge is now writing by me at the same table. I need not say how ardently he joins with me in this wish, and how deeply interested he is in e[very]thing relating to you. We have a

---

[1] S. T. C. (see List of Correspondents), whom W. W. had met two years before, was completing his tragedy *Osorio* for Drury Lane, with the encouragement of William Lisle Bowles (see List of Correspondents).

[2] See List of Correspondents.

delightful scheme in agitation, which is rendered still more delightful by a probability which I cannot exclude from my mind that you may be induced to join in the party. We have come to a resolution, Coleridge, Mrs. Coleridge, my Sister and myself of going into Germany, where we purpose to pass the two ensuing years in order to acquire the German language, and to furnish ourselves with a tolerable stock of information in natural science. Our plan is to settle if possible in a village near a university, in a pleasant, and, if we can a mountainous, country; it will be desirable that this place should be as near as may be to Hamburg on account of the expense of travelling. What do you say to this? I know that Cecilia Baldwin[1] has great activity and spirit, may I venture to whisper a wish to her that she would consent to join this little colony? I have not forgotten your apprehensions from Sea-sickness; there may be many other obstacles which I cannot divine. I cannot, however, suppress wishes which I have so ardently felt. Where is Tweddel?[2] Will you have the goodness to write to him, and to request that he would inform you what places he has seen in Germany, which he thinks eligible residence for persons with such views: either from accidental or permanent advantages; also, if he could give any information respecting the prices of board, lodging, house-rent, provisions, etc upon which we should be justified in proceeding it would be highly useful.

I have not yet seen any numbers of the *Economist*,[3] though I requested Cottle to transmit them to me. I have been tolerably industrious within the last few weeks. I have written 1300 lines of a poem which I hope to make of considerable utility; its title will be *The Recluse or views of Nature, Man, and Society*.[4] Let me hear from you immediately. My Sister begs her kind remembrances. I am, dear Losh, your affecte. Friend,

W. Wordsworth

[1] Losh's fiancée, whom he had in fact married the previous month.
[2] A Cambridge friend of Losh and Wrangham.
[3] A Newcastle journal to which Losh contributed.
[4] W. W. had now composed the preamble to *The Recluse*, the long poem of which only the second part, *The Excursion*, was completed. He had also expanded *The Ruined Cottage* (which eventually became Bk. i of *The Excursion*).

11. *To* Joseph Cottle

Alfoxden, 12th April, 1798.

My dear Cottle,

. . . You will be pleased to hear that I have gone on very rapidly adding to my stock of poetry.[1] Do come and let me read it to you, under the old trees in the park. We have a little more than two months to stay in this place. Within these four days the season has advanced with greater rapidity than I ever remember, and the country becomes almost every hour more lovely. God bless you,

Your affectionate friend,

W. Wordsworth

12. *To* Thomas Poole

Hamburg October 3 [1798]

My dear Poole,

It was my intention to have written to you from England to bid you farewell. I was prevented by procrastination and I now take up the pen to assure you that my sister and myself both retain the most lively recollection of the many kindnesses which we have received from you and your family. I believe my letter would be more acceptable to you if instead of speaking on this subject I should tell you what we have seen during our fortnight's residence at Hamburg. It is a *sad* place. In this epithet you have the soul and essence of all the information which I have been able to gather. We have however been treated with unbounded kindness by Mr. Klopstock the brother of the poet[2] and I have no doubt this city contains a world of good and honest people, if one had but the skill to find them. I will relate to you an anecdote. The other day I went into a Bakers shop. Put into his hand two pieces of money for which I ought to have had five loaves but I thought the pieces had only been worth two loaves each. I took up four loaves. The baker would not permit this, upon which I took from his hand one of the pieces, and pointed to two loaves, and then re-offering to him the

---

[1] The earliest of the *Lyrical Ballads*.

[2] Friedrich Klopstock (1724–1803), author of *Der Messias*.

piece I took up two others: he dashed the loaves from my hand into the basket in the most brutal manner. I begged him to return the other piece of money, which he refused to do, nor would he let me have any bread into the bargain. So I left the shop empty-handed and he retained the money. Is there any baker in England who would have done this to a foreigner? I am afraid we must say, yes. Money, money is here the god of universal worship. And rapacity and extortion among the lower classes and the classes immediately above them, are just sufficiently common to be a matter of glory and exultation.

The situation of the town is upon the whole pleasant: the ramparts present many agreeable views of the river and the adjoining country. The banks of the Elbe are thickly sown with houses built by the merchants for Saturday and Sunday retirement. The English merchants have set the example, the style is in imitation of the English garden, imitated as Della Crusca[1] might imitate Virgil. It is however something gained, the dawning of a better day.

We set off this evening by the diligence for Brunswick. We shall be two days and two nights constantly travelling in a vehicle compared with which Tanlin's long coach[2] is a very chariot of the Gods—patience patience. We have one comfort travelling in this way, a very great one for poor. viz. that we cannot be cheated. Coleridge has most likely informed you that he and Chester[3] have settled at Ratzeburg. Dorothy and I are going to speculate farther up in the country.

I have seen Klopstock the poet. [There] is nothing remarkable either in his conversation or appearance, except his extreme gaiety with legs swelled as thick as your thigh. He is in his 74th year. He began his Messiah at 17. Not the composition for the plan employed him 3 years.

I sent a copy of my tragedy[4] by Wade.[5] Ward[6] will transcribe it as soon as he can and you have the goodness to transmit the original to Wade. It is in a sad incorrect state. Ward must use his

[1] The pen-name of Robert Merry, writer of inflated and sentimental verse.
[2] The Bridgwater coach.   [3] S. T. C.'s travelling companion.
[4] *The Borderers* (publ. 1842).
[5] Josiah Wade, linen draper of Bristol, S. T. C.'s early friend.
[6] Poole's apprentice.

best eyes and his best sagacity in decyphering it. Pray have the goodness to remove those boxes of ours from that damp room at Mr Coleridges, and lodge them in some perfectly *dry* place at Stowey. I could wish also that they might be well aired, I mean on the outside as I am afraid the things may have already sustained some injury. Either let them be put in the sunshine or before a large fire.

My sister joins me in kindest remembrances to yourself and your mother, nor forgetting Ward. I hope Mrs Coleridge is well and the children.[1]

Yours most affectionately,

Wm Wordsworth

I have one word to say about Allfoxden: pray keep your eye upon it. If any series of accidents should bring it again into the market we should be glad to have it, if we could manage it.

13. *To* Josiah Wedgwood

Goslar February 5th 1799

Dear Sir,

I have received, as you probably have been already informed, the value of forty pound sterling from Mr Krause of Brunswick. I do not think I shall have occasion to give you any more trouble of this kind. I have written to request of my Brother to pay into your hands all the money which he has received belonging to me. I fear I have overdrawn my ability at least fifteen pounds; if so I must remain your debtor till the end of the summer. Knowing as I do your goodness I should not have taken this liberty had I not been going into Upper Saxony, where I should have had no further means of supplying myself, and though it is probable that we are going to make rather a *tour* than a residence yet I was unwilling to be driven into port by sheer lack of provisions.

We have had a pleasant residence at Goslar where we have been for eighteen weeks. Our progress in the language has been very, very far short of what it would have been, had we been richer. The

[1] Hartley (1796–1849), the poet, and Berkeley Coleridge.

practice of taking people *en pension* is a thing almost unknown in Germany, and consequently, a price is demanded far above our calculations and our means; on this account that time which I expected would have been the most profitable has with respect to attaining the language been utterly useless, as we have been compelled to be together alone at meal-times etc, etc. Goslar is a venerable, (venerable I mean as to its external appearance) decayed city. It is situated at the foot of some small mountains, on the edge of the Harts forest. It was once the residence of Emperors, and it is now the residence of Grocers and Linen-drapers who are, I say it with a feeling of sorrow, a wretched race; the flesh, blood, and bone of their minds being nothing but knavery and low falshood. We have met with one dear and kind creature, but he is so miserably deaf that we could only play with him games of cross-purposes, and he likewise labours under a common German infirmity, the loss of teeth, so that with bad German, bad English, bad French, bad hearing, and bad utterance you will imagine we have had very pretty dialogues but the creature is all kindness and benevolence, and I shall never forget him. On Sunday Morning we set off to Nordhausen. Our present plan is to return to Hamburgh when the mild weather comes on, whence we shall shortly set sail for England unless we meet with some opportunity of learning the language more favorable than we have reason to expect. I mean by learning the language not merely the knowing that "Liebe" is German for "love", and "darum" for "therefore" etc but the having your mind in such a state that the several German idioms and phrases without any act of thought or consideration shall immediately excite feelings analogous to those which are excited in the breasts of the natives. Unless our minds *are* in this state, what we call knowledge of languages is a wretched self-delusion; words are a mere dead letter in the mind. I have received two very kind letters from Mr Krause with most obliging offers of civility. I hope to have the pleasure of making my personal acknowledgements to him on my return to Hamburgh. I remain, with sentiments of great respect and esteem,

Yours affectionately
Wm Wordsworth

14. *To* Joseph Cottle

24th June [1799]
Sockburn[1] near Northallerton, Yorkshire,
To be left at Smeaton.

My dear Cottle,

I received your letter enclosing a 5 £ Bank note. I am in want of money. I shall therefore be obliged to you if you will remit to *me* (not to my Brother as I before requested) that remaining 15 £ as soon as you can without inconvenience. Most probably your statement is accurate; for myself I recollect nothing about it. What I told you was from Dorothy's memory, and she is by no means certain about it.

You tell me the poems have not sold ill. If it is possible, I should wish to know *what number* have been sold. From what I can gather it seems that The Ancyent Mariner[2] has upon the whole been an injury to the volume, I mean that the old words and the strangeness of it have deterred readers from going on. If the volume should come to a second Edition I would put in its place some little things which would be more likely to suit the common taste.

When you send the money pray look over this letter and reply to this part of it.

I shall be obliged to you if you will send me three copies of the Ballads enclosed in your parcel to Charles Lloyd.[3] I shall easily get them from Penrith.

We are highly gratified by the affectionate wish which you express to see us again in Somersetshire. We are as yet not determined where we shall settle; we have no particular house in view, so it is impossible for us to say when we shall have the pleasure of meeting you.

Dorothy sends her very kind love to you. God bless you, my dear Cottle.

Your affectionate Fd
W. Wordsworth

[1] The Hutchinsons' farm, where W. W. now renewed his acquaintance with his future wife Mary.

[2] S. T. C.'s chief contribution to *Lyrical Ballads*, omitted from the 2nd edn.

[3] Charles Lloyd (1775–1839), author of *Edmund Oliver*, who had lodged with S. T. C. at Bristol in 1796.

We thank you for your care of our box. We do not at present want any of its contents.

We have never heard from Coleridge since our arrival in England—we are anxious for news of him. I hope he is coming home as he does not write to us

15. *To* S. T. Coleridge

Christmas Eve, [and 27 Dec.] Grasmere [1799].

My dearest Coleridge

We arrived here last Friday, and have now been four days in our new abode[1] without writing to you, a long time! but we have been in such confusion as not to have had a moment's leisure. We found two Letters from you one of which I had heard of at Sockburne. I do not think there is much cause to be uneasy about Cookes[2] affair, but as he has not answered my Letter I cannot say but I am sorry I mentioned your name: feeling so forcibly as I did that, if any man had reason to suppose I could be of service to him, he would gain incalculably by the proposed change, I was betrayed into language not sufficiently considerate and reserved. If it is in my power to remedy any part of the evil by writing again to Cooke, or in any other way, pray mention it to me.

I arrived at Sockburn the day after you quitted it, I scarcely knew whether to be sorry or no that you were no longer there, as it would have been a great pain to me to have parted from you. I was sadly disappointed in not finding Dorothy; Mary was a solitary housekeeper and overjoyed to see me. D. is now sitting by me racked with the tooth-ache. This is a grievous misfortune as she has so much work for her needle among the bedcurtains etc that she is absolutely buried in it. We have both caught troublesome colds in our new and almost empty house, but we hope to make it a comfortable dwelling. Our first two days were days of fear as one of the rooms upstairs smoked like a furnace, we have since learned that it is uninhabitable as a sitting room on this account; the other room however which is fortunately the one we intended for our *living* room promises uncommonly well; that is, the chimney draws

---

[1] Dove Cottage.   [2] A friend of Basil Montagu.

perfectly, and does not even smoke at the first lighting of the fire. In particular winds most likely we shall have *puffs* of *inconvenience*, but this I believe will be found a curable evil, by means of devils as they are called and other beneficent agents which we shall station at the top of the chimney if their services should be required. D is much pleased with the house and *appurtenances* the orchard especially; in imagination she has already built a seat with a summer shed on the highest platform in this our little domestic slip of mountain. The spot commands a view over the roof of our house, of the lake, the church, helm cragg, and two thirds of the vale. We mean also to enclose the two or three yards of ground between us and the road, this for the sake of a few flowers, and because it will make it more our own. Besides, am I fanciful when I would extend the obligation of gratitude to insensate things? May not a man have a salutary pleasure in doing something gratuitously for the sake of his house, as for an individual to which he owes so much. The manners of the neighbouring cottagers have far exceeded our expectations; They seem little adulterated; indeed as far as we have seen not at all. The people we have uniformly found kind-hearted frank and manly, prompt to serve without servility. This is but an experience of four days, but we have had dealings with persons of various occupations, and have had no reason whatever to complain. We do not think it will be necessary for us to keep a servant. We have agreed to give a woman who lives in one of the adjoining cottages two shillings a week for attending two or three hours a day to light the fires wash dishes etc etc In addition to this she is to have her victuals every Saturday when she will be employed in scouring, and to have her victuals likewise on other days if we should have visitors and she is wanted more than usual. We could have had this attendance for eighteen pence a week but we added the sixpence for the sake of the poor woman, who is made happy by it. The weather since our arrival has been a keen frost, one morning two thirds of the lake were covered with ice which continued all the day but to our great surprize the next morning, though there was no intermission of the frost had entirely disappeared. The ice had been so thin that the wind had broken it up, and most likely driven it to the outlet of the lake. Rydale is covered with ice, clear as polished steel, I have procured a pair of skates and tomorrow mean to give my body to the wind,—not however without reasonable caution. We are looking for John[1] every day; it will [be] a pity, if he should come, that D. is so much engaged, she has scarcely been out since our arrival; one evening I tempted her forth; the planet Jupiter was on the top of the hugest of the Rydale mountains, but I had reason to repent of having seduced her from her work as she returned with a raging tooth-ache. We were highly pleased with your last short letter which we had confidently and eagerly expected at Sockburn. Stuarts conduct is liberal and I hope it will answer for him.[2] You make no mention of your health. I was uneasy on that account when you were with us: upon recollection it seemed to me that the fatigues, accidents, and exposures attendant upon our journey, took greater hold of you than they ought to have done had you[r] habit of body been such as not to render caution necessary for it. Your account of Pinney is not more than I should have expected as I know him to be an excellent man. I received a Letter from him enclosing a five pound note, and informing me he hoped soon to be able to render me more substantial assistance. I wrote to him requesting him to use all his interest to induce M.[3] to repay the principal, etc. and, that if it was his intention to do any-thing to disentangle M. from his embarrassments, I recom-mended to him to consider my claim. We shall be glad to receive the German books though it will be at least 3 weeks before D. will have any leisure to begin. Your selection of names in your history of the eminent men with whom you dined entertained me much a wretched Painter, a worse Philosopher,[4] and a respectable bonesetter. This last I mention merely for the sake of ekeing out my sentence, as I venerate the profession of a Surgeon, and deem it the only one which has anything that deserves the name of utility in it. I suspect that it may partly be owing to something like unconscious affectation, but in honest truth I feel little disposed to notice what you say of the Lyrical Ballads though the account when I first read it gave me pleasure. The said Mr. G. I have often heard described as a puppy, one of the fawning, flattering kind in short, a polite liar, often perhaps without knowing himself to be so. Accordingly he would snatch at an opportunity of saying anything agreeable to

[1] Their 'sailor' brother.
[2] Daniel Stuart (see List of Correspondents) had offered S. T. C. further employment on the *Morning Post.*
[3] Montagu.   [4] William Godwin.

your friend Fox[1] ergo the account is smoke or something near it.
You do not speak of your travelling conversations,[2] I have begun
the pastoral of *Bowman*:[3] in my next letter I shall probably be able
to send it to you. I am afraid it will have one fault that of being too
long. As to the Tragedy and Peter Bell,[4] D. will do all in her power
to put them forward. Composition I find invariably pernicious to
me, and even penmanship if continued for any length of time at one
sitting. I shall therefore wish you good night my beloved friend, a
wish, with a thousand others, in which D. joins me. I am afraid half
of what I have written is illegible, farewell. Friday Ev: We have
been overhead in confusion, painting the rooms, mending the
doors, and heaven knows what! This however shall not prevent me
from attempting to give you some account of our Journey hither.
We left Sockburne tuesday before last early in the morning, D. on a
double horse behind that good creature George,[5] and I upon Lilly,
or Violet as Cottle calls her. We cross'd the Tees in the Sockburn
fields by moonlight. George accompanied us eight miles beyond
Richmond and there we parted with sorrowful hearts. We were
now in Wensley dale and D and I set off side by side to foot it as far
as Kendal. A little before sunset we reached one of the waterfalls of
which I read you a short description in Mr Taylor's tour I meant to
have attempted to give you a picture of it but I feel myself too lazy
to execute the task. Tis a singular scene; such a performance as you
might have expected from some giant gardiner employed by one of
Queen Elizabeth's Courtiers, if this same giant gardiner had
consulted with Spenser and they two had finish'd the work
together. By this you will understand that with something of
vastness or grandeur it is at once formal and wild. We reach'd the
town of Askrigg, 12 miles, about six in the evening, having walked
the three last miles in the dark and two of them over hard-frozen
road to the great annoyance of our feet and ancles. Next morning
the earth was thinly covered with snow, enough to make the road
soft and prevent its being slippery. On leaving Askrigg we turned
aside to see another waterfall 'twas a beautiful morning with
driving snow-showers that disappeared by fits, and unveiled the

---

[1] Probably Charles James Fox (see List of Correspondents).
[2] A proposed account of his recent trip to the Lake District.
[3] *The Brothers*.   [4] Composed 1798, publ. 1819.
[5] George Hutchinson, Mary's younger brother.

east which was all one delicious pale orange colour. After walking through two fields we came to a mill which we pass'd and in a moment a sweet little valley opened before us, with an area of grassy ground, and a stream dashing over various lamina of black rocks close under a bank covered with firs. The bank and stream on our left, another woody bank on our right, and the flat meadow in front from which, as at Buttermere, the stream had retired as it were to hide itself under the shade. As we walked up this delightful valley we were tempted to look back perpetually on the brook which reflected the orange light of the morning among the gloomy rocks with a brightness varying according to the agitation of the current. The steeple of Askrigg was between us and the east, at the bottom of the valley; it was not a quarter of a mile distant, but oh! how far we were from it. The two banks seemed to join before us with a facing of rock common to them both, when we reached this point the valley opened out again, two rocky banks on each side, which, hung with ivy and moss and fringed luxuriantly with brush-wood, ran directly parallel to each other and then approaching with a gentle curve, at their point of union presented a lofty waterfall, the termination of the valley. Twas a keen frosty morning, showers of snow threatening us but the sun bright and active; we had a task of twenty one miles to perform in a short winter's day, all this put our minds in such a state of excitation that we were no unworthy spectators of this delightful scene. On a nearer approach the water seemed to fall down a tall arch or rather nitch which had shaped itself by insensible moulderings in the wall of an old castle. We left this spot with reluctance but highly exhilarated. When we had walked about a mile and a half we overtook two men with a string of ponies and some empty carts. I recommended to D. to avail herself of this opportunity of husbanding her strength, we rode with them more than two miles, twas bitter cold, the wind driving the snow behind us in the best stile of a mountain storm. We soon reached an Inn at a place called Hardraw, and descending from our vehicles, after warming ourselves by the cottage fire we walked up the brook side to take a view of a *third* waterfall. We had not gone above a few hundred yards between two winding rocky banks before we came full upon it. It appeared to throw itself in a narrow line from a lofty wall of rock; the water which shot manifestly to some distance from the rock seeming from the extreme height of the fall to be dispersed before it reached the bason, into a thin shower of snow that was toss'd about like snow blown from the roof of a house. We were disappointed in the cascade though the introductory and accompanying banks were a noble mixture of grandeur and beauty. We walked up to the fall and what would I not give if I could convey to you the images and feelings which were then communicated to me. After cautiously sounding our way over stones of all colours and sizes encased in the clearest ice formed by the spray of the waterfall, we found the rock which before had seemed a perpendicular wall extending itself over us like the cieling of a huge cave; from the summit of which the water shot directly over our heads into a bason and among fragments of rock wrinkled over with masses of ice, white as snow, or rather as D. says like congealed froth. The water fell at least ten yards from us and we stood directly behind it, the excavation not so deep in the rock as to impress any feeling of darkness, but lofty and magnificent, and in connection with the adjoining banks excluding as much of the sky as could well be spared from a scene so exquisitely beautiful. The spot where we stood was as dry as the chamber in which I am now sitting, and the incumbent rock of which the groundwork was limestone veined and dappled with colours which melted into each other in every possible variety. On the summit of the cave were three festoons or rather wrinkles in the rock which ran parallel to each other like the folds of a curtain when it is drawn up; each of them was hung with icicles of various length, and nearly in the middle of the festoons in the deepest valley made by their waving line the stream shot from between the rows of icicles in irregular fits of strength and with a body of water that momently varied. Sometimes it threw itself into the bason in one continued curve, sometimes it was interrupted almost midway in its fall and, being blown towards us, part of the water fell at no great distance from our feet like the heaviest thunder shower. In such a situation you have at every moment a feeling of the presence of the sky. Above the highest point of the waterfall large fleecy clouds drove over our heads and the sky appeared of a blue more than usually brilliant. The rocks on each side, which, joining with the sides of the cave, formed the vista of the brook were chequered with three diminutive waterfalls or rather veins of water each of which was a miniature of all that summer and winter can produce of delicate beauty. The rock in the centre of these falls where the water was most abundant, deep black, the adjoining parts yellow white purple violet and dove colour'd, or covered with water-plants of the most vivid green, and hung with streams and fountains of ice and icicles that in some places seemed to conceal the verdure of the plants and the variegated colours of the rocks and in some places to render their hues more splendid. I cannot express to you the enchanted effect produced by this Arabian scene of colour as the wind blew aside the great waterfall behind which we stood and hid and revealed each of these faery cataracts in irregular succession or displayed them with various gradations of distinctness, as the intervening spray was thickened or dispersed. In the luxury of our imaginations we could not help feeding on the pleasure which in the heat of a July noon this cavern would spread through a frame exquisitely sensible. That huge rock of ivy on the right! the bank winding round on the left with all its living foliage, and the breeze stealing up the valley and bedewing the cavern with the faintest imaginable spray. And then the murmur of the water, the quiet, the seclusions, and a long summer day to dream in! Have I not tired you? With difficulty we tore ourselves away, and on returning to the cottage we found we had been absent an hour. Twas a short one to us, we were in high spirits, and off we drove, and will you believe me when I tell you that we walked the next ten miles, by the watch over a high mountain road, thanks to the wind that drove behind us and the good road, in two hours and a quarter, a marvellous feat of which D. will long tell. Well! we rested in a tempting inn, close by Garsdale chapel, a lowly house of prayer in a charming little valley, here we stopp'd a quarter of an hour and then off to Sedbergh 7 miles farther in an hour and thirty five minutes, the wind was still at our backs and the road delightful. I must hurry on, next morning we walked to Kendal, 11 miles, a terrible up and down road, in 3 hours, and after buying and ordering furniture, the next day by half past four we reached Grasmere in a post chaise. So ends my long story. God bless you,

W. W.

Take no pains to contradict the story that the L. B. are entirely yours. Such a rumour is the best thing that can befall them. Poor Cottle![1] of this enough.[2]

16. *To* Dorothy Wordsworth

[*c*. late May 1800?]

When you are writing to France say all that is affectionate to A. and all that is fatherly to C.[3]

17. *To* Charles James Fox

Grasmere, Westmoreland January 14th 1801

Sir,

It is not without much difficulty, that I have summoned the courage to request your acceptance of these Volumes.[4] Should I express my real feelings, I am sure that I should seem to make a parade of diffidence and humility.

Several of the poems contained in these Volumes are written upon subjects, which are the common property of all Poets, and which, at some period of your life, must have been interesting to a man of your sensibility, and perhaps may still continue to be so. It would be highly gratifying to me to suppose that even in a single instance the manner in which I have treated these general topics should afford you any pleasure; but such a hope does not influence me upon the present occasion; in truth I do not feel it. Besides, I am convinced that there must be many things in this collection, which may impress you with an unfavorable idea of my intellectual powers. I do not say this with a wish to degrade myself; but I am sensible that this must be the case, from the different circles in which we have moved, and the different objects with which we have been conversant.

[1] Cottle was in financial difficulties.
[2] D. W. adds a PS before W. W.'s.
[3] Annette Vallon and Wordsworth's 'French' daughter Caroline. The letter to which this is a PS has not survived.   [4] The 2nd edn. of *Lyrical Ballads*.

Being utterly unknown to you as I am, I am well aware, that if I am justified in writing to you at all, it is necessary, my letter should be short; but I have feelings within me which I hope will so far shew themselves in this letter, as to excuse the trespass which I am afraid I shall make. In common with the whole of the English people I have observed in your public character a constant predominance of sensibility of heart. Necessitated as you have been from your public situation to have much to do with men in bodies, and in classes, and accordingly to contemplate them in that relation, it has been your praise that you have not thereby been prevented from looking upon them as individuals, and that you have habitually left your heart open to be influenced by them in that capacity. This habit cannot but have made you dear to Poets; and I am sure that, if since your first entrance into public life there has been a single true poet living in England, he must have loved you.

But were I assured that I myself had a just claim to the title of a Poet, all the dignity being attached to the word which belongs to it, I do not think that I should have ventured for that reason to offer these volumes to you: at present it is solely on account of two poems in the second volume, the one entitled "The Brothers," and the other "Michael," that I have been emboldened to take this liberty.

It appears to me that the most calamitous effect, which has followed the measures which have lately been pursued in this country, is a rapid decay of the domestic affections among the lower orders of society. This effect the present Rulers of this country are not conscious of, or they disregard it. For many years past, the tendency of society amongst almost all the nations of Europe has been to produce it. But recently by the spreading of manufactures through every part of the country, by the heavy taxes upon postage, by workhouses, Houses of Industry, and the invention of Soup-shops etc. etc. superadded to the encreasing disproportion between the price of labour and that of the necessaries of life, the bonds of domestic feeling among the poor, as far as the influence of these things has extended, have been weakened, and in innumerable instances entirely destroyed. The evil would be the less to be regretted, if these institutions were regarded only as palliatives to a disease; but the vanity and pride of their promoters are so subtly interwoven with them, that they are deemed great discoveries and blessings to humanity. In the mean time parents are separated from their children, and children from their parents; the wife no longer prepares with her own hands a meal for her husband, the produce of his labour; there is little doing in his house in which his affections can be interested, and but little left in it which he can love. I have two neighbours, a man and his wife, both upwards of eighty years of age; they live alone; the husband has been confined to his bed many months and has never had, nor till within these few weeks has ever needed, any body to attend to him but his wife. She has recently been seized with a lameness which has often prevented her from being able to carry him his food to his bed; the neighbours fetch water for her from the well, and do other kind offices for them both, but her infirmities encrease. She told my Servant two days ago that she was afraid they must both be boarded out among some other Poor of the parish (they have long been supported by the parish) but she said, it was hard, having kept house together so long, to come to this, and she was sure that "it would burst her heart." I mention this fact to shew how deeply the spirit of independence is, even yet, rooted in some parts of the country. These people could not express themselves in this way without an almost sublime conviction of the blessings of independent domestic life. If it is true, as I believe, that this spirit is rapidly disappearing, no greater curse can befal a land.

I earnestly entreat your pardon for having detained you so long. In the two Poems, "The Brothers" and "Michael" I have attempted to draw a picture of the domestic affections as I know they exist amongst a class of men who are now almost confined to the North of England. They are small independent *proprietors* of land here called statesmen, men of respectable education who daily labour on their own little properties. The domestic affections will always be strong amongst men who live in a country not crowded with population, if these men are placed above poverty. But if they are proprietors of small estates, which have descended to them from their ancestors, the power which these affections will acquire amongst such men is inconceivable by those who have only had an opportunity of observing hired labourers, farmers, and the manufacturing Poor. Their little tract of land serves as a kind of permanent rallying point for their domestic feelings, as a tablet upon which they are written which makes them objects of memory in a thousand instances when they would otherwise be forgotten. It is a fountain fitted to the nature of social man from which supplies of affection, as pure as his heart was intended for, are daily drawn. This class of men is rapidly disappearing. You, Sir, have a consciousness, upon which every good man will congratulate you, that the whole of your public conduct has in one way or other been directed to the preservation of this class of men, and those who hold similar situations. You have felt that the most sacred of all property is the property of the Poor. The two poems which I have mentioned were written with a view to shew that men who do not wear fine cloaths can feel deeply. "Pectus enim est quod disertos facit, et vis mentis. Ideoque imperitis quoque, si modo sint aliquo affectu concitati, verba non desunt."[1] The poems are faithful copies from nature; and I hope, whatever effect they may have upon you, you will at least be able to perceive that they may excite profitable sympathies in many kind and good hearts, and may in some small degree enlarge our feelings of reverence for our species, and our knowledge of human nature, by shewing that our best qualities are possessed by men whom we are too apt to consider, not with reference to the points in which they resemble us, but to those in which they manifestly differ from us. I thought, at a time when these feelings are sapped in so many ways that the two poems might co-operate, however feebly, with the illustrious efforts which you have made to stem this and other evils with which the country is labouring, and it is on this account alone that I have taken the liberty of thus addressing you.

Wishing earnestly that the time may come when the country may perceive what it has lost by neglecting your advice, and hoping that your latter days may be attended with health and comfort.

I remain, With the highest respect and admiration
Your most obedient and humble Servt
W Wordsworth

[1] See Quintilian, *Inst. Orat.* x. vii. 15.

18. *To* Anne Taylor

Grasmere April 9th. 1801

Madam,

I have great reason to congratulate myself on the pleasure which my poems have afforded you; and I ought to have thanked you sooner for your kindness in communicating it. But I have been prevented by indisposition, a violent cold, which threw me back in some indispensible business; which circumstance, I hope, will plead my excuse.

You do me too much honor when you express a desire to learn from me an account of such events in my life as may have had an influence in forming my present opinions. With this request I should have complied with great pleasure, had the task been more difficult, but the history of my life is very short. I was born at Cockermouth, about twenty-five miles from the place where I now dwell. Before I was nine years of age I was sent to the Grammar School of Hawkshead, a small market-village near the Lake of Esthwaite: there I continued till the beginning of my eighteenth year, at which time I went to Cambridge, where I remained three years and a half. I did not, as I in some respects greatly regret, devote myself to the studies of the University. This neglect of university studies will be easily comprehended by you, when I inform you, that I employed the last of my summer vacations in a pedestrian tour in the Alps. Since I left Cambridge, my time has been spent in travelling upon the Continent, and in England: and in occasional residences in London, and in different parts of England and Wales. At present I am permanently fixed in my native country. I have taken a house in the Vale of *Grasmere*, (a very beautiful spot of which almost every body has heard), and I live with my Sister, meaning, if my health will permit me, to devote my life to literature. It may be proper to add that my Father was by profession an Attorney, and that he and my Mother both died when I was a Boy.

In what I have said I am afraid there will be little which will throw any light on my writings, or gratify the wish which you entertain, to know how I came to adopt the opinions which I have expressed in my preface;[1] and to write in the style in which my

[1] To the 2nd edn. of *Lyrical Ballads*.

poems are written: but in truth my life has been unusually barren of events, and my opinions have grown slowly and, I may say, insensibly.

You ask me if I have always thought so independently. To this question I am able to give you a satisfactory answer by referring you to two poems, which I published in the beginning of the year 1793. The one is entitled "Descriptive Sketches made during a pedestrian Tour in the Italian, Grison, Swiss, and Savoyard Alps", the other "an Evening Walk, an Epistle addressed to a Young Lady"; both published, with my name, by Johnson St Paul's Churchyard. They are juvenile productions, inflated and obscure, but they contain many new images, and vigorous lines; and they would perhaps interest you, by shewing how very widely different my former opinions must have been from those which I hold at present. It would have given me great pleasure to have sent you copies of these poems, if I had been possessed of them. Johnson has told some of my Friends who have called for them, that they were out of print: this must have been a mistake. Unless he has sent them to the Trunk-maker's they must be lying in some corner of his Warehouse, for I have reason to believe that they never sold much.

You flatter me, Madam, that my style is distinguished by a genuine simplicity. Whatever merit I may have in this way I have attained solely by endeavouring to look, as I have said in my preface, steadily at my subject. If you read over carefully the Poem of the Female Vagrant,[1] which was the first written of the Collection (indeed it was written several years before the others) you will see that I have not formerly been conscious of the importance of this rule. The diction of that Poem is often vicious, and the descriptions are often false, giving proofs of a mind inattentive to the true nature of the subject on which it was employed. Hoping that it may afford you some amusement I will write down a few corrections of this poem in which I have endeavoured to bring the language nearer to truth. I think, if you will take the trouble of comparing these corrections with the correspondent passages in the printed poem, you will perceive in what manner I have attempted gradually to purify my diction.

Omit the first stanza entirely and begin the poem with the 2nd, omit the 3rd and 4th Stanzas. Page 70 the Line "His little range of

---

[1] W. W. had published part of the Salisbury Plain poem under this title.

water was denied" must have another substituted for it which I
have not written. Page 72 For, "with proud parade," Read, "day
after day", the next line For "*to sweep* the streets" Read "*and clear'd*
the streets".

Page 73 read the first stanza thus

> "There long were we neglected; and we bore
> Much sorrow ere the fleet its anchor weigh'd.
> Green fields before us, and our native shore,
> We breath'd a pestilential air that made
> Ravage for which no knell was heard—We pray'd
> For our departure; wish'd and wish'd, nor knew
> 'Mid that long sickness, and those hopes delay'd,
> That happier ["] etc. Omit the first stanza of page 74.

Page 75 after the 4th line read thus

> I too was calm—though heavily distress'd!
> O me! how quiet sky and ocean were!
> My heart was heal'd within me, I was bless'd
> And look'd, and look'd etc. etc. Page 76 Read first Stanza

thus

> At midnight once the storming army came:
> Yet do I see the miserable sight,
> The bayonet, the Soldier, and the flame
> That follow'd us, and fac'd us, in our flight:
> When Rape and Murder by the ghastly light
> Seiz'd their joint prey, the Mother and the child!
> But I must leave these thoughts—From night to night
> From day to day the air breath'd soft and mild
> And on the gliding vessel heaven and ocean smil'd.

Page 77—Read the first stanza thus

> And oft I thought, (my fancy was so strong)
> That I, at last, a resting-place had found:
> Here will I dwell said I, my whole life long
> Roaming the illimitable waters round;
> Here will I live: of every friend disown'd,
> Here will I roam about the ocean-flood—
> To break my dream etc etc—

In the next stanza of the same page for "*How dismal* toll'd" Read "*Dismally* toll'd".

I am afraid you may have found the perusal of these fragments tedious and uninteresting. I have no other apology to make, but that I wished, in a way however imperfect, to comply with the request with which you honored me.

I remain, Madam,

Your obliged and faithful Servant

W Wordsworth

19. *To* S. T. Coleridge

[Grasmere, 16 Apr. 1802]

My dear Coleridge

I parted with Mary on Monday afternoon about six oclock, a little on this side of Rushy-ford.[1] Poor Creature! she would have an ugly storm of sleet and snow to encounter and I am anxious to hear how she reached home. Soon after I missed my road in the midst of the storm, some people at a house where I called directed me how to regain the road through the fields, and alas! as you may guess I fared worse and worse. With the loss of half an hour's time, and with no little anxiety I regained the road. Unfortunately, not far from St. Helen's Auckland the Horse came down with me on his knees, but not so as to fall overhead himself or to throw me. Poor beast it was no fault of his! a Chaise-driver of whom I inquired the next day told me it was a wonder he could travel at all, he wanted shoeing so sadly, and his hoofs cleaning and paring. I was so ignorant as not to know that a horse might stand in need of new shoes, though the old ones might not be loose. Except for this accident he carried me very well, better 20 times over than could be expected from a Horse in that condition. The Horse is certainly well worth what Calvert[2] asks for him, and not in my estimation to be at all worse thought of for this accident. I would wish you to buy him on this account if you can conveniently, and I will make up any loss if he should not happen to suit you. He seems shy as if he

---

[1] Nr. Bishop Middleham, where George Hutchinson now farmed.
[2] William Calvert of Greta Bank, Keswick.

had not been well broken, but I did not discover any vice in him. Between the beginning of Lord Darlington's park at Raby and two or three miles beyond Staindrop, I wrote the Poem which you will find on the opposite page. I reached Barnard Castle about half past ten, but I mistook the Inn; I was however well treated, but I wished to have been at the old one where we were together. Between eight and nine next Evening I reached Eusemere,[1] more tired than I should otherwise have been, on account of not being able to ride fast for the horses shoes. Yesterday after dinner we set off on foot meaning to sleep at Paterdale; a storm came on when we were within two miles of the Inn and we were sadly wet: we had a good supper and good beds, but they and the breakfast cost us seven shillings; too much! This morning was delightful; we set off about half past ten and walked slow with many rests; I wrote the little description you will find over leaf[2] during one of them; at Ambleside we called on the Luffs[3] to see how Luff was but learning that the Boddingtons[4] were upstairs we did not see either Luff or his Wife. He has been dangerously ill but is now recovering fast. We reached home at dusk: so ends my story. Now for a word about yourself. I am very sorry indeed you have been poorly. Let us see you as soon as ever you find an inclination to come over.[5] I was much pleased with your verses in Ds letter; there is an admirable simplicity in the language of the first fragment, and I wish there had been more of the 2nd; the fourth line wants mending sadly, in other respects the lines are good. The extract from Pliny is very judicious, I remember having the same opinion of Plinys Letters which you have express'd when I read them many years ago. Farewell, my dear, dear friend.

> Among all lovely things my Love had been,
> Had noted well the stars, all flow'rs that grew
> About her home, but She had never seen
> A Glow-worm, never once—and this I knew.

[1] Home of the Clarksons (see List of Correspondents).
[2] D. W. has copied in 'The cock is crowing' at the end of this letter, with a PS.
[3] Local friends.   [4] Hawkshead friends.
[5] From Greta Hall, Keswick.

While I was riding on a stormy night,
Not far from her abode, I chanced to spy
A single Glowworm once; and at the sight
Down from my Horse I leapt—great joy had I.

I laid the Glowworm gently on a leaf,
And bore it with me through the stormy night
In my left hand—without dismay or grief
Shining, albeit with a fainter light.

When to the Dwelling of my Love I came,
I went into the Orchard quietly,
And left the Glowworm, blessing it by name,
Laid safely by itself, beneath a tree.

The whole next day I hop'd, and hop'd with fear:
At night the Glowworm shone beneath the tree;
I led my Emma to the place,—"Look here!"—
O joy it was for her, and joy for me![1]

The incident of this Poem took place about seven years ago .
between Dorothy and me.

I have sent Thels Book,[2] tell me something about it.

20. *To* John Wilson

[Grasmere, 7 June 1802]

My dear Sir,

Had it not been for a very amiable modesty you could not have
imagined that your letter could give me any offence. It was on
many accounts highly grateful to me. I was pleas'd to find that I
had given so much pleasure to an ingenuous and able mind and I
further considered the enjoyment which you had had from my poems
as an earnest that others might be delighted with them in the same
or a like manner. It is plain from your letter that the pleasure which
I have given you has not been blind or unthinking you have studied

---

[1] *The Glow Worm.*
[2] Probably John Thelwall's *Poems Chiefly Written in Retirement.*

the poems and prove that you have entered into the spirit of them. They have not given you a cheap or vulgar pleasure therefore I feel that you are entitled to my kindest thanks for having done some violence to your natural diffidence in the communication which you have made to me.

There is scarcely any part of your letter that does not deserve particular notice, but partly from a weakness in my stomach and digestion and partly from certain habits of mind I do not write any letters unless upon business not ev[en] to my dearest Friends. Except during absence from my own family I ha[ve] not written five letters of friendship during the last five years. I have mentioned this in order that I may retain your good opinion should my le[tter] be less minute than you are entitled to expect. You seem to be desirous [of] my opinion on the influence of natural objects in forming the character of nati[ons]. This cannot be understood without first considering their influence upon men in [general?] first with reference to such subjects as are common to all countries: and {next?} such as belong exclusively to any particular country or in a greater d[egree] to it than to another. Now it is manifest that no human being can be so besotted and debased by oppression, penury or any other evil which unhum[anizes] man as to be utterly insensible to the colours, forms, or smell of flowers, the [voices?] and motions of birds and beasts, the appearances of the sky and heavenly bodies, the [genial?] warmth of a fine day, the terror and uncomfortableness of a storm, etc etc. How dead soever many full-grown men may outwardly seem to these thi[ings] they all are more or less affected by them, and in childhood, in the first practice and exercise of their senses, they must have been not the nourish[ers] merely, but often the fathers of their passions. There cannot be a doubt that in tracts of country where images of danger, melancholy, grandeur, or loveliness, softness, and ease prevail, that they will make themselves felt powerfully in forming the characters of the people, so as to produce a uniformity of national character, where the nation is small and is not made up of men who, inhabiting different soils, climates, etc by their civil usages, and relations materially interfere with each other. It was so formerly, no doubt, in the Highlands of Scotland but we cannot perhaps observe much of it in our own island at the present day, because, even in the most sequestered places, by manufactures, traffic, religion, Law, interchange of inhabitants etc distinctions are done away which would otherwise have been strong and obvious. This complex state of society does not, however, prevent the characters of individuals from frequently receiving a strong bias not merely from the impressions of general nature, but also from local objects and images. But it seems that to produce these effects in the degree in which we frequently find them to be produced there must be a peculiar sensibility of original organization combining with moral accidents, as is exhibited in *The Brothers* and in *Ruth*—I mean, to produce this in a marked degree not that I believe that any man was ever brought up in the country without loving it, especially in his better moments, or in a district of particular grandeur or beauty without feeling some stronger attachment to it on that account than he would otherwise have felt. I include, you will observe, in these considerations the influence of climate, changes in the atmosphere and elements and the labours and occupations which particular districts require.

You begin what you say upon the Idiot Boy with this observation, that nothing is a fit subject for poetry which does not please. But here follows a question, Does not please whom? Some have little knowledge of natural imagery of any kind, and, of course, little relish for it, some are disgusted with the very mention of the words pastoral poetry, sheep or shepherds, some cannot tolerate a poem with a ghost or any supernatural agency in it, others would shrink from an animated description of the pleasures of love, as from a thing carnal and libidinous some cannot bear to see delicate and refined feelings ascribed to men in low conditions of society, because their vanity and self-love tell them that these belong only to themselves and men like themselves in dress, station, and way of life: others are disgusted with the naked language of some of the most interesting passions of men, because either it is indelicate, or gross, or [vu]lgar, as many fine ladies could not bear certain expressions in The [Mad] Mother and the Thorn, and, as in the instance of Adam Smith, who, we [are] told, could not endure the Ballad of Clym of the Clough, because the [au]thor had not written like a gentleman; then there are professional[, loca]l and national prejudices forevermore some take no interest in the [descri]ption of a particular passion or quality, as love of solitariness, we will say, [gen]ial activity of fancy, love of nature, religion, and so forth, because they have [little or?] nothing of it in themselves, and so on without end. I return then to [the] question, please whom? or what? I answer, human nature, as it has been [and eve]r will be. But where are we to find the best measure of this? I answer, [from with]in; by stripping our own hearts naked, and by looking out of ourselves to[wards me]n who lead the simplest lives most according to nature men who [ha]ve never known false refinements, wayward and artificial desires, false criti[ci]sms, effeminate habits of thinking and feeling, or who, having known these [t]hings, have outgrown them. This latter class is the most to be depended upon, but it is very small in number. People in our rank in life are perpetually falling into one sad mistake, namely, that of supposing that human nature and the persons they associate with are one and the same thing. Whom do we generally associate with? Gentlemen, persons of fortune, professional men, ladies persons who can afford to buy or can easily procure books of half a guinea price, hot-pressed, and printed upon superfine paper. These persons are, it is true, a part of human nature, but we err lamentably if we suppose them to be fair representatives of the vast mass of human existence. And yet few ever consider books but with reference to their power of pleasing these persons and men of a higher rank few descend lower among cottages and fields and among children. A man must have done this habitually before his judgment upon the Idiot Boy would be in any way decisive with me. I *know* I have done this myself habitually; I wrote the poem with exceeding delight and pleasure, and whenever I read it I read it with pleasure. You have given me praise for having reflected faithfully in my poems the feelings of human nature I would fain hope that I have done so. But a great Poet ought to do more than this he ought to a certain degree to rectify men's feelings, to give them new compositions of feeling, to render their feelings more sane pure and permanent, in short, more consonant to nature, that is, to eternal nature, and the great moving spirit of things. He ought to travel before men occasionally as well as at their sides. I may illustrate this by a reference to natural objects. What false notions have prevailed from generation to generation as to the true character of the nightingale. As far as my Friend's Poem[1] in the

[1] S. T. C.'s 'conversation poem', *The Nightingale*.

Lyrical Ballads, is read it will contribute greatly to rectify these. You will recollect a passage in Cowper where, speaking of rural sounds, he says—

> "and *even* the boding Owl
> That hails the rising moon has charms for me."[1]

Cowper was passionately fond of natural objects yet you see he mentions it as a marvellous thing that he could connect pleasure with the cry of the owl. In the same poem he speaks in the same manner of that beautiful plant, the gorse; making in some degree an amiable boast of his loving it, "*unsightly* and unsmooth" as it is.[2] There are many aversions of this kind, which, though they have some foundation in nature, have yet so slight a one, that though they may have prevailed hundreds of years, a philosopher will look upon them as accidents. So with respect to many moral feelings, either of [lo]ve or dislike what excessive admiration was payed in former times to personal prowess and military success it is so with [the] latter even at the present day but surely not nearly so much as hereto[fore]. So with regard to birth, and innumerable other modes of sentiment, civil and religious. But you will be inclined to ask by this time how all this applies to the Idiot Boy. To this I can only say that the loathing and disgust which many people have at the sight of an Idiot, is a feeling which, though having som[e] foundation in human nature is not necessarily attached to it in any vi[rtuous?] degree, but is owing, in a great measure to a false delicacy, and, if I [may] say it without rudeness, a certain want of comprehensiveness of think[ing] and feeling. Persons in the lower classes of society have little or nothing [of] this: if an Idiot is born in a poor man's house, it must be taken car[e of] and cannot be boarded out, as it would be by gentlefolks, or sent [to a] public or private receptacle for such unfortunate beings. [Poor people] seeing frequently among their neighbours such objects, easily [forget what]ever there is of natural disgust about them, and have t[herefore] a sane state, so that without pain or suffering they [perform] their duties towards them. I could with pleasure pursue this subj[ect, but] I must now strictly adopt the plan which I proposed [to my]self when I began to write this letter, namely, that

---

[1] *The Task*, i. 205–6.   [2] Ibid. i. 527 (misquoted).

of setting down a few hints or memorandums, which you will think of for my sake.

I have often applied to Idiots, in my own mind, that sublime expression of scripture that, "*their life is hidden with God.*" They are worshipped, probably from a feeling of this sort, in several parts of the East. Among the Alps where they are numerous, they are considered, I believe, as a blessing to the family to which they belong. I have indeed often looked upon the conduct of fathers and mothers of the lower classes of society towards Idiots as the great triumph of the human heart. It is there that we see the strength, disinterestedness, and grandeur of love, nor have I ever been able to contemplate an object that calls out so many excellent and virtuous sentiments without finding it hallowed thereby and having something in me which bears down before it, like a deluge, every feeble sensation of disgust and aversion.

There are in my opinion, several important mistakes in the latter part of your letter which I could have wished to notice; but I find myself much fatigued. These refer both to the Boy and the Mother. I must content myself simply with observing that it is probable that the principle cause of your dislike to this particular poem lies in the *word* Idiot. If there had been any such word in our language, *to which we had attached passion*, as lack-wit, half-wit, witless etc I should have certainly employed it in preference but there is no such word. Observe, (this is entirely in reference to this particular poem) my Idiot is not one of those who cannot articulate and such as are usually disgusting in their persons—

> "Whether in cunning or in joy"
> "And then his words were not a few" etc

and the last speech at the end of the poem. The Boy whom I had in my mind was, by no means disgusting in his appearance quite the contrary and I have known several with imperfect faculties who are handsome in their persons and features. There is one, at present, within a mile of my own house remarkably so, though there is something of a stare and vacancy in his countenance. A Friend of mine, knowing that some persons had a dislike to the poem such as you have expressed advised me to add a stanza describing the person of the Boy [so a]s entirely to separate him in the imaginations of my Readers from [that] class of idiots who are disgusting in their persons, but the narration [in] the poem is so rapid and impassioned that I could not find a place [in] which to insert the stanza without checking the progress of it, and [so lea]ving a deadness upon the feeling. This poem has, I know, frequently produced [the s]ame effect as it did upon you and your Friends but there are many [peo]ple also to whom it affords exquisite delight, and who indeed, prefer [it] to any other of my Poems. This proves that the feelings there delineated [are] such as all men *may* sympathize with. This is enough for my purpose. [It] is not enough for me as a poet, to delineate merely such feelings as all men *do* sympathise with but, it is also highly desirable to add to these others, such as all men *may* sympathize with, and such as there is reason to believe they would be better and more moral beings if they did sympathize with.   `

I conclude with regret, because I have not said one half of [what I inten]ded to say: but I am sure you will deem my excuse suf[ficient when I] inform you that my head aches violently, and I am, in [other respect]s, unwell. I must, however, again give you my warmest [thanks] for your kind letter. I shall be happy to hear from you again [and] do not think it unreasonable that I should request a letter from you when I feel that the answer which I may make to it will not perhaps, be above three or four lines. This I mention to you with frankness, and you will not take it ill after what I have before said of my remissness in writing letters.

I am, dear Sir
With great Respect,
Yours sincerely W Wordsworth

21. *To* Sara Hutchinson[1]

[14 June 1802]

My dear Sara

I am exceedingly sorry that the latter part of the Leech-gatherer[2] has displeased you, the more so because I cannot take to myself (that being the case) much pleasure or satisfaction in having

---

[1] Part of a joint letter of D. W. and W. W. to Mary and Sara H.
[2] i.e. *Resolution and Independence*.

pleased you in the former part. I will explain to you in prose my feeling in writing that Poem, and then you will be better able to judge whether the fault be mine or yours or partly both. I describe myself as having been exalted to the highest pitch of delight by the joyousness and beauty of Nature and then as depressed, even in the midst of those beautiful objects, to the lowest dejection and despair. A young Poet in the midst of the happiness of Nature is described as overwhelmed by the thought of the miserable reverses which have befallen the happiest of all men, viz Poets—I think of this till I am so deeply impressed by it, that I consider the manner in which I was rescued from my dejection and despair almost as an interposition of Providence. 'Now whether it was by peculiar grace A leading from above'. A person reading this Poem with feelings like mine will have been awed and controuled, expecting almost something spiritual or supernatural—What is brought forward? 'A lonely place, a Pond' 'by which an old man *was*, far from all house or home'—not stood, not sat, but '*was*'—the figure presented in the most naked simplicity possible. This feeling of spirituality or supernaturalness is again referred to as being strong in my mind in this passage—'*How came he here* thought I or what can he be doing?' I then describe him, whether ill or well is not for me to judge with perfect confidence, but this I can *confidently* affirm, that, though I believe God has given me a strong imagination, I cannot conceive a figure more impressive than that of an old Man like this, the survivor of a Wife and ten children, travelling alone among the mountains and all lonely places, carrying with him his own fortitude, and the necessities which an unjust state of society has entailed upon him. You say and Mary (that is you can say no more than that) the Poem is *very well* after the introduction of the old man; this is not true, if it is not more than very well it is very bad, there is no intermediate state. You speak of his speech as tedious: everything is tedious when one does not read with the feelings of the Author—'*The Thorn*' is tedious to hundreds; and so is the *Idiot Boy* to hundreds. It is in the character of the old man to tell his story in a manner which an *impatient* reader must necessarily feel as tedious. But Good God! Such a figure, in such a place, a pious self-respecting, miserably infirm, and [   ] Old Man telling such a tale!

My dear Sara, it is not a matter of indifference whether you are pleased with this figure and his employment; it may be comparatively so, whether you are pleased or not with *this Poem*; but it is of the utmost importance that you should have had pleasure from contemplating the fortitude, independence, persevering spirit, and the general moral dignity of this old man's character. Your feelings upon the Mother, and the Boys with the Butterfly, were not indifferent: it was an affair of whole continents of moral sympathy. I will talk more with you on this when we meet—at present, farewell and Heaven for ever bless you!

W. W.

22. *To* Richard Wordsworth

[Grasmere] Saturday Even: July 3d 1802

My dear Brother,

I have this evening received two Letters from you, one of the 26th, the other the 29th June.

Before I say any thing in answer to what relates to business in them, I feel it proper to inform you that I must disapprove of the tone which pervades your second Letter. Many parts of it are totally deficient in that respect with which Man ought to deal with Man, and Brother with Brother. You seem to speak to me as if you were speaking to a Child: this is very unbecoming on your part: and it is not fit that I should hear it without informing you, that it is your duty to guard against any thing of the kind in future. I hope this is the last time I shall have occasion to speak on this subject.

It gives me great pleasure to say that I entirely approve of the Letter which you have addressed to Mr Richardson.[1] It is the very thing which I myself should have done, and done in the very way in which I should have done it.

You say "*If I had the least doubt about the proper steps to be taken, I am sure I would instantly ask your advice.*" This I approve; but remember that it may happen to be a great misfortune, that you *have no* doubts about the proper method to be taken. You say further, "*I fortunately*

---

[1] Agent to the new Viscount Lowther, later created 1st Earl of Lonsdale (see List of Correspondents), who was preparing to discharge the debts (including debts to the Wordsworths) incurred by his predecessor the 'bad' Earl.

have very favourable opportunities of procuring information on the subject." I am glad to hear this, though I wish that they had been of such a nature that they might have been communicated to me, in order that I might have known thoroughly on what grounds you stand, and have been sure that you are not misled. Do not imagine that there is any thing disrespectful to you in these apprehensions; far from it; but I have too much reason to be afraid that you are disposed to conduct the affair as a mere man of business. We see what Lawyers and Attornies have done in it already; and depend upon it if you proceed according to the letter in this track we are ruined. Though the affair must be bottomed no doubt upon a right in Law, that right will be lost to us, and we shall draw no advantage from it whatsoever, if we do not constantly bear in mind that our hopes of success (both in the conduct and in the final settlement) must depend entirely upon our combining with this right certain principles of natural justice, and considering the affair as an affair betwixt man and man.

The memorial of which I spoke has given you, it appears, much needless alarm. As soon as I was *certain* that we had still a right in Law, I never entertained a thought of making any use of a memorial in the first instance, nor till there appeared to be a manifestation of an intention on the part of Lord Lowther or his agents to act unhandsomely or unjustly. Should this not be the case, a memorial cannot be necessary perhaps in any stage of the business; but should there unfortunately now be such manifestation from any quarter, then it is my cool and determined opinion that a concise yet not imperfect statement of the whole proceedings ought to be laid before Lord Lowther, and a forcible appeal made to him in his personal character, as a man of honour and justice.

You exhort me to be patient: I feel that I should not stand in need of patience in your sense of the word, where it would do us any good. But you must know as well as I that such exhortations are the common language of hackney men of business. "We must take time" "we must not be in a hurry." All this is a sort of mechanic rule which they lay down, easy to adhere to: and thus they cheaply purchase to themselves the applause of being methodical, circumspect, and temperate men. But if there ever was a case that called aloud for promptness and decision it is the present: it must be plain to common sense that Lord L— will be most likely to act worthily and justly, I will not say nobly and generously, while the freshness of his new situation is upon him, while he is *studious* of popularity, and before he is tired out by the burthen of his duties. Besides, at this particular time on the eve of a general election, these probabilities become particularly strong.

I have nothing further to say at present: but I must beg that you will write to me punctually informing me of the steps which are taken. I again exhort you to avoid every thing like a shew of a disposition to contest the matter in a court of justice. Firmness is a very different thing from ostentatious parade of right, and rash confidence. As to myself, I have no thing further to say than to inform you of the principle of action which I have laid down to myself, in this case, and which I shall act up to with the utmost vigour.

No step of the nature of a proceeding in law shall be taken with my approbation. If without previously consulting me such step be taken, or any measures resorted to which seem manifestly to lead thereto, I apprise you that I immediately divide from you upon the business, and shall act singly upon my own judgement. I am with kind remembrances and best love of Dorothy and myself your affectionate Br

W Wordsworth

Do not fail to write to me as soon as you receive Mr Richardsons answer.[1]

W W

23. *To* [?] Charles Lamb

Nov 1802.

Tell John[2] when he buys Spenser, to purchase an edition which has his 'State of Ireland' in it.[3] This is in prose. This edition may be scarce, but one surely can be found.

Milton's Sonnets (transcribe all this for John, as said by me to him) I think manly and dignified compositions, distinguished by

---

[1] D. W. adds a PS. above W. W.'s.   [2] The 'sailor' brother.
[3] Spencer's *View of the State of Ireland*, written 1596; publ. in *Works*, 1679.

simplicity and unity of object and aim, and undisfigured by false or vicious ornaments. They are in several places incorrect, and sometimes uncouth in language, and, perhaps, in some, inharmonious; yet, upon the whole, I think the music exceedingly well suited to its end, that is, it has an energetic and varied flow of sound crowding into narrow room more of the combined effect of rhyme and blank verse than can be done by any other kind of verse I know of. The Sonnets of Milton which I like best are that to *Cyriack Skinner*; on his *Blindness*; *Captain or Colonel*; *Massacre of Piedmont*; *Cromwell* except two last lines; *Fairfax*, etc.

24. *To* Thomas De Quincey

Grasmere July 29th 1803
near Kendal
Westmoreland

Dear Sir

Your Letter dated May 31 (owing I presume to the remissness of Messeurs Longman and Rees[1] in forwarding it) I did not receive till the day before yesterday. I am much concerned at this as though I am sure you would not suppose me capable of neglecting such a Letter, yet still my silence must needs have caused you some uneasiness.

It is impossible not to be pleased when one is told that one has given so much pleasure: and It is to me a still higher gratification to find that my poems have impressed a stranger with such favorable ideas of my character as a man. Having said this which is easily said I find some difficulty in replying more particularly to your Letter.

It is needless to say that it would be out of nature were I not to have kind feelings towards one who expresses sentiments of such profound esteem and admiration of my writings as you have done. You can have no doubt but that these sentiments however conveyed to me must have been acceptable; and I assure you that they are still more welcome coming from yourself. You will then perceive that the main end which you proposed to yourself in

[1] W. W.'s publishers.

writing to me is answered, viz. that I am already kindly disposed towards you. My friendship it is not in my power to give: this is a gift which no man can make, it is not in our own power: a sound and healthy friendship is the growth of time and circumstance, it will spring up and thrive like a wildflower when these favour, and when they do not, it is in vain to look for it.

I do not suppose that I am saying any thing which you do not know as well as myself. I am simply reminding you of a common place truth which your high admiration of me may have robbed perhaps of that weight which it ought to have with you. And this leads me to what gave me great concern, I mean the very unreasonable value which you set upon my writings, compared with those of others. You are young and ingenuous and I wrote with a hope of pleasing the young the ingenuous and the unworldly above all others, but sorry indeed should I be to stand in the way of the proper influence of other writers. You will know that I allude to the great names of past times, and above all to those of our own Country. I have taken the liberty of saying this much to hasten on the time, when you will value my poems not less, but those of others, more. That time I know would come of itself; and may come sooner for what I have said, which at all events I am sure you cannot take ill.

How many things are there in a mans character of which his writings however miscellaneous or voluminous will give no idea. How many thousand things which go to making up the value of a frank and moral man concerning not one of which any conclusion can be drawn from what he says of himself or of others in the Worlds Ear. You probably would never guess from any thing you know of me, that I am the most lazy and impatient Letter writer in the world. You will perhaps have observed that the first two or three Lines of this sheet are in a tolerably fair, legible hand, and, now every Letter, from A to Z, is in complete route, one upon the heals of the other. Indeed so difficult Do I find it to master this ill habit of idleness and impatience, that I have long ceased to write any Letters but upon business. In justice to myself and you I have found myself obliged to mention this, lest you should think me unkind if you find me a slovenly and sluggish Correspondent.

I am going with my friend Coleridge and my Sister upon a tour into Scotland for six weeks or two months. This will prevent me hearing from you as soon as I could wish, as most likely we shall set off in a few days. If however you write immediately I may have the pleasure of receiving your Letter before our departure; if we are gone, I shall order it to be sent after me. I need not add that it will give me great pleasure to see you at Grasmere if you should ever come this way. I am dear sir with great sincerity and esteem

Yours sincerely,
W. Wordsworth

P.S. I have just looked my letter over, and find that towards the conclusion I have been in a most unwarrantable hurry, especially in what I have said on seeing you here. I seem to have expressed myself absolutely with coldness. This is not in my feelings I assure you. I shall indeed be very happy to see you at Grasmere; if you ever find it convenient to visit this delightful country. You speak of yourself as being very young; and therefore may have many engagements of great importance with respect to your wor[l]dly concerns and future happiness in life. Do not neglect these on any account; but if consistent with these and your other duties, you could find time to visit this country which is no great distance from your present residence[1] I should, I repeat it, be very happy to see you.

W. W.

25. *To* Sir George Beaumont

Grasmere, 14th October, 18[03].

Dear Sir George,

If any Person were to be informed of the particulars of your kindness to me, if it were described to h[im] in all its delicacy and nobleness, and he should afterwards [be] told that I suffered eight weeks to elapse without writ[ing] to you one word of thanks or acknowledgement, he would deem it a thing absolutely *impossible*.

[1] De Quincey was living near Liverpool, pending his matriculation at Oxford.

It is nevertheless true. T[his is,] in fact, the first time that I have taken up a pen, not [for] writing Letters, but on any account whatsoever, except onc[e,] since Mr Coleridge shewed me the writings of the Apple[thwaite] Estate,[1] and told me the little history of what you had d[one] for me, the motives, etc. I need not say that it gave [me] the most heartfelt pleasure, not for my own sake [chiefly,] though in that point of view it might well be m[ost] highly interesting to me, but as an act which, cons[idered] in all its relations as to matter and manner, it [would] not be too much to say, did honour to human n[ature;] at least, I felt it as such and it overpowered me.

Owing to a set of painful and uneasy sensations which [I have,] more or less at all times about my chest, from a disease which chiefly affects my nerves and digestive organs, and which makes my aversion from writing little less than madness, I deferred writing to you, being at first made still more uncomfortable by travelling, and loathing to do violence to my self, in what ought to be an act of pure pleasure and enjoyment; viz the expression of my deep sense of your goodness. This feeling was indeed so strong in me, as to make me look upon the act of writing to you, not as a work of a moment, but as a business with something little less than awful in it, a task, a duty, a thing not to be done but in my best, my purest, and my happiest moments. Many of these I had, but then I had not my pen and ink, my paper before me, my conveniences, "my appliances and means to boot"[2] all which, the moment that I thought of them, seemed to disturb and impair the sanctity of my pleasure. I contented my self with thinking over my complacent feelings, and breathing forth solitary gratulations and thanksgivings, which I did in many a sweet and many a wild place, during my late Tour. In this shape, procrastination became irresistible to me; at last I said I will write at home, from my own fireside, [w]hen I shall be at ease and in comfort. I have now been more than [a] fortnight at home, but the uneasiness in my chest has made [me] beat off the time when the pen was to be taken up. I do not know from what cause it is, but during the last three [y]ears I have never had a pen in my hand for five minutes, [b]efore my whole frame

---

[1] i.e. the title deeds of the estate at the foot of Skiddaw, which his new friend, Sir George Beaumont, had presented to W. W. so that he might be nearer S. T. C. at Keswick.   [2] *2 Henry IV*, III. i. 29.

becomes one bundle of uneasiness, [a] perspiration starts out all over me, and my chest is [o]ppressed in a manner which I can not describe. [T]his is a sad weakness, for I am sure, though, it is chiefly [o]wing to the state of my body, that by exertion of mind [I] might in part control it. So however it is, and I mention it, because I am sure when you are made acquainted with the circumstances, though the extent to which it exists nobody can well conceive, you will look leniently upon my silence, and rather pity than blame me: Though I must still continue to reproach myself, as I have done bitterly every day for these last eight weeks. One thing in particular has given me great uneasiness, it is, lest in the extreme delicacy of your mind, which is well known to me, you for a moment may have been perplexed by a single apprehension that there might be any error, any thing which I might misconceive, in your kindness to me. When I think of the possibility of this I am vexed beyond measure that I had not resolution to write immediately. But I hope that these fears are all groundless, and that you have, (as I know your nature will lead you to do) suspended your judgement upon my silence, blaming me indeed but in that qualified way in which a good man blames what he believes will be found an act of venial infirmity, when it is fully explained. But I have troubled you far too much with this; such I am however and deeply I regret that I am such. I shall conclude with solemnly assuring you, late as it is, that nothing can wear out of my heart, as long as my faculties remain, the deep feeling which I have of your delicate and noble conduct towards me.

It is now high time to speak of the estate, and what is to be done with it. It is a most delightful situation, and few things would give me greater pleasure than to realise the plan which you had in view for me of building a house there. But I am afraid, I am sorry to say, that the chances are very much against this, partly on account of the state of my own affairs, and still more from the improbability of Mr Coleridge's continuing in the Country. The writings are at present in my possession, and what I sh[ould] wish is, that I might be considered at present as Steward of the land with liberty to lay out the rent in plant[ing] or any other improvement which might be thought [advi]sable with a view to building upon it. And if it should [be] out of my power to pitch my own tent there, I would then request that you would give me leave [to] restore the property to your own hands, in order tha[t] you might have the opportunity of again presen[ting] it to some worthy person who might be so fortu[nate] as to be able to make that pleasant use of it which it was your wish that I should have done.

Mr. Coleridge informed me that immediately after you left Keswick, he had as I requested, returne[d] you thanks for those two elegant drawings which you were so [good] as to leave for me. The present is valuable in itsel[f,] and I consider it as a high honour conferred on m[e.] How often did we wish for five minutes' command [of your] pencil while we were in Scotland! or rather that [you] had been with us. Sometimes, I am sure, you would [have] been highly delighted. In one thing Scotland is superior to every country I have travelled in; I mean the grace[ful] beauty of the dresses and figures; there is a tone of imagination about them beyond any thing I have seen elsewhere.

Mr Coleridge, I understand, has written to you several times lately, so of course he will have told you when and why he left us. I am glad he did, as I am sure the solitary part of his tour did him much the most service. He is still unwell, though wonderfully strong; he is attempting to bring on a fit of the gout, which he is sure will relieve him greatly. I was at Keswick last Sunday and saw both him and Mr Southey,[1] whom I liked very much. Coleridge looks better, I think, than when you saw him; and is, I also think, upon the whole much better. Lady Beaumont will be pleased to hear that our Carriage, (though it did not suit Mr Coleridge, the noise of it being particularly unpleasant to him,) answered wonderfully well for my Sister and me, and that the whole tour far surpassed our most sanguine expectations.

They are sadly remiss at Keswick in putting themselves to trouble in defence of the Country; they came forward very chearfully some time ago, but were so thwarted by the orders and counter orders of the Ministry and their Servants that they have thrown up the whole in disgust. At [G]rasmere, we have turned out almost to a Man.[2] [We] are to go to Ambleside on Sunday to be mustered, [a]nd put on, for the first time our military [ap]parel. I

---

[1] The Southeys had recently moved to Greta Hall.

[2] W. W. had been active in setting up the Grasmere Volunteers to counter threats of a French invasion.

remain dear Sir George, with the most affectionate and respectful regard for you and Lady [B]eaumont,

> yours sincerely,
> W. Wordsworth

[My] sister will transcribe three sonnets, which I do not send [you] from any notion I have of their merit, but merely because [the]y are the only Verses I have written since I had the [pl]easure of seeing you and Lady Beaumont. At the sight [of] Kilchurn Castle, an antient Residence of the Breadalbanes, [up]on an island in Loch Awe I felt a real poetical [im]pulse: but I did not proceed. I began a Poem (apostrophising [the] Castle) thus:

> "Child of loud-throated War the mountain Stream
> Roars in thy hearing, but thy hour of rest
> Is come, and thou art silent in thine age."

but I stopp'd.[1]

If you think either you or Lady Beaumont that these two last Sonnets are worth publication, would you have the goodness to circulate them in any way you like?[2]

26. *To* Walter Scott

Grasmere near Keswick Cumberland. October 16th, 1803.

My dear Sir,

I am a wretched Sinner in Letter writing, and have taken off the whole grace from the present letter by my procrastination. A petty alteration which I wished to make in the sonnet[3] prevented me from writing immediately on our arrival, and the first step being made in transgression the rest followed of course.

We had a delightful journey home, delightful weather, and a sweet country to travel through. We reached our little cottage in

[1] This poem was finished 'long after'. D. W. transcribes at this point early versions of 'Degenerate Douglas!', *To the Men of Kent*, and *Anticipation*.

[2] *Anticipation* was subsequently published in *The Poetical Register* and *The Anti-Gallican*.

[3] 'Degenerate Douglas!' (see previous letter), copied by D. W. in its earlier version at the foot of this letter.

high spirits and thankful to God for all his bounties. My Wife and Child were both well, and as I need not say, we had all of us a happy meeting.

We past Branxholme, your Branxholme we supposed, about 4 miles on this side of Hawick, it looks better in your Poem[1] than in its present realities: the situation however is delightful, and makes amends for an ordinary mansion. The whole of the Teviot, and the pastoral steeps about Mosspaul pleased us exceedingly. The Esk below Langholm is a delicious River, and we saw it to great advantage. We did not omit noticing Johnnie Armstrongs[2] Keep, but his hanging place we miss'd, to our great regret. We were indeed most truly sorry that we could not have you along with us into Westmoreland. The country was in its full glory, the verdure of the valleys, in which we are so much superior to you in Scotland, was but little tarnished by the season, and the trees were putting on their most beautiful looks. My Sister was quite enchanted, and we often said to each other what a pity Mr Scott is not with us!

I had the pleasure of seeing both Coleridge and Southey at Keswick last Sunday. Southey whom I never saw much of before I liked much better than I expected; he is very pleasant in his manners, and a man of great reading, in old books, poetry, Chronicles, memoirs, etc., particularly Spanish and Portuguese. By the Bye, he occasionally reviews and he has at present, among other things, a Poem to review of that very Tytler[3] who made the illiberal attack upon him and Coleridge in the Edinburgh Magazine which I showed you at Liswaide, so no mercy for poor Tytler. He has also to review a Vol. of Poems by a somebody Bayley[4] Esqr which contains a long dull Poem in ridicule of the Idiot Boy, and in which Squire Bayley has mentioned by name "Mr Wordsworth that most simple of all simple Poets", so no mercy for Squire Bayley. But enough of this nonsense. My sister and I often talk of the happy days which we passed in your Company, such things do not occur often in life. If we live, we shall meet again that is my consolation when I think of these things. Do

---

[1] *The Lay of the Last Minstrel* (publ. 1805), parts of which Scott had read to W. W. and D. W. during their recent visit to Lasswade.

[2] The freebooter, celebrated in the *Minstrelsy of the Scottish Border*.

[3] Dr Henry William Tytler, translator.

[4] *Poems*, by Peter Bayley, Jun. Esq., 1803.

write to me and promise you will come and see us here, and bring Mrs Scott if you can. At all events we shall look for you certainly. Scotland and England sound like division, do what you can, but we really are but neighbours; if you were no farther off and in Yorkshire, we should think so. Farewell. My Sister joins with me in best remembrances to you and Mrs Scott. God prosper you and all that belongs to you. Your sincere Friend, for such I will call myself, though slow to use a word of such solemn meaning to any one,

W. Wordsworth

Poor Coleridge was prevented by ill health from walking over to Leswaide.

27. *To* Francis Wrangham

Grasmere, late Jan. *or* early Feb. 1804]

My dear Wrangham,

It is something less than ten minutes since I received your Pacquet of songs and kind admonishment accompanying them, for both of which receive my best thanks. I have indeed behaved very uncourteously to you, I will not say unkindly because that would be unjust, inasmuch as my own apparent neglect of you has called out more kind feelings towards you than I ever could have had, if I had done my duty. You do not know what a task it is to me, to write a Letter; I absolutely loath the sight of a Pen when I am to use it. I have not written Three Letters except upon indispensable business during the last three years. I should not mention a circumstance so discreditable to me, were it not to justify myself from any apprehension on your part that I may have slighted You. It is not in my Nature to neglect old Friends, I live too much in the past for anything of that kind to attach to me. You wrote me a very friendly and pleasant letter long since, with a copy of verses which were very amusing; for both of these, if thanks late be better than thanks never at all, I now make you my acknowledgements. I have hurried through your songs which I think admirably adapted for the intended purpose. "A song or a story may drive away care" etc pleased me best but I shall be able to judge better upon a more leisurely perusal. You enquire how I am and what doing. As to the first I am tolerably well, and for the second, I have great things in meditation but as yet I have only been doing little ones. At present I am engaged in a Poem on my own earlier life[1] which will take five parts or books to complete, three of which are nearly finished. My other meditated works are a Philosophical Poem and a narrative one. These two will employ me some I ought to say several years, and I do not mean to appear before the world again as an Author till one of them at least be finished.

As to my private affairs you would probably hear at Gallow Hill[2] if you called there that I have a Son;[3] and a noble one too, he is as ever was seen. He is a great Comfort and pleasure to us in this lonely place. My sister continues to live with me. I read walk, doze a little now and then in the afternoon, and live upon the whole what you may call a tolerably rational life, I mean as the world goes.

But should this letter grow in length as it has grown in dullness, the Muses have mercy on you! but I will spare you! Farewell. Do not fail to present my kind remembrances to Mrs Wrangham[4] and believe me in spite of my remissness and Letter-Phobia (forgive the uncouth wedlock of this compound) your very sincere and affectionate

Friend
W. Wordsworth

P.S. I shall send you on the other side 3 Sonnets the first and 3rd of which I believe have been printed though I myself have never seen them in Print.[5] I sent them to Sir George Beaumont who informed me that he would forward them to some of the Newspapers. The two or three last lines in the last I have altered from the copy sent to Sir George; if you think it worth while to circulate them with your own Ballads and songs or otherwise you are perfectly at liberty to do so. They are however heavy armed Troops and might perhaps stand in the way of the movements of your flying artillery. I conjecture that you have more songs to follow, do not fail on any account to transmit them to me. Let me know also what you are

---

[1] *The Prelude.*   [2] Thomas Hutchinson's farm, nr. Scarborough.
[3] John (b. June, 1803).   [4] Wrangham had remarried in 1801.
[5] The second sonnet was *In the Pass of Killicranky.*

doing, and how yourself and family are. I cannot promise to be a correspondent I know my own infirmity too well. Therefore perhaps you may think this a request little less than impudent viz that you should write to me upon such terms. Poor Coleridge who has very miserable health is now in London whither he is gone with a view, of trying to arrange matters for a voyage to Madeira for benefit of Climate. Farewell, and all happiness attend you.

W. W.

My Wife and Sister send their best respects to you and Mrs Wrangham.

28. *To* Thomas De Quincey

Grasmere, March 6th, [1804]

My dear Sir,

Your last amiable Letter ought to have received a far earlier answer: I have been indeed highly culpable in my procrastination. It arrived just before we set off on our Scotch Tour, and I am so sadly dilatory in matters of this kind, that, unless I reply to a letter immediately, I am apt to defer it till the thought becomes painful, taking the shape of a duty rather than a pleasure, and then Heaven knows when I may set myself to rights again by doing what I ought to do. While I am on this subject, I must however say what you will be sorry to hear, that I have a kind of derangement in my stomach and digestive organs which makes writing painful to me, and indeed almost prevents me from holding correspondence with any body: and this (I mean to say the unpleasant feelings which I have connected with the act of holding a Pen) has been the chief cause of my long silence.

Your last Letter gave me great pleasure; it was indeed a very amiable one; and I was highly gratified in the thought of being so endeared to you by the mere effect of my writings. I am afraid you may have been hurt at not hearing from me, and may have construed my silence into neglect or inattention, I mean in the ordinary sense of the word. I assure you this has by no means been the case; I have thought of you very often and with great interest and wished to hear from you again, which I hope I should have done, had you not perhaps been apprehensive that your Letter might be an intrusion. I should have been very glad to hear from you; and another Letter might have rouzed me to discharge sooner the duty which I had shoved aside.

We had a most delightful Tour of six Weeks in Scotland; our pleasure however was not a little dashed by the necessity under which Mr. Coleridge found himself of leaving us, at the end of something more than a fortnight, from ill health; and a dread of the rains, (his complaint being Rheumatic) which then, after a long drought, appeared to be setting in. The weather however on the whole was excellent, and we were amply repaid for our pains.

As most likely you will make the Tour of the Highlands some time or other, do not fail to let me know, beforehand, and I will tell you what we thought most worth seeing, as far as we went. Our Tour, though most delightful, was very imperfect, being nothing more than what is commonly called the Short Tour, with considerable deviations. We lef[t] Loch Ness the Fall of Foyers, etc etc unvisited.

By this time I conclude you have taken up your abode at Oxford: I hope this Letter, though sent at random partly, will be forwarded, and that it will find you. I am anxious to hear how far you are satisfied with yourself at Oxford;[1] and, above all, that you have not been seduced into unworthy pleasures or pursuits. The State of both the Universities is, I believe, much better than formerly in respect to the morals and manners of the Students. I know that Cambridge is greatly improved since the time when I was there, which is about thirteen years ago. The manners of the young men were very frantic and dissolute at that time and Oxford was no better or worse. I need not say to you that there is no true dignity but in virtue and temperance, and, let me add, chastity; and that the best safeguard of all these is the cultivation of pure pleasures, namely, those of the intellect and affections. I have much anxiety on this head, from a sincere concern in your welfare, and the melancholy retrospect which forces itself upon one of the number of men of genius who have fallen beneath the evils that beset them: I do not mean to preach; I speak in simplicity and tender apprehension as one lover of Nature and of Virtue speaking

---

[1] De Quincey was now at Worcester College.

to another. Do not on any account fail to tell me whether you are satisfied with yourself since your migration to Oxford; if not, do your duty to yourself immediately; love Nature and Books; seek these and you will be happy; for virtuous friendship, and love, and knowledge of mankind, must inevitably accompany these, all things thus ripening in their due season. I am now writing a Poem on my own earlier life; and have just finished that part in which I speak of my residence at the University:[1] it would give me great pleasure to read this work to you at this time. As I am sure, from the interest you have taken in the L. B. that it would please you, and might also be of service to you. This Poem will not be published these many years, and never during my lifetime, till I have finished a larger and more important work to which it is tributary. Of this larger work I have written one Book and several scattered fragments: it is a moral and Philosophical Poem; the subject whatever I find most interesting, in Nature Man Society, most adapted to Poetic illustration. To this work I mean to devote the Prime of my life and the chief force of my mind. I have also arranged the plan of a narrative Poem. And if I live to finish these three principal works I shall be content. That on my own life, the least important of the three, is better [than] half complete: viz 4 Books amounting to about 2500 lines. They are all to be in blank verse. I have taken the liberty of saying this much of my own concerns to you, not doubting that it would interest you. You have as yet had little knowledge of me but as a Poet; but I hope, if we live, we shall be still more nearly united.

I cannot forbear mentioning to you the way in which a wretched creature of the name of Peter Bailey has lately treated the author of your favourite Book, the Lyrical Ballads. After pillaging them in a style of Plagiarism I believe unexampled in the history of modern Literature, the wretch has had the baseness to write a long poem in ridicule of them, chiefly of the Idiot Boy; and, not content with this, in a note annexed to the same Poem, has spoken of me, *by name* as the *simplest* i.e. the most contemptible of all Poets. The complicated baseness of this (for the Plagiarisms are absolutely by wholesale) grieved me to the heart for the sake of poor human Nature: that any body could combine (as this man in some way or other must have done) an admiration and love of those poems,

[1] *The Prelude*, Bk. iii.

72

with moral feelings so detestable hurt me beyond measure. If this Unhappy Creature's Volume should ever fall in your way, you will find the Plagiarisms chiefly in two Poems, one entitled The *Evening in the Vale of Festiniog*, which is a wretched Parody throughout of the *Tintern Abbey*, and the other the *Ivy Seat*, also in the *Forest Fay* and some others.

I must now conclude, not omitting however to say that Mr Coleridge and my sister were much pleased with your kind remembrances of them, which my Sister begs me to return. Mr C— is at present in London, sorry I am to say on account of the very bad health under which he labours. Believe me to be Dear Sir your very affectionate Friend.

W Wordsworth

P. S. Do not fail to write to me as soon as you can find time.

29. *To* Sir George Beaumont

Grasmere July 20th 1804

Dear Sir George,

Lady Beaumont in a Letter to my Sister told her some time ago that it was your intention to have written to me, but knowing my aversion to Letter writing you were unwilling to impose upon me the trouble of answering. I am much obliged to you for the honour you intended me, and deeply sensible of your delicacy. If a man were what he ought to be, with such feelings and such motives as I have, it would be as easy for him to write to Sir George Beaumont as to take his food when he was hungry or his repose when he was weary. But we suffer bad habits to grow upon us, and that has been the case with me as you have had reason to find and forgive already. I cannot quit the subject without regretting that any weakness of mine should have prevented me hearing from you, which would always give me great delight, and though I cannot presume to say that I should be a *punctual* correspondent, I am sure I should not be insensible of your kindness, but should also do my best to deserve it.

A few days ago I received from Mr Southey your very acceptable present of Sir Joshua Reynolds works, which with the life I have nearly read through. Several of the discourses I had read before though never regularly together: they have very much added to the high opinion which I before entertained of Sir Joshua Reynolds. Of a great part of them, never having had an opportunity of *studying* any pictures whatsoever I can be but a very inadequate judge: but of such parts of the Discourses as relate to general philosophy I may be entitled to speak with more confidence, and it gives me great pleasure to say to you knowing your great regard for Sir Joshua, that they appear to me highly honourable to him. The sound judgement universally displayed in these discourses is truly admirable, I mean the deep conviction of the necessity of unwearied labour and diligence, the reverence for the great men of his art, and the comprehensive and unexclusive character of his taste. Is it not a pity Sir George that a Man with such a high sense of the *dignity* of his art, and with such industry, should not have given more of his time to the nobler departments of painting. I do not say this so much on account of what the world would have gained by the superior excellence and interest of his pictures, though doubtless that would have been very considerable, but for the sake of example. It is such an animating sight to see a man of Genius, regardless of temporary gains whether of money or praise, fixing his attention solely upon what is intrinsically interesting and permanent, and finding his happiness in an entire devotion of himself to such pursuits as shall most ennoble human nature. We have not yet seen enough of this in modern times, and never was there a period in society when such examples were likely to do more good than at present. The industry and love of truth which distinguish Sir Joshua's mind are most admirable, but he appears to me to have lived too much for the age in which he lived and the people among whom he lived, though this in an infinitely less degree than his friend Burke, of whom Goldsmith said, with such truth, long ago

> "that born of the universe, 'he narrowed his mind'
> And to party gave up what was meant for mankind."[1]

I should not have said thus much of Reynolds, which I have not said without pain, but because I have so great a respect for his

---

[1] *Retaliation*, lines 31–2.

character and because he lived at a time, when being the first Englishman distinguished for excellence in the higher department of painting, he had the field fairly open for him to have given an example upon which all eyes needs must have been fixed of a man preferring the cultivation and exertion of his own powers in the highest possible degree to any other object of regard.

My writing is growing quite illegible. I must therefore either mend it, or throw down the pen. How sorry we all are under this roof that we cannot have the pleasure of seeing you and Lady Beaumont down this summer! The weather has been most glorious, and the country of course most delightful. Our own valley in particular was last night by the light of the full moon, and in the perfect stillness of the Lake a scene of loveliness and repose as affecting as was ever beheld by the eye of man. We have had a day and a half of Mr. Davys[1] company at Grasmere, and no more; he seemed to leave us with great regret being post-haste on his way to Edinborough. I went with him to Paterdale on his road to Penrith where he would take coach. We had a deal of talk about you and Lady Beaumont: he was in your debt a Letter as I found, and exceedingly sorry that he had not been able to get over to see you; having been engaged at Mr Coke's sheep-shearing,[2] which had not left him time to cross from the Duke of Bedfords to your place. We had a very pleasant interview though far too short. He is a most interesting man whose views are fixed upon worthy objects.

That Loughrigg Tarn beautiful Pool of Water as it is, is a perpetual mortification to me when I think that you and Lady Beaumont were so near having a summernest there. This is often talked over among us, and we always end the subject with a heigh ho! of regret. But I must think of concluding. My Sister thanks Lady Beaumont for her last Letter and will write to her in a few days: but I must say to her myself how happy I was to hear that her sister had derived any consolation from Coleridge's poems and mine. I must also add how much pleasure it gives me that Lady Beaumont is so kindly so affectionately disposed to my dear and good Sister, and also to the other unknown parts of my family. Could we but have Coleridge back among us again![3] There is no happiness in this life but in intellect and virtue. Those were very

---

[1] Humphry, later Sir Humphry, Davy (1778–1829), the scientist.
[2] At Holkham.   [3] S. T. C. was now in Malta in search of health.

pretty verses which Lady Beaumont sent, and we were much obliged to her for them.

What shocking bad writing I have sent you; I don't know [how] it is but [it] seems as if I could not write any better.

Farewell. Believe me, with the sincerest love and affection for you and Lady Beaumont,

yours,
Wm Wordsworth

30. *To* Sir George Beaumont

Grasmere Monday 11th Febry —05

My dear Friend

The public papers will already have broken the shock which the sight of this Letter will give you; you will have learned by them the loss of the Earl of Abergavenny East Indiaman, and along with her and a great proportion of the crew, that of her Captain Our Brother:[1] and a most beloved Brother he was. This calamitous news we received at 2 o clock today, and I write to you from a house of mourning. My poor Sister, and Wife who loved him almost as we did (for he was one of the most amiable of men) are in miserable affliction, which I do all in my power to alleviate; but heaven knows I want consolation myself. I can say nothing higher of my ever dear Brother than that he was worthy of his Sister who is now weeping beside me, and of the friendship of Coleridge; meek, affectionate, silently enthusiastic, loving all quiet things, and a Poet in every thing but words. Alas! what is human life! This present moment I thought this morning would have been devoted to the pleasing employment of writing a Letter to amuse you in your confinement. I had singled out several little fragments, descriptions merely, which I purposed to have transcribed from my Poems, thinking that the perusal of them might give you a few minutes gratification and now I am called to this melancholy office.

I shall never forget your goodness in writing so long and interesting [a] Letter to me under such circumstances. This Letter

[1] John, drowned in Weymouth Bay on 5 Feb.

also arrived by the same Post which brought the unhappy tidings of my Brother's death, so that they were both put into my hands at the same moment.

I cannot but turn to you to thank you for your goodness, and to congratulate you and Lady Beaumont on your recovery, assuring you at the same time that I and all my family pray earnestly that your valuable life may long be preserved. When the state of my feelings will permit I shall write to you at length, in the mean time let me thank Lady Beaumont in my sister's name for her two Last Letters; We were certain that something uncommon had befallen you, and of course apprehended evil; Lady Bs Letter though bringing distressing tidings of your illness, nevertheless relieved us from much anxiety. Again my dear Sir George farewell; do not fail to write as soon as you can without injury to yourself; but not before on any account.

Your affectionate friend W. Wordsworth

I shall do all in my power to sustain my Sister under her sorrow, which is and long will be bitter and poignant. We did not love him as a Brother merely, but as a man of original mind, and an honour to all about him. Oh! dear Friend forgive me for talking thus.

We have had no tidings of Coleridge. I trembled for the moment when he is to hear of my Brothers death, it will distress him to the heart, and his poor body cannot bear sorrow. He loved my Brother, and he knows how we at Grasmere loved him.

31. *To* Robert Southey

Grasmere, Tuesday Evening, [12 Feb.] 1805.

We see nothing here that does not remind us of our dear brother; there is nothing about us (save the children, whom he had not seen) that he has not known and loved.

If you could bear to come to this house of mourning to-morrow, I should be forever thankful. We weep much to-day, and that relieves us. As to fortitude, I hope I shall show that, and that all of us will show it, in a proper time, in keeping down many a silent pang hereafter. But grief will, as you say, and must, have its course;

there is no wisdom in attempting to check it under the circumstances which we are all of us in here.

I condole with you, from my soul, on the melancholy account of your own brother's situation;[1] God grant you may not hear such tidings! Oh! it makes the heart groan, that, with such a beautiful world as this to live in, and such a soul as that of man's is by nature and gift of God, we should go about on such errands as we do, destroying and laying waste; and ninety-nine of us in a hundred never easy in any road that travels towards peace and quietness! And yet, what virtue and what goodness, what heroism and courage, what triumphs of disinterested love everywhere; and human life, after all, what is it! Surely, this is not to be forever, even on this perishable planet! Come to us tomorrow, if you can; your conversation, I know, will do me good. . . .

All send best remembrances to you all.

Your affectionate friend,
W. Wordsworth

32. *To* James Losh

Grasmere, March 16th 1805.

My dear Losh,

The distress of mind under which we are at present labouring is not to be measured by any living person but one, and that is poor Coleridge, who is now far from us, at Malta. Our Brother was so modest and shy a man, that not a tenth part of his worth, above all, his Taste, Genius, and intellectual merits was known to anybody but ourselves and Coleridge who had an opportunity of seeing him familiarly during several months under our roof and at C's own house. C. knew what he was in himself and what he was to us nobody else, not even our other Brothers had or now have the faintest idea of it. John as a Sailor being accustomed to live with Men with whom he had little sympathy and who did not value or understand what he valued and having been from his earliest infancy of most lonely and retired habits (my Father in allusion to

---

[1] Thomas Southey was on active service in the West Indies.

this part of his disposition used to call him Ibex, the shyest of all the beasts) had lived all his life with all the deepest part of his nature shut up within himself. When he came to Grasmere somewhat better than five years ago he found in his Sister and me and Coleridge and in my Wife and a Sister of hers whom at that time he had an opportunity of seeing much of,[1] all that was wanting to make him completely happy; accordingly he gave up his heart to us, and we had the unexpected delight of finding in him a Friend who had a perfect sympathy with all our pleasures. After staying eight months with us he left us to take the command of this unfortunate Ship: we had at that time little to live upon and he went to sea high in hope and heart that he should soon be able to make his Sister independant and contribute to any wants which I might have. He encouraged me to persist in the plan of life which I had adopted; I will work for you was his language and you shall attempt to do something for the world. Could I but see you with a green field of your own and a Cow and two or three other little comforts I should be happy. (observe this was long before my marriage and when I had no thoughts of marrying and also when we had no hope about the Lowther debt) He went to sea with these hopes and poor fellow instead of gaining any thing he lost about £1000. We saw him (for the last time) in London at his return; he said to us where I have had one depressing thought in my own account, my ill success has made me think of you a thousand times. He went to sea again, with the same hope of being useful to us the ruling feeling of his heart, and was also unsuccessful though not quite in the same degree. Then came this lamentable voyage upon which he entered with far better grounded hopes: his bad success had rouzed him, and he had procured many powerful friends, got himself appointed to a voyage which by many was thought the best in the service, had an investment of £20,000, and had he returned he was next season to have had his choice of all the voyages in the service. He wrote to us from Portsmouth about 12 days before this disaster full of hopes saying that he was to sail tomorrow, of course at the time when we heard this deplorable news we imagined that he was as far on his voyage as Madeira. It was indeed a thunderstroke to us! The language which he held was always so encouraging, saying that Ships were in nine instances out of ten

[1] Sara Hutchinson.

lost by mismanagement: he had indeed a great fear of Pilots and I have often heard him say that no situation could be imagined more distressing than that of being at the mercy of these men; oh said he it is a joyful time for us when we get rid of them. His fears alas! were too well founded his own ship was lost while under the management of the Pilot, whether mismanaged by him or not I do not know; but know for certain, which is indeed our great consolation, that our dear Brother did all that man could do, even to the sacrifice of his own life. The newspaper accounts were grossly inaccurate indeed that must have been obvious to any person who could bear to think upon the subject for they were absolutely unintelligible. There are two pamphlets upon the subject; one a mere transcript from the Papers, the other may be considered as to all important particulars as of authority, it is by a person high in the India house and contains the deposition of the surviving officers concerning the loss of the Ship. The pamphlet I am told is most unfeelingly written, I have only seen an extract from it containing Gilpin's deposition, the 4th Mate. From this it appears that every thing was done that could be done under the circumstances, for the safety of the lives and the Ship: my poor Brother was standing on the hen-coop (which is placed upon the Poop and is in the most commanding situation in the Vessel) when she went down: and was thence washed overboard by a huge sea which sunk the Ship, he was seen struggling with the waves some time afterwards having laid hold, it is said, of a rope. He was an excellent swimmer, but what could it avail in such a sea encumbered with his cloaths and exhausted in body as he must have been. He was seen talking with the 1st Mate with apparent chearfulness a few minutes before the Ship went down. Such my dear Losh was the end of this brave and good man, if ever a human being existed who deserved to attain the end he had in view, this was the person. He had not one vice of his profession; never did I hear an oath or even an indelicate allusion from his mouth; he was pure as the purest woman. There is nothing remarkable in the courage or presence of mind which he shewed at his death, thousands would have done the same. But it is a noble object of contemplation that a man of his gentle and meek and happy temper a man in the prime of health and strength (he was only 32 years of age) with every thing in prospect which could make life dear, beloved and honored to the height of love and honor by his nearest friends and kindred and respected and liked by every body that knew him; that such a man having the anguish which he knew he would leave behind him, should nevertheless die calm and resigned; this is surely a noble spectacle. Oh! my friend I shall never forget him! his image if my senses remain, will be with me at my last hour and I will endeavour to die as he did, and what is of still more consequence perhaps, to live as he did: for he was innocent as he was brave, his whole life was dignified by prudence and firmness and self-denial—as far as my knowledge goes never did a man live who had less to repent of than he. He was steady to his duty in all situations. I praise him in a manner that would have shocked him, but I fall far, far, below the truth.

For myself I feel that there is something cut out of my life which cannot be restored, I never thought of him but with hope and delight, we looked forward to the time not distant as we thought when he would settle near us when the task of his life would be over and he would have nothing to do but reap his reward. But that time I hoped also that the chief part of my labours would be executed and that I should be able to shew him that he had not placed a false confidence in me. I never wrote a line without a thought of its giving him pleasure, my writings printed and manuscript were his delight and one of the chief solaces of his long voyages. But let me stop—I will not be cast down were it only for his sake I will not be dejected. I have much yet to do and pray God to give me strength and power—his part of the agreement between us is brought to an end, mine continues and I hope when I shall be able to think of him with a calmer mind that the remembrance of him dead will even animate me more than the joy which I had in him living.

I wish you would procure the pamphlet I have mentioned; you may know the right one by its having a motto from Shakespeare from Clarence's dream; I wish you to see it that you may read G's statement and be enabled if the affair should ever be mentioned in your hearing to correct the errors which they must have fallen into who have taken their ideas from the newspaper accounts. I have dwelt long, too long I fear upon this subject but I could not write to you upon any thing else till I had unburthened my heart. We have great consolations from the sources you allude to but alas! we have much yet to endure. Time only can give us regular tranquillity; we neither murmur nor repine but sorrow we must; we should be senseless else.

We have lost so much hope and gladsome thought; John who was almost perpetually in our minds was always there as an object of pleasure, never was presented to us in any other point of view; in this he differed from all our friends, from Coleridge in particular, in connexion with whom we have many melancholy, fearful, and unhappy feelings,[1] but with John it was all comfort and expectation and pleasure. We have lost him at a time when we are young enough to have been justified in looking forward to many happy years to be passed in his Society and when we are too old to outgrow the loss.

[*Unsigned*]

33. *To* Sir George Beaumont

Grasmere June 3d 1805

My dear Sir George,

I write to you from the Moss-Hut at the top of my orchard, the Sun just sinking behind the hills in front of the entrance, and his light falling upon the green moss of the side opposite me. A Linnet is singing in the tree above, and the Children of some of our neighbours who have been today little John's Visitors are playing below, equally noisy and happy; the green fields in the level area of the Vale and part of the lake, lie before me in quietness. I have just been reading two newspapers, full of fractious brawls about Lord Melville[2] and his delinquencies, ravages of the French in the West Indies, victories of the English in the East, Fleets of ours roaming the sea in search of enemies whom they cannot find, etc etc etc, and I have asked myself more than once lately If my affections can be in the right place caring as I do so little about what the world seems to care so much for. All this seems to me "a tale told by an Idiot full of sound and fury signifying nothing".[3] It is pleasant in such a mood to turn ones thoughts to a good Man and a Dear Friend. I have

---

[1] A reference to the breakdown of S. T. C's marriage, his love for S. H., and his growing opium addiction.

[2] First Lord of the Admiralty, impeached in 1806.   [3] *Macbeth*, v. v. 27.

therefore taken up the pen to write to you. And first let me thank you (which I ought to have done long ago, and should have done but that I knew I had a licence from you to procrastinate) for your most acceptable present of Coleridge's portrait, welcome in itself, and more so as coming from you. It is as good a resemblance as I expect to see of Coleridge, taking it all together, for I consider C—'s as a face absolutely impracticable. Mrs Wordsworth was overjoy'd at the sight of the Print,[1] Dorothy and I much pleased. We think it excellent about the eyes and forehead which are the finest parts of C—'s face, and the general contour of the face is well given, but to my Sister and me, it seems to fail sadly about the middle of the face particularly at the bottom of the nose: Mrs W— feels this also; and my Sister so much, that except when she covers the whole of the middle of the face it seems to her so entirely to alter the expression, as rather to confound than revive in her mind the remembrance of the original. We think, as far as mere likeness goes Hazlitt's[2] is better; but the expression in Hazlitt's is quite dolorous and funereal, that in this, much more pleasing though certainly falling far below what one would wish to see infused into a picture of C.

Mrs C received a day or two ago a Letter from a Friend who had letters from Malta not from Coleridge, but a Miss Stoddart who is there with her Brother.[3] These letters are of the date of the fifth of March, and speak of him as looking well and quite well, and talking of coming home, but doubtful whether by land or sea.

I have the pleasure to say that I finished my Poem[4] about a fortnight ago, I had looked forward to the day as a most happy one; and I was indeed grateful to God for giving me life to complete the work, such as it is; but it was not a happy day for me I was dejected on many accounts; when I looked back upon the performance it seemed to have a dead weight about it, the reality so far short of the expectation; it was the first long labour that I had finished, and the doubt whether I should ever live to write the Recluse and the sense which I had of this Poem being so far below what I seem'd capable

---

[1] From James Northcote's portrait (1804).
[2] William Hazlitt (1778–1830), the essayist. It was painted for Sir George Beaumont at Keswick in 1803.
[3] John, later Sir John, Stoddart (see List of Correspondents). His sister later married Hazlitt.   [4] *The Prelude.*

of executing, depressed me much: above all, many heavy thoughts of my poor departed Brother hung upon me; the joy which I should have had in shewing him the Manuscript and a thousand other vain fancies and dreams. I have spoken of this because it was a state of feeling new to me, the occasion being new. This work may be considered as a sort of portico to the Recluse, part of the same building, which I hope to be able erelong to begin with, in earnest; and if I am permitted to bring it to a conclusion, and to write, further, a narrative Poem of the Epic kind, I shall consider the *task* of my life as over. I ought to add that I have the satisfaction of finding the present Poem not quite of so alarming a length as I apprehended.

I wish much to hear from you, if you have leisure, but as you are so indulgent to me it would be the highest injustice were I otherwise to you.

We have read Madoc,[1] and been highly pleased with it; it abounds in beautiful pictures and descriptions happily introduced, and there is an animation diffused through the whole story though it cannot perhaps be said that any of the characters interest you much, except perhaps young Llewellyn whose situation is highly interesting, and he appears to me the best conceived and sustained character in the piece. His speech to his Uncle at their meeting in the Island is particularly interesting. The Poem fails in the highest gifts of the poet's mind Imagination in the true sense of the word, and knowledge of human Nature and the human heart. There is nothing that shows the hand of the great Master: but the beauties in description are innumerable; for instance that of the figure of the Bard towards the beginning of the convention of the bards, receiving the poetic inspiration, that of the wife of Tlalalu the Savage going out to meet her husband; that of Madoc and the Aztecan King with the long name preparing for battle, everywhere, indeed, you have beautiful descriptions, and it is a work which does the Author high credit, I think. I should like to know your opinion of it. Farewell best remembrances and love to Lady Beaumont. Believe me my dear Sir George your most sincere Friend

W. Wordsworth

---

[1] Southey's poem.

My Sister thanks Lady Beaumont for her Letter and will write in a few days. I find that Lady B— has been pleas'd much by Madoc.

34. *To* Sir George Beaumont

Feb^{ry} 11th [1806]

My dear Sir George,

Upon opening this letter you must have seen that it is accompanied with a copy of Verses;[1] I hope they will give you some pleasure, as it will be the best way in which they can repay me for a little vexation of which they have been the cause. They were written several weeks ago and I wished to send them to you but could not muster up resolution, as I felt that they were so unworthy of the subject. Accordingly I kept them by me from week to week with a hope (which has proved vain) that in some happy moment a new fit of inspiration would help me to mend them: and hence my silence which with your usual goodness I know you will excuse—

You will find that the Verses are allusive to Lord Nelson,[2] and they will shew that I must have sympathized with you in admiration of the Man, and sorrow for our loss. Yet considering the matter coolly there was little to regret. The state of Lord Nelson's health I suppose was such that he could not have lived long, and the first burst of exultation upon landing in his native Country, and his reception here, would have been dearly bought, perhaps, by pain and bodily weakness; and distress among his friends which he could neither remove nor alleviate. Few men have ever died under circumstances so likely to make their death of benefit to their Country: it is not easy to see what his life could have done comparable to it. The loss of such men as Lord Nelson is indeed great and real; but surely not for the reason which makes most people grieve, a supposition that no other such man is in the Country: the Old Ballad has taught us how to feel on these occasions:

> I trust I have within my realm
> Five Hundred good as he.[3]

---

[1] *The Character of the Happy Warrior.*   [2] d. 21 Oct. 1805 at Trafalgar.
[3] From 'The more modern Ballad of Chevy Chase' in Percy's *Reliques*.

But this is the evil that nowhere is merit so much under the power of what (to avoid a more serious expression) one may call that of fortune as in military and naval service; and it is five hundred to one that such men will [not] have attained situations where they can shew themselves so, that the Country may know in in whom to trust. Lord Nelson had attained that situation; and therefore, I think, (and not for the other reason) ought we chiefly to lament that he is taken from us.

Mr. Pitt[1] is also gone! by tens of thousands looked upon in like manner as a great loss. For my own part, as probably you know, I have never been able to regard his political life with complacency: I believe him, however, to have been as disinterested a Man, and as true a lover of his Country as it was possible for so ambitious a man to be. His first wish (though probably unknown to himself) was that his Country should prosper under his administration; his next, that it should prosper: could the order of these wishes have been reversed, Mr. Pitt would have avoided many of the grievous mistakes into which, I think, he fell. I know my dear Sir George, you will give me credit for speaking without arrogance; and I am aware it is not unlikely you may differ greatly from me in these points. But I like in some things to differ with a Friend, and that he should *know* I differ from him; it seems to make a more healthy friendship, to act as a relief to those notions and feelings which we have in common and to give them a grace and spirit which they could not otherwise possess.

There were some parts in the long Letter which I wrote about laying out grounds, in which the expression must have been left imperfect. I like splendid mansions in their proper places, and have no objection to large or even obtrusive houses in themselves. My dislike is to that system of gardening which, because a house happens to be large or splendid and stands at the head of a large domain, establishes it therefore as a principle that the house ought to *dye* all the surrounding country with a strength of colouring, and to an extent proportionate to its own importance. This system I think is founded in false taste, false feeling, and its effects disgusting in the highest degree. The Reason you mention as having induced you to build[2] was worthy of you, and gave me the

---

[1] The younger Pitt, Prime Minister 1783–1801, and in 1804.
[2] Beaumont was rebuilding Coleorton Hall.

highest pleasure. But I hope God will grant you and Lady Beaumont life to enjoy yourselves the fruit of your exertions for many years.—

We have lately had much anxiety about Coleridge. What can have become of him? It must be upwards of three months since he landed at Trieste. Has he returned to Malta, think you, or what can have befallen him? He has never since been heard of.

Lady Beaumont spoke of your having been ill of a cold; I hope you are better: we have all here been more or less deranged in the same way.

We have to thank you for a present of Game, which arrived in good time.

Never have a moment's uneasiness about answering my Letters.—We are all well at present and unite in affectionate wishes to you and Lady Beaumont. Believe me,

your sincere friend,
W. Wordsworth

I have some thoughts of sending the Verses to a Newspaper.

35. *To* Basil Montagu

Grasmere July 25th [1806]

My dear Montagu,

I was from home when your Letter came. I am very sorry to find that you continue to be so disturbed in mind, and the more so because I know how utterly impossible it is in these cases to administer any effectual consolation.[1] Effort may do something and change of situation and pursuit but nothing is to be greatly depended upon but time.—

We can accommodate you with a bed in our House, but you will be very ill off in other respects; I mean as to a sitting-room; I have none myself as you will remember: our house is so small that we shall be unable to winter in it and whither to go I know not—

Come as soon as you can and with Basil; I think it would certainly be of great service to you. Farewell. believe us all

sincerely yours W Wordsworth

[1] Montagu had just lost his second wife.

36. *To* Sir George Beaumont

Grasmere, August 1st, 1806.

My dear Friend,

It was very good in you to write to me, much more than I deserved, as I have shown by suffering your Letter to remain so long unanswered; I deserve your friendship, I hope, but not your Letters, indeed, I am unworthy of any Body's, being a Correspondent intolerably remiss. I am glad you liked the verses,[1] I could not but write them with feeling with such a subject, and one that touched me so nearly: your delicacy in not leading me to the Picture did not escape me. It is a melancholy satisfaction to me to connect my dear Brother with anybody whom I love much; and I knew that the verses would give you pleasure as a proof of my affection for you. The picture was to me a very moving one; it exists in my mind at this moment as if it were before my eyes. We have been looking every day for a Letter from Lady Beaumont with a hope still remaining that we may see you this summer. Lady Beaumont speaks in her last of your health being better; we were much concerned to hear that you had not been so well as usual; you need not fear that any inability on your part thoroughly to enjoy the country would make your company less acceptable; you would certainly enjoy much, and we should have the pleasure of contributing to your pleasure, with the hope of seeing you better, which would brighten everything.

I do not know whether my sister has written since we had another account of Coleridge;—I am sorry I cannot say *from* him. He was at Leghorn with a friend on their way to England: so that we still continue to look for him daily. He has lost *all* his papers; *how* we are not told. This grieves and vexes me much; probably (but it is not on this account—his loss being I daresay irreparable—that I am either much vexed or grieved) a large collection of my poems is gone with the rest; among others five books of the Poem upon my own life, but of all these I have copies; he, I am afraid, has none of his old writings.

Within this last month I have returned to the Recluse, and have

---

[1] *Elegiac Stanzas suggested by a Picture of Peele Castle in a Storm.* W. W. had recently seen Beaumont's picture in London.

written 700 additional lines.[1] Should Coleridge return, so that I might have some conversation with him upon the subject, I should go on swimmingly. We have been very little interrupted with Tourist-Company this summer, and, of course, being for the most part well, have enjoyed ourselves much. I am now writing in the Moss hut, which is my study, with a heavy thunder shower pouring down before me. It is a place of retirement for the eye (though the Public Road glimmers through the apple-trees a few yards below), and well suited to my occupations. I cannot however refrain from smiling at the situation in which I sometimes find myself here; as, for instance, the other morning when I was calling some lofty notes out of my harp, chaunting of Shepherds, and solitude, etc., I heard a voice, which I knew to be a male voice, whose also it was, crying out from the road below, in a tone exquisitely effeminate, 'Sautez, sautez, apportez, apportez; vous ne le ferez pas, venez donc Pandore, venez, venez'. Guess who this creature could be, thus speaking to his Lap-dog in the midst of our venerable mountains? It is one of two nondescripts who have taken the Cottage for the summer which we thought you might occupy, and who go about parading the valley in all kinds of fantastic dresses, green leather caps, turkey half-boots, jackets of fine linnen, or long dressing-gowns, as suit them. Now you hear them in the roads; now you find them lolling in this attire, book in hand, by a brook-side—then they pass your window in their Curricle,—to-day the Horses Tandem-wise, and to-morrow abreast; or on Horseback, as suits their fancies. One of them we suspect to be painted, and the other, though a pale-cheeked Puppy, is surely not surpassed by his blooming Brother. If you come you will see them, and I promise you they will be a treat to you.

We still think it possible that we may winter at Coleorton, but we shrink from the thought of going so far without seeing you, and if we [can] procure a House in this neighbourhood we certainly shall. We are the more willing to be kept in a state of suspense as long as Coleridge is unarrived. I don't know that after expressing my thanks for your many kindnesses to me when under your roof, and at all times, and the happiness I derive from your friendship, I

[1] W. W. was now at work on *The Excursion*, 'a portion of *The Recluse*' (publ. 1814).

can fill this Paper better than by adding a sonnet from Michael Angelo,[1] translated some time since. Farewell.

Yours most affectionately,
W. Wordsworth

37. *To* S. T. Coleridge[2]

Coleorton[3] near Ashby de la Zouche
November 7th 1806

Dearest Coleridge

We had some hopes of a Letter from you today; being most anxious to hear of you.

I write now to entreat that you would not on any account entangle yourself with any engagement to give Lectures in London, and to recommend your coming hither where you may sit down at leisure and look about you before you decide. You might bring Hartley with you and live here as long as you liked free of all expense but washing, you would be altogether uninterrupted and might proceed as rapidly as you liked with your Book of Travels, which would be certain of a great sale. Other things might be planned when we are together. Do write immediately. We had the Beaumont's company from Thursday Evening till Monday: they are the best of people, and their kindness to us most delicate and unbounded; their love of you is very great and they are most anxious to hear from you—write to them if possible; they continue in London—

38. *To* Sir George Beaumont

Coleorton November 10th 1806

My dear Sir George,

I was moved even to weakness by your Letter; it is indeed a great happiness to me to be beloved by you, and to think upon what

---

[1] 'The prayers I make will then be sweet indeed.'
[2] S. T. C. had returned to England in August.
[3] The Wordsworths were passing the winter at the Hall Farm.

foundation that love rests.—We were as sorry to part with you as you could be to part with us; perhaps even more so, as I believe is almost always the case with those who are left behind. We did not see the rising Sun which you describe so feelingly; but the setting was as glorious to us as to you. We looked at it with great delight from your fireside; but were foolish enough, at least I was, to believe that we should have such every night; that it was a gift of our new situation, and so the colours and motions which touched you so much were thrown away upon me; at least it seems so now. You know that at Grasmere the high mountains conceal from us in a great measure the splendour of a western sky at sunset; we have often regretted this; and we congratulated ourselves that evening on the opportunity which our present comparatively flat situation would give us of enjoying a sight from which we had long been excluded. We have had one or two fine evenings since but nothing like that first; which was I think the most magnificent I ever beheld. The whole day had been uncommonly fine.—We have not yet rambled much about; once I have been at the fir-wood with Miss Hutchinson, once at the pool with Mrs. W., and once had a long walk with my Sister, about the House and in the Kitchen Garden. Much engaged as the Females have been, some of the party would have been at Grace-dieu[1] before this time, but upon enquiry we found that an Ass was wanting which Mr Bailey[2] is to procure, I believe today or tomorrow. Your new Building and its immediate neighbourhood improve upon me much; I am particularly pleased with the spot, a discovery since your departure! which Lady Beaumont has chosen, I conjecture, for a winter garden. It will be a delightful place. By the bye, there is a pleasing paper in the Spectator (in the 7th Vol., No 477) upon this subject, the whole is well worth reading, particularly that part which relates to the Winter Garden. He mentions Hollies and Horn-beam as Plants which his Place is full of. The Horn-beam I do not know but the Holly I looked for in Lady B's ground and could not find: for its own beauty and for the sake of the Hills and crags of the north, let it be scattered here in profusion. It is of slow Growth, no doubt, but not so slow as generally supposed; and then it does grow, and somebody, we hope, will enjoy it.—Among the Barbarisers of our

---

[1] The neighbouring priory ruins.
[2] The bailiff.

beautiful Lake-region, of those who bring and those who take away, there are few whom I have execrated more than an extirpator of this beautiful shrub, or rather tree the Holly; this Worthy thank heaven! is not a Native, but he comes from far; and his business is to make bird-lime, and so down go these fair Creatures of Nature wherever he can find them. (You know probably that bird-lime is made of the bark of the Holly.) I would also plant Yew, which is of still slower growth.—One thought struck me, too, relating to the grounds which I will mention. I should not be for planting many forest trees about the House, by the side of those which are already at their full growth; when I planted at all, there, I should rather choose thickets of underwood, hazels, wild roses, honeysuckle, hollies, thorns, trailing plants, such as Traveller's joy etc. My reason, in addition to the beauty of these is that they would never be compared with the grown up trees; whereas young trees of the same kind will; and must appear insignificant. Observe my remark only applies to placing these young trees *by the side* of the others; where there is an open space of any size it does not hold.—

Miss Hutchinson and I were at Church yesterday; we were pleased with the singing; and I have often heard a far worse Parson, I mean as to reading. His sermon was, to be sure, as Village sermons often are, very injudicious; a most knowing discourse about the Gnostics, and other hard names of those who were '*h*adversaries to Christianity and *H*enemies of the Gospel.' How strangely injudicious this is! and yet nothing so frequent. I remember hearing Coleridge say that he was once at Keswick Church, and Mr Denton, you know him, was very entertaining in guarding his Hearers against the inordinate vice of ambition, what a shocking thing it was to be a Courtier, and sacrifice a man's hopes in heaven for wordly state and power. I don't know that I ever heard in a Country pulpit a sermon that had any especial bearing on the condition of the majority of the Audience. I was sorry to see at Coleorton few middle aged men, or even Women; the congregation consisted almost entirely of old persons particularly Old Men, and Boys and Girls.—The Girls were not well dressed; their clothes were indeed clean, but not *tidy*; they were in this respect a striking contrast to our Congregation at Grasmere.— I think I saw the old man (not he with the Spectacles) whose face, especially the eyes Mr Dawe[1] has drawn so well. Lady Beaumont will remember that I objected to the Shoulders in the drawing as being those of a young Man. This is the case in nature, in this instance I mean; for I never saw before such shoulders and unwithered arms with so aged a face as in the person I allude to.—I have talked much Chit-chat, I have chosen to do this rather than give way to my feelings which were powerfully called out by your affecting and beautiful Letter. I will say this, and this only, that I esteem your friendship one of the best gifts of my life; I and my family owe much to you and Lady Beaumont, I need not say that I do not mean any addition to our comforts or happiness, which, with respect to external things, you have been enabled to make; but I speak of soul indebted to soul—I entirely participate your feelings upon your Birthday: it is a trick of Kings and people in power to make Birthdays matter of rejoicing. Children, too, with their Holiday and plum-pudding rejoice; but to them in their inner hearts it is a day

> That tells of time misspent, of comfort lost,
> Of fair occasions gone for every by.

I long to see Wilkie's Picture;[2] from Lady Beaumont's account it seems to have surpassed your utmost expectations. I am glad of this, both because the Picture is yours, and as it is an additional promise of what he is to do hereafter. No doubt you will read him my Orpheus of Oxford Street,[3] which I think he will like. In a day or two I mean to send a sheet of my intended Volume to the Press; it would give me pleasure to desire the Printer to send you the sheets as they are struck off if you could have them free of expense. There is no forming a true estimate of a Vol of *small* Poems by reading them all together; one stands in the way of the other. They must either be read a few at once, or the Book must remain some time by one before a judgement can be made of the quantity of thought and feeling and imagery it contains, and what, and what variety of moods and mind it can either impart or is suited to—My Sister is writing to Lady Beaumont and will tell her how comfortable we are here, and every thing relating thereto.—Alas

---

[1] George Dawe (1781–1829), portrait painter.
[2] *The Blind Fiddler*, painted for Sir George Beaumont.
[3] i.e. W. W.'s poem *Power of Music*.

we have had no tidings of Coleridge, a certain proof that he continues to be very unhappy. Farewell, my dear Friend most faithfully and affectionately yours

Wm Wordsworth

39. *To* Lady Beaumont

[Coleorton]
[late Jan. 1807]

My dear Lady Beaumont,

We are all truly distressed for the situation of your sister; and sincerely sympathize with you in your dejection on her account. We hope that her health will strengthen as the mild weather comes on; she would then also suffer less from sea sickness which is dreadful in a stormy season even to the strongest. We were sorry to hear that you yourself had suffered from headaches: they have been caused, most likely, by the anxiety of mind; and if that were removed would probably cease.—

Lord Redesdale's[1] Letter contains several things that will be of use to us; I must however make two or three remarks upon it. Our Garden is to be a winter Garden, a place of comfort and pleasure from the fall of the leaf to its return; nearly half of the year. Great part of this time you now perhaps pass in London, but if you live, that probably will not always be so. Infirmities come on with age, that render tranquillity every year more welcome and more necessary. Lord Redesdale seems to have overlooked this, as far as the greatest part of his Letter applies only to a summer garden. His plan of avoiding expense in digging, weeding, and mowing, particularly the last may be carried too far; a wilderness of shrubs is a delightful thing as part of a garden, but only as a part. You must have open space of Lawn, or you lose all the beauty of outline in the different tufts or islands of shrubs, and even in many instances their individual forms. This lawn cannot be had without mowing. Digging and weeding ought to be avoided as much as possible; and his method is a good one. With his Lordship I should wish my strength to lie in perennial plants and flowers; but a small

---

[1] Lawyer and politician: Lord Chancellor of Ireland from 1802.

quantity of annuals such as flower very late may with little trouble and great advantage be interspersed among the others. His objection to an over-arched walk of *evergreens* except for summer at first appears well founded; but there is an oversight in it. In summer you may have a shade of *deciduous* trees or plants; but what are you to do in April or March, and sometimes even in February, when the heat and glare of the sun are often oppressive; notwithstanding the general cloudiness of our climate. For my own part I can say with truth that in the month of April I have passed many an hour under the shade of a green Holly, glad to find it in my walk and unwilling to quit it because I had not the courage to face the sun—Our winter Garden is four parts out of five planned for the Sun; if the alley or Bower, the only parts exclusively designed for shade should appear too damp or gloomy, you pass them by; but I am sure this will not always be the case; and even in those times when it is so, will not a peep into that gloom make you enjoy the sunshine the more? But the Alley I designed for March and April when there is often a heat in the sun, and a conflict of sun and wind which is both unpleasant and dangerous, and from which neither walls nor bare leafless trees can protect you.—His Lordship's practical Rules about making walks, propagating plants, etc, seem all to be excellent, and I like his plan of a covered walk of vines; but not for our own Winter Garden.—I shall read the whole to Mr Craig;[1] he and I propose to borrow Mr Bailey's Gig and go to a Nursery Garden about fourteen miles off to procure such plants as we are most likely to want. I would not have them bought of any great size; it is a needless expense; and surely it will be some pleasure to see them grow up as from infancy. I never saw any American plants growing with their Bog earth about them, and know not whether it has an unsightly appearance: if not it certainly would be advisable to have some of the most brilliant in the first compartment of the Garden; I mean that under the wall. This is to be the most splendid and adorned. I have removed the rubbish from under the wall; part of it is thrown upon the ridge running from the wall on the right, and part against the straight hedge between the two ivied Cottages. I am afraid we must give up the Fountain, as Mr Craig tells me the quantity of water will be too small to produce any effect even in winter: this consideration does

---

[1] The gardener.

not sway with me much; but Captn Bailey told me there would be little or *none* sometimes in summer, and upon reflection I think this would be so melancholy, and would make such open declaration of the poverty of the land, that it is better to abandon the idea. We may easily have enough for as many pools or basons as we like. Before I conclude I will add two or three words in further explanation of my general plan. The first Compartment as I have said is to be as splendid as possible; to be divided by a fence of shrubbery twelve feet in width, interspersed with Cypress. My present thought is to have that side of this fence which looks towards the first Compartment to consist probably all together of Laurustinus rather than of a variety of plants; plants in rows or masses in this way always are more rich and impressive. The next Compartment of which the ivied Cottage is to be the master object, I meant in contrast to the preceeding one to present the most delightful assemblage of English winter shrubs and flowers, intermingled with some foreign shrubs as are so common in english cottage Gardens as to be almost naturalized. Then comes the 2nd Cottage which I cannot find in my heart to pull down; and I am sure it may be repaired in a manner that will give no offense. I do not mean the encircling path to pass *through* the glade with the gold or silver fish but only on one side of it, so that it may be entered or not at pleasure.—The Quarry will be a delightful spot; but this with the English Spire that will so feelingly adorn it I would have in all its ornaments entirely English; from it we should pass to the clipped holly or Boxwood Hedge and its accompanying glade, and this should be mixed; and elaborate in its ornaments; something midway betwixt the compartment under the wall and the rest of the Garden. Farewell most affectionately yours and Sir Georges

Wm Wordsworth

40. *To* Walter Scott

[Coleorton]
[late Feb. 1807]

My dear Scott,

I am much obliged to you for your Gaelic information,[1] which

---

[1] For *The Blind Highland Boy.*

answers my purpose completely; nothing but kindness like yours could have encouraged me to trouble you on so trifling an occasion.—

We are all exceedingly happy in your promise of visiting us in your Road to town. Coleridge talks of leaving us in a fortnight, but as he is of a procrastinating habit, there is great probability of meeting him here, he desires me to give his best respects and to say how happy he will be to see you. Coming this way, of course you will have to take the Carlisle and Lancashire Road; if you come by Coach take your place only to Derby; which is only 14 miles from this place; the Innkeeper will be for sending you round by Buxton which is 6 miles about, this under pretence of the badness of the road, but the short Road is as good as the long one; and if he should refuse to bring you this way, threaten him with taking a Chaise from another Inn and he will immediately comply. They sent us round and Sir George Beaumont was exceedingly angry; and I have heard from several persons that the short Road is not a whit worse than the other. The coach would bring you to Lough-borough which is only eleven Chaise miles from us, but as it is 14 or 16 miles beyond Derby it cannot be worth while to be boxed up in the Coach so long for little or no advantage.

I am very glad to hear that Flodden Field is to be celebrated by you:[1] As you say you think of publishing your Poem is probably in a state of great forwardness, I mean as to composition for which I am still more glad: as your memory is so excellent we all hope to be gratified with the recitation of some of it when you come hither.

The day before yesterday I made an excursion of 20 miles from this place, as far as Nottingham which is an interesting town and neighbourhood; and even would be something more so to a Scotchman as its appearance and situation are somewhat like Stirling or Edingborough: a Castle (but unfortunately the old one is demolished and a new modern edifice with Corinthian pillars built upon its site) perched upon a Rock, a lofty bare rock, with the Town sloping down from it on the same ridge, and below a vast extent of fertile meadow at this time 'green as an emerald', a magnificent savanna with the Trent one of the grandest, if not the grandest, of our English Rivers winding through it. By the bye speaking of Nottingham have you read Mrs Hutchinson's Life of

[1] In *Marmion* (publ. 1808).

Colonel Hutchinson, her Husband; he was Governor of Nottingham Town and Castle in the time of the civil Wars; it is a most delightful Book.—

I have not yet received your Vol: of Ballads;[1] we are here in a bye place and the means which I took to have them conveyed safely have been the very cause of my not yet having received them at all. My Printer seems to have added one more to the number of the Seven Sleepers; I have not had a Sheet these thirteen days. farewell as I am to see you so soon; affectionately yours

Wm Wordsworth

You must enquire for Sir George Beaumont's new Farm House near Coleorton Hall.

41. *To* Lady Beaumont

Coleorton, Tuesday May 21st 1807.

Pray excuse this villainous paper, I cannot find any other of the folio size.

My dear Lady Beaumont,

Though I am to see you so soon I cannot but write a word or two, to thank you for the interest you take in my Poems[2] as evinced by your solicitude about their immediate reception. I write partly to thank you for this and to express the pleasure it has given me, and partly to remove any uneasiness from your mind which the disappointments you sometimes meet with in this labour of love may occasion. I see that you have many battles to fight for me; more than in the ardour and confidence of your pure and elevated mind you had ever thought of being summoned to; but be assured that this opposition is nothing more than what I distinctly foresaw that you and my other Friends would have to encounter. I say this, not to give myself credit for an eye of prophecy, but to allay any vexatious thoughts on my account which this opposition may have produced in you. It is impossible that any expectations can be lower than mine concerning the immediate effect of this little work

---

[1] *Ballads and Lyrical Pieces*, 1806.　　　　[2] *Poems in Two Volumes*, 1807.

upon what is called the Public. I do not here take into consideration the envy and malevolence, and all the bad passions which always stand in the way of a work of any merit from a living Poet; but merely think of the pure absolute honest ignorance, in which all worldlings of every rank and situation must be enveloped, with respect to the thoughts, feelings, and images, on which the life of my Poems depends. The things which I have taken, whether from within or without,—what have they to do with routs, dinners, morning calls, hurry from door to door, from street to street, on foot or in Carriage; with Mr. Pitt or Mr. Fox, Mr. Paul or Sir Francis Burdett, the Westminster Election,[1] or the Borough of Honiton; in a word, for I cannot stop to make my way through the hurry of images that present themselves to me, what have they to do with endless talking about things nobody cares anything for except as far as their own vanity is concerned, and this with persons they care nothing for but as their vanity or *selfishness* is concerned; what have they to do (to say all at once) with a life without love? in such a life there can be no thought; for we have no thought (save thoughts of pain) but as far as we have love and admiration. It is an awful truth, that there neither is, nor can be, any genuine enjoyment of Poetry among nineteen out of twenty of those persons who live, or wish to live, in the broad light of the world—among those who either are, or are striving to make themselves, people of consideration in society. This is a truth, and an awful one, because to be incapable of a feeling of Poetry in my sense of the word is to be without love of human nature and reverence for God.

Upon this I shall insist elsewhere; at present let me confine myself to my object, which is to make you, my dear Friend, as easy-hearted as myself with respect to these Poems. Trouble not yourself upon their present reception; of what moment is that compared with what I trust is their destiny, to console the afflicted, to add sunshine to daylight by making the happy happier, to teach the young and the gracious of every age, to see, to think and feel, and therefore to become more actively and securely virtuous; this is their office, which I trust they will faithfully perform long after we (that is, all that is mortal of us) are mouldered in our graves. I am well aware how far it would seem to many I overrate my own

[1] In which Paull and Burdett, both radicals, had been rivals.

exertions when I speak in this way, in direct connection with the Volumes I have just made public.

I am not, however, afraid of such censure, insignificant as probably the majority of those poems would appear to very respectable persons; I do not mean London wits and witlings, for these have too many bad passions about them to be respectable even if they had more intellect than the benign laws of providence will allow to such a heartless existence as theirs is; but grave, kindly-natured, worthy persons, who would be pleased if they could. I hope that these Volumes are not without some recommendations, even for Readers of this class, but their imagination has slept; and the voice which is the voice of my Poetry without Imagination cannot be heard.

Leaving these, I was going to say a word to such Readers as Mr. Rogers.[1] Such!—how would he be offended if he knew I considered him only as a representative of a class, and not as unique! 'Pity,' says Mr. R., 'that so many trifling things should be admitted to obstruct the view of those that have merit;' now, let this candid judge take, by way of example, the sonnets, which, probably, with the exception of two or three other Poems for which I will not contend appear to him the most trifling, as they are the shortest, I would say to him, omitting things of higher consideration, there is one thing which must strike you at once if you will only read these poems,—that those to Liberty, at least, have a connection with, or a bearing upon, each other, and therefore, if individually they want weight, perhaps, as a Body, they may not be so deficient, at least this ought to induce you to suspend your judgement, and qualify it so far as to allow that the writer aims at least at comprehensiveness. But dropping this, I would boldly say at once, that these Sonnets, while they each fix the attention upon some important sentiment separately considered, do at the same time collectively make a Poem on the subject of civil Liberty and national independence, which, either for simplicity of style or grandeur of moral sentiment, is, alas! likely to have few parallels in the Poetry of the present day. Again, turn to the 'Moods of my own Mind'. There is scarcely a Poem here of above thirty Lines, and very trifling these poems will appear to many; but, omitting to speak of them individually, do they not, taken collectively, fix the attention

[1] Samuel Rogers (see List of Correspondents).

upon a subject eminently poetical, viz., the interest which objects in nature derive from the predominance of certain affections more or less permanent, more or less capable of salutary renewal in the mind of the being contemplating these objects? This is poetic, and essentially poetic, and why? because it is creative.

But I am wasting words, for it is nothing more than you know, and if said to those for whom it is intended, it would not be understood.

I see by your last Letter that Mrs. Fermor[1] has entered into the spirit of these 'Moods of my own Mind.' Your transcript from her Letter gave me the greatest pleasure; but I must say that even she has something yet to receive from me. I say this with confidence, from her thinking that I have fallen below myself in the Sonnet beginning—'With ships the sea was sprinkled far and nigh.' As to the other which she objects to, I will only observe that there is a misprint in the last line but two, 'And *though* this wilderness' for 'And *through* this wilderness'—that makes it unintelligible. This latter Sonnet for many reasons, though I do not abandon it, I will not now speak of; but upon the other, I could say something important in conversation, and will attempt now to illustrate it by a comment which I feel will be very inadequate to convey my meaning. There is scarcely one of my Poems which does not aim to direct the attention to some moral sentiment, or to some general principle, or law of thought, or of our intellectual constitution. For instance in the present case, who is there that has not felt that the mind can have no rest among a multitude of objects, of which it either cannot make one whole, or from which it cannot single out one individual, whereupon may be concentrated the attention divided among or distracted by a multitude? After a certain time we must either select one image or object, which must put out of view the rest wholly, or must subordinate them to itself while it stands forth as a Head:

> Now glowed the firmament
> With living sapphires! Hesperus, that *led*
> The starry host, rode brightest; till the Moon,
> Rising in clouded majesty, at length,
> Apparent *Queen*, unveiled *her peerless* light,
> And o'er the dark her silver mantle threw.[2]

---

[1] Lady Beaumont's sister.   [2] *Paradise Lost*, iv. 694–9.

Having laid this down as a general principle, take the case before us. I am represented in the Sonnet as casting my eyes over the sea, sprinkled with a multitude of Ships, like the heavens with stars, my mind may be supposed to float up and down among them in a kind of dreamy indifference with respect either to this or that one, only in a pleasurable state of feeling with respect to the whole prospect. 'Joyously it showed,' this continued till that feeling may be supposed to have passed away, and a kind of comparative listlessness or apathy to have succeeded, as at this line, 'Some veering up and down, one knew not why.' All at once, while I am in this state, comes forth an object, an individual, and my mind, sleepy and unfixed, is awakened and fastened in a moment. 'Hesperus, that *led* The starry host,' is a poetical object, because the glory of his own Nature gives him the pre-eminence the moment he appears; he calls forth the poetic faculty, receiving its exertions as a tribute; but this Ship in the Sonnet may, in a manner still more appropriate, be said to come upon a mission of the poetic Spirit, because in its own appearance and attributes it is barely sufficiently distinguish[ed] to rouse the creative faculty of the human mind; to exertions at all times welcome, but doubly so when they come upon us when in a state of remissness. The mind being once fixed and rouzed, all the rest comes from itself; it is merely a lordly Ship, nothing more:

> This ship was nought to me, nor I to her,
> Yet I pursued her with a lover's look.

My mind wantons with grateful joy in the exercise of its own powers, and, loving its own creation,

> This ship to all the rest I did prefer,

making her a sovereign or a regent, and thus giving body and life to all the rest; mingling up this idea with fondness and praise—

> where she comes the winds must stir;

and concluding the whole with

> On went She, and due north her journey took.

Thus taking up again the Reader with whom I began, letting him know how long I must have watched this favorite Vessel, and inviting him to rest his mind as mine is resting.

Having said so much upon a mere 14 lines, which Mrs. Fermor did not approve, I cannot but add a word of two upon my satisfaction in finding that my mind has so much in common with hers, and that we participate so many of each other's pleasures. I collect this from her having singled out the two little Poems, the Daffodils, and the Rock crowned with snowdrops.[1] I am sure that whoever is much pleased with either of these quiet and tender delineations must be fitted to walk through the recesses of my poetry with delight, and will there recognise, at every turn, something or other in which, and over which, it has that property and right which knowledge and love confer. The line, 'Come, blessed barrier, etc.,' in the sonnet upon Sleep,[2] which Mrs. F. points out, had before been mentioned to me by Coleridge, and indeed by almost everybody who had heard it, as eminently beautiful. My letter (as this 2nd sheet, which I am obliged to take, admonishes me) is growing to an enormous length; and yet, saving that I have expressed my calm confidence that these Poems will live, I have said nothing which has a particular application to the object of it, which was to remove all disquiet from your mind on account of the condemnation they may at present incur from that portion of my contemporaries who are called the Public. I am sure, my dear Lady Beaumont, if you attach any importance [to it] it can only be from an apprehension that it may affect me, upon which I have already set you at ease, or from a fear that this present blame is ominous of their future or final destiny. If this be the case, your tenderness for me betrays you; be assured that the decision of these persons has nothing to do with the Question; they are altogether incompetent judges. These people in the senseless hurry of their idle lives do not *read* books, they merely snatch a glance at them that they may talk about them. And even if this were not so, never forget what I believe was observed to you by Coleridge, that every great and original writer, in proportion as he is great or original, must himself create the taste by which he is to be relished; he must teach the art by which he is to be seen; this, in a certain degree, even to all persons, however wise and pure may be their

---

[1] i.e. 'Who fancied what a pretty sight?'

[2] The third sonnet *To Sleep*, beginning 'A flock of sheep that leisurely pass by'.

lives, and however unvitiated their taste; but for those who dip into books in order to give an opinion of them, or talk about them to take up an opinion—for this multitude of unhappy, and misguided, and misguiding beings, an entire regeneration must be produced; and if this be possible, it must be a work of *time*. To conclude, my ears are stone-dead to this idle buzz, and my flesh as insensible as iron to these petty stings; and after what I have said I am sure yours will be the same. I doubt not that you will share with me an invincible confidence that my writings (and among them these little Poems) will co-operate with the benign tendencies in human nature and society, wherever found; and that they will, in their degree, be efficacious in making men wiser, better, and happier. Farewell; I will not apologise for this Letter, though its length demands an apology. Believe me, eagerly wishing for the happy days when I shall see you and Sir George here, most affectionately yours,

Wm Wordsworth

Do not hurry your coming hither on our account: my Sister regrets that she did not press this upon you, as you say in your Letter, 'we cannot *possibly* come before the first week in June'; from which we infer that your kindness will induce you to make sacrifices for our sakes. Whatever pleasure we may have in thinking of Grasmere, we have no impatience to be gone, and think with full as much regret at leaving Coleorton. I had, for myself, indeed, a wish to be at Grasmere with as much of the summer before me as might be, but to this I attach no importance whatever, as far as the gratification of that wish interferes with any inclination or duty of yours. I could not be satisfied without seeing you here, and shall have great pleasure in waiting.

42. *To* Walter Scott

Grasmere Jan^{ry} 18. 1808

My dear Scott,

   I am two Letters in your debt, and therefore ought to write: particularly as you spoke of some painful affairs in which you have

been entangled, I hope you have gotten fairly through them by this
time—I guess from the advertizements that your Poem[1] is nearly
out: how comes on the Dryden?[2]—I think the character of the
Annus Mirabilis as a Poem might be illustrated by some extracts
from a long sermon entitled God's terrible voice in the City, in
which the fire of London is minutely described; Dryden's is a sorry
Poem, and the Sermonist though with a world of absurdity has
upon the whole greatly the advantage of him.—There is in
Echard's History a most laughable account of Ogilby,[3] who, by the
bye, was a countryman of yours. Echard at the end of each year
gives an account of every eminent man who had died in the course
of it; and Ogilby makes one of a list, he died in Charles the second's
time.—

'Tom the second reigns like Tom the first'[4] is a fling at Shadwell.
'Tom Sternhold's or Tom Shadwell's rhymes will serve'[5]—In
Harte's Poems[6] Anderson's edition are two or three notes upon
Dryden which might be worth looking at—Harte had read
Dryden's works with exceeding care but very little profit.—I have
a life of Shaftsbury entitled I believe Rawleigh Redivivus, should
you like to see it?—I am curious to see your notes on Dryden's
political Poems, which are in my opinion far the best of his works,
though there is very great merit in his two translations from
Boccaccio—Chaucer I think he has entirely spoiled, even
wantonly deviating from his great original, and always for the
worse.—Of his plays I do not mean to speak as I know very little
about them—As a Translator from the antient classics he succeeds
the best with Ovid, next with Juvenal, next with Virgil, and worst
of all with Homer.—He has however done some things with spirit
from Horace, and in one or two passages with first-rate
excellence.—I have a very high admiration of the talents both of
Dryden and Pope, and ultimately, as from all good writers of
whatever kind, their Country will be benefited greatly by their
labours. But thus far I think their writings have done more harm
than good. It will require yet half a century completely to carry off
the poison of Pope's Homer; but too much of this.—I must say a

---

[1] *Marmion.*   [2] Scott's edition.   [3] John Ogilby (1600–76), translator.
[4] Dryden, *To my dear Friend, Mr. Congreve*, line 48.   [5] *Religio Laici*, line 456.
[6] Walter Harte (1709–74), *Poems*, 1727. (For Anderson, see List of Correspondents.)

word of my own employments; after I left you[1] I had a thoroughly idle summer; and part of the Autumn was as idle—but latterly I have been busy, though with many interruptions; and have written a narrative Poem of about 1700 lines;[2] I finished it two days ago—I am nearly at the end of my sheet and must say one word of Mr. Jefferay;[3] in passing through Penrith I had an opportunity of seeing his last Review. I had before skimmed over, some time ago, what he had written in the article on Thalaba, I then set him down in my mind as a poor Creature, and he has in this last performance shewn himself so utterly contemptible that I should not have adverted to him at all had it not been that I am writing to one personally connected with him.—To you therefore I must observe, that in the first sentence of what he has said upon my Poems he has shewn a gross want of the common feeling of a British Gentleman. He was cordially received by Southey at his home in this Country, and takes the first opportunity of repaying that civility by a base attempt to hold him up to ridicule for residing in that very country where he had entertained the said Jefferay. If Mr. J. continues to play tricks of this kind, let him take care to arm his breech well for assuredly he runs desperate risque of having it soundly kicked—affectionately yours, pray let me hear from you soon.

W. Wordsworth

43. *To* Francis Wrangham

Grasmere, June 5th, 1808.

My dear Wrangham,

I have this moment received your Letter. Montagu is a most provoking Fellow; very kind, very humane, very generous, very ready to serve with a thousand other good qualities; but in the practical business of life the arrantest Mar-plan that ever lived. When I first wrote to you, I wrote also to him, sending the statement which I sent to you, and begging his exertions *among his*

---

[1] At Coleorton.

[2] *The White Doe of Rylstone* (publ. 1815).

[3] Francis Jeffrey (1773–1850) had ridiculed Southey's *Thalaba* (1802), and more recently W. W.'s *Poems in Two Volumes*, in the *Edinburgh Review*.

friends.[1] By and by comes back my statement having undergone a rifaciamento from his hands, etc., *printed*; with an accompanying Letter saying that if some of the principal people in this neighbourhood who had already subscribed, would put their names to this Paper testifying that this was a proper case for charitable interference; or that the *Persons mentioned were proper objects of Charity*, that he would have the printed Paper inserted in the public Newspapers, etc. etc. Upon which my Sister wrote to him that in consequence of what had been already subscribed, and what we had reason to expect from those Friends who were privately stirring in the business, among whom we chiefly alluded to you, in our own minds, as one on whom we had most dependance, that there would be no necessity for *public advertisements*; but that if amongst his private Friends he could raise any thing for us, we should be *very glad* to receive it. And upon this does he write to you in this (what shall I call it, for I am really vexed) blundering manner!!! I will not call upon you to undertake the awkward task of rebuilding that part of the Edifice which Montagu has destroyed, but let what remains be preserved, and if a little could be added there would be no harm.—I must request you to transmit the money to me with the Names of the Persons to whom we are obliged, in order that they may be inserted in the Book which is lodged with the Treasurer!—

With regard to the latter, and more important part of your letter I am under many difficulties. I am writing from a window which gives me a view of a little Boat gliding quietly about upon the surface of our Bason of a lake. I should like to be in it, but what could I do with such a Vessel in the heart of the Atlantic Ocean? As this Boat would be to that Navigation, so is a letter to the subject upon which you would set me afloat. Let me however say, that I have read your sermon (which I lately received from Longman) with much pleasure. I only gave it a cursory perusal, for since it arrived our family has been in great confusion, we having removed to another House,[2] in which we are not yet half settled. The Appendix I had received before in a frank, and of that I feel myself more entitled to speak, because I had read it more at leisure.

I am entirely of accord with you, in chiefly recommending

---

[1] On behalf of the orphaned children of George and Sarah Green of Grasmere, who had perished on the fells.   [2] Allan Bank.

religious Books for the Poor, but of many of those which you recommend I can neither speak in praise nor blame, as I have never read them. Yet, as far as my own observation goes, which has been mostly employed upon agricultural Persons in thinly-peopled districts, I cannot find that there is much disposition to read among the labouring Classes, or much occasion for it. Among Manufacturers and Persons engaged in sedentary employments it is, I know, very different. The labouring man in agriculture generally carries on his work either in solitude, or with his own Family, persons whose minds he is thoroughly acquainted with, and with whom he is under no temptation to enter into discussions, or to compare opinions. He goes home from the field, or the Barn, and within and about his own house, he finds a hundred little jobs which furnish him with a change of employment, which is grateful and profitable; then comes supper, and to bed. This for week-days: for Sabbaths he goes to Church, with us mostly twice a day; on coming home some one turns to the Bible, finds the Text and probably reads the chapter whence it is taken, or perhaps some other; and in the afternoon the Master or Mistress frequently reads the Bible, if alone; and on this day the Mistress of the house *almost always* teaches the children to read, or as they express it, hears them a Lesson; or, if not thus employed, they visit their neighbours or receive them in their own houses as they drop in, and keep up by the hour a slow and familiar chat. This kind of life of which I have seen much, and which I know will be looked upon with little complacency by many religious persons, from its bearing no impression of their particular modes of faith and from its want of fervent Piety and habitual Godliness, is peaceable; and as innocent as (the frame of society and the practices of Government being what they are) we have a right to expect; besides, it is much more intellectual than a careless observer would suppose. One of our Neighbours, who lives as I have described, was yesterday walking with me, and as we were pacing on, talking about indifferent matters, by the side of a Brook, he suddenly said to me with great spirit and a lively smile: 'I like to walk where I can hear the sound of a Beck' (the word as you know in our dialect for a Brook)—I cannot but think that this Man, without being conscious of it, has had many devout feelings connected with the appearances which have presented themselves to him in his employment as a

Shepherd, and the pleasure of his heart at that moment was an acceptable offering to the divine Being. But to return to the subject of Books; I find, among the people I am speaking of, half-penny Ballads, and penny and two-penny histories, in great abundance; these are often bought as charitable tributes to the poor Persons who hawk them about (and it is the best way of procuring them); they are frequently stitched together in tolerably thick volumes, and such I have read; some of the contents, though not often religious, very good; others objectionable, either for the superstition in them (such as prophecies, fortune-telling, etc.) or more frequently for indelicacy. I have so much felt the influence of these straggling papers, that I have many a time wished that I had talents to produce songs, poems, and little histories, that might circulate among other good things in this way, supplanting partly the bad; flowers and useful herbs to take place of weeds. Indeed some of the Poems which I have published were composed not without a hope that at some time or other they might answer this purpose. The kind of Library which you recommend would not, I think, from the reasons given above, be of much direct use in any of the agricultural or pastoral districts of Cumberland or Westmorland with which I am acquainted, though almost every person can read: I mean of *general* use as to morals or behaviour; it might however with individuals do much in awakening enterprize, calling forth ingenuity, and fostering genius. I have known several Persons who would eagerly have sought, not after these Books merely, but *any* Books, and would have been most happy in having such a collection to repair to. The knowledge thus acquired would also have spread, by being dealt about in conversation among their Neighbours, at the door, or by the fireside—so that it is not easy to foresee how far the good might extend; and harm I can see none which would not be greatly over-balanced by the advantage.—

The situation of Manufacturers is deplorably different. The monotony of their employments renders some sort of stimulus, intellectual or bodily, absolutely necessary for them. Their work is carried on in clusters, Men from different parts of the world, and perpetually changing; so that every individual is constantly in the way of being brought into contact with new notions and feelings, and of being unsettled in his own accordingly. A select Library therefore, in such situations, may be of the same use as a public

Dial, keeping every Body's clock in some kind of order. Besides, contrasting the Manufacturer with the Agriculturalist, it may be observed that he has much more leisure, and in his over-hours (not having other pleasant employment to turn to) he is more likely to find reading a relief. What then are the Books which should be put in his way? Without being myself a clergyman, I have no hesitation in saying, chiefly religious ones; though I should not go so far as you seemed inclined to do, excluding others because they are not according to the letter or in the spirit of your profession. I, with you, feel little disposed to admire several of those mentioned by Gilbert Burns,[1] much less others which you name as having been recommended; in G. Burns' collection there may be too little religion; and I should fear that you like all other Clergymen, may confine yourself too exclusively to that concern which you justly deem the most important, but which by being exclusively considered can never be thoroughly understood. I will allow with you that Religion is the eye of the Soul, but if we would have successful Soul-oculists, not merely that organ, but the general anatomy and constitution of the intellectual frame must be studied; farther, the powers of that eye are affected by the general state of the system. My meaning is, that piety and religion will be best understood by him who takes the most comprehensive view of the human mind, and that for the most part, they will strengthen with the general strength of the mind; and that this is best promoted by a due mixture of direct and indirect nourishment and discipline. For example, Paradise Lost and Robinson Crusoe might be as serviceable as Law's Serious Call,[2] or Melmoth's Great Importance of a Religious Life;[3] at least, if the books be all good, they would mutually assist each other.

In what I have said, though following my own thoughts merely as called forth by your Appendix, is *implied* an answer to your request that I would give you 'half an idea upon education as a national object'. I have only kept upon the surface of the question; but you must have deduced, that I deem any plan of national education in a country like ours most difficult to apply to practice. In Switzerland, or Sweden, or Norway, or France, or Spain, or anywhere but Great Britain it would be comparatively easy.

[1] Brother of Robert Burns.
[2] *A Serious Call to a Devout and Holy Life*, 1728.   [3] Publ. 1711 (anon.).

Heaven and Hell are scarcely more different from each other than Sheffield and Manchester, etc. differ from the plains and Vallies of Surrey, Essex, Cumberland, or Westmorland. We have mighty Cities and Towns of all sizes, with Villages and Cottages scattered everywhere. We are Mariners, Miners, Manufacturers in tens of thousands: Traders, Husbandmen, everything. What form of discipline; what Books or doctrines, I will not say would equally suit all these; but which, if happily fitted for one, would not perhaps be an absolute nuisance in another?—You will also have deduced that nothing romantic can be said with truth of the influence of education upon the district in which I live. We have thank heaven free schools, or schools with some endowment, almost everywhere, and almost every one can read; but not because we have free or endowed schools, but because our land is far more than elsewhere tilled by Men who are the Owners of it; and as the population is not over-crowded and the vices which are quickened and cherished in a crowded population do not therefore prevail, Parents have more ability and inclination to send their Children to School; much more than in Manufacturing districts, and also, though in a less degree, more than in Agricultural ones, where the Tillers are not proprietors.—

If in Scotland the Children are sent to School, where the Parents have not the advantage I have been speaking of, it is chiefly because their labour can be turned to no account at home. Send among them Manufacturers; or Farmers on a large scale, and, you may indeed substitute Sunday-schools, or other modes of instructing them, but the ordinary parish Schools will be neglected. The influence of our schools in this neighbourhood can never be understood if this their connection with the state of landed property be overlooked. In fact that influence is not striking. The people are not habitually religious in the common sense of the word, much less godly. The effect of their schooling is chiefly seen in the activity with which the young Persons emigrate, and the success attending it; and at home, by a general orderliness and gravity, with habits of independence and self-respect; nothing obsequious or fawning is ever to be seen amongst them. It may be added that this ability (from the two causes, Land and Schools) of giving their children instruction contributes to spread a respect for Scholarship through the Country. If in any Family one of the

Children should be quicker at his Book or fonder of it than others he is often marked out in consequence for the profession of a Clergyman; this (before these mercantile or manufacturing employments held out such flattering hopes) very generally happened; so that the schools of the North were the great nurseries of Curates, several of whom got forward in their profession; some with, and others without, the help of a University education; and in all instances such connection of families (all the members of which lived in the humblest and plainest manner, working with their own hands as labourers) with a learned and dignified profession assisted (and still does, though in a less degree) not a little to elevate their feelings, and conferred importance on them in their own eyes.

But I must stop. My dear Wrangham, begin your Education at the top of society; let the head go in the right course and the tail will follow. But what can you expect of national education conducted by a Government which for twenty years resisted the abolition of the Slave Trade; and annually debauches the morals of the people by every possible device? holding out the temptation with one hand, and scourging with the other. The distilleries and Lotteries are standing records that the Government cares nothing for the morals of the People, and that all they want is their money.—But Wisdom and Justice are the only true sources of the revenue of a people—preach this, and may you not preach in vain! Wishing you success in every good work I remain your affectionate friend

Wm Wordsworth

Thanks for your enquires about our little boy. He is well, though not yet quite strong.

This is a Copy of my Letter which was so ill penned that you could not have read it.

44. *To* Richard Sharp

Grasmere, September 27 [1808]

My dear Sharp,

I am much obliged to you for taking the trouble to send me Mackintosh's[1] opinion of my Poems; if you think it worth while, tell him I was happy to have given a man like him so much pleasure, especially at such a distance from his own Country, and in these distressful times; the sonnet beginning "Two voices are there,"[2] you will remember is the one which I mentioned to you as being the best I had written.—

It gave me real pleasure to hear that your health had been so much benefited, and I should have been glad if you had added that you were resolved to be upon your guard against late hours, crowded rooms, etc. during the ensuing winter.—

Two subjects are likely to be discussed in Parliament in which I fell interested; the one, lotteries, in which I know you will bear a part, and which is surely of infinite importance—and the other, copyright of Authors.[3]—I am told that it is proposed to extend the right from 14 years, as it now stands, after the decease of authors, till 28, this I think far too short a period; at least I am sure that it requires much more than that length of time to establish the reputation of original productions, both in Philosophy and Poetry, and to bring them consequently into such circulation that the authors, in the Persons of their Heirs or posterity, can in any degree be benefited, I mean in a pecuniary point of view, for the trouble they must have taken to produce the works.—The law as it now stands merely consults the interest of the useful drudges in Literature, or of flimsy and shallow writers, whose works are upon a level with the taste and knowledge of the age; while men of real power, who go before their age, are deprived of all hope of their families being benefited by their exertions. Take for instance in philosophy, Hartley's book upon Man,[4] how many years did it sleep in almost entire oblivion! What sale had Collins' Poems during his lifetime, or during the fourteen years after his death, and

---

[1] Sir James Mackintosh (1765–1832), reformer and historian, now a judge in India.   [2] *Thoughts of a Briton on the Subjugation of Switzerland.*

[3] An issue to which W. W. returned in 1836.

[4] David Hartley, *Observations on Man*, 1749.

how great has been the sale since! the product of it if secured to his family, would have been an independence to them.—Take a still stronger instance, but this you may say proves too much, I mean Milton's minor Poems; it is nearly 200 years since they were published, yet they were utterly neglected till within these last 30 years, notwithstanding they had, since the beginning of the last century, the reputation of the Paradise Lost to draw attention towards them. Suppose that Burns or Cowper had left at their deaths each a child a few months old, a daughter for example, is it reasonable that those children, at the age of 28, should cease to derive benefit from their Father's works, when every Bookseller in the Country is profiting by them?—I merely remind you of these things, which cannot but have passed through your active mind; if you can be of any service to Literature in this case I know you will not let slip the opportunity.—

I was much pleased with your speech upon the Copenhagen business,[1] and think that the language of the declaration of Ministers was horrible: at the same time I must say that I deem it too probable that the Danes would have joined with our enemies; and the conduct of the Danish government since towards the disarmed part of the Spanish troops, while it strengthens this belief, very much diminishes any regret which I felt for our treatment of Copenhagen. Surely the Danish Government has behaved infamously towards these brave and much injured men, and towards their more fortunate fellow-soldiers who have escaped from Gallic Thraldom, under [the] conduct of the Marquess of Romagna.

Rogers has sent me £31. 8, including 5 guineas from himself—it is very handsome.—

I remain dear Sharp yours very sincerely,
W. Wordsworth

We are all here cut to the heart by the conduct of Sir Hew and his Brother Knight in Portugal[2]—for myself, I have not suffered so much upon any public occasion these many years.

Pray send the enclosed for Rogers to the twopenny Post.

[1] The bombardment of Copenhagen and the capture of the Danish fleet (Sept. 1807).

[2] Sir Hew Dalrymple and Sir Henry Burrard, whose cautious policy in the Peninsula led to the Convention of Cintra (see letter 46 below).

45. *To* Samuel Rogers

Grasmere, Sept^br 29, 1808.

My dear Sir,

I am greatly obliged to you for your kind exertions in favour of our Grasmere Orphans, and for your own contribution. It will give you pleasure to hear that there is the best prospect of the children being greatly benefited in every respect by the sum which has been received, amounting to nearly 500£. They are placed in three different Houses in the Vale of Grasmere, and are treated with great tenderness; they will be carefully taught to read and write, and when they are of a proper age care will be taken to put them forward in life in the most adviseable manner.

The bill you sent me, £31:8—I have already paid into the hands of the secretary.

I was glad to hear that our Friend Sharp was so much benefited in health by his late visit to our beautiful Country. We passed one pleasant day together, but we were unlucky upon the whole in not seeing much of each other; as a more than usual part of his time was spent about Keswick and Ulswater. I am happy to find that we coincide in opinion about Crabbe's *verses*; for *poetry* in no sense can they be called. Sharp is also of the same opinion. I remember that I mentioned in my last that there was nothing in the last publication[1] so good as the description of the Parish workhouse, Apothecary, etc. This is true—and it is no less true that the passage which I commended is of no great merit, because the description, at the best of no high order, is in the instance of the apothecary, inconsistent, that is, false. It, no doubt, sometimes happens, but, as far as my experience goes, very rarely, that Country Practitioners neglect, and brutally treat, their Patients; but what kind of men are they who do so?—not Apothecaries like Crabbe's Professional, pragmatical Coxcombs, 'generally neat, all pride, and business, bustle, and conceit,' no, but drunken reprobates, frequenters of boxing-matches, cock-fightings, and horse-races— these are the men who are hard-hearted with their Patients, but any man who attaches so much importance to his profession as to have strongly caught, in his dress and manner, the outward formalities of it, may easily indeed be much occupied with himself,

[1] *The Parish Register*, 1807.

but he will not behave towards his 'Victims,' as Mr. Crabbe calls them, in the manner he has chosen to describe. After all, if the Picture were true to nature, what claim would it have to be called Poetry? At the best, it is the meanest kind of satire, except the merely personal. The sum of all is, that nineteen out of 20 of Crabbe's Pictures are mere matters of fact; with which the Muses have just about as much to do as they have with a Collection of medical reports, or of Law cases.

How comes it that you never favour these mountains with a visit? You ask how I have been employed; you do me too much honour, and I wish I could reply to the question with any satisfaction. I have written since I saw you about 500 lines of my long Poem,[1] which is all I have done. What are you doing? My Wife and Sister desire to be remembered by you, and believe me, my dear Sir,

with great truth, yours,
Wm Wordsworth

We are here all in a rage about the Convention in Portugal; if Sir Hew were to shew his face among us, or that other doughty Knight, Sir Arthur,[2] the very Boys would hiss them out of the Vale.

46. *To* Francis Wrangham

[late Mar. 1809]

My dear Wrangham,

You will think I am afraid that I have used you ill in not replying sooner to your last letter; particularly as you were desirous to be informed in what Newspaper my pamphlet was printing. I should not have failed to give you immediately any information on this subject which could be of use but in fact, though I began to publish in a newspaper, viz., the *Courier*, an accidental loss of two or three sheets of the Manuscript prevented me from going on in that mode of publication, after two sections had appeared. The Pamphlet will be out in less than a fortnight, entitled at full length, Concerning the Relations of Great Britain, Spain and Portugal, to each other

---

[1] *The Excursion*.　　　[2] Wellesley.

and to the common Enemy, at this crisis, and specifically as affected by the Convention of Cintra,[1] the whole brought to the Test of those Principles by which alone the independence and freedom of Nations can be preserved or recovered. This is less a Title than a Table of Contents, I give it you at full length in order that you may set your fancy at work (if you have no better employment for it) upon what the Pamphlet may contain.—I sent off the last sheets only a day or two since, else I should have written to you sooner; it having been my intention to pay my debt to you the moment I had discharged this debt to my Country, and to the virtuous of all Countries. What I have written has been done according to the best light of my Conscience; it is indeed very imperfect, and will I fear be little read, but, if it is read, it cannot I hope fail of doing some good—though I am aware it will create me a world of enemies, and call forth the old yell of Jacobinism.—I have not sent it to any personal friends as such; therefore I have made no exception in your case. I have ordered it to be sent to two, the Spanish and Portuguese Ambassadors, and to three or four other public men, and Members of Parliament, but to nobody of my friends and relations. It is printed with my name, and I believe will be published by Longman.

Verses have been out of my Head for some time; but in some inspiring moment should such be vouchsafed, I may not be unmindful of the request which you do me the honour to make. You must permit me to return the same request on my part to you; there may not be much invention in this, the sincerity of it may make amends.

I am very happy that you have not been inattentive to my suggestion on the subject of Topography. When I ventured to recommend this pursuit to you, I did not for a moment suppose that it was to interfere with your appropriate duties as a parish priest—far otherwise—but I know you are of an active mind; and I am sure that a portion of your time might be thus employed without any deduction from that which was due to your professional engagements. It would be a recreation to you—and

---

[1] The agreement of 30 Aug., by which the French had been allowed to evacuate Portugal and return home in British ships, was widely regarded as a humiliating defeat. W. W.'s critique developed into an indictment of Napoleonic policy in the Peninsula, and a call to the Spanish to rise against their oppressors.

also it does appear to me that records of this kind ought to be executed by some body or other, both for the instruction of those now living and for the sake of posterity; and if so, the duty devolves more naturally upon Clergymen than upon other persons; as their opportunities and qualifications are, both, likely to be better than those of other men. If you have not seen White's[1] and Whitaker's[2] books, do procure a sight of them.—

I was aware that you would think me fair game upon the Catholic Question—but really I should be greatly obliged to any man who would help me over the difficulty I stated. If the Catholics upon the plea of their being the majority merely (which implies an admission on our part that their profession of faith is in itself as good as ours, as consistent with civil liberty), if they are to have these requests accorded, how can they be refused (consistently) the further prayer, of being constituted upon the same plea, the established Church? I confess I am not prepared for this—with the Methodists on one side and the Catholics on the other, what is to become of the poor Church and people of England, to both of which I am most tenderly attached, and to the former, not the less on account of the pretty little spire of Brompton Parish Church, under which you and I were made happy men, by the gift from providence of two excellent wives. To Mrs Wrangham present my cordial regards, and believe me dear Wrangham

Your very sincere and affectionate Friend,

W. Wordsworth

47. *To* S. T. Coleridge

[5 May 1809]

My dear Coleridge,

I am very sorry to hear of your being taken ill again, were it only on account of the effect these seizures may have upon the work in which you are engaged.[3] They prove that it is *absolutely necessary* that you should always be *beforehand* with your work. On the

---

[1] *Natural History and Antiquities of Selborne*, 1789.
[2] *The History and Antiquities of Cleveland in the North Riding of Yorkshire*, 1808.
[3] His periodical *The Friend*.

general question of your health, one thing is obvious, that health of mind, that is, resolution, self-denial, and well-regulated conditions of feeling, are what you must depend upon; and that Doctors can do you little or no good, and that Doctors' stuff has been one of your greatest curses; and of course, of ours through you.—I should not speak now upon this subject were it not on account of what you say about Mr. Harrison. You must know better than Mr. Harrison, Mr. King, or any Surgeon what is to do you good; what you are to do, and what to leave undone. Do not look out of yourself for that stay which can only be found within. I have had a strong inclination to walk over to Keswick lately, for many reasons; one of which you will scarcely guess. Turning over an old Magazine three or four days ago I hit upon a paragraph stating that B. Flower had been fined £100, and committed to Newgate for 4 months, for reflecting on the Union with Ireland, in some comments upon a Speech of the Bishop of Llandaff. This brought Gilbert Wakefield to my mind and his four years' imprisonment in Dorsetshire Gaol; and led me to review in my thoughts what I had written in the Pamphlet, not without a reference to the possibility of my being subject to the like chastisement of an incensed Government, or prosecution of an angry individual. I could not recollect any passage but one from which there seemed much to apprehend. It is as follows. 'I say that we (the people of England) did not look for the punishment of the men who had signed and ratified the convention to gratify any feelings of vindictive justice, for these, if they could have existed in such a case, had been abundantly appeased already, for what punishment could be greater than to have brought upon themselves the *unremovable hatred and contempt* of their countrymen, but etc.' I cannot remember what follows, but it is to this purpose that by judicial punishment of the authors our detestation of the fact might be more emphatically expressed, or made more signally manifest.—The words marked in Italics I fear for; and on this account. It has pleased his Majesty's Ministers to their utter disgrace to send back Wellesley to Portugal, and to make him General in Chief there; when I bear in mind that Sidmouth[1] said in the house of Lords, that the character of Sir Arthur W. and some others were precious deposits in the hands of their Country, I cannot doubt with what dispositions the

[1] The former Prime Minister.

government would regard expressions of this kind. Mr. De
Quincey says in his last letter that he hopes the Pamphlet would be
out the day before yesterday: it was not till that very day that these
thoughts struck me in this light, and I immediately wrote to
Stuart[1] to request he would look over the pamphlet to see if there
was anything in it for which it was likely I should be prosecuted,
and if it should not be published, to cancel *this* leaf if he thought
proper and soften the expression. Now the reason which induced
me to use this language was not intemperate indignation, but a
deep conviction of the importance of keeping—in cases of this
kind—as close a connection as possible in the minds of men
between disapprobation or hatred of vice and of the vitious person,
of crime and of the criminal. In private life where we may have
been personally piqued or injured, it may be well to encourage
relenting and forgiving dispositions, for many reasons, and for this
not the least that in cases which only concern ourselves we are
much more likely to form precipitate and erroneous notions. But in
public offences, under settled Governments, there is no feeling
more to be dreaded than this disposition to forgive and to relent; it
approaches the mind under the mask of charity and humanity and
so forth; and in fact is at the bottom nothing but remissness
indolence weakness and cowardice; an inability to keep the mind
steadfastly fixed on its object; the sensations wound up to their
proper tone. Accordingly duties which it would be laborious to
discharge, and difficulties which it would be hard to overcome, are
all gotten rid of at once with this flattering promise that the future
will make amends and set all things right of itself. And so were it
merely to avoid the trouble of changing we start afresh with the
same crazy or vitious cattle as before.—I have no doubt that one
victory gained by Sir A. W. would blot out all remembrance of his
former transactions, and yet what would ten victories avail if the
moral spirit continues the same?—You would see the proclamation published by the Portuguese Government guarding the nation
against insidious persons who were propagating reports to the
prejudice of the English in respect to their intentions towards the
Portuguese, and denouncing the severest punishment against
those who should spread or countenance such calumnies.—
Neither the English nor the sound part of the Portuguese Nation

[1] Daniel Stuart.

need have cared a straw for these reports, had the English behaved
with common decency towards the Portuguese, but they are
formidable engines indeed when backed by an instrument like the
Convention of Cintra. But Politicians (and alas! it is too much the
case with the mass of mankind when the matter does not come
home to their own concerns) only look at things in the gross; the
spirit always escapes their notice. Upon this I have insisted with
effect I think in the pamphlet. But to return to the libel, do not be
alarmed, for I assure you I am not; I am confident there is no
passage more objectionable than this, and this will be corrected
probably if my letter has not arrived too late. 'That they had
brought upon themselves hatred and contempt is known to the
whole nation; that it was or *ought* to be *unremovable*, I have proved,
because it is a fundamental position that no subsequent judicial
investigation could affect anything that was *material* in our notions
of the offence.'—Mary tells me that I ought not to have written to
you upon this subject, as it will turn your thoughts from the Friend.
I should be very sorry to think so humbly of your command over
your thoughts upon such an occasion. My reason for writing was
merely to know your opinion how far these words were actionable
in themselves, and next how far it is likely in the present temper of
the times that I should be prosecuted for them. This was all which
I proposed to do when I began the subject, and I have dwelt so
long upon it merely because my pen chose to move in that track.—

I am half in mind to destroy this scrawl, and half in mind to
scribble another sheet upon another subject, viz. my published
Poems, and the arrangment which I mean to place them in if they
are ever republished during my lifetime.[1] I should begin thus,
Poems relating to childhood, and such feelings as rise in the mind
in after life in direct contemplation of that state; to these I should
prefix the motto 'the Child is father of the man—etc.' The class
would begin with the simplest dawn of the affections or faculties, as
the Foresight, or Children gathering flowers, the Pet Lamb, etc.
and would ascend in a gradual scale of imagination to Hartley,[2]
'there was a Boy', and it would conclude with the grand ode,
'There was a time',[3] which perhaps might be preceded by We are

[1] This is a first sketch of the arrangement which was followed in the edition of
1815. It was not fundamentally altered thereafter.
[2] i.e. *To H.C. Six Years Old.*   [3] *Intimations of Immortality.*

Seven, if it were not advisable to place that earlier. This class would contain Gathering Flowers, Pet Lamb, Alice Fell, Lucy Gray, We are Seven, Anecdote for Fathers, Rural Architecture, Idle Shepherd Boys, to H. C. Six Years Old, There was a Boy, Ode. There may be others which I forget. (I am doubtful whether I should place the Butterfly and Sparrow's nest here or elsewhere.) The 2nd class would relate to the fraternal affections, to friendship and to love and to all those emotions, which follow after childhood, in youth and early manhood. Here might come the Sparrow's Nest, etc., the Butterflies, those about Lucy, 'She was a phantom', Louisa, 'Dear child of nature', 'There is a change, and I am poor'. This class to ascend in a scale of imagination or interest through ''Tis said that some have died for love' Ellen Irwin—and to conclude with Ruth or The Brothers, printed with a separate Title as an adjunct, or this last might be placed elsewhere.—

Then 3d class Poems relating to natural objects and their influence on the mind either as growing or in an advanced state, to begin with the simply human and conclude with the highly imaginative as the Tintern Abbey to be immediately preceded by the Cuckoo Poems, the Nutting, after having passed through all stages from objects as they affect the mere human being from properties with which they are endowed, and as they affect the mind by properties conferred; by the life found in them, or their life given. Here would come (I place them at Random) The daisies, the Celandines, The daffodils, the Nightingale and Stockdove, The green linnet, Waterfall and Eglantine, Oak and Broom, poor Susan perhaps, Poem on Rydale Island, on Grasmere, I heard a thousand blended notes, the Whirlblast from behind the hill, The Kitten and the falling leaves, Fidelity, those concerning Tom Hutchinson's dog; but with respect to the two or three last I am not sure that they may not be arranged better elsewhere.—The above class would be numerous, and conclude in the manner mentioned above with Tintern Abbey.

Next might come the Naming of Places, as a Transition to the Poems relating to human life; which might be prettily connected, harmoniously I may say, by Poor Susan mentioned before, and better perhaps placed here, Beggars, Simon Lee, last of Flock, Goody Blake, etc. to ascend through a regular scale of imagination to the Thorn, The Highland Girl, The Leech-gatherer, Hartleap

Well. This class of poems I suppose to consist chiefly of objects most interesting to the mind not by its personal feelings or a strong appeal to the instincts or natural affections, but to be interesting to a meditative and imaginative mind either from the moral importance of the pictures or from the employment they give to the understanding affected through the imagination and to the higher faculties. Then might come, perhaps, those relating to the social and civic duties, and chiefly interesting to the imagination through the understanding, and not to the understanding through the imagination, as the political Sonnets, Character of Happy Warrior, Rob Roy's Grave, Personal talk, Poet's epitaph, Ode to Duty, To Burns' Sons, etc. Then perhaps those relating to Maternal feeling, connubial or parental, Maternal to ascend from The Sailor's mother through The Emigrant Mother, Affliction of M—[1], to The Mad Mother, to conclude with the Idiot Boy.

Finally, the class of old age—Animal tranquillity and decay, The Childless Father, Though narrow be that old man's cares, and near, The Two Thieves, The Matron of Jedborough, those relating to Mathew, The Cumberland Beggar, to conclude perhaps with Michael, which might conclude the whole. The Blind Highland Boy ought to take its place among the Influences of Natural Objects, (the sense of the eye being wanting) to produce an [? effect] of imagination, and to throw the humblest [person] into sublime situations; feeling consecrating form, and form ennobling feeling.—This may have sufficed to give you a notion of my views. The principle of the arrangement is that there should be a scale in each class and in the whole, and that each poem should be so placed as to direct the Reader's attention by its position to its *primary* interest. I am writing illegibly.

Sara is, I think, full as well as usual.

Most affectionately your friend,
W. Wordsworth

[1] Margaret.

48. *To* Thomas Poole

[30 May 1809]

My dear Poole,

Before I wrote my last letter to you, the last sheet of my Pamphlet was sent off to the Printer, since which time I have not altered a word in it, or added one; judge then, when I say that at that time 100 pages were printed off, how I must have been used! In fact my patience is completely wearied out. I will explain to you the mystery as far as I can. Mr. De Quincey, some time before the time I have mentioned, took his departure from my house to London, and, in order to save time and expense, I begged that instead of sending the sheets down to me to be corrected, they should be transferred directly to him for that purpose; and I determined to send the remaining portions of the MSS to him as they were finished; to be by him transmitted to the Press. This was a most unfortunate resolution; for at the time as the subject of punctuation in prose was one to which I had never attended and had of course settled no scheme of it in my own mind, I deputed that office to Mr. De Quincey. Hinc illae lacrymæ! He had been so scrupulous with the Compositor, in having his own plan rigorously followed by an iota, that the Man took the Pet, and whole weeks elapsed without the Book's advancing a step. And, as if there were some fatality attending it, now that it has been entirely printed off full ten days, I have reason to believe it is not published! And this is owing to the Printer (I conceive) having neglected to inform Mr. Stuart that the Printing was finished; Mr. Stuart having undertaken to advertize and have it published. So that the Pamphlet has been lying ten days (and ten days at this season, and after so long delay!) like a ship in a dry dock—Now is not this provoking? But I write the account to you not for sympathy but to clear myself from any imputations of indolence and procrastination, which otherwise you would be justified in throwing upon me. My hands in fact have been completely tied. I should the less have regretted the late appearance of the work if I had been at liberty to employ the time in adding to its value; but in fact as I expected its appearance every day, I abandoned every thought of the kind.—I must take up with the old proverb, 'What cannot be cured must be endured!'—The pamphlet was sent off to me ten days ago, and the world may perhaps not see it these ten weeks!

I have yet another and far more important reason for writing to you; connected as no doubt you will guess, with Coleridge. I am sorry to say that nothing appears to me more desirable than that his periodical essay should never commence. It is in fact *impossible* utterly impossible—that he should carry it on; and, therefore, better never begin it; far better, and if begun, the sooner it stop, also the better—the less will be the loss, and not greater the disgrace. You will consider me as speaking to you now in the most sacred confidence, and as under a strong sense of duty; from a wish to save you from anxiety and disappointment; and from a further and still stronger wish that, as one of Coleridge's nearest and dearest Friends, you should take into most serious consideration his condition, above all with reference to his children. I gave it to you as my deliberate opinion, formed upon proofs which have been strengthening for years, that he neither will nor can execute any thing of important benefit either to himself his family or mankind. Neither his talents nor his genius mighty as they are nor his vast information will avail him anything; they are all frustrated by a derangement in his intellectual and moral constitution—In fact he has no voluntary power of mind whatsoever, nor is he capable of acting under any *constraint* of duty or moral obligation. Do not suppose that I mean to say from this that The Friend may not appear—it may—but it cannot go on for any length of time. I am *sure* it cannot.

C. I understand has been three weeks at Penrith whither he went to superintend the publication and has since never been heard of (save once on his first arrival) though frequently written to—I shall say no more at present, but I do earnestly wish that you would come down hither this summer in order that something may be arranged respecting his children, in case of his death, and also during his life-time. I must add, however, that it answers no purpose to advise her[1] to remonstrate with him, or to represent to him the propriety of going on or desisting. The disease of his mind is that he perpetually looks out of himself for those obstacles to his utility which exist only in himself. I am sure that if any friend whom he values were, in consequence of such a conviction as I

[1] Mrs Coleridge.

have expressed, to advise him to drop his work, he would immediately ascribe the failure to the damp thrown upon his spirits by this interference. Therefore in this way nothing can be done, nor by encouraging him to attempt anything else—he would catch eagerly perhaps at the advice—and would be involved in new plans—new procrastination, and new expenses.

I am dear Poole most sincerely yours
W Wordsworth

49. *To* John Miller

Grasmere Jany. 4 [1810]

Dear Sir,

I have to ask your pardon for not having replied immediately to the letter with which you honoured me. I feel myself obliged to you by the Communication which you have made, your friend also is of course entitled to my thanks. In answer to the elegant Sonnet which he has addressed to me, I have not much to say: it asks what temper the various censures which have been so properly poured on my Poems have excited in me? What can I say to this that would be understood in the sense I should wish my words to bear but by a man who might have had opportunities to know more of my character than it is possible can be collected from my writings. Shall I be believed when I say that in ninety nine cases out of a hundred praise and censure are things to me of equal indifference and that I attach no interest to my poems in their connection with the world further than as I think they are fitted to communicate knowledge, to awaken kindly or noble dispositions, or to strengthen the intellectual powers; in a word to promote just thinking and salutary feelings. With this habit of mind how can I be in the slightest degree affected by what this scribbler, whether simple dunce or compound of dunce and malignant, says or thinks of them; or this or that goodnatured man who thinks no more of Poetry than our Parish Clerk of Hebrew. If my Poems are inspired by Genius and Nature they will live, if not, they will be forgotten and the sooner the better; this being so, and their Author habitually feeling that it must be so, what matters it who is pleased or displeased, except he gives proof by the manner in which his approbation or displeasure is expressed, and by the grounds upon which it is rested that his opinion may demand attention as affecting the question of the vitality of the performances themselves. Now unfortunately for me all those who have given their judgment in public are such contemptible creatures in their intellectual power, moral qualities, and in their attainments, that whether they censure or praise, I am compelled alike to say in all the instances that I have seen—

> foedissima turba—
> Non vestri sum iuris ego.

I have spoken sincerely because the question was put to me in sincerity. Let it not however be concluded that I have not received pleasure from praise in some instances when, as upon the present occasion it has been accompanied with evidence that what I write is really understood in the spirit in which it was written. But let us turn to a more agreeable subject. The Vision of the Brothers has the merits and defects which it is pleasing to see in the composition of a young man as I take the author to be; it is vigorous, in some places elegant, but it is also uncouth often, and obscure, faults which I like to see in a young author as they are of good omen when conjoined with such excellencies as this poem contains. . . . The first stanza is dark and led me to expect an allegory; the second is pleasingly and vigorously written, save that it is obscure in the passage about the angel, and the word *weakened* is feeble. The next stanza is elegant, the character well delineated, and the relation of the two brothers towards each other highly interesting. Towards the conclusion there is again obscurity; a passage occurs leading you back to the idea of allegory, and it is by no means so well written as the Stanzas above. I have [told] you my feeling, and I have pleasure in saying that I think both the Poems do their author great credit. I am obliged to conclude in extreme haste which you and your friend will have the kindness to excuse,

I remain, Dear Sir
Yours with great truth
W. Wordsworth

Mr de Quincey has taken a Cottage[1]

---

[1] Dove Cottage, former home of the Wordsworths.

50. *To* Richard Wordsworth

[early May 1810]

My dear Brother,

I have received instructions about Algernon[1] and he will be well taken care of. I am very happy to hear that you are so well.—As you talk only of staying a month,[2] and do not make mention of coming hither I am afraid we shall not see you.—This will give me concern—for it hurts me that you should have so little knowledge of my family; life is very uncertain for us all; and should I be cut off I could not but think with pain that those I should leave behind me, have [se]en so little of you or you of them.—But enough of this—I should have come over wi[th] your servant—but Mary expects every [day] to be confined—and therefore it is impossible [that] I can quit home till that eve[nt][3] . . . who had suffered it to stuff its stomach with an immense quantity of raw carrots, before breakfast. The Child is however mending apace. Dorothy will be very sorry that she cannot come over; I say *will* be for I have not yet seen her. She quite longs to see you. I shall come over as soon as ever Mary is evidently doing well.—Your affectionate Brother

W. Wordsworth

51. *To* Mary Wordsworth

Hindwell[4]—Saturday August 11th [1810]

I arrived here at 10 this morning; where I found all well, Sara wonderfully improved in look and Joanna[5] quite fat, Sara indeed also. The house is comfortable, and its situation beside the pool, and the pool itself quite charming, and far beyond my expectation. Having said this, let me turn at once to thee my love of loves and to thy dearest of Letters which I found here, and read with a beating heart. O my blessing, how happy was I in learning that my Letter

---

[1] Basil Montagu's second son, at school in Ambleside.
[2] At Sockbridge, nr. Penrith.
[3] The birth of William. Several lines, describing Catharine's recent seizure, are hereafter torn away.
[4] Thomas Hutchinson's farm, nr. Radnor.   [5] S. H.'s sister.

had moved thee so deeply, and thy delight in reading had if possible been more exquisite than mine in writing. You seem to have been surprized at the receipt of my Letter, and surely it is odd that I did not mention to you I should avail myself of some opportunity, and as strange that you did not take for granted that I should. My Letter had been written three or four days before I could find the means of sending it off, which was the reason of its arriving so late; you would notice also that it was somewhat worn, for I had carried it about with me in my pocket.—I was sure that you would be most happy in receiving from me such a gift from the whole undivided heart for your whole and sole possession; and the Letter in answer which I have received from you today I will entrust to your keeping when I return, and they shall be deposited side by side as a bequest for the survivor of us. Every day every hour every moment makes me feel more deeply how blessed we are in each other, how purely how faithfully how ardently, and how tenderly we love each other; I put this last word last because, though I am persuaded that a deep affection is not uncommon in married life, yet I am confident that a lively, gushing, thought-employing, spirit-stirring, passion of love, is very rare even among good people. I will say more upon this when we meet, grounded upon recent observation of the condition of others. We have been parted my sweet Mary too long, but we have not been parted in vain, for wherever I go I am admonished how blessed, and almost peculiar a lot mine is.—

You praised the penmanship of my last; I could wish that this should be legible also, but I fear I shall wish in vain; for I must write in a great hurry having only an hour allotted to me. Let me then first communicate the facts in which you may be interested, relating to my journey etc otherwise if I give way to the emotions of my heart first you will hear nothing of these.—On Monday morn: at 9 o'clock Sir G. B.[1] and I left Ashby in a chaise. Sir G— had a wish to see the Leasowes[2] with me; I had never been there and he had not seen the place these thirty years; I reserve the detail of this journey till we meet. We slept the first night at Hagley returned to Birmingham next day at 4 afternoon, went together to the play, and the next morning walked about the Town, and I accompanied

---

[1] Sir George Beaumont.
[2] The poet Shenstone's estate in Worcestershire.

Sir G. back on his way as far as four miles which brought me to within 2 miles a 1/2 of Castle Bromwich, Mr. Blairs.[1] At Mr Blairs, I found a note from my Br Chrisr who had accidentally heard of my intention of being at Mr Blairs. I was greatly surprized at this, as I had confidently concluded that he was either gone from Birm: or had never come thither from his not having answered the Letter inviting him to Coleorton. On Thursday he came over to Mr Blairs, dined with us, and I returned with him, and supped at Lloyds,[2] where I found Priscilla looking I thought not very well. The children were gone to bed and asleep so of course I can have no accurate image of them: their faces were heated and they seemed bloomed, but their natural complexions, are sallow. The eldest is the handsomest, much, the 2nd the stoutest, and the third the plainest; so it appeared as they slept and so, I was told, it is; Christopher looked uncommonly; but I am sorry to say that he is likely to have great trouble (at least I fear so) from the state of his wifes health and the nature of her malady; great expense also which at present he can ill bear,—for his living[3] has entangled him in two law suits; and you will grieve to hear that he has been much deceived as the income of it; it is some hundreds lower than he had reason to expect, so that he will be not a little pinched, unless it should please God to take the Bishop. But not a word of these particulars to any body.

On friday Morning, I was called a little after three, having had two hours feverish sleep, got on the top of the Coach, it began to rain before we were out of Birming: and rained for two hours and a half; my umbrella and coat however protected me pretty well; when we were half way to Worcester the weather cleared up and I had a pleasant ride through a fine Country to that City, which stands charmingly upon the Severn, at no great distance from the Malvern hills. These hills which are a fine object brought Joseph Cottle to my mind, and dearest Dorothy, who had travelled this way when she came from Newcastle to meet me at Bristol whence we journeyd to Racedown; but though much endeared to me on this latter account, I looked at them with a trembling which I cannot describe when I thought that *you* had not seen them, but *might* have seen, if you had but taken the road through Bristol when

---

[1] John Wilson's friend.
[2] Charles Lloyd, snr., father of C. W.'s wife Priscilla.   [3] Bocking, Essex.

you left Racedown;[1] in which case I should certainly have accompanied you as far as Bristol; or further, perhaps: and then I thought, that you would not have taken the coach at Bristol, but that you would have walked on Northwards with me at your side, till unable to part from each other we might have come in sight of those hills which skirt the road for so many miles, and thus continuing our journey (for we should have moved on at small expense) I fancied that we should have seen so deeply into each others hearts, and been so fondly locked in each others arms, that we should have braved the worst and parted no more. Under that tree, I thought as I passed along we might have rested, of that stream might have drank, in that thicket we might have hidden ourselves from the sun, and from the eyes of the passenger; and thus did I feed on the thought of bliss that might have been, which would have [been] intolerable from the force of regret had I not felt the happiness which waits me when I see you again. O Mary I love you with a passion of love which grows till I tremble to think of its strength; your children and the care which they require must fortunately steal between you and the solitude and the longings of absence—when I am moving about in travelling I am less unhappy than when stationary, but then I am at every moment, I will not say reminded of you, for you never I think are out of my mind 3 minutes together however I am engaged, but I am every moment seized with a longing wish that you might see the objects which interest me as I pass along, and not having you at my side my pleasure is so imperfect that after a short look I had rather not see the objects at all. But I must return to my journey. I left Worcester at half past ten, reached Leominster at 5, and there was 20 miles to Hindwell, without coach—Luckily two other persons were going part of the same way; so we took chaise for 14 miles, I slept at Presteigne 5 miles from hence, hired a Guide who bore my luggage, and I arrived here before eleven.

I have read to Sara the parts of your Letter intended for her, and all the rest which I could read; she will reply to these of course herself. How happy am I [to] learn that thou art so well, and untormented with that cruel pain in thy mouth! May it never return! if it does fail not to apply to Dr Dicks remedies: for my account for really I have suffered much in this cruel complaint of

[1] After her visit in 1797.

thine—I have thought of it ten thousand times since we parted and sometimes I have fancied that I was caressing thee, and thou couldst not meet me with kindred delight and rapture from the interruption of this distressing pain. But far oftener for less selfish reasons has it employed my mind with an anxiety which I cannot describe; for every thing about you that is indicative of weakness or derangement of health affects me when I [am] absent from you, and cannot see how you look, beyond what it is in the power of words to describe. O take care of yourself for all our sakes—but I cannot bear to look that way, and I know you will do nothing to hurt yourself for my sake.—

My stomach failed about a fortnight since from too much talking, or rather from not being sufficiently alone—before I left C—[1] by taking more care I brought it about; and except in my eyelids I look well, and am well; but certainly though not weak far from being so strong as I should have been but for my old enemy: that has troubled me more than ever.—I agree with you that it was unreasonable in the B's to expect me to go to C— again next summer; be assured, I shall not do it on any account nor will I go any where without thee. I cannot but think knowing how the little ones would be taken care of but that we might be happy supremely happy together in a tour of a few weeks if our circumstances would allow; but this will never, I fear be the case, nor am I anxious about this; but I never will part from you for more than a week or a *fort*night at the very utmost, unless when I [am] compelled by a sense of duty that leaves no choice—I cannot and ought not; if I could lay in a stock of health and strength to enable me to work more vigorously when I return there might be some plea for this but the contrary is the case; for my longing day and night to see you again is more powerful far, as I said before than when you were at Middleham; and when I am away from you I seem to have heart for nothing and no body else—But this theme is endless; I must content myself with your Letters for a short time; and oh most dearly shall I prize them, till I consign them to your care to be preserved whatever else we lose.

I have not yet said a word about the time I purpose to stay here; but I came with a resolution not to extend it beyond a fortnight, for a hundred reasons which will crowd in upon your mind. At all

---

[1] Coleorton.

events I shall move heaven and earth to be with you by this day
three weeks. I shall not stop a moment at Liverpool more than I
can help, if I go that way. You may guess how eager I am to be at
home, when I tell you that Christophers entreaties and my own
wishes, could not prevail upon me to stay half a day at
Birmingham.—Certainly I parted from him with great regret, as
he and I are likely to be so much divided. I will satisfy Sara's claim
upon me and let me add a little too for Joanna and Mary
Monkhouse[1] especially, and then I shall take wing and oh for the
sight of dear Grasmere, and how I shall pant up the hill, and then
for dear little W. and his beloved Mother, and how shall we pour
out hearts together in the lonely house, and in the lonely and to *us*
thrice dear Season.

Thank you for your pretty tales of Dorothy and strin[g]-loving
Thomas[2] bless [him] he shall be contented if possible, I will bring
him string from his Godmother, string for his Uncle, for Mr
Addison[3] and for myself adieu adieu adieu, for I am told I have not
a moment to lose, and that the post will be lost— this must not be
again and again farewell—a thousand kisses for you all, yourself
first, John Dorothy, Thomas, Catharine, W^m. dear little Catharine
I have not mentioned her, but she has often been here in my
thoughts again and again farewell—I fear for her Take care.

52. *To* William Godwin

Grasmere March 9th 1811

Dear Sir,

I received your Letter and the accompanying Booklet yesterday.—Some one recommended to Gainsborough a subject for a
Picture, it pleased him much but he immediately said with a sigh,
'What a pity I did not think of it myself!' Had I been as much
delighted with the Story of the Beauty and the Beast as you appear
to have been, and as much struck with its fitness for Verse, still
your proposal would have occasioned in me a similar regret. I have
ever had the same sort of perverseness, I cannot work upon the

---

[1] M. W.'s cousin, Thomas H.'s future wife.
[2] W. W.'s elder daughter and younger son.   [3] A lawyer friend.

suggestion of others however eagerly I might have addressed myself to the proposed subject if it had come to me of its own accord. You will therefore attribute my declining the task of versifying the Tale to this infirmity, rather than to an indisposition to serve you. Having stated this, it is unnecessary to add, that in my opinion things of this sort cannot be even decently done without great labour, especially in our language. Fontaine acknowledges that he found 'les narrations en vers très mal-aisées', yet he allowed himself in point of metre and versification, every kind of liberty, and only chose such subjects, as (to the disgrace of his Country be it spoken) the french language is peculiarly fitted for.—This Tale, I judge from its name, is of french Origin; it is not however found in a little collection which I have in that tongue; mine only includes Puss in Boots, Cinderella, Red riding hood, and two or three more. I think the shape in which it appears in the little Book you have sent me has much injured the story. Mrs. Wordsworth and my Sister both have an impression of the story being told differently and to them much more pleasantly though they do not distinctly recollect the variations. I confess there is to me something disgusting in the notion of a human Being consenting to *Mate* with a Beast, however amiable his qualities of heart. There is a line and a half in the Paradise Lost upon this subject which always shocked me,—

> 'for which cause
> Among the Beasts no Mate for thee was found.'[1]

These are objects to which the attention of the mind ought not to be turned even as things in possibility.—I have never seen the Tale in french, but as every body knows, the word Bete in french conversation perpetually occurs as applied to a stupid, senseless, half idiotic Person—bêtise in like manner stands for stupidity. With us Beast and bestial excite loathsome and disgusting ideas; I mean when applied in a metaphorical manner; and consequently something of the same hangs about the literal sense of the words. *Brute* is the word employed when we contrast the intellectual qualities of the inferior animals with our own, the brute creation, etc. 'Ye of *brute human*, we of *human Gods*.'[2] Brute metaphorically used, with us designates ill-manners of a coarse kind, or insolent

---

[1] *Paradise Lost*, viii. 593–4.   [2] Ibid. ix. 712 (misquoted).

and ferocious cruelty—I make these remarks with a view to the difficulty attending the treatment of the story in our tongue, I mean in verse, where the utmost delicacy, that is, true philosophic permanent delicacy is required.

Wm. Taylor of Norwich[1] took the trouble of versifying Blue Beard some years ago; and might perhaps not decline to assist you in the present case, if you are acquainted with him or could get at him. He is a Man personally unknown to me, and in his literary character doubtless an egregious Coxcomb; but he is ingenious enough to do this if he could be prevailed upon to undertake it.—

Permit me to add one particular. You live and have lived long in London and therefore may not know at what rate Parcels are conveyed by Coach. Judging from the diminutive size of yours, you probably thought the expence of it would be trifling. You remember the story of the poor Girl who being reproached with having brought forth an illegitimate Child said it was true, but added that it was a very little one; insinuating thereby that her offence was small in proportion. But the plea does not hold good. As it is in these cases of morality so is it with the Rules of the Coach Offices. To be brief, I had to pay for your tiny parcel 4/9 and should have no more to pay if it had been 20 times as large. The weight till it amount to several pounds is no object with these People; a small Parcel requires as much trouble to receive, to lodge, and to deliver as a large one, and probably more *care* on account of its very smallness. [Excuse my frankness when I say I really grudged this sum *erased*]. I deem you therefore from inattention or want of knowledge my debtor, and will put you in a way of being quits with me. If you can command a Copy of your book upon Burial,[2] which I have never seen, let it be sent to Lamb's for my use who in the course of this Spring will be able to forward it to me free of expense—[I assure you I am no less than yourself, obliged to look to these little matters. I have five children, and follow a Work to me utterly unprofitable, and which will ever continue to be so. *Erased*] Remember me kindly to Mrs. Godwyn, and believe me with great truth

Yours

W. Wordsworth

---

[1] The German scholar.   [2] *Essay on Sepulchres*, 1809.

53. *To* Francis Wrangham

Grasmere, March 27th [1811]

My dear Wrangham,

Your last Letter which I have left so long unanswered, found me in a distressed state of mind with one of my children[1] lying nearly as I thought at the point of death. It recovered however after some time. This put me off answering your Letter, when otherwise I might have done my duty; and then my procrastinating habits interfered, making bad far worse. As to Coleridge, there is no accounting for his apparent neglect of any body, except in the common way in which I have accounted for my own apparent neglect of you. He left this Country in October for London where he has since resided, and I have never heard *from* him since, though I have heard several times *of* him. It is said, he is looking well.—I should certainly have answered your Letter immediately had I known any thing of the Mr W [?] whom you enquire after. But I do not mix with the Gentry of this neighbourhood, and therefore never saw him. I have heard him spoken of as an excellent Musician, and this is all the knowledge I have of him. You return to the Catholic Question. I am decidedly of opinion that no further concessions should be made. The Catholic Emancipation is a mere pretext of ambitious and discontented men. Are you prepared for the next step, a Catholic Established Church?—I confess I dread the thought. As to the Bible Society;[2] my view of the subject is as follows. 1st distributing Bibles is a good thing; 2ndly more Bibles will be distributed in consequence of the existence of the Bible Society; therefore so far as that goes the existence of the Bible Society is good;—But 3dly as to the *indirect* benefits expected from it, in producing a golden age of unanimity among Christians, all that I think fume and emptiness, nay far worse; so deeply am I persuaded that discord and artifice, and pride and ambition would be fostered by such an approximation and unnatural alliance of sects that I am inclined to think the evil thus produced would do more than outweigh the good done by dispersing the Bibles. I think the last 50 or 60 Pages of my Brother's pamphlet[3] merit the serious

---

[1] Catharine.   [2] Founded 1804.
[3] C. W.'s *Reasons for declining to become a Subscriber to the British and Foreign Bible Society*, 1810.

consideration of all persons of the established Church who have connected themselves with Sectaries for this purpose.

The Montagus[1] were down here in the autumn; neither of them looking very well. M. has put himself I think upon too abstemious a regimen. He is, (as you know no doubt) advancing rapidly in his profession. Algernon is at school at Ambleside, and Alfred is to come in summer. You see what a hand I write, and therefore will not wonder that I am slow to put my friends to the trouble of decyphering it; especially when the matter is of so little value. Entreating your pardon for my long delay in answering your last, let me conclude with assuring you that I remain with

great truth your affectionate Friend

W. Wordsworth

54. *To* C. W. Pasley

Grasmere, March 28, 1811.

My dear Sir,

I address this to the Publishers of your 'Essay'[2] not knowing where to find you. Before I speak of the instruction and pleasure which I have derived from your work, let me say a word or two in apology for my own apparent neglect of the Letter with which you honoured me some time ago. In fact I was thoroughly sensible of the value of your Correspondence, and of your kindness in writing to me, and took up the Pen to tell you so. I wrote half of a pretty long Letter to you, but I was so disgusted with the imperfect and feeble expression which I had given to some not uninteresting Ideas, that I threw away the unfinished sheet, and could not find resolution to resume what had been so inauspiciously begun. I am ashamed to say, that I write so few Letters, and employ my pen so little in any way, that I feel both a lack of words such words I mean as I wish for and of [mechan]ical skill, extremely discouraging to me. I do [not plead] these disabilities on my part as an excuse; but I wish you to know that they have been the sole [cause] of my silence, and not a want of sense of the honour done me by your

---

[1] Montagu had remarried in 1808.
[2] *The Military Policy and Institutions of the British Empire*, 1810.

Correspondence, or an ignorance of what good breeding required of me. But enough of my trespasses; let me only add, that I addressed a letter of some length to you when you were lying ill at Middleborough; this probably you never received.

Now for your book. I had expected it with great impatience, and desired a Friend to send it down to me immediately on its appearance, which he neglected to do. On this account, I did not see it till a few days ago. I have read it through twice, with great care, and many parts three or four times over. From this you will conclude that I must have been much interested; and I assure you that I deem myself also in a high degree instructed. It would be a most pleasing employment to me to dwell, in this Letter, upon those points in which I agree with you, and to acknowledge my obligations for the clearer views you have given of truths which I before perceived, though not with that distinctness in which they now stand before my eyes. But I could wish this Letter to be of some use to you; and that end is more likely to be attained if I advert to those points in which I think you are mistaken. These are chiefly such as though very material in themselves, are not at all so to the main object you have in view, viz. that of proving that the military power of France may by us be successfully resisted, and even overthrown. In the first place then; I think that there are great errors in the survey of the comparative strength of the two Empires, with which you begin your book, and on which the first 160 pages are chiefly employed. You seem to wish to frighten the People into exertion; and in your ardour to attain your object, that of rousing our Countrymen by any means, I think you have caught far too eagerly at every circumstance with respect to revenue, navy, etc. that appears to make for the French. This I think was unnecessary. The People are convinced that the Power of France is dangerous, and that it is our duty to resist it to the utmost. I think you might have commenced from this acknowledged fact; and, at all events, I cannot help saying, that the first 100 pages or so of your book, contrasted with the brilliant prospects towards the conclusion, have impressed me with a notion that you have written too much under the influence of feelings similar to those of a Poet or novelist, who deepens the distress in the earlier part of his work, in order that the happy catastrophe which he has prepared for his hero and heroine may be more keenly relished. Your object is to conduct us to Elysium, and, lest we should not be able to enjoy the pure air and purpurial sunshine, you have taken a peep at Tartarus on the road. Now I am of your mind, that we ought not to make peace with France on any account till she is humiliated and her power brought within reasonable bounds. It is our duty and our interest, to be at war with her; but I do not think with you that a state of peace would give to France that superiority which you seem so clearly to foresee. In estimating the resources of the two Empires, as to revenue, you appear to make little or no allowance for what I deem of prime and paramount importance, the characters of the two nations, and of the two Governments. Was there ever an instance, since the world began, of the peaceful arts thriving under a despotism so oppressive as that of France is and must continue to be, and among a people so unsettled, so depraved, and so undisciplined in civil arts and habits as the French nation must now be? It is difficult to come at the real revenue of the French Empire; but it appears to me certain, absolutely certain, that it must diminish rapidly every year. The armies have hitherto been maintained chiefly from the contributions raised upon the conquered countries, and from the plunder which the soldiers have been able to find. But that harvest is over. Austria, and particularly Hungary, may have yet something to supply; but the French Ruler will scarcely quarrel with them for a few years at least. But from Denmark, and Sweden, and Russia, there is not much to be gained. In the mean while, wherever his iron yoke is fixed, the spirits of the people are broken; and it is in vain to attempt to extort money which they do not possess, and cannot procure. Their bodies he may command, but their bodies he cannot move without the inspiration of *wealth*, somewhere or other; by wealth I mean superfluous produce, something arising from the labour of the inhabitants of countries beyond what is necessary to their support. What will avail him the command of the whole population of the Continent, unless there be a security for Capital somewhere existing, so that the mechanic arts and inventions may thereby be applied in such a manner as that an overplus may arise from the labour of the Country which shall find its way into the pocket of the State for the purpose of supporting its military and civil establishments? Now,—when I look at the condition of our Country, and compare it with that of France, and reflect upon the length of the time, and the infinite combination of favorable circumstances which have been necessary to produce the laws, the regulations, the customs, the moral character, and the physical enginery of all sorts, through means, and by aid of which, labour is carried on in this happy Land; and when I think of the wealth and population (concentrated too in so small a space) which we must have at command for military purposes,—I confess I have not much dread, looking either at war or peace, of any power which France, with respect to us, is likely to attain for years,—I may say for generations. Whatever may be the form of a government, its spirit, at least, must be mild and free before agriculture, trade, commerce, and manufactures can thrive under it; and if these do not prosper in a State, it may extend its empire to right and to left, and it will only carry poverty and desolation along with it, without being itself permanently enriched. You seem to take for granted, that because the french revenue amounts to so much at present it must continue to keep up to that height. This, I conceive impossible, unless the spirit of the government alters, which is not likely for many years. How comes it that we are enabled to keep, by sea and land, so many men in arms?—Not by our foreign commerce, but by our domestic ingenuity, by our home labour, which, with the aid of capital and the mechanic arts and establishments, has enabled a few to produce so much as will maintain themselves, and the hundreds of thousands of their Countrymen whom they support in arms. If our foreign trade were utterly destroyed, I am told that not more than one-sixth of our trade would perish. The Spirit of Buonaparte's government is, and must continue to be, like that of the first Conquerors of the new world who went raving about for gold—gold! and for whose rapacious appetites the slow but mighty and sure returns of any other produce could have no charms. I cannot but think that generations must pass away before France, or any of the Countries under its thraldom, can attain those habits, and that character, and those establishments which must be attained before it can wield its population in a manner that will ensure our overthrow. This (if we conduct the war upon principles of common sense) seems to me impossible, while we continue at war; and should a peace take place (which, however, I passionately deprecate), France will long be compelled to pay tribute to us, on account of our being so far before her in the race of genuine practical philosophy and true liberty. I mean that the *mind* of the Country is so far before that of France, and that *that* mind has empowered the *hands* of the country to raise so much national wealth, that France must condescend to accept from us what she will be unable herself to produce. Is it likely that any of our manufacturing capitalists, in case of a peace, would trust themselves to an arbitrary government like that of France, which, without a moment's warning, might go to war with us and seize their persons and their property; nay—if they should be so foolish as to trust themselves to its discretion, would be base enough to pick a quarrel with us for the very pupose of a pretext to strip them of all they possessed? Or is it likely—if the native French manufacturers and traders were capable of rivalling us in point of skill, that any Frenchman would venture upon that ostentatious display of wealth which a large Cotton Mill, for instance, requires, when he knows that by so doing he would only draw upon himself a glance of the greedy eye of government, soon to be followed by a squeeze from its rapacious hand?—But I have dwelt too long upon this. The sum of what I think, by conversation, I could convince you of is, that your comparative estimate is erroneous, and materially so, inasmuch as it makes no allowance for the increasing superiority which a State, supposed to be independent and equitable in its dealings to its subjects, must have over an oppressive government; and none for the time which is necessary to give prosperity to peaceful arts, even if the government should improve. Our Country has a mighty and daily-growing forest of this sort of wealth; whereas, in France, the trees are not yet put into the ground. For my own part, I do not think it possible that France, with all her command of territory and coast, can outstrip us in naval power,—unless she could previously, by her land power, cut us off from timber and naval stores, necessary for the building and equipment of our Fleet. In that intellectual superiority which I have mentioned we possess over her, we should find means to build as many ships as she could build, and also could procure sailors to man them. The same energy would furnish means for maintaining the men; and if they could be fed and maintained, they would surely be produced. Why then am I for *war* with France?—1st. Because I think our naval superiority may be more cheaply maintained, and more easily, by war than by peace; and because I think that, if the war were conducted upon those principles of martial policy which you so admirably and nobly enforce, united with (or rather bottomed upon) those notions of justice and right, and that knowledge of and reverence for the moral sentiments of mankind, which, in my Tract, I attempted to pourtray and illustrate—the tide of military success would immediately turn in our favour; and we should find no more difficulty in reducing the French Power than Gustavus Adolphus did in reducing that of the German Empire in his day. And here let me express my zealous thanks for the spirit and beauty with which you have pursued, through all its details, the course of martial policy which you recommend. Too much praise cannot be given to this which is the great body of your work. I hope that it will not be lost upon your Countrymen. But (as I said before) I rather wish to dwell upon those points in which I am dissatisfied with your Essay. Let me then come at once to a fundamental principle. You maintain, that as the military power of France is in progress, ours must be so also, or we must perish. In this I agree with you. Yet you contend also, that this increase or progress can only be brought about by conquest permanently established upon the Continent; and, calling in the doctrines of the writers upon the law of Nations to your aid, you are for beginning with the conquest of Sicily, and so on, through Italy, Switzerland, etc. etc. Now it does not appear to me, though I should rejoice heartily to see a British army march from Calabria triumphantly to the heart of the Alps, and from Holland to the centre of Germany,—yet it does not appear to me that the conquest and permanent possession of these Countries is necessary either to produce those resources of men or money which the security and prosperity of our country requires. All that is absolutely needful, for either the one or the other, is a large, experienced, and seasoned *army*,—which we cannot possess without a field to fight in, and that field must be somewhere upon the Continent. Therefore, as far as concerns *ourselves* and our security, I do not think that so wide a space of conquered country is desirable; and as a Patriot I have no wish for it. If I desire it, it is not for our sakes directly, but for the benefit of those unhappy nations whom we should rescue, and whose prosperity would be reflected back upon ourselves. Holding these notions, it is natural—highly as I rate the importance of military power, and deeply as I feel its necessity for the protection of every excellence and virtue—that I should rest my hopes with respect to the emancipation of Europe more upon moral influence, and the wishes and opinions of the people of the respective nations, than you appear to do. As I have written in my pamphlet—'On the moral qualities of a people must its salvation ultimately depend. Something higher than military excellence must be taught *as* higher; something more fundamental, *as* more fundamental.' Adopting the opinion of the writers upon the laws of Nations, you treat of *Conquest* as if *conquest* could in itself, nakedly and abstractedly considered, confer rights. If we once admit this proposition, all morality is driven out of the world. We conquer Italy, that is, we raise the British standard in Italy—and by the aid of the Inhabitants we expel the French, subdue the country, and have a right to keep it for ourselves. This, if I am not mistaken, is not only implied, but explicitly maintained in your Book. Undoubtedly—if it be clear that the possession of Italy is necessary for our security—we have a right to keep possession of it, if we should ever be able to master it by the sword. But not because we have gained it by conquest, therefore may we keep it;—no; the sword, as the sword, can give no rights; but because a great and noble Nation, like ours, cannot prosper or exist without such possession. If the fact *were* so, we should then have a right to keep possession of what by our valour we had acquired—not otherwise. If these things were matter of mere speculation, they would not be worth talking about; but they are not so. The spirit of conquest, and the ambition of the sword, never can confer true glory and happiness upon a nation that has attained power sufficient to protect itself. Your favorites, the Romans, though no doubt having the fear of the Carthaginians before their eyes, yet were impelled to carry their arms out of Italy by ambition far more than by a rational apprehension of the danger of their condition. And how did they enter upon their career? By an act of atrocious injustice. You are too well read in history for me to remind you what that act was. The same disregard of morality followed too closely their steps everywhere. Their ruling passion, and sole steady guide, was the glory of the Roman name, and the wish to spread the Roman power. No wonder, then, if their armies and military leaders, as soon as they had destroyed all foreign enemies from whom anything was to be dreaded, turned their swords upon each other. The ferocious cruelties of Sylla and Marius, of Catiline, and of Antony and Octavius, and the despotism of the empire, were the necessary consequences of a long course of action pursued upon such blind and selfish principles. Therefore, admiring as I do your scheme of martial policy, and agreeing with you that a British military power may, and that the *present* state of the world requires that it *ought* to be, predominant in Italy, and Germany, and Spain,—yet still, I am afraid that you look with too much complacency upon conquest by British arms, and upon British military influence upon the Continent, for *its own sake*. Accordingly, you seem to regard Italy with more satisfaction than Spain. I mean you contemplate our possible exertions in Italy with more pleasure, merely because its dismembered state would probably keep it more under our sway—in other words, more at our mercy. Now, I think there is nothing more unfortunate for Europe than the condition of Germany and Italy in these respects; could the barriers be dissolved which have divided the one nation into Neapolitans, Tuscans, Venetians, etc., and the other into Prussians, Hanoverians, etc., and could they once be taught to feel their strength, the French would be driven back into their own Land immediately. I wish to see Spain, Italy, France, Germany, formed into independent nations; nor have I any desire to reduce the power of France further than may be necessary for that end. Woe be to that country whose military power is irresistible! I deprecate such an event for Great Britain scarcely less than for any other Land. Scipio foresaw the evils with which Rome would be visited when no Carthage should be in existence for her to contend with. If a nation have nothing to oppose or to fear without, it cannot escape decay and concussion within. Universal triumph and absolute security soon betray a State into abandonment of that discipline, civil and military, by which its victories were secured. If the time should ever come when this Island shall have no more formidable enemies by land than it has at this moment by sea, the extinction of all that it previously contained of good and great would soon follow. Indefinite progress, undoubtedly, there ought to be somewhere; but let that be in knowledge, in science, in civilization, in the increase of the numbers of the people, and in the augmentation of their virtue and happiness; but progress in conquest cannot be indefinite; and for that very reason, if for no other, it cannot be a fit object for the exertions of a people, I mean beyond certain limits, which, of course, will vary with circumstances. My prayer, as a Patriot, is, that we may always have, somewhere or other, enemies capable of resisting us, and keeping us at arms's length. Do I, then, object that our arms shall be carried into every part of the Continent? no: such is the present condition of Europe, that I earnestly pray for what I deem would be a mighty blessing. France has already destroyed, in almost every part of the Continent, the detestable Governments with which the nations have been afflicted; she has extinguished one sort of tyranny, but only to substitute another. Thus then have the countries of Europe been taught, that domestic oppression, if not manfully and zealously repelled, must sooner or later be succeeded by subjugation from without; they have tasted the bitterness of both cups; have drunk deeply of both. Their spirits are prepared for resistance to the foreign Tyrant, and, with our help, I think they may shake him off, and, under our countenance, and following (as far as they are capable) our example, they may fashion to themselves, making use of what is best in their own ancient laws and institutions, new forms of government, which may secure posterity from a repetition of such calamities as the present age has brought forth. The materials of a new balance of power exist in the language, and name, and territory of Spain, in those of France, and those of Italy, Germany, Russia, and the British Isles. The smaller States must disappear, and merge in the large nations and wide-spread languages. The possibility of this remodelling of Europe I see clearly; earnestly do I pray for it; and I have in my mind a strong conviction that your invaluable work will be a powerful instrument in preparing the way for that happy issue. Yet still we must go deeper than the nature of your labour requires you to penetrate. Military policy merely will not perform all that is needful, nor mere military virtues. If the Roman State was saved from overthrow by the attack of the slaves and of the gladiators, through the excellence of its armies, yet this was not without great difficulty; and Rome would have been destroyed by Carthage, had she not been preserved by a civic fortitude in which she surpassed all the nations of the earth. The reception which the Senate gave to Terentius Varro after the battle of Cannae is the sublimest event in human history. What a contrast to the wretched conduct of the Austrian Government after the battle at Wagram![1] England requires, as you have shown so eloquently and ably, a new system of martial policy; but England, as well as the rest of Europe, requires what is more difficult to give it,—a new course of education, a higher tone of moral feeling, more of the grandeur of the imaginative faculties, and less of the petty processes of the unfeeling and purblind understanding, that would manage the concerns of nations in the same calculating spirit with which it would set about building a house. Now a State ought to be governed (at least in these times)—the labours of the statesman ought to advance—upon calculations and from impulses similar to those which give motion to the hand of a great Artist when he is preparing a picture, or of a mighty Poet when he is determining the proportions and march of a Poem. Much is to be done by rule; the great outline is previously to be conceived in distinctness, but the consummation of the work must be trusted to resources that are not tangible, though known to exist. Much as I admire the political sagacity displayed in your work, I respect you still more for the lofty spirit that supports it, for the animation and courage with which it is replete, for the contempt, in a just cause, of death and danger by which it is ennobled, for its heroic confidence in the valour of your countrymen, and the absolute determination which it everywhere expresses to maintain in all points the honour of the soldier's profession, and that of the noble Nation of which you are a member—of the Land in which you were born. No insults, no indignities, no vile stooping, will your politics admit of, and therefore, more than for any other cause, do I congratulate my country on the appearance of a book which, resting—in this point—our national safety upon the purity of our national character, will (I trust) lead naturally to make us, at the same time, a more powerful and a more highminded nation.

Affectionately yours,

W. Wordsworth

[1] In 1809.

55. *To* Sara Hutchinson[1]

[Sept. 1811]

My dear Sara,

We reached home on Sunday morning having slept at Tamar Turner's, Fanny's Sister, in Eugh-dale.[2] Everybody thinks Catharine *greatly* improved; all cry out how much she is *grown* during her less than six weeks absence, and Dorothy and everybody else says confidently that her lameness is very much relieved. Mary and I think so too; but for my own part, I ascribe this improvement mainly to the influence of the glorious weather which we have had during the last ten days; and cannot but fear some degree of relapse when the damp and cold weather returns. We are, however this may be, very thankful for the advance she has made, and I cannot but hope with encreasing confidence, that she will outgrow all visible traces of this infirmity. She is certainly a tall and stout child for her age; and Dorothy who was not an admirer of the cast of her features now says that she is growing handsome, and like her elder Sister. William stumps about the floor most stoutly, and with his broad chest and his round bonnet turned up on one side looks not unlike Henry the 8th. We had very bleak and broken weather during our residence by the seaside,[3] save the last 4 days, and as many intermingled ones, which were beautiful. We have made an arrangement for all the family's being received next year, the greatest part of us in a house close to the sea shore, with a noble beach in front at low water. Don't imagine from this that Mary has abandoned the thought of Hindwell for next year; she purposes a visit there in Spring as soon as inviting weather comes on, if the journey can be accomplished; want of cash is the only difficulty which stands in the way of the thought.

Mary and I returned from Duddon Bridge, up the Duddon and through Seathwaite, the children with Fanny taking the direct road through Coniston. We dined in the Porch of Ulpha Kirk, and passed two Hours there and in the beautiful churchyard. Our pace was so slow and our halts so many and long that it was half past 4 in the afternoon before we reached New Field (the public House in

---

[1] Part of a joint letter of W. W. and M. W. to S. H. at Hindwell.
[2] Yewdale, between Coniston and Ambleside.
[3] At Bootle, nr. Ravenglass.

Seathwaite) though we had left Duddon Bridge at nine. The next day we took as long a time to reach Eugh-dale, over that long and steep ascent which you will remember to have passed with Coleridge and me a few years ago.

The ivy Cottage retains its beauty, but many trees have been felled about New Field, and Seathwaite Chapel, so that they are both much injured in their appearance. The vale of Seathwaite was not so beautiful as when we saw it, on account of the trees having not yet begun to put on their autumnal varieties—When we reached home Dorothy and John were at Church. I was the first who espied two things set out upon the table of the larger Parlour, a lovely Desk and upon that a Silver tea Pot, which had been there set forth in state, in order that upon our first coming we might be saluted by them. Mary's pleasure was somewhat damped when she heard from Sarah[1] that they were presents from you. Had they been from somebody less near and dear to her they would have had the air of something gained or acquired; in the present case, though they are both useful things, there is a large draw-back in the knowledge that your slender purse was the power that conveyed them into our House. When I first saw the writing Desk I thought it had come from Montagu to me, as I mentioned to him while he was talking about some present for me, that a writing Desk was what I most wanted. Now don't *you* think of buying me one or any thing else indeed; as to the Desk I will have one from M. and as to anything else I may want I must have it, if at all, from those who have more to spare than you.

Now for my journey to meet you. I think of it with great Pleasure, and wish the difficulty of the Horse were got over. I have today written to Richard, but he has sold the grey Horse that Tom saw. He got it for 70 Guineas, and I much fear that I shall not succeed in my application to him. Nothing will then remain but to hire a Kendal Hack. Be assured that the moment I have procured a Horse, I shall write to you, and do you immediately on the receipt of my Letter write back, fixing your own selves where and *when* I am to meet you. I leave this entirely to yourselves; and remember, that taking chances of Horse and Man together you must not calculate on my accomplishing more than thirty miles per day upon an average. I shall be most happy to meet Mary Monkhouse

[1] The maid.

and hope the ride will be of service to her. John, I must not forget to say, greatly prefers the writing-desk to the Silver tea-pot, which he cannot perceive has any advantages over a common one. The Misses De Quincey have just called, and I must walk with them to the Waterfall at Ghyll-side, so I shall leave this letter to be finished by Mary or Dorothy. Most affectionately

Yours
W. W.

56. *To* the Earl of Lonsdale

Grasmere Febry 6th 1812

My Lord,

It is not without considerable difficulty that I can bring my mind to address your Lordship in the present occasion. I shall be brief; while I cannot write at all without a hope that I may be justified in trespassing a few minutes upon your Lordship's time, though in a matter relating wholly to myself. Last autumn I was on my way to wait upon your Lordship at Lowther Castle when I heard that you had left it for the winter. My intention was at that time, with your Lordship's permission, to have represented to you, viva voce, my situation; in order that when you were in possession of a few facts, which it is not likely would ever be known to you unless they came from myself, you might act towards me in respect to the matter in question as to your Lordship's Judgement might seem proper.

I regret that it is not in my power to wait upon you personally; as the experience which I have had of your Lordship's gracious manners would have rendered quite pleasing to me the delicate task, which, through the means of a Letter, I am undertaking not without some reluctance. But to come to the point. I need scarcely say that Literature has been the pursuit of my Life; a Life-pursuit justified (as I believe are those of most men distinguished by any particular features of character) partly through passionate liking and partly through calculations of judgement; and in some small degree through circumstances, in which my Youth was passed; that threw great difficulties in the way of my adopting that Profession to which I was most inclined and for which I was perhaps best qualified.[1] I long hoped, depending upon my moderate desires, that the profits of my literary labours added to the little which I possessed would have answered to the rational wants of myself and my family. But in this I have been disappointed; and for these causes; 1st the unexpected pressure of the times falling most heavily upon men who have no regular means of increasing their income in proportion; and 2ndly I had erroneously calculated upon the degree in which my writings were likely to suit the taste of the times; and, lastly, much the most important part of my efforts cannot meet the public eye for many years through the comprehensiveness of the subject. I may also add (but it is scarcely worth while) a fourth reason, viz. an utter inability on my part to associate with any class or body of literary men, and thus subject myself to the necessity of sacrificing my own judgement, and of lending even indirectly countenance or support to principles either of taste, politics, morals, or religion, which I disapproved; and your Lordship is not ignorant that except writers engaged in mere drudgery, there are scarcely any authors but those associated in this manner, who find literature, at this day, an employment attended with pecuniary gain.

The statement of these facts has been made, as your Lordship will probably have anticipated, in order that if any Office should be at your Lordship's disposal[2] (the duties of which would not call so largely upon my exertions as to prevent me from giving a considerable portion of time to study) it might be in your Lordship's power to place me in a situation where with better hope of success I might advance towards the main object of my life; I mean the completion of my literary undertakings; and thereby contribute to the innocent gratification, and perhaps (as the Subjects I am treating are important) to the solid benefit of many of my Countrymen.

I have now discharged what I deemed to be a duty to myself; and, allow me to say, what I deem to be a duty I owed to your Lordship. I have been emboldened to make this statement from a remembrance that my Family has for several generations been honoured by the regard of that of your Lordship; and that, in particular, my father and grandfather did conscientiously, I

[1] Apparently, the army.
[2] W. W. was appointed Distributor of Stamps for Westmorland in 1813.

believe, discharge such trusts as were reposed in them through that connection. But *my* situation is a peculiar one; and I have been chiefly encouraged by a knowledge of your Lordship's attachment to Literature, and by the particular marks of kindness with which you have distinguished me.

Having been disappointed in my intention of making the above representation last autumn, I purposed to defer it till I had the honour of waiting upon you in London next spring. But I have this day been informed that, by the recent death of Mr Richardson,[1] certain Offices have become vacant, which has awakened my regret at not having made known to you my feelings earlier; as a Letter, at this time upon such a subject, cannot but add to the trouble which must be pressing upon you from many quarters. And, for my own part, I confess that upon this incitement I have written with some reluctance, as I wished that what I had to say should be confined to general representation, and should by no means assume the aspect of particular application; but an opportunity may exist at present which may not soon occur again; and to this possibility and to your Lordship's candour I trust for my excuse.

I have the honour to be
with great truth
my Lord, your Lordship's
most obedient and obliged servant
Wm Wordsworth

57. *To* Catherine Clarkson

Grosvenor Square, Tuesday, May 6th [1812]

My dear Friend,

. . .I came to Town with a *determination* to confront Coleridge and Montagu upon this vile business.[2] But Coleridge is most averse to it; and from the difficulty of procuring a fit person to act as referee in such a case, and from the hostility which M. and C. feel towards

---

[1] Agent at Lowther.

[2] W. W. had given Montagu a frank account of S. T. C.'s habits, to which the latter had taken violent exception. A long estrangement followed.

each other, I have yielded to C.'s wish, being persuaded that much more harm than good would accrue from the interview. I have not seen C., nor written to him. Lamb has been the medium of communication between us. C. intimated to me by a letter addressed to Lamb that he would transmit to me a statement, begun some time ago, in order to be sent to Miss Hutchinson, but discontinued on account of his having heard that she had 'already *decided* against him.' A very delicate proposal! Upon this I told Lamb that I should feel somewhat degraded by consenting to read a paper, begun with such an intention and discontinued upon such a consideration. Why talk about '*deciding*' in the case? Why, if in this decision she had judged amiss, not send the paper to rectify her error? or why draw out a paper at all whose object it was to win from the sister of my wife an opinion in his favour, and therefore to my prejudice, upon a charge of *injuries*, grievous injuries, done by me to him; before he had openly preferred his complaint to myself, the supposed author of these injuries? All this is unmanly, to say the least of it.

Upon coming home yesterday I found, however, a letter from him, a long one, written apparently and sent before he could learn my mind from Lamb upon this proposal. The letter I have not opened; but I have just written to Lamb that if Coleridge will assure me that this letter contains nothing but a naked statement of what he believes Montagu said to him, I will read it and transmit it to Montagu, to see how their reports accord. And I will then give my own, stating what I believe myself to have said, under what circumstances I spoke, with what motive, and in what spirit. And there, I believe, the matter must end; only I shall admonish Coleridge to be more careful how he makes written and public mention of injuries done by me to him.

There is some dreadful foul play, and there are most atrocious falsehoods, in this business; the bottom of which, I believe, I shall never find, nor do I much care about it. All I want is to bring the parties for once to a naked and deliberate statement upon the subject, in order that documents may exist, to be referred to as the best authority which the case will admit . . .

58. *To* Mary Wordsworth[1]

Saturday night 10 oclock.
[9–13 May 1812]

My dearest Love,

I have just returned from a walk of an hour and a half, for it has taken that time to go to and come from Baldwyns gardens, whither I went with the intention of sitting an hour with Johnsy,[2] had I found him at home. My way back led me by the end of Newman street where the Montagu's live, and I had an hour and a half of the night to spare, but I preferred coming home, where I knew I should be alone, in order to write to thee, which is the most grateful of my occupations. To day I have sent off a hasty Letter to thee, abruptly closed; and have also received one with which I find no fault but that it is too short. But is it not strange that I hear nothing from Grasmere? Surely a Letter must have miscarried; I wrote to them last Thursday. I hope all is well, but if I do not hear soon I shall begin to be alarmed.—

Do not put Thomas his flannel on again; I understand that every body who has worn a flannel in the night, perspires for some time after they leave it off, the same as when they wore it. That is the habit of perspiration continues: It is not however unlikely considering how weak Tom is that he may continue to perspire, during the greatest part of the summer; but I am sure that he would be much worse if he wore flannel.—I will call on Thom Monkhouse[3] about the beginning of the ensuing week, and also upon the Addison's.—I wish to hear again from Annette[4] before I attempt to send her any money.—I am less tormented by my old enemy than when I wrote last, though not free from inconvenience, and my stomach is I think some thing stronger. How happy should I hear that thou hast grown a little fatter with this exercise and improvement of appetite. Oh could I but see thee again in this respect which thou wert when thou came down the Lane to meet at Gallow Hill on my return with D— from france.[5] Never shall I

---

[1] At Hindwell.
[2] William Johnson, schoolmaster, formerly curate of Grasmere.
[3] M. W.'s cousin, a merchant.   [4] Vallon.
[5] Shortly before his marriage, W. W. had taken D. W. to visit Annette and his 'French' daughter at Calais.

forget thy rich and flourishing and genial mien and appearance. Nature had dressed thee out as if expressly that I might receive thee to my arms in the full blow of health and happiness. I remind thee of that time in order that thou mayst try to put thyself into the same train as produced those delightful and cheering effects. Then thou hadst only me and D— to think of, now thou hast Me to think of, little Thomas to behold, and all our dear ones at Grasmere to play before thy memory, with our sweet little William, and all his pretty looks and harmonious tones to entertain and soothe and support and nourish and cherish thee. Tell me thou my love that thou dost some credit to this picture. Thou sayst that thou art the blessedest of Women and surely I am the most blessed of Men. The life which is led by the fashionable world in this great city is miserable; there is neither dignity nor content nor love nor quiet to be found in it. If it was not [for] the pleasure I find under this roof,[1] and that I am collecting something to think about; I should be unable to resist my inclination to set off to morrow, to walk with thee by the woody side of that quiet pool, near which thy days and nights are passed. O. my Mary, what a heavenly thing is pure and ever growing Love; such do I feel for thee, and D— and S— and all our dear family.—Write thou to me long and tenderly, thy next letter, may be under cover to Sharp, and the next after to Lambe, to whom I shall say that I have desired thee to direct for me.—His Sister,[2] he writes me, is returned, but much weakened by her long and sharp illness.

Sunday Morning. Here I was interrupted last night by the arrival of the Beaumont's. I waked this morning before 7, and lay half an hour in bed thinking of thee and Grasmere; I then rose, washed myself from head to foot in cold water, shaved etc, and now, the above occupations having employed me near an hour I sit down to continue my Letter to thee.—I find, that the hours in London agree with me better than those we keep in the country. I rise as you see something earlier breakfast between 9 and ten, have a luncheon, as it may happen from 12 to 3, dine as may happen between 5 and half past six, take a cup of tea or Coffee after but never any supper, so that if I do not chance to overeat myself at breakfast, my stomach is never over-burthened. I am still very

---

[1] The Beaumonts'.
[2] Mary.

costive, but in other respects I am considerably better, and look I think better.—

I hear nothing of interest in politics, except that [it] is apprehended that these riots may still become more general. It was feared, by government that a kind of general rising would have taken place in the manufacturing districts upon the 4th Ins.^{nt} but it has been prevented. I suppose by this time that the number of troops quartered in the discontented parts is very considerable.— But I hear little of politics; and therefore cannot write any thing which would prove generally interesting in that way.—Henry Robinson,[1] tells me with regret, that the number of Spaniards serving in Bonapartes armies in Spain is considerable; not he believes voluntarily but frightened and forced by the French to bear arms against their Country Men.—He gives a most favorable account of the state of North Germany, and does not doubt that if our troops had gone thither instead of that miserable expedition to Walcheren the whole Country would have appeared in open insurrection against the french.—I shall go to the House of Commons some other day to hear Canning, and some others. De Quincey is in town as I learn from Mrs M—[2] I wonder he has not found me out. Mrs M— says that he took fire at some thing that you said to him about the possession of the house, and retired from their House in great Indignation. He is quite mad with pride. Mrs M— says he looks very ill.—

I shall now lay down the pen for breakfast, when I again take it up I hope to tell you that I have seen Coleridge; as I expect Robinson this morning. Ever tenderly yours. Kiss little Totts for me; I will try to find out Mr Curwen[3] perhaps Sharp will be able to tell me. I saw Tuffin[4] yesterday, he has a trifle for me for the Greens.

My dear Love, it is now 9 o clock Wednesday Morning; I have been in Berner's street to call on C— but he has gone down to the Courier Off: to assist Stuart in writing upon the late most dreadful event the Assassination of Mr Perceval[5] in the Lobby of the House of Commons. He was shot dead there on Monday last about five in

---

[1] See List of Correspondents.
[2] Montagu.
[3] J. C. Curwen, MP, of Workington Hall, and Belle Isle, Windermere.
[4] A friend of Rogers.   [5] The Prime Minister.

the afternoon, by a man named Bellingham, formerly a Merchant of Liverpool.—

The business between C— and me is settled by a Letter. He stated, which I will send to you some future day an account of what Montagu said, Part of which I denied utterly, that is the most material part, and the rest though I allowed it had something of the form, I utterly denied that it had any of the spirit of Truth. But you shall have the correspondence. I hope to see Coleridge to day; his lectures[1] are put off, on account of this event which has struck all London as I hope it would the whole Island with horror; that is all except a few of the lowest rabble—for they I am shocked to say are rejoiced. Last night I was at the play with Miss Lamb and her Brother. To day I dine at Ruffs[2] with Christopher.

I have already seen Christopher, who is, and looks well. I breakfasted with Dr Bell[3] and Johnsy yesterday morning; Johnsy will have a good deal of vexation in his new situation, but I hope in the end it will answer. Dr Bell changes his mind, I fear, often, and has something of a plaguy manner, but he is a most excellent Creature—I have heard nothing yet from Grasmere, and therefore am sure that some letters must have miscarried. I am very uneasy upon this subject. I shall write a brief note to day to them; I should much oftener but I only procure franks by chance, though Sharp made me so kind an offer, yet I do not like to abuse his kindness. Do you however address to him still.—Tell me if Thomas's difficulty in making water continues—and I shall speak to some medical person. I am considerably better myself in health, but when I have made a conquest of my old complaint some of those injurious accidents occur and throw me back. I am now doing well, but I fear a relapse from the same cause—I have undertaken a disagreeable employment for Dr Bell; viz to select and compose with Mr Johnson's assistance 20 pages of monosyllabic lessons for Children.—

Montagu tells me that the Policy left by Luff as a security for the £100 is not worth a straw for me. Of course I cannot think of advancing the money; I called yesterday on Woodriff[4]—to carry him to Montagus that he might hear this opinion; he (Woodriff) was not at home, and I waited in vain upwards of an hour for his

---

[1] On Shakespeare.
[2] C. W.'s lawyer friend.
[3] The educationalist.
[4] Lamb's friend.

arrival—I am now writing in the gesso rooms where I have breakfasted with Bowles the Poet who is just gone: he is a man of simple undisguised manners, but of mean appearance, and no strength in his conversation but it is impossible not to be pleased with his frank and ingenuous manner. This Letter will be franked by Lord Byron, a Man who is now the rage in London, in consequence of his Late Poem Childe Haroldes pilgrimage. He wrote a satire[1] some time since in which Coleridge and I were abused, but these are little thought of; and the other day I met him here and indeed it was from his mouth that Rogers first heard, and in his presence told us, the murder of Perceval.—

I wish I could make my Letters more entertaining, but I have such a number of disconnected particulars in my mind, that it is impossible to treat any of them with grace or interest. Besides, I feel as if every word, my Darling was thrown away, unless it mention some intelligence of importance relating to Friends, or unless it be employed in giving vent to the feelings of my heart towards thee. Oh my Joy and my comfort, my hope and my repose, what awful thoughts passed through my mind of thee and Dorothy and home soon after I heard, first or almost in the moment in which I heard, of Mr Perceval's death. I saw him only ten short days before his death upon the floor of the house of Commons, and admired the spirit and animation with which he suppressed and chastized that most dangerous and foolish Demogogue Sir Francis Burdett. It is most probable that the murderer on that very day was about the House of Commons, for he has been lurking there for more than a fortnight, watching an opportunity to perpetrate the execrable Deed. The debate which I heard on that day, must have had no inconsiderable influence upon the mind of this detestable fanatic; and the lower orders of the People in London cry out Burdett for ever in the Pot houses, deeming him their champion and the Man who is rid them of all their sufferings real and imaginary. The country is no doubt in a most alarming situation; and if much firmness be not displayed by the government confusion and havoc and murder will break out and spread terribly. I am glad that I am in London at this crisis, I shall see and hear all I can; but I am melancholy in finding how one's time slips away in going after people whom one cannot find; besides this ugly

---

[1] *English Bards and Scotch Reviewers,* 1809.

affair of Coleridge which I hope may now be considered as settled, has hampered me grievously; and defrauded me of many days and hours of days.—

My sweet Love how I long to see thee; think of me, wish for me, pray for me, pronounce my name when thou art alone, and upon thy pillow; and dream of me happily and sweetly.—I am the blessedest of Men, the happiest of husbands—How often does that passage of Milton come to my mind; "I chiefly who enjoy so far the happier lot, enjoying thee, preeminent etc"—apologize for me to Mary Monkhouse and John for not having seen their Brother,[1] but I have been really run off my Legs or a Prisoner in the House by appointments. On Sunday Morning Josiah Wedgewood called and sate above an hour with me; he has not had any communication with Coleridge for seven years, He spoke very kindly of him, and offered himself as a mediator, disagreeable as it was, the subject having been mentioned to him by Mrs. M—. I will not quarrel with Mrs M— but such has been her conduct in this case and others, and towards us all, that I must find some excuse for not placing myself under her roof. More of this when we meet. Tell me frankly can you puzzle out this wretched writing; if not do say so and I will write better; there is nothing which I would not do to give you pleasure, I would sit up all night, I would rise at midnight, nay any thing could I bring myself to without difficulty, which you would not condemn as injurious to me. My soul is all day long full of tenderness to you and my dear Grasmere friends.—

Miss Lamb looks far better than could be expected and enjoyed herself much at the play; a stupid opera, called "the Devils Bridge", but the Farce "High Life below Stairs" was very entertaining; it is an excellent Piece. It is now half past 12 and at two I must be in Grosvenor Square to meet Johnsy, upon the subject of those monosyllabic books. at a quarter after three I must start for Ruffs, where I dine at four. I now proceed to write to Grasmere; how uneasy I am in never hearing from them, what can be the cause I sometimes fear a relapse of this frightful [?complaint]. I shall write again I hope on Saturday; and as often as ever I can. A thousand tender kisses, do write long and often Love to every body. Kiss Thomas. W W—

[1] i.e. Thomas Monkhouse, brother of Mary and John.

59. *To* Catherine Clarkson

Thursday June 4th [1812]
Grosvenor Square

My dear Friend,

Excuse this Note; it is the only sort of paper I have upon my Table, and if I go down stairs in search of larger I may be detained, and miss the opportunity of this day's post, the morning being already far advanced. Let me tell you then at once which I do with great joy, that on Monday I depart for Bocking with Chris^r: meaning on the Saturday or Sunday following at latest to be with you at Bury.—I should have written to thank you for your last much sooner, but I wished to let you know that this interesting point was settled.

I saw Mr Clarkson for two minutes yesterday; having unfortunately found him at dinner; it was not then fixed when I should take my departure. Mr C. was looking uncommonly well. I shall let him know by twopenny Post tomorrow when I depart for Bocking.—As to public affairs; they are most alarming. The different parties cannot agree; the ——[1] seems neither respected nor beloved; and the lower orders have been for upwards of thirty years accumulating in pestilential masses of ignorant population; the effects now begin to show themselves, and unthinking people cry out that the national character has been changed all at once, in fact the change has been silently going on ever since the time we were born; the disease has been growing, and now breaks out in all its danger and deformity.

—As to the ministry; there is no likelihood at present that the old opposition will come in. An administration, weak in parliament, but strong enough to keep things going in a languid and interrupted course, will be formed of Wellesley, Canning, Moira, and the remains of the Perceval administration;[2] at least such I think will be the issue; but how long this composition will keep together it is impossible to foresee.—I shall have much to say to you upon these things, and the general state of the Country.

I hear often from Wales and from Grasmere, and nothing but well. This week is employed by Mary and Joanna and T. H. in a

[1] Apparently the Prince Regent.
[2] Lord Liverpool formed a new administration, including these statesmen.

Tour in South Wales, chiefly upon the Wye. I however had a Letter from [*name omitted*] dated Hereford and put into the office last Monday evening the day their Tour began.—I shall tell you all that has passed between Coleridge and me. Upon the whole he appears more comfortable and seems to manage himself much better than when he was at Grasmere. I have seen him several times, but not much alone; one morning we had, however a pleasant walk to Hampstead together—I shall [not] advert in the hearing of any body to what you communicated in your last concerning him.

He certainly would not wish to wound you; he is sensible that he has used you ill, and fear, and dislike to encounter disagreeable sensations, a dislike which augments in proportion as it is his *duty* to face them; these are the regulators and governours of his actions to a degree that is pitiable and deplorable—Believe me with an earnest desire to see you

Your most affectionate Friend
W. Wordsworth

I will give you a Line from Bocking.

60. *To* Thomas De Quincey

[Hindwell]
[Saturday, 20 June 1812]

My dear Friend,

I arrived here on Sunday, after a journey as pleasant as my state of mind would permit. I found Mrs W— in great distress and dejection; nor have we yet made any perceptible progress in raising her mind.—I am therefore much at a loss what to do; whether to return to Grasmere, or continue here awhile with a hope of restoring her to some degree of chearfulness and tranquillity.—At all events we cannot move immediately as she is at present much reduced, and indeed very weak, too weak to have the fatigues of the journey.—Thomas is very well and looks charmingly.—

I have little hope that Mrs W would derive benefit from any excursion in North Wales, or deviation from the direct route home.

Her mind seems too full of fears least she should lose some other of her children during her absence; and she appears too intent upon the thought of performing many tender offices of sorrow to the memory of her departed child[1] to tolerate any proposal of the kind.—

Excuse the shortness of this; I have deferred writing to all my friends with a hope that I might have better news to give. And today I shall write to all. My address for ten days probably will [be] here.—I shall be glad [to] know that you were remembered [at] Grasmere.

Your affectionate friend
W. Wordsworth

Mary had a melancholy satisfaction in thinking of the degree to which you would participate her distress and feel a loss from this same cause. She inquired after this with as lively interest as I have seen her take in any thing.—

61. *To* Robert Southey

[Grasmere]
Wednesday Evening
[2 Dec. 1812]

My dear Friend,

Symptoms of the measles appeared upon my Son Thomas last Thursday; he was most favorable [*sic*] held till tuesday, between ten and eleven at that hour was particularly lightsome and comfortable; without any assignable cause a sudden change took place, an inflammation had commenced on the lungs which it was impossible to check and the sweet Innocent yielded up his soul to God before six in the evening. He did not appear to suffer much in body, but I fear something in mind as he was of an age to have thought much upon death a subject to which his mind was daily led by the grave of his Sister. My Wife bears the loss of her Child with striking fortitude. My Sister was not at home but is returned to day, I met her at Threlkeld. Miss Hutchinson also supports her

[1] Catharine.

sorrow as ought to be done. For myself dear Southey I dare not say in what state of mind I am; I loved the Boy with the utmost love of which my soul is capable, and he is taken from me—yet in the agony of my spirit in surrendering such a treasure I feel a thousand times richer than if I had never possessed it. God comfort and save you and all our friends and us all from a repetition of such trials—O Southey feel for me! If you are not afraid of the complaint, I ought to have said if you have had it come over to us! Best love from everybody—you will impart this sad news to your Wife and Mrs Coleridge and Mrs Lovel[1] and to Miss Barker[2] and Mrs Wilson.[3] Poor woman! she was most good to him—Heaven reward her.

> Heaven bless you
> Your sincere Friend
> W. Wordsworth

Will Mrs Coleridge please to walk up to the Calverts and mention these afflictive news with the particulars. I should have written but my sorrow over-powers me.

62. *To* Elizabeth Monkhouse

Grasmere Sunday Dec^br 6th [1812]

My dear Madam,

I write this to you, I mean I address it to you, in consequence of having been very uneasy at having omitted your name when I wrote my last most unhappy Letter: in fact, when I begged Mr Monkhouse[4] to communicate the sad tidings to the family at Hindwell, it escaped my recollection that you were resident there. But I have already said too much of this; you cannot for a moment suppose that I could be insensible to the degree in which you would be afflicted by our loss; often have I thought of it and suffered for you much and heavily; as indeed I have suffered in some degree for every body who knew him; as no loving creature ever did without

---

[1] Sister of Mrs Southey and Mrs S. T. C.
[2] A local friend.   [3] Nurse to S. T. C.'s children.
[4] One of her nephews, either Thomas or John.

loving him.—Sweet Lamb he was laid by the side of his sister yesterday, and we all support ourselves by the blessing of God better than before he died, far better than we could have ventured to hope. But it is not to be concealed that our loss is dreadful, and would be insupportable but that we acknowledge in it the will of God and feel that it is our duty to submit.—None of the other three children have yet sickened and though John and Dorothy have at times after the manner of children been grievously distressed, they have also thrown off their sorrow as lightly, and are at this moment quite chearful. God grant that they pass safely through, we are not alarmed, and we repose upon God's mercy.—

Sara's health has somewhat suffered; the pain in her side returned upon her last night, but it is gone to day, and I do not fear that by riding exercise, for which the weather is at present quite favorable, she will be able to keep it down.—Never child was more deeply or generally deplored than our sweet Thomas; he was the darling of old and young; his little Schoolfellows weep for him, and his new Master was stricken with heart felt sorrow when he heard that his Favorite was no more. This is a melancholy consolation but a consolation in some degree it is; nothing however can sustain us under our affliction but reliance in God's Goodness, and a firm belief that it is for *our* Good, as we cannot doubt it was for his, that he should be removed from this sinful and troublesome world. He was too good for us; we did not deserve such a blessing—and we must endeavour to correct and amend every thing that is wrong in us and our bitter sorrow will in time become sweet and kindly, and never such, at no moment such, as we should wish to part with—Farewell, best love to all—Yours very affectionately
W. W.

63. *To* the Earl of Lonsdale

Grasmere Jan.^ry 8 1813

My Lord

The last Post brought me your Lordship's Letter enclosing a draft for £100; for which I beg leave to offer my faithful acknowledgements. It is your general desire that this act of kindness should be retrospective; but if an assurance on my part that, in the spirit of your Lordship's wishes I will 'call upon you whenever I have occasion to do so;' if this may reconcile you to my declining further assistance at present, I have no difficulty in giving such assurance.—But as a decisive backwardness to meet your most liberal suggestion would be unworthy of me and would not accord with the delicacy of your conduct towards me, I submit in this point to what may be most satisfactory to your Lordship's mind.

I cannot forbear, my Lord, to add that you have been the means of relieving my mind, in a manner that, I am sure, will be gratifying to your Heart.—The House which I have for some time occupied is the Parsonage of Grasmere. It stands close by the Churchyard; and I have found it absolutely necessary that we should quit a Place, which, by recalling to our minds at every moment the losses we have sustained in the course of the last year, would grievously retard our progress towards that tranquillity of mind which it is our duty to aim at. By your Lordship's goodness we shall be enabled to remove, without uneasiness from some additional Expense of Rent, to a most desirable Residence soon to be vacant at Rydale.[1] I shall be further assisted in my present depression of mind (indeed I have already been so) by feeling myself at liberty to recur to that species of intellectual exertion which only I find sufficiently powerful to rouze me, and which for some time I could not have yielded to, on account of a task undertaken for profit. This I can now defer without imprudence till I can proceed with it more heartily than at present would be possible. I have troubled your Lordship with this detail, being conscious that this is the best way of expressing my thanks to a mind like yours.

Your sympathy and that of your family in our distress much affects me and mine. I have a heartfelt Pleasure in saying that my Little-one is quite recovered.

I have the honour to be

> with affectionate respect
> my Lord
> your Lordship's obliged and
> faithful ser[vt]
> Wm Wordsworth

[1] Rydal Mount.

64. *To* Dorothy Wordsworth[1]

Perth, Sunday Morn. 10 oclock
August 19 or 20 [1814]

My dearest Dorothy,

As our Letter from Dunkeld would inform you our Tour has advanced much more slowly than we expected. Yesterday we walked on both sides [of] the Tay; but only ascended the high ground on the side approach[ing] the Town. You have a beautiful view of the Abbey from the bridge, and see it also very pleasingly, as you walk up the river side, when you have crossed. We were unusually pleased, I should say delighted with the view from the high ground, up and down the Tay; it is magnificent and lovely at the same time.—I was much more struck with this than I recalled to have been when we saw it together.[2] Our Car met us near Rumbling Bridge, and we slept at Amelrig. Passed the narrow Glen, about 8, yesterday morning—an hour too late; a very fine morning, but the Scene not so interesting as when we saw it. When we had ascended to the top of the hill we turned with the Course of the Almond towards Perth. Unfortunately we were misdirected by a Man upon the spot and went a mile and a half about, two miles and past up a steep hill instead of half a mile. Came to the Bridge of Buckarty, a beautiful little spot with a mill, Rocks and a Waterfall upon the Almond, thence 4 or five miles over a moor, an[d] rejoined the Almond, at Lyne-dock. General Graham,[3] the place from which he takes his title, visited here the burial place of Bessy Bell and Mary Gray, which I shall describe to you when we see you. Arrived at Perth about six, dined and walked about the Town. Rose this morning at six; Mary and I walked to the summit of Kinnoul-Hill—not quite a mile and a half; and had an extensive and fine view of the course of the Tay seawards. This is a fine prospect in all directions, almost, but the sky was disturbed and threatening, and a sullen haze concealed two thirds of the prospect. We mean to stay at Perth to day; and tomorrow, weather permitting, shall go to Kinross, near Lock Leven, thence to Stirling by Clackmannon and Alloa. I do not exactly know the distance. Yesterday was much the finest day for weather we have had, the

---

[1] Part of a joint letter of W. W. and M. W.   [2] In 1803.
[3] Gen. Thomas Graham, Lord Lyndoch (1748–1843).

narrow Glen was less solemn than when we saw it; but very attractive, Cattle grazing peacefully along its bottom, with a [?] sweet image of the Ideal of pastoral Life.

The Course of the Almond is naturally very interest[ing] if the Road had kept near the River, but unfortunately it shews little or nothing of it, going over a [?] Country now under a course of interesting improvement; and the River ungraciously concealing itself in its own rough Bed.—Perth disappointed me, not the county which is fine, but the town, it has only two Churches, not large, with beggarly steeples, and no kind of public Buildings to crown the Body of the Town, which with the exception of these two sorry steeples, presents to view nothing but Roofs and Chimneys. There is a bridge very respectable but much inferior to the new one at Dunkeld. Dunkeld is indeed vastly improved since we saw it together and the Duke[1] is going to build a splendid mansion. The weather was delightful from Blair to Dunkeld and the Garry, Tay and Tummel delighted us. The Tay is unquestionably the noblest river in Britain for its own dignity and the beauty and variety of the scenes it flows through.—We are sadly disheartened about the state of the weather to day, quite mortifying, as yesterday we confidently calculated upon a course of fine days, which would have carried us sure enough into Harbor at Edinburgh.—I forgot to say, that I stepped yesterday evening into a Bookseller's shop with a sneaking hope that I might hear something about the Excursion,[2] but not a word; on the contrary, inquiry of the Bookseller what a poetical parcel which he was then opening consisted of, he said, that it was a new Poem, called Lara, a most exquisite thing, supposed to be written by Lord Byron, and that all the world were running wild after it: this parcel they had down by the Coach—they had received one the day before which was carried off immediately. Now don't you think I am quite a hero not to be envious. You I assume yet bring philosophy as proof against all this. I took the book in my hand, and saw 'Jacqueline' in the same volume with Lara; what's this, oh said the bookseller, Jacqueline is a sweet Thing supposed to be by Rogers the author of The Pleasures of Memory. Here was another rap for poor me if I had been of the commonly supposed poetic constitution. You remember that when I wrote to Rogers last, I said that it was

---

[1] Of Athol.   [2] Just published.

impossible for any honest Poet to thrive while his friend Lord B. was flourishing daily at such a rate—Here I must stop, as we are going to Church to hear the *grunting* Priest of the old Kirk. This elegant portrait is supplied by Miss H. I am better of my complaint.—

65. *To* Robert Anderson

Rydale Mount near
Ambleside
September 17th 1814

Dear Sir,

Literature is much indebted to you for the, at that time, unexampled comprehensiveness of the Edition of English Poetry of which you were the Editor. I have no doubt that if your wishes had been complied with, this Collection would have included many valuable works of our elder Poets which have no place there. Chalmers' Edition,[1] which would probably never have existed without the Example of yours, is also very incomplete. The Public therefore is still unprovided with an entire Body of English Poetry; which might be furnished at a reasonable rate, if a few volumes were added to your Collection, with such Biographical Notes and Critical Notices as your Researches and your taste would furnish. I have long wished this to be done; and have talked with several of my Friends Messieurs Coleridge and Southey in particular upon the subject who both participate my desire to see your Edition adequately enlarged; tho regretting however at the same time that so valuable a work should have been printed so incorrectly. A few days ago I had a conversation with Mr Southey on this subject, and we both agreed that it would be a fortunate thing for the interests of Literature; if the Proprietors of your Edition would encourage you to supply what is yet wanting to make the work complete, by furnishing a few additional volumes.—We drew out a list[2] of the following authors, and works, which I take the liberty of

---

[1] Publ. 1810.

[2] The list which follows illustrates the range of W. W.'s knowledge of his literary predecessors, many of them almost forgotten today.

submitting to your consideration; only observing, that if the scheme be judged feasible, the fewer of the following that are excluded the better.—1st all that are in Chalmers and not in yours, adding to the works of Skelton many pieces which have lately come to light which C. has not included. Mr. Heber[1] has most or all of them. And to the works of Turberville may be added what Chalmers has omitted, His letters from Russia which are in Hackluyt.

Occleve	Watson	Chalkhill	Quarles
Minot	Willoby	A. Fraunce	May
Hawes	Southwell	Sir P. Sydney	Herbert
—	B. Googe	Lord Brooke	Herrick
Churchyard	N. Breton	Sylvester	Lovelace
Constable	Chapman	Best parts of Wither	Henry More
Chamberlain	Cleveland	Randolph	Marvel

including in the works of Marvel the Poems which the Quarto Edition of his Prose Works contains—

> Norris of Bemerton
> Lady Winchelsea
> A selection from Tom D'Urfey
> A volume of Ballads and state Poems
> A volume of Metrical Romances
> P. Ploughman's Vision and Creed and [*seal*]
> Miscellanies of the age of Tudor.

Of old Translations the following are desireable,
> Chapman's Homer
> Fairfax's Tasso
> Goulding's Ovid
> Phaer's Virgil
> May's Lucan

_And as a curiosity the few books of Stanyhurst's Virgil— —

Now Sir I should be much obliged to you if you could prevail upon the Proprietors of your Edition, to enlarge so as to include as many of the above as possible. The present possessors of your Collection, I think, would almost all become purchasers. Many

[1] The bibliophile.

also who have bought Chalmers would be glad to complete its deficiencies by your Volumes. And if the work were correctly printed I have little doubt that it would answer; I am certain that it would meet with patronage amongst my literary Friends. Hoping that you will excuse this Liberty, I beg leave to subscribe myself
With gratitude
Your obliged and humble servant
W. Wordsworth

66. *To* Richard Wordsworth

Rydal Mount
October 13th 1814.

My dear Richard,

I was over at Lowther some little time since, and called at Sockbridge, but you were then at Allonby.—

It hurts me very much, and surprizes me not a little, that I never hear from you on the subject of our affairs. There is something apparently very unbrotherly in this silence, which neither Dorothy or I seem to have the power to induce you to break—

Have you ever done us the justice to ask yourself what situation our affairs would be in if you should happen to die? If you have provided for the accident pray let us know immediately, and in what manner; if you have not, for heaven's sake, do [not] omit any longer to do what is right. I have told you what is our wish—to have the money[1] at our command.—At present I suppose it is holden in your name, and we have no power over it independent of you.

I shall probably be at Sockbridge in the course of the next month, towards the beginning of it—Let me entreat of you to be prepared to satisfy me on these points, by that time.

I am dear Brother most faithfully yours
Wm Wordsworth

---

[1] The repayment of the Lowther debt.

67. *To* Christopher Wordsworth

Nov. 26th [1814]

My dear Brother,

   Not hearing from you I had some apprehensions (as the Booksellers are not the most attentive persons in the world to directions given them) that my intentions in sending you *The Excursion* might not have been fulfilled. But a few days before the receipt of yours I learned from Mrs Lloyd that the Work had reached you. I should have been sorry had you not been pleased with it; sorry both as a Poet and an Englishman. I hear from many quarters high commendations and not a few from the members of your Profession. Yesterday I had a letter from Sir George Beaumont in which he says the Bishop of London is enchanted with the Excursion, and indeed I hear but one opinion on the subject! The Printers have just begun the 2nd Volume of my Poems,[1] so that I hope they will be ready for Publication about the beginning of Janry. Many delays have taken place, for none of which I was accountable, or they might have been before the public ere this time. I have not yet heard anything of the Sale of the Excursion; which I should have done had it been such as was likely to lead the way to the steady demand of a second Edition which many Persons are waiting for; and I should be sorry if their disappointment be of long continuance, as must be the case if the work does not go off in reasonable time.—I see that you have some sermons ready for Publication; Why did not you mention this to me? I remember that I am in your debt for a bound set of your Ecclesiastical History[2] which was presented to Mr. Johnson; and which you shall be paid for the first convenient opportunity; therefore pray let me know the amount.—Dorothy is in S. Wales with Mr. Hutchinson's family; we expect her home by the next moon: She is well. I saw Richard and his Bride at Sockbridge; he was pretty well and she is a very decent and comely person, but he has done a foolish thing in marrying one so young; not to speak of the disgrace of forming such a connection with a servant, and that, one of his own. Mrs Lloyd is but poorly, and Charles has not been well lately; though when we saw him a few days ago he was

---

[1] *Poems including Lyrical Ballads,* 2 vols., 1815.
[2] C. W.'s *Ecclesiastical Biography,* 1810.

unusually so. He has printed his Alfieri,[1] and composed a novel recently with his usual rapidity. I have not seen it.—Mary is well and so are the children except that Wm has a bad cold; which always somewhat alarms us, as his colds never fail to be accompanied with considerable difficulty in breathing, and a croupy sound in the throat which is most painful to hear. He is a stout lively and healthy child, of great promise. His sister is quick and clever. She is very careless and inattentive, but capable of learning rapidly would she give her mind to it. John is for book-attainments the slowest Child almost I ever knew. He has an excellent judgment and well regulated affections; but I am much disappointed in my expectations of retracing the Latin and Greek classics with him. Incredible pains has been taken with him, but he is to this day a deplorably bad reader of *English* even. You do not mention your farming. How does it answer, verily and truly?

With best love from Mary to yourself and our sister Priscilla I remain my dear Christopher most faithfully yours

W. Wordsworth

Our neighbour the Bishop[2] is declining gradually but more in mind than in body. Pray tell how your expectations stand as to succeeding him. Do not forget this.

68. *To* Catherine Clarkson

[Jan. 1815]

My dear Friend,

I don't know that it is quite *fair* to sit down to answer a letter of friendship the moment it is received; but allow me to do so in this case.—Unitarian hymns must by their dispassionate monotony have deprived your Friend's ear of all compass, which implies of all discrimination. To you I will whisper, that the Excursion has one merit if it has no other, a versification to which for *variety* of musical effect no Poem in the language furnishes a parallel. Tell Patty

---

[1] His translation, publ. 1815.

[2] Bishop Watson of Calgarth, on Windermere: Professor of Divinity at Cambridge.

Smith[1] this (the name is a secret with me and make her stare); and exhort her to study with her fingers till she has learned to confess it to herself. Miss S's notion of poetical imagery is probably taken from the Pleasures of Hope or Gertrude of Wyoming[2] see for instance stanza first of said poem. There is very little imagery of that kind; but, I am far from subscribing to your concession that there is little imagery in the Poem; either collateral in the way of metaphor coloring the style; illustrative in the way of simile; or directly under the shape of description or incident: there is a great deal; though not quite so much as will be found in the other parts of the Poem where the subjects are more lyrically treated and where there is less narration; or description turning upon manners, and those repeated actions which constitute habits, or a course of life.—Poetic Passion (Dennis[3] has well observed) is of two kinds imaginative and enthusiastic; and merely human and ordinary; of the former it is only to be feared that there is too great a proportion. But all this must inevitably be lost upon Miss P. S.—

The Soul, dear Mrs C. may be re-given when it had been taken away, my own Solitary is an instance of this; but a Soul that has been dwarfed by a course of bad culture cannot after a certain age, be expanded into on[e] of even ordinary proportion.—Mere error of opinion, mere apprehension of ill consequences from supposed mistaken views on my part, could never have rendered your correspondent blind to the innumerable analogies and types of infinity, insensible to the countless awakenings to noble aspiration, which I have transfused into that Poem from the Bible of the Universe as it speaks to the ear of the intelligent, as it lies open to the eyes of the humble-minded. I have alluded to the Ladys errors of opinion—she talks of my being a worshipper of Nature—a passionate expression uttered incautiously in the Poem upon the Wye[4] has led her into this mistake, she reading in cold-heartedness and substituting the letter for the spirit. Unless I am greatly mistaken, there is nothing of this kind in the Excursion. There is indeed a passage towards the end of the 4th. Book where the

[1] Daughter of William Smith, MP.
[2] Poems by Thomas Campbell (1777–1834).
[3] John Dennis (1657–1734), the critic.
[4] *Tintern Abbey.*

Wanderer introduces the simile of the Boy and the Shell, and what follows, that has something, ordinarily but absurdly called *Spinosistic*. But the intelligent reader will easily see the *dramatic* propriety of the Passage. The Wanderer in the beginning of the book had given vent to his own devotional feelings and announced in some degree his own creed; he is here preparing the way for more distinct conceptions of the Deity by reminding the Solitary of such religious feelings as cannot but exist in the minds of those who affect atheism. She condemns me for not distinguishing between nature as the work of God and God himself. But where does she find this doctrine inculcated? Where does she gather that the Author of the Excursion looks upon nature and God as the same? He does not indeed consider the Supreme Being as bearing the same relation to the universe as a watch-maker bears to a watch. In fact, there is nothing in the course of religious education adopted in this country and in the use made by us of the holy scriptures that appears to me so injurious as the perpetually talking about *making* by God—Oh! that your Correspondent had heard a conversation which I had in bed with my sweet little Boy, four and a half years old, upon this subject the other morning. 'How did God make me? Where is God? How does he speak? He never spoke to *me*.' I told him that God was a spirit, that he was not like his flesh which he could touch; but more like his thoughts in his mind which he could *not* touch.—The wind was tossing the fir trees, and the sky and light were dancing about in their dark branches, as seen through the window—Noting these fluctuations he exclaimed eagerly—'There's a bit of him I see it there!' This is not meant entirely for Father's prattle; but, for Heaven's sake, in your religious talk with children say as little as possible about *making*. One of the main objects of the Recluse is, to reduce the calculating understanding to its proper level among the human faculties—Therefore my Book must be disliked by the Unitarians, as their religion rests entirely on that basis; and therefore is, in fact, no religion at all—but—I won't say what. I have done little or nothing towards your request of furnishing you with arguments to cope with my antagonist. Read the Book if it pleases you; the construction of the language is uniformly perspicuous; at least I have taken every possible pains to make it so, therefore you will have no difficulty here. The impediment you may meet with will be of two kinds, such as exist in the ode[1] which concludes my 2ᵈ volume of poems. This poem rests entirely upon two recollections of childhood, one that of a splendour in the objects of sense which is passed away, and the other in indisposition to bend to the law of death as applying to our own particular case. A Reader who has not a vivid recollection of these feelings having existed in his mind in childhood cannot understand that poem. So also with regard to some of those elements of the human soul whose importance is insisted upon in the Exⁿ. And some of those images of sense which are dwelt upon as holding that relation to immortality and infinity which I have before alluded to; if a person has not been in the way of receiving these images, it is not likely that he can form such an adequate conception of them as will bring him into lively sympathy with the Poet. For instance one who has never heard the echoes of the flying Raven's voice in a mountainous Country, as described at the close of the 4ᵗʰ Book will not perhaps be able to relish that illustration; yet every one must have been in the way of perceiving similar effects from different causes;—but I have tired myself, and must have tired you—

One word upon ordinary or popular passion. Could your correspondent read the description of Robert, and the fluctuations of hope and fear in Margaret's mind, and the gradual decay of herself and her dwelling without a bedimmed eye then I pity her. Could she read the distress of the Solitary after the loss of his Family and the picture of his quarrel with his own conscience (though this tends more to meditative passion) without some agitation then I envy not her tranquillity. Could the anger of Ellen before she sate down to weep over her babe, though she were but a poor serving-maid, be found in a book, and that book be said to be without passion, then, thank Heaven! that the person so speaking is neither my wife nor my Sister, nor one whom (unless I could work in her a great alteration) I am forced to daily converse with. What thinks she of those Relatives about the little Infant, who was unexpectedly given, and suddenly taken away? But too much of this—Farewell. I wish I could have written you a more satisfactory letter. Lamb is justifiably enraged at the spurious Review which his Friends expect to be his. No Newmarket jockey, no horse-stealer was ever able to play a hundredth part of the tricks

[1] *Intimations of Immortality.*

upon the person of an unhappy beast that the Bavius of the Quarterly Review[1] has done for that sweet composition. So I will not scruple to style it, though I never saw it. And worst of all, L[amb kept no copy] and the original M S [we] fear, destroyed.—As [to the Ed Review] I hold the Author [of it in entire] contempt, and therefore shall not pollute my fingers [with the touch] of it.[2] There is one sentence in the Ex^n. ending in 'sublime att[ractions] of the grave' which,—if the poem had contained nothing else that [I valued,] would have made it almost a matter of religion with me to [keep out] of the way of the best stuff which so mean a mind as Mr [Jeffrey's] could produce in connection with it. His impertinences, to us[e the] mildest te[rm,] if once they had a place in my memory, would, for a [time] at least, [sti]ck there. You cannot scower a spot of this kind ou[t of] your mind as you may a stain out of your clothes. If the m[ind] were under the power of the will I should read Mr J^s merely to expose his stupidity to his still more stupid admirers. This not being the case, as I said before, I shall not pollute my fingers with touching his book. Give my affectionate regards to Henry Robinson, and the sa[me] to Mr Clarkson. Remember me also kindly to your Father.—I am sure you are competent to write the Review as well as I could wish to have it done. I am very sorry for the indisposition under which your last was written. Headaches are plaguey things, I hope you are better—Sunday Morning—I have just read over this Letter; it is a sad jumble of stuff and as ill expressed.—I should not send it but in compliance with the wish of Mary and Dorothy.[3] The reason of the thing being so bad is that your Friends remarks were so monstrous. To talk of the offense of writing the Ex^n and the difficulty of forgiving the Author is carrying audacity and presumption to a heigth of which I did not think any *Woman* was capable. Had my Poem been much coloured by Books, as many parts of what I have to write must be, I should have been accused as Milton has been of pedantry, and of having a mind which could not support itself but by other mens labours.—Do not you perceive that my conversations almost all take place out of Doors, and all with grand objects of nature surrounding the speakers for the

[1] William Gifford, who had mangled Lamb's review.
[2] Jeffrey had recently reviewed *The Excursion*.
[3] Who had taken down the earlier parts of this letter from W. W.'s dictation.

express purpose of their being alluded to in illustration of the subjects treated of. *Much* imagery from books would have been an impertinence and an incumbrance: where it was required it is found. As to passion; it is never to be lost sight of, that the Excursion is *part* of a work; that in its plan it is conversational; and that if I had introduced stories exciting curiosity, and filled with violent conflicts of passion and a rapid interchange of striking incidents, these things could have never harmonized with the rest of the work and all further discourse, comment, or reflections must have been put a stop to.—This I write for you and not for your friend; with whom if you would take my advice, you will neither converse by letter nor *viva voce* upon a subject which she is [in every] respect disqualified to treat. farewell.

[?Your most] affectionate friend   W. W.

You had sent a promise that Mr C would give me an account of the impression my Book made on him.

69. *To* Thomas Poole

Rydal Mount Ambleside
March 13 1815.

My dear Poole,

A few days ago I was at Keswick, where I learned that Hartley[1] was to go to Oxford about Easter. Mrs. Coleridge wished me to write to you and mention this, and also that if it were not inconvenient to you, that the ten pounds which you were so kind as to offer, would be convenient at this time;—as she has not the means of fitting him out, and she does not like to apply to his Uncles in the first instance. He is to go to Merton College, where his Cousins or Uncles (I am not sure which) have procured him an office, the title of it, Postmaster, which is to bring him in £50 per annum, which with his Uncle's £40, Lady B.'s[2] £30, and your ten, it is hoped will maintain him. Cottle also allows £5 per annum; if more be wanted, Southey and I must contrive to advance it. I have

---

[1] Hartley Coleridge.   [2] Beaumont's.

done all in my power to impress upon H.'s mind the necessity of not trusting vaguely to his talents, and to an irregular sort of knowledge, however considerable it may be, in some particulars; and of applying himself zealously and perseveringly to those studies which the University points out to him. His prime object ought to be to gain an independence; and I have striven to place this truth before his understanding in the clearest point of view; and I took the opportunity of speaking to him on the subject in the presence of his uncle Southey, who confirmed and enforced all that I said. So that if good advice have any virtue in it, he has not been left unfurnished with it.—Southey means to look out for a place in some public office for Derwent;[1] he hopes to succeed in the Exchequer where the situations are very good. Sara[2] has made great progress in Italian under her mother; and is learning French and Latin. She is also instructed in music by Miss Barker, a friend of Southey's, who is their near neighbour; so that should it be *necessary* she will be well fitted to become a Governess in a nobleman's or gentleman's family, in course of time; she is remarkably clever; and her musical Teacher says that her progress is truly astonishing. Her health unfortunately is but delicate.

It was my intention to write to you if Mrs. C. had not requested it, and I am happy to give this account of our Friend's children, who are all very promising. Nevertheless, I have some fears for Hartley, as he is too much inclined to the eccentric. But it is our *duty* to hope for the best. Coleridge, we have learnt, is still with the Morgans, but removed from the neighbourhood of Bath to Colne or Caln in Wiltshire. His friends in this Country hear nothing from him directly. A sister of my Wife's, who was staying at Bath, walked over to call upon him, but found the family removed. His late Landlady was very communicative, and said that Mr. C. used to talk with her of his children, and mentioned that his Eldest was going to college. So that you see he expects the thing to take place, though he wished to put it off when you conversed with him on the subject. I rejoice to hear of your thriving School. I have not yet seen your Relation's pamphlet which you recommend; I have heard it praised by others, and shall procure it.—If you have read my Poem, the 'Excursion', you will there see what importance I attach

---

[1] Derwent Coleridge (1800–83), schoolmaster and divine.
[2] See List of Correspondents.

to the Madras System.[1] Next to the art of Printing it is the noblest invention for the improvement of the human species. Our population in this neighbourhood is not sufficient to apply it on a large scale; but great benefit has been derived from it even upon a small one.—If you *have* read my Poem, I should like to have a record of your feelings during the perusal, and your opinion afterwards; if it has not deeply interested you, I should fear that I have missed my aim in some important particulars.—I had the hope of pleasing you in my mind during the composition in many parts, especially those in which I have alluded to the influence of the manufacturing spirit; and in the pictures, in the last book but one, which I have given of Boys in different situations in life: the manufacturer, the boy of the yeomanry, and the Clergyman's or Gentleman's son. If you can conscientiously recommend this expensive work to any of your wealthier friends, I will thank you, as I wish to have it printed in a cheaper form, for those who cannot afford to buy it in its present shape. And, as it is in some places a little abstruse, and in all, serious, without any of the modern attractions of glittering style, or incident to provoke curiosity, it cannot be expected to make its way without difficulty, and it is therefore especially incumbent on those who value it to exert themselves in its behalf. My opinion as to the execution of the minor parts of my works is not in the *least altered*. My Poems are upon the point of being republished in two vols octavo, with a new preface, and several additions, though not any pieces of length. I should like to present you with a copy as a testimony of my regard, if you would let me know where you wish to have it sent; or if you could call, or desire anybody to call, for it at Longmans. Pray give me your notions upon the Corn Laws; what restricted price you think high enough: some one seems indispensable.

Most faithfully yours,
W. Wordsworth

[1] The educational system devised by Dr Bell, in which senior pupils taught the juniors.

70. *To* Sara Hutchinson

Thursday 16ᵗʰ March [1815]
Dearest Sara—I will repeat in other words what D has said[1] of the
Corn Laws. The opinion that importation should [?not] be
restricted is monstrous; I wish you could see Mr Wilberforce's[2]
speech, it is almost word for word what I had said by our fireside
before—I have not sufficient knowledge of facts to fix upon the best
restrictive price; but it is clear that rents have had an unnatural
rise; and if they keep at their present pitch by aid of the present
price of 80 shillings, I have no hesitation in saying that the price is
too high—and I could have wished that a sum below 80 shillings
had been tried; though with 80 shillings corn I should expect
would not be saleable at that price for any length of time together;
because it must fall from the moment that importation is likely to
take place—so that it is possible that the price may answer for the
good of the community. Nothing can be more deplorable than the
errors of the mob; who seem never to have had a thought, that
without a restriction upon importation no corn could be grown in
this country, and consequently that it would become insupportably dear; and perhaps could not be got at all—The advocates for the
Corn Laws are in fact the friends of the poor; though as I have said
they may be mistaken as to the best price to fix upon. If
Buonaparte were a man of genuine talents, such is the present state
of Italy I am persuaded he might yet atchieve a noble work, which
would almost redeem him in my estimation; I mean the making
and consolidating the several states of that divided Kingdom into
one;[3] and if this were done the independence [of] that people would
be established—one of the most desirable political events that
could possibly take place. The Italians have been abominably
used, in being transferred to Austria, to the King of Sardinia and
the rest of those vile Tyrants. B's is a strange adventure, he must
doubtless have very many adherents in France, but I must be in
deplorable ignorance of facts, if it be possible that such an

[1] In the earlier part of this joint letter to S. H. at Hindwell.
[2] William Wilberforce (see List of Correspondents).
[3] The Napoleonic Kingdom of Italy had been dismembered in 1814. Now, after
Napoleon's escape from Elba, his brother-in-law Murat had revived the ideal of
unification.

Enterprize should succeed. I quit the pen to walk with Mary very affectionately yours W. W.

71. *To* Robert Gillies

Rydal Mount, April 25, 1815

My dear Sir,

I think of starting for London in a few days with Mrs. Wordsworth, and as I wish to leave home with as clear a conscience as I can, I sit down to atone for one of my offences in not having replied sooner to your kind letter. Your health, I hope, is better, and if it be much improved, what should prevent you from taking a trip as far south as we think of going, and meeting us in town? We shall be in lodgings somewhere at the west-end, and may easily be heard of, by inquiries at Sir George Beaumont's, corner of North Audley Street, Grosvenor Square.

You ought to have received my two volumes of poems long before this, if Longman has done his duty. I ordered a copy likewise to be sent to Walter Scott. I cannot but flatter myself that this publication will interest you. The pains which I have bestowed on the composition can never be known but to myself, and I am very sorry to find, on reviewing the work, that the labour has been able to do so little for it. You mentioned *Guy Mannering* in your last. I have read it. I cannot say that I was disappointed, for there is very considerable talent displayed in the performance, and much of that sort of knowledge with which the author's mind is so richly stored. But the adventures I think not well chosen or invented, and they are still worse put together; and the characters, with the exception of Meg Merrilies, excite little interest. In the management of this lady the author has shown very considerable ability, but with that want of taste, which is universal among modern novels of the Radcliffe[1] school, which, as far as they are concerned, this is. I allude to the laborious manner in which everything is placed before your eyes for the production of picturesque effect.

[1] Mrs Ann Radcliffe, the Gothic novelist.

The reader, in good narration, feels that pictures rise up before his sight, and pass away from it unostentatiously, succeeding each other. But when they are fixed upon an easel for the express purpose of being admired, the judicious are apt to take offence, and even to turn sulky at the exhibitor's officiousness. But these novels are likely to be much overrated on their first appearance, and will afterwards be as much undervalued. *Waverley* heightened my opinion of Scott's talents very considerably, and if *Mannering* has not added much, it has not taken much away. Infinitely the best part of *Waverley* is the pictures of Highland manners at Mac Ivor's castle, and the delination of his character, which are done with great spirit. The Scotch baron, and all the circumstances in which he is exhibited, are too peculiar and *outré*. Such caricatures require a higher condiment of humour to give them a relish than the author of *Waverley* possesses. But too much of this gossip. I heard casually the other day that Mr Mackenzie[1] might take up his residence in our neighbourhood during some part of the approaching summer. I am sorry for the occasion, which I am told is the delicate health of one of his daughters. Houses and lodgings might be had hereabouts if applied for early in the season, otherwise are difficult to find. I mention this in order that if you happen to see Mr Mackenzie, you may repeat it to him, and add that I should be happy to be of service to him on this occasion. My sister will continue at Rydale Mount during Mrs Wordsworth's and my absence; and if Mr Mackenzie has no friend to whom he can apply, she would be happy to transmit to him any information that she thought likely to be useful.

Excuse this Dull and hasty letter, and believe me

Most sincerely yours
William Wordsworth

[1] Probably Henry Mackenzie, the Scottish novelist.

72. *To* S. T. Coleridge

24 Edward Street
Cavendish Sq^{re}
Monday Morn: 22nd May 1815

My dear Coleridge,

Let me beg out of kindness to me that you would relinquish the intention of publishing the Poem addressed to me after hearing *mine* to you.[1] The commendation would be injurious to us both, and my work when it appears, would labour under a great disadvantage in consequence of such a precursorship of Praise.

I shall be thankful for your remarks on the Poems, and also upon the Excursion, only begging that whenever it is possible references may be made to some passages which have given rise to the opinion whether favourable or otherwise; in consequence of this not having been done (when indeed it would have been out of Place) in your Letter to Lady B— I have rather been perplexed than enlightened by your *comparative* censure. One of my principal aims in the Ex^{n}: has been to put the commonplace truths, of the human affections especially, in an interesting point of view; and rather to remind men of their knowledge, as it lurks inoperative and unvalued in their own minds, than to attempt to convey recondite or refined truths. Pray point out to me the most striking instances where I have failed, in producing poetic effect by an overfondness for this practice, or through inability to realize my wishes.

I am happy to hear that you are going to press.[2]

And believe me my dear Coleridge in spite of your silence

Most affectionately yours
W. Wordsworth

I hope to send you the White Doe in a few days. Some prefatory Lines have found their way into the Courier, much to my regret, and printed with vile incorrectness. I remain in Town nearly three weeks longer.

---

[1] S. T. C.'s lines, *To William Wordsworth*, composed at Coleorton in Dec. 1806, after hearing W. W. read aloud *The Prelude*.

[2] The publication of *Biographia Literaria* and *Sibylline Leaves* was in fact delayed until 1817.

73. *To* William Wilberforce

24th May 1815
24 Edward Street
Cavendish Sq[re]

My dear Sir,

I am very sorry that I am engaged for breakfast every day this week, although on Friday only conditionally. If on that day Mr Heber and Mr Walter Scott should be at liberty, I am under promise to meet them at Sir George Beaumont's to breakfast, thence to proceed to the City with Sir George and Lady Beaumont to view an original Portrait of Milton (a very fine one) recently rescued from the dust of a Broker's Shop.—

If this arrangement cannot be effected, it will give me great pleasure to wait upon you on Friday, otherwise I must defer that gratification till Monday Morning—In the mean while permit me to thank you for your most kind note, and to express my regret on account of your illness, and earnest wishes for your speedy and perfect recovery.

I have the honor to be
my dear Sir
With great respect
Your obedient Ser[vt]
W[m] Wordsworth

74. *To* Christopher Wordsworth

Friday Night, Kendal
[13 Oct. 1815]

My dear Brother,

I am just returned home, after accompanying Charles and Sophia to Manchester, where we arrived last night. I saw them into the Birmingham Mail; Mrs Lloyd will no Doubt give you an account of [the] journey [and] the state of her Husband's health[1]—after his arrival at Birmingham whither it was absolutely necessary that he should go.

---

[1] Charles Lloyd had gone mad.

Your Letter my dear Brother affected us all deeply; we received it on Wednesday night; and I have not since had time to sit down and write to you, as I could wish; scarcely have I had ten minutes that I could call my own—Dorothy is at Brathay with the Children,[1] but I left her most anxious to contribute to your present support. Let us hear from you immediately; and who you have with you; some female friend I trust. If you wish that Dorothy should come to Bocking she will do so, as soon as you desire—Heaven preserve you, and what remains to you on earth of yours: for her who is gone[2] she is among the blessed—farewell, our prayers shall not be wanting on your behalf—for myself as a Husband I feel for you to the utmost—I would write more could I suggest any consolation; I only can assure you, of what you well know, our heart-felt sympathy and our wish to relieve you, in any way you can point out—

Your ever affectionate Brother—
Wm Wordsworth

75. *To* Robert Southey

[?autumn 1815]

Dear Southey,

  . . . My opinion in respect to epic poetry is much the same as that of the critic whom Lucien Bonaparte[3] has quoted in his preface. Epic poetry, of the highest class, requires in the first place an action eminently influential, an action with a grand or sublime train of consequences; it next requires the intervention and guidance of beings superior to man, what the critics, I believe, call machinery; and lastly, I think with Dennis that no subject but a religious one can answer the demand of the soul in the highest class of this species of poetry. Now Tasso's is a religious subject, and in my opinion a most happy one; but I am confidently of opinion that the movement of Tasso's poem rarely corresponds with the essential character of the subject; nor do I think it possible that, written in stanzas, it should. The celestial movement cannot, I

---

[1] i.e. Lloyd's.   [2] C. W.'s wife Priscilla had just died.
[3] Napoleon's brother, author of *Charlemagne*, 1814.

think, be kept up, if the sense is to be broken in that despotic manner at the close of every eight lines. Spenser's stanza is infinitely finer than the *ottava rima*, but even Spenser's will not allow the epic movement as exhibited by Homer, Virgil, and Milton. How noble is the first paragraph of the *Aeneid* in point of sound, compared with the first stanza of the *Jerusalem Delivered*! The one winds with the majesty of the Conscript Fathers entering the Senate House in solemn procession; and the other has the pace of a set of recruits shuffling on the drill-ground, and receiving from the adjutant or drill-serjeant the command to halt at every ten or twenty steps. Farewell.

Affectionately yours,
W. Wordsworth

76. *To* Bernard Barton

Rydal Mount, near Ambleside,
Jan. 12, 1816.

Dear Sir,

Though my sister, during my absence, has returned thanks in my name for the verses which you have done me the honour of addressing to me, and for the obliging letter which accompanies them, I feel it incumbent on me, on my return home, to write a few words to the same purpose with my own hand.

It is always satisfaction to me to learn that I have given pleasure upon *rational* grounds; and I have nothing to object to your poetical panegyric but the occasion which called it forth. An admirer of my works, zealous as you have declared yourself to be, condescends too much when he gives way to an impulse proceeding from the—,[1] or indeed from any other Review. The writers in these publications, while they prosecute their inglorious employment, cannot be supposed to be in a state of mind very favourable for being affected by the finer influences of a thing so pure as genuine poetry; and as to the instance which has incited you to offer me this tribute of your gratitude, though I have not seen it, I doubt not but that it is a splenetic effusion of the Conductor of that Review who has taken a

[1] The *Edinburgh*.

perpetual Retainer from his own incapacity to plead against my claims to public approbation.

I differ from you in thinking that the only poetical lines in your address are 'stolen from myself'. The best Verse, perhaps, is the following:

> Awfully mighty in his impotence,

which, by way of repayment, I may be tempted to steal from you on some future occasion.

It pleases, though it does not surprize me, to learn that, having been affected early in life by my verses, you have returned again to your old Loves after some little infidelities, which you were shamed into by commerce with the scribbling and chattering part of the World. I have heard of many who, upon their first acquaintance with my poetry, have had much to get over before they could thoroughly relish it; but never of one who, having once learned to enjoy it, had ceased to value it or survived his admiration. This is as good an external assurance as I can desire that my inspiration is from a pure source, and that my principles of composition are trustworthy.

With many thanks for your good wishes, and begging leave to offer mine in return, I remain, dear sir,

Respectfully yours,
Wm Wordsworth

77. *To* B. R. Haydon

Rydale Mount   Jan^ry 13 [1816]
near Ambleside

My dear Sir,

On my return home my Sister delivered to me your Letter, which on many accounts gave me great pleasure. Mrs W— and I had been absent some time; and indeed I have been much unsettled by business during the best part of this winter. It gratifies me much that the Sonnets, especially the one addressed to yourself,[1] find favor in your eyes, and those of your friends.—As to

---

[1] 'High is our calling, Friend!'

your request for permission to publish them I cannot refuse to comply with it. In regard to that addressed to yourself, you deserve a much higher Compliment; but from the nature of the subject it may be found pretty generally interesting. The two others, particularly the Snow-crested Mountain,[1] full surely are morsels only for the few. But if Mr Scott[2] desires it, he is at liberty to give them a place in his Journal when and how he likes. At the same time my own feelings urge me to state in sincerity, that I naturally shrink from solicitation of public notice. I never publish any thing without great violence to my own disposition which is to shun, rather than court, regard. In this respect we Poets are much more happily situated than our Brother Labourers of the Pencil; who cannot, unless they be born to a Fortune, proceed in their employments without public countenance.

I thank you for the Number of the Champion; after being found worthy of such eulogy as is there bestowed upon you, the next enviable thing is the ability to praise merit in so eloquent a style.—There is also an excellent political essay of Scott at the head of the same number.—Pray give my regards to him; and I will take this occasion of stating, that it may be agreeable to Mr Hunt to learn that his Mask[3] has been read with great pleasure by my Wife and her Sisters under this peaceful Roof. They commend the style in strong terms; and though it would not become *me* to say that their taste is correct, I have often witnessed with pleasure and an entire sympathy, the digust with which in this particular they are affected by the main part of contemporary productions.

I am glad to learn that your Picture[4] advances.—It is as grand a subject as could be selected. The feelings to be excited are adoration and exultation, and subordinate to them, astonished suspension of mind. In all the Evangelists it is written, that our blessed Lord was accompanied with hosannas. These a silent Picture cannot express, and but imperfectly indicate; but Garments may be spread, and boughs may be carried in triumph, and prostrate forms exhibited, as you have done. From the manner in which I have dwelt upon these images you will infer that I think you have done well in rejecting the character of the supercilious

[1] 'How clear, how keen, how marvellously bright'.
[2] John Scott of *The Champion* (see List of Correspondents).
[3] Leigh Hunt's *Descent of Liberty*.   [4] *Christ's Entry into Jerusalem*.

Prude.—I cannot but think such a person discordant with the piece. One of the Evangelists says that the Pharisees called on Jesus to rebuke his disciples, and this is the only feeling mentioned that does not fall directly in with the general triumph and exultation. For there is nothing discordant with these in the Question, who is this? immediately succeeded by the answer, 'The King of Jerusalem;' in fact in no stronger manner could the overwhelming presence of Jesus Christ be expressed. The request of the Pharisees has *indirectly* the same tendency, they wished that the Disciples should be rebuked; and why? because their pride was wounded and their indignation raised by the homage which the multitude paid with such fervor to Jesus on his approach to Jerusalem.—A character like that of the haughty prude belongs rather to the higher kinds of Comedy, such as the works of Hogarth, than to a subject of this nature, which to use Milton's expression is 'more than heroic'.—I coincide with you in opinion as to Raphael's characters, but depend upon it he has erred upon the safer side. Dramatic diversities aid discrimination, [and] should never be produced upon sublime subjects by the sacrifice of sublime effect. And it is better that expression should give way to beauty than beauty be banished by expression. Happy is he who can hit the exact point, where grandeur is not lowered but heightened by detail, and beauty not impaired, but rendered more touching and exquisite by Passion.—This has been done by the great artists of antiquity, but not frequently in modern times; yet much as I admire those productions I would on no account discourage your efforts to introduce more of the diversities of actual humanity into the management of sublime and pathetic subjects. Much of what Garrick is reported to have done for the stage, may by your Genius be effected for the Picture Gallery.— But in aiming at this object, proceed with reflection, and if you are in *doubt*—decide in favour of the course which Raphael pursued.

Before I conclude, I have one word to say of the mode of publishing the Sonnet addressed to you. I could wish that it should appear, that the thing was not first addressed to you through the medium of a Public journal, but was a private communication of Friendship. Don't you think that the Sonnet on the sight of a beautiful Picture,[1] the second I believe, it stands in my large

[1] 'Praised be the art'.

edition, would come with effect if paired with the one addressed to yourself.—It is a favorite of mine, and I think not unworthy of the subject, which was a picture painted by our Friend Sir George Beaumont; though this is not mentioned in the title of the Piece.—The Editor might add in a foot note, that the Landscape which had suggested the verses, was he understood from the pencil of Sir George.—My poems are not so extensively known but that a Reprint of this piece would be new to a great majority of the Readers of the Champion.

You do not speak of your eyes; I trust, therefore, they are much better.—

My Wife and Miss Hutchinson send their kindest regards; and join with me in best wishes for your health happiness and success. This last word reminds me of your desire that my merits as a Poet might be acknowledged during my life-time. I am quite satisfied on this head—with me it must be a work of time; but I frequently receive acknowledgements of gratitude from persons unknown, in all quarters of the Island.

faithfully yours
W Wordsworth

Remember that the frame of the Study[1] you so kindly promised me is to be at my expense, but I wish you to procure it because you will know what sort of one will best suit the picture, and also though this is an occasion on which I am not scrupulous about economy, because the dealer will let you have it cheaper. What is the price of one of my busts?[2]

78. *To* John Scott

Rydal Mount, Tuesday, June 11, [1816]

My dear Sir,

I am only just returned after more than a week's absence upon painful and anxious business, which has devolved upon me as trustee under the will of my eldest brother, recently deceased. He

---

[1] For the portrait of W. W. in Haydon's picture.
[2] By Leigh Hunt's brother John.

has left an only child, a boy sixteen months old, and a widow not twenty-seven years, and though his property is considerable, yet the affairs are in an intricate and perplexed situation, so that much of my time and more of my thoughts will in future be taken up by them; and I need scarcely say to you that I am wholly inexperienced in things of this kind. But to return to your situation and prospects. My best wishes will follow you to the Continent, and I shall be anxious to hear that your hopes keep their ground and strength from the influence of a milder climate. I have no doubt that the world will be benefited by your observations abroad; yet in a public point of view I cannot but regret your departure from your own country. It would give me pleasure could I say that I have any acquaintances in the literary world, through whom I could hope to aid you in disposing of *The Champion*. It will be very difficult, I fear impossible, to place the work in such hands as would support its present reputation, after you have resigned the management of it; and therefore I cannot but think you judge well and prudently in being desirous to *sell* the property, rather than entrust it to an editor or partner during your absence. But I have not a single acquaintance except Southey, to whom it would be advisable even to make known your intentions; for there is a disadvantage, as well as an advantage, in publicity upon occasions of this sort. . . . The queries you put to me upon the connection between genius and irregularity of conduct may probably induce me to take up the subject again, and yet it scarcely seems necessary. No man can claim indulgence for his transgressions on the score of his sensibilities, but at the expense of his credit for intellectual powers. All men of *first* rate genius have been as distinguished for dignity, beauty, and propriety of moral conduct. But we often find the faculties and qualities of the mind not well balanced; something of prime importance is left short, and hence confusion and disorder. On the one hand it is well that dunces should not arrogate to themselves a pharisaical superiority, because they avoid the vices and faults which they see men of talent fall into. They should not be permitted to believe that they have more understanding merely on that account, but should be taught that they are preserved probably by having less feeling, and being consequently less liable to temptation. On the other hand, the man of genius ought to know that the cause of his vices is, in fact, his deficiencies, and not, as he fondly imagines, his superfluities and superiorities. All men ought to be judged with charity and forbearance after death has put it out of their power to explain the motives of their actions, and especially men of acute sensibility and lively passions. This was the scope of my letter to Mr. Gray.[1] Burns has been cruelly used, both dead and alive. The treatment which Butler[2] and others have experienced has been renewed in him. He asked for bread—no, he did not *ask* it, he endured the want of it with silent fortitude—and ye gave him a stone. It is worse than ridiculous to see the people of Dumfries coming forward with their pompous mausoleum, they who persecuted and reviled him with such low-minded malignity. Burns might have said to that town when he was dying, 'Ingrata—non possidebis ossa mea!'[3] On this and a thousand other accounts his monument ought to have been placed in or near to Edinburgh; 'stately Edinburgh throned on crags.' How well would such an edifice have accorded with the pastoral imagery near St. Anthony's Well and under Arthur's Seat, while the metropolis of his native country,—to which his writings have done so great honour—with its murmuring sounds, was in distinct hearing! . . .

I must not conclude without a word upon politics. . . . I will not at present recur to our military disagreement, further than to repeat the expression of my own belief, that no danger to the civil liberties of the country—in the present state of public information, and with our present means of circulating truth—is to be apprehended from such scientific military establishments as appear to be eligible. And surely you will allow that martial qualities are the natural efflorescence of a healthy state of society. All great politicians seem to have been of this opinion; in modern times Machiavel, Lord Brooke,[4] Sir Philip Sydney, Lord Bacon, Harrington,[5] and lastly Milton, whose tractate of education never loses sight of the means of making man perfect, both for contemplation and action, for civil and military duties. But you are persuaded that if you take care of our civil privileges, they will

---

[1] *A Letter to a Friend of Robert Burns*, 1816.

[2] Samuel Butler (1612–80), author of *Hudibras*.

[3] The epitaph of Scipio Africanus, inscribed on his tomb near Naples after his rejection from Rome.

[4] Sir Fulke Greville, Lord Brooke (1554–1628), poet and courtier.

[5] James Harrington (1611–77), republican: author of *Oceana*.

generate all that can be needed of warlike excellence; and here only we differ. My opinion is that much of immediate fitness for warlike exploit may co-exist with a perfect security of our rights as citizens. Nay, I will go farther, and affirm that tendencies to degradation in our national chivalry may be counteracted by the existence of those capabilities for war in time of peace. But this point I do not wish to press. War we shall have, and I fear shortly—and alas! we are little fit to undertake it. At present there is nothing relating to politics, on which I should so much like to converse with you, as the conduct which it is desirable that the king of France should pursue. The French nation is less fitted than any other to be governed by moderation. Nothing but heat and passion will have any sway with them. Things must pass with them, as they did with us, in the first and second Charles's time, from one extreme to the other. Something to this effect is thrown out in a late number of *The Courier*; and I confess I have myself been long of that opinion. The reforming Royalists in Charles the First's time vanished before the Presbyterians, they before the Independents, they before the Army, and the Army before Cromwell; then things ran to the opposite extreme, with a force not to be resisted. Louis the Eighteenth stands as the successor of Cromwell, and not like our Revolution William. The throne of a James-the-Second Louis cannot I fear stand, but by the support of the passions of an active portion of his subjects; and how can such passions be generated but by deviation into what a moderate man would call ultra-royalist. Justice in the settlement of affairs has been cruelly disappointed, and this feeling it is which gives strength and a seeming reasonableness to these passions. The compromises *once* were intolerable . . .

79. *To* Henry Crabb Robinson

Rydale Mount near Ambleside.
August 2nd 1816

My dear Sir,

It gave me much pleasure to see your Friend Mr Cargill; though I am sorry to say that his looks and appearance were so much altered by delicate not to say bad health that I did not at first recollect him.—In fact he had found himself so far untuned on his arrival at Kendal as to deem it adviseable to halt there for two days: and in consequence of this consumption of his time he could only spare one day for this neighbourhood, being anxious to reach Edingh[1] as quickly as possible. I need not say that I found his manners and conversation answer the promises of your introductory letter, and that I parted from him with regret, which was not a little encreased by an impression upon my mind that the rest would have been a better thing for him than Eñborogh bustle, or a fatiguing and harassing journey among the bad and widely-parted Inns of the Highlands.

The hope of seeing you here is very grateful to me; and upon a supposition that you propose to take some pains in seeing the Country I will proceed to give you directions for doing it to the best advantage. London, Manchester, *Lancaster*, (the Castle is extremely well worth your notice): at this Town, instead of proceeding by the Coach to Kendal, enquire about the best mode of crossing the Sands to Ulverstone; a Coach used to go, but whether it runs now or not, I cannot say: of course you must take care to cross these sands at a proper time, or you will run a risk of being drowned, a catastrophe to which I would not willingly be instrumental. At Ulverstone you will be within 7 or 8 miles of the celebrated abbey of St Mary's, commonly called Furness Abbey. These Ruins are very striking, and in an appropriate situation; if you should think it worth while to go and see them, the best way would be for you and your Friend to hire a Chaise, as by so doing you would preserve your strength, and only need consume three hours in the Expedition. Should you not deem this sight [? to your] taste (for you would have to go and to come back by the same way), you will proceed straight from Ulverstone to Coniston Water, by Penny Bridge, where is a decent Inn; at the head of Coniston Lake a very good one delightfully situated. If so inclined, you might pass a whole day very pleasantly there, the morning rowing upon the water, the afternoon walking up and through Eugh-dale into Tilberthwaite and taking care to return from Tilberthwaite, by a house called the Eugh-tree, and up a road which will lead you near another Farmhouse called Tarn Hows, at a point in this Road you

[1] Edinburgh.

will suddenly come upon a fine prospect of Coniston Lake, looking
down it. From Coniston to Hawkshead; At Hawkshead walk up
into the Churchyard, and notice below you the School House,
which has sent forth many northern lights, and among others your
humble servant. From Hawkshead proceed to the Ferry-House
upon Windermere, and less than a quarter of a mile before you
reach it stop, and put yourself under the guidance of an old
Woman, who will come out to meet you if you ring or call for her at
a fantastic sort of gateway, an appurtenance to a *Pleasure-House* of
that celebrated Patriot Mr Curwen, called the Station. The Ferry
Inn is very respectable, and that at Bowness excellent. Cross at the
Ferry, and proceed by Bowness up the lake towards Ambleside;
you will pass Low-wood, an excellent Inn also, but here you would
be within four miles of Rydale Mount, where I shall be most happy
to see you and furnish you with a bed as long as you like; but I am
sorry to say it will [not] be in my power to accommodate your
Friend, who nevertheless shall be welcome for your sake. Here you
will have further directions. I shall do everything in my power to be
at home when you come, but many engagements have devolved
upon me in consequence of the lamented death of my Brother,[1] and
some, I fear, are too likely to press upon me about the time of your
intended Tour.

The Road I have chalked out is much the best for commencing
the Tour, but few take it. The usual way is to come on directly to
Kendal, but I can assure you that this deviation from the common
course will amply repay you.

I am glad that you were pleased with my Odes etc [?][2] They were
poured out with much feeling, but from mismanagement of myself
the labour of making some verbal corrections cost me more health
and strength than anything of that sort ever did before. I have
written nothing since—and as to Publishing I shall give it up, as
no-body will buy what I send forth: nor can I expect it seeing what
stuff the public appetite is set upon. As to your advice about *touring*,
that subject we will talk of when we meet. My whole soul was with
those who were resolved to fight it out with Bonaparte; and my
heart of hearts set against those who had so little confidence in the
power of justice or so small discernment concerning its nature, as
to be ready at any moment to accept of such a truce, as under the

[1] Richard.   [2] *Thanksgiving Ode . . . with Other Short Pieces*, 1816.

name of peace he might condescend to bestow. For the personal
character of the present ministry, with the exception of Lord
Hawksbury[1] I cannot say to you that I entertain any high respect,
but I do conscientiously believe that they have not been wanting in
efforts to economise and that the blame of unnecessary expendi-
ture, wherever that exists, rests with the Prince Regent. Adieu.

Faithfully yours,
W Wordsworth

The ladies under my roof join in best regards and remembrance—[2]

80. *To* Charles Lamb

Rydal Mount 21st Nov^r [1816]

Dear Lamb,

Miss H. writes that you may *read*.—W. H.[3] is much such a
drawer of characters, as, judging from the specimens of art which
he has left in this country, he is a portrait painter. He tried his hand
upon me. My brother Richard happened to come into the room
where his work was suspended, saw, stopt, I believe recoiled, and
exclaimed *God Zounds!* a criticism as emphatic as it was concise. He
was literally *struck* with the strength of the sign-board likeness; but
never, till that moment, had he conceived that so much of the
diabolical lurked under the innocent features of his quondam
playmate, and respected Friend and dear Brother. Devils may be
divided into two large classes, first, the malignant and mis-
chievous,—those who are bent upon all of evil-doing that is prayed
against in the Litany; and secondly those which have so thorough a
sense of their own damnation, and the misery consequent upon
it, as to be incapable of labouring a thought injurious to the
tranquillity of others. The pencil of W. H. is potent in delineating
both kinds of physiognomy. My Portrait was an example of the
one; and a Picture of Coleridge, now in existence at Keswick (mine

---

[1] Now Lord Liverpool, the Prime Minister.   [2] D. W. adds a PS.
[3] William Hazlitt, who had painted portraits of W. W. and S. T. C. in 1803 (see
also Letter 33 above), had recently attacked S. T. C. and his *Statesman's Manual*, in
the *Examiner*.

has been burnt) is of the other. This piece of art is not producable for fear of fatal consequences to married Ladies, but is kept in a private room, as a special treat to those who may wish to sup upon horrors. As H. served the person of Coleridge, fifteen years ago, now has he served his mind; a likeness, it must be acknowledged there is, but one takes refuge from the spectacle in detestation (in this latter instance) of the malevolence by which the monstrous caricature was elaborated.

By the bye, an event has lately occured in our neighbourhood which would raise the character of its population in the estimation of that roving God Pan, who some years ago made his appearance among us. You will recollect, and Mr Henry Robinson will more easily recollect, that a little Friend of our's was profuse in praises of the 'more than beauty'—'the angelic sweetness'—that pervaded the features of a fair young Cottager dwelling upon the banks of Rydal mere. To be brief, Love and opportunity have wrought so much upon the tender frame of this terrestrial angel, that, to the surprize of Gods, Men, and Matrons, she has lately brought forth a Man child to be known, and honored, by the name of *William*, and so called after a deceased Brother of its acknowledging Father Thomas de Q—.[1] Such, in these later times, are the fruits of philosophy ripening under the shelter of our Arcadian mountains. A marriage is expected by some; but, from the known procrastination of one of the parties, it is not looked for by others till the commencement of the millenium. In the meanwhile he has a proud employment in nursing the new-born.

Let me hear that the Shoemaker has not bullied you out of your intention of completing the meditated Essays. Southey, of whom H. affects to talk contemptuously, beats us all hollow in interesting and productive power. If he reads, if he talks, if he is talked to, he turns it all to account: behold! it is upon paper, it is in print; and the whole world reads, or many read it, sure of being always entertained, and often instructed. If the attainment of just notions be an evidence of ability, Southey will be cherished by posterity when the reputation of those, who now so insolently decry him, will be rotted away and dispersed upon the winds. I wish to hear from you, and not unfrequently. You are better off than we—inasmuch as London contains one person whose conversation is worth

[1] De Quincey married Margaret Simpson the following February.

listening to—whereas here we are in an utter desert, notwithstanding we have a very amiable and edifying Parson; an intelligent Doctor; an honest Attorney (for he is without practice); a Lady of the Manor, who has a Spice of the romantic; Landscape Painters who are fraught with admiration, at least of their own works; Irish Refugees, and Liverpool Bankrupts, without number.—Have you seen a thing advertized called the *Poetic Mirror*? a parody which selects, as a Subject for my Muse, 'The flying Taylor'. You will call to mind that I told you there was a person, in this neighbourhood, who from his agility, had acquired this name—hence a thought crossed my mind that the Author of this *Skit* might be of your acquaintance; but as he has selected *three* Scotch Poets—Hogg,[1] Scott, and Wilson—to the exclusion of English ones of near equal eminence and more merit, I conclude that he is some Sawney ayont the Tweed, who has been resident in this Country and probably about the time when the annual sports bring the flying Taylor into notice. To conclude—I remain, in good health, and not bad spirits notwithstanding the bad weather and hard times,

Your friend to command,

Wm Wordsworth

81. *To* Daniel Stuart

April 7, 1817, Rydale Mount.

My dear Sir,

It was only two days ago that I received an acknowledgement from France of the money having been received, otherwise I should have thanked you before for your obliging Letter. You make mention only of £30; in fact I ordered £35 to be paid to you, and on application to the Bank of Kendal they tell me that Sum was paid, and I dare say you remitted to Mr Beaudouin[2] to that amount, though his Letter does not specify the sum he received, but simply says 'la Rente'. I should like to know *at your leisure*, whether you actually received and remitted 30 or 35, for I do not like, for particular reasons, to ask him what sum he received.—30 pounds

---

[1] James Hogg (1770–1835), 'the Ettrick Shepherd'.

[2] Husband of W. W.'s 'French' daughter Caroline. W. W. paid her an annual allowance after her marriage.

was the sum you had sent on my account the year before, and probably that occasioned the mistake in your recollection.—

Many thanks for your communications on the subject of Politics. There has been a general outcry among sensible people in this neighbourhood against the remissness of Government in permitting the free circulation of injurious writings. It has been especially felt in regard to the blasphemous parodies upon the Liturgy; no one can comprehend why these things should not be suppressed and the Authors or publishers punished. The suspension of the Habeas Corpus Act is a measure approved by all the well disposed, who are a large majority of the influential part of the Country. In fact also the spirit among the labouring classes (with the exception of the populace of Carlisle) is incomparably better than it was in 1794 and 5. The agricultural population of Cumberland and Westmoreland is at present sound; but I would not engage that it will continue so, in case rebellion should get the upper hand in other parts of the Island. A Revolution will, I think, be staved off for the present, nor do I even apprehend that the disposition to rebellion may not without difficulty be suppressed, notwithstanding the embarrassments and heavy distresses of the times. Nevertheless I am like you, an alarmist and for this reason, I see clearly that the principal ties which kept the different classes of society in a vital and harmonious dependence upon each other have, within these 30 years either been greatly impaired or wholly dissolved. Everything has been put up to market and sold for the highest price it would bring. Farmers used formerly to be attached to their Landlords, and labourers to their Farmers who employed them. All that kind of feeling has vanished—in like manner, the connexion between the trading and landed interests of country towns undergoes no modification whatsoever from personal feeling, whereas within my memory it was almost wholly governed by it. A country squire, or substantial yeoman, used formerly to resort to the same shops which his father had frequented before him, and nothing but a serious injury real or supposed would have appeared to him a justification for breaking up a connexion which was attended with substantial amity and interchanges of hospitality from generation to generation. All this moral cement is dissolved, habits and prejudices are broken and rooted up; nothing being substituted in their place but a quickened selfinterest, with more extensive views,—and wider dependencies,—but more lax in proportion as they are wider. The ministry will do well if they keep things quiet for the present, but if our present constitution in church and state is to last, it must rest as heretofore upon a moral basis; and they who govern the country must be something superior to mere financiers and political economists. Farewell do let me hear from you,

> I remain very faithfully yours,
> W. Wordsworth

(turn over)

Southey is going to Town shortly on his way for a short trip on the Continent. I saw him a few days ago quite well, and preparing a Rod for Mr Wm Smith.[1]

82. *To* J. P. Collier

> [London]
> Wednesday [Dec. 1817 *or* Jan. 1818]

My dear Sir,

Coleridge,[2] to whom all but certain reviewers wish well, intends to try the effect of another course of Lectures in London on poetry generally, and on Shakespeare's poetry particularly. He gained some money and reputation by his last effort of the kind, which was, indeed, to him no effort, since his thoughts as well as his words flow spontaneously. He talks as a bird sings, as if he could not help it: it is his nature. He is now far from well in body or spirits: the former is suffering from various causes, and the latter from depression. No man ever deserved to have fewer enemies, yet, as he thinks and says, no man has more, or more virulent. You have long been among his friends; and as far as you can go, you will no doubt prove it on this as on other occasions. We are all anxious on his account. He means to call upon you himself, or write from Highgate, where he now is.

> Yours sincerely,
> W. Wordsworth

[1] The MP, who had attacked Southey's *Wat Tyler*.
[2] S. T. C. had now become a permanent inmate of the Gillman household at Highgate, where he was to remain for the rest of his days.

83. *To* the Earl of Lonsdale

Rydal Mount
10 Feb^{ry} 1818

My Lord,

The Committee have now entered into the thing in earnest,[1] and begin to understand the business, in which they were unavoidably inexperienced, at first. Everything looks brighter. The day after I had the honor of your Lordship's of the 4th Ins^t, I went over to Kendal, and on a suggestion of Lord Lowther, that I would consider if the Editor of the Kendal Paper[2] could not be induced to deal fairly with our cause,—I saw him, and represented to him how ill his promises of impartiality had been kept; and entered so fully into every branch of the subject, that I trust good will result from the Interview, as he acknowledged the reasonableness of what I said. He engaged to publish a notice to correspondents that nothing defamatory or personal should be admitted from either side; and that the accounts of proceedings, to the best of his judgement, should be fair. He pleaded hurry (having only just entered on his office) for what I complained of; and said that no paper in support of the Lowther interest had been refused admittance.—Much of the abuse, which to my knowledge has done great mischief, found its way into the Paper, under the shape of Letters, often inserted for mere want of matter to fill the Columns. Being a dissenter the present Editor has naturally a strong bias to opposition, and complaint; but he is no approver of Mr Brougham, deems him unfit to represent any county, and regards him as a trading Publican. He has refused Mr B. his vote, and means to vote on neither side, unless (a reservation which is suspicious) he is provoked by the Intemperance of either Party.

In consequence of what I gathered, concerning the difficulty of filling the Paper, I have urged our friends to write, and shall write myself, were it only to keep others out.—I have prepared two addresses to the Freeholders,[3] one of which is left for publication in the paper, and the other shall follow next week, at least part of it.

As the Com. have struck off another thousand of the paper

---

[1] In the impending Westmorland election, Henry Brougham (1778–1868), the radical, was standing against Lord Lonsdale's sons Lord Lowther and Col. H. C. Lowther, the Tory candidates.   [2] The *Kendal Chronicle*.   [3] Publ. 1818.

signed, a Friend to Consistency,[1] I presume they have found it serviceable notwithstanding my fears; indeed, I was told so, but I begged they would look carefully to the subject.

Not to exclude or give offence to Dissenters, who are very powerful in Kendal, I recommended 'King and Constitution' in preference to 'Church and King' as the latter part of the Lowther motto.

I saw Mr Isaac Wilson,[2]—his report is favorable; but many inwardly well-inclined hang back through fear that by a too hasty shew of strength, they should be disappointed of a journey to Appleby, and the riotous pleasure of an Election.

I should have met Lord Lowther and the Col: at Kendal, but as the pretext of this outcry is Independence, I thought it better, considering the office which I hold, by Your Lordship's patronage, to keep out of the way.[3] I wish much for half an hour's quiet conversation, with either of the Members; and will wait upon them at their convenience.

Mr B's correspondence with Mr W[4] may be turned forcibly against him; but your Lordship's dignified reply ought to go along with it, to give the thing its full effect.

I rejoice to hear that Lady Mary[5] is better.

> I have the honor to be
> with highest respect
> My Lord
> Your Lordship's
> faithfully and truly
> W Wordsworth

84. *To* Viscount Lowther

[*c.* 14 Apr. 1818]

My dear Lord Lowther,

As Lord Lonsdale and yourself approve of the *doctrines* and Spirit of the Addresses, I will set them afloat in their present shape in

[1] By W. W.: publ. in the *Kendal Chronicle* and as a handbill.
[2] A Lowther supporter.
[3] As a civil servant, W. W. was not allowed to take part in elections.
[4] Wilberforce. Brougham had sought his help at a previous election.
[5] Lord Lonsdale's daughter.

such directions as seem most likely to make them serviceable; which need not prevent their being given piecemeal according to the plan recommended by you, in the Carlisle Patriot.

The notes upon Brougham's Speech, I have not seen, unless they be those from the pen of Mr De Quincey[1] of Grasmere, which, in your hurry, you may have fogotten that we read together at Kendal,—and that a passage was interwoven by me, at that time. It related to facts.

Nothing material has lately occurred in this neighbourhood. I hear from Kendal that Brougham has hurt himself in several quarters, by the violence and jacobinical character of his late Speeches in Westmorland.

Calvert[2] thinks that they will not be able to carry on the Election for want of money. I did not hear this opinion from himself, but from good authority. He is likely to know what is the state of their funds.

The delay of the new Kendal Paper,[3] is much to be regretted.

Your Lordship's intention about the allowance for the Princes is very prudent. It seems impolitic in the Ministers to bring things of this sort forward, on the Eve of a general Election.

James Brougham[4] is expected in this neighbourhood, on Monday next. I have written to Col. Lowther, urging him to come among us as soon as possible.

I have the honor to be
my dear Lord Lowther
very faithfully yours
W. Wordsworth

Be so good as to cast your eye over the Enclosed to Mr Wilkin.[5]

85. *To* J. Forbes Mitchell

Rydal Mount, Apr. 21st 1819.

Sir,

The letter with which you have honoured me, bearing date the 31st of March, I did not receive until yesterday; and therefore

---

[1] His pamphlet *Close Comments on a Straggling Speech.*   [2] William Calvert.

[3] *The Westmorland Gazette*, which De Quincey was to edit.

[4] Brougham's brother.   [5] A Lowther supporter.

could not earlier express my regret that, notwithstanding a cordial approbation of the *feeling* which has prompted the undertaking, and a genuine sympathy in admiration with the Gentlemen who have subscribed towards a Monument for Burns, I cannot unite my humble efforts with theirs in promoting this object. Sincerely can I affirm that my respect for the motives which have swayed these gentlemen has urged me to trouble you with a brief statement of the reasons of my dissent. In the first place, Eminent poets appear to me to be a Class of men who, less than any others, stand in need of such marks of distinction, and hence I infer that this mode of acknowledging their merits is one for which they would not, in general, be themselves solicitous. Burns did, indeed, erect a monument to Ferguson;[1] but I apprehend that his gratitude took this course because he felt that Ferguson had been prematurely cut off, and that his fame bore no proportion to his deserts. In neither of these particulars can the fate of Burns justly be said to resemble that of his Predecessor, his years indeed were few, but numerous enough to allow him to spread his name far and wide, and to take permanent root in the affections of his Countrymen: in short he has raised for himself a Monument so conspicuous, and of such imperishable materials, as to render a local fabric of Stone superfluous, and therefore comparatively insignificant. But why, if this be granted, should not his fond admirers be permitted to indulge their feelings, and at the same time to embellish the Metropolis of Scotland? If this may be justly objected to, and in my opinion it may, it is because the showy Tributes to Genius are apt to draw of[f] attention from those efforts by which the interests of Literature might be substantially promoted; and to exhaust public spirit in comparatively unprofitable exertions, when the wrongs of literary men are crying out for redress on all sides. It appears to me that towards no class of his Majesty's Subjects are the laws so unjust and oppressive.—The attention of Parliament has lately been directed by petition to the exaction of copies of newly published Works for certain Libraries; but this is a trifling evil compared with the restrictions imposed upon the duration of Copyright, which in respect to Works profound in philosophy, or elevated, abstract, and refined in imagination, is tantamount almost to an exclusion of all pecuniary recompense for the Author,

[1] Robert Ferguson (1750–74), the Scottish poet.

and even where Works of imagination and manners are so constituted as to be adapted to immediate demand, as in the case of those of Burns, justly may it be asked what reason can be assigned that an Author who dies young should have the prospect before him of his Children being left to languish in Poverty and Dependence, while Booksellers are revelling in luxury upon gains derived from Works which are the delight of many Nations.

This subject might be carried much further, and we might ask, if the course of things insured immediate wealth, and accompanying rank and honours, honours and wealth often entailed on their families to Men distinguished in the other learned professions, why the laws should interfere to take away those pecuniary emoluments which are the natural Inheritance of the posterity of Authors whose pursuits, if directed by genius and sustained by industry, yield in importance to none in which the Members of a Community can be engaged.

But to recur to the proposal in your letter:—I would readily assist, according to my means, in erecting a Monument to the memory of Chatterton,[1] who with transcendent genius was cut off by his own hand while he was yet a Boy in years; this, could he have anticipated the tribute, might have soothed his troubled spirit; as an expression of general belief in the existence of those powers which he was too impatient and too proud to develop. At all events it might prove an awful, and a profitable warning—I should also be glad to see a monument erected on the banks of Lochleven to the memory of the innocent, and tender-hearted Michael Bruce,[2] who, after a short life spent in poverty and obscurity, was called away too early to leave behind him more than a few trustworthy promises of pure affections and unvitiated imagination.

Let the Gallant Defenders of our Country be liberally rewarded with Monuments: their noble Actions cannot speak for themselves as the Writings of Men of genius are able to do; gratitude in respect to them stands in need of admonition; and the very multitude of Heroic competitors, which increase the demand for this sentiment towards our Naval and Military defenders considered as a Body, is injurious to the claims of Individuals.—Let our great Statesmen

[1] Thomas Chatterton (1752–70).
[2] Michael Bruce (1746–67), whose *Poems* were published posthumously.

and eminent Lawyers, our learned and eloquent Divines, and they who have successfully devoted themselves to the abstruser Sciences, be rewarded in like manner; but towards departed Genius, exerted in the fine Arts and more especially in Poetry, I humbly think, in the present state of things, the sense of our obligation to it may more satisfactorily be expressed by means pointing directly to the general benefit of Literature.

Trusting that these opinions of an Individual will be candidly interpreted, I have the honour to be,

Your obedient servant
Wm Wordsworth

86. *To* the Earl of Lonsdale

Rydal Mount
Sept 22nd [1819]

My Lord,

Prince Leopold[1] may be inclined to visit Keswick from Lowther: should this be the intention of his R.H:, allow me, in the absence of Mr Southey, to suggest that the Lake is seen to great advantage from General Peachey's House upon the Island, and also from Friar's Crag on the opposite shore.—Mr Gray's[2] account of the lakes printed as an Appendix to Mr West's Guide, is the best. Treating of Keswick Vale, he speaks in high terms of the view from the Hersing-block close to the Vicarage. Plantations made since his time have hindered a just proportion of the lake being seen from this point. The view is now much better from the neighbourhood of Ormathwaite and from the *new road* close under Skiddaw by Applethwaite—proceeding towards Bassenthwaite less than $\frac{1}{2}$ a mile and returning the same way. Lowdore and Borrowdale as far as Bowder Stone are well worth visiting returning to Keswick by the opposite side of the Lake. In the Vale of Grasmere, if there should be 10 minutes to spare, when the Swan Inn is reached enquire for a small Hill called Butterlip How, it commands a panorama view of this celebrated Vale—thence proceeding by the

---

[1] Uncle of Queen Victoria, and later King of the Belgians.
[2] Thomas Gray.

Church to rejoin the road, leading to Ambleside by Rydal. The Valley of Ambleside is perhaps nowhere better seen than from the Terrace at Rydal Mount—the grounds of Rydal Hall with their Waterfalls are known to everyone. Your Lordship will infer from this letter that I am not much relieved. Greatly regretting my inability to be with you to-morrow I have the honour

My Lord, your faithful

Friend and Serv[t]

Wm Wordsworth

87. *To* B. R. Haydon

Rydale Mount near Ambleside. 16th January, 1820

My dear Friend,

Mr Monkhouse[1] has probably informed you how far I have suffered under the same malady as yourself.—I am better so far as to be able to use my eyes by day; but I neither write nor read by Candle light.—I do most sincerely rejoice in *your* recovery—and congratulate you with all my heart on the completion of your Picture;[2] of which I hear from our common Friends the Beaumonts the most excellent accounts. Indeed they speak of it in the highest terms.—Your most valuable Drawing[3] arrived, when I was unable to enjoy it as it deserved. I did not like to employ an Amanuensis to thank you for it; as I hoped for a speedy recovery:—a hope I shall not indulge in again as I am convinced that the organ of sight is with me in a precarious state; that is very irritable and subject to inflammation. Under these circumstances as I was sure of your painful sympathy I ran the risk of incurring your displeasure, as the less evil of the two—Your drawing is much admired as a work of art; some think it a stodgy likeness; but in general it is not deemed so—for my own part I am proud to possess it as a mark of your regard, and for its own merits.

I purpose being in London in the Spring; when I trust I shall find you well and prosperous. Do you ever hear of John

[1] Thomas Monkhouse, M. W.'s cousin.
[2] *Christ's Entry into Jerusalem.*
[3] The chalk drawing (1818), now in the National Portrait Gallery.

Scott—pray how is he? and where; if you are in communication with him let him know that I am much interested in his welfare.—Mr Monkhouse, I understand, you see occasionally, and through him we hear of you; always with lively interest. Now that you have recovered your eyes, paint, and leave writing to the dunces and malignants with which London swarms—You have taken too much trouble about them.—How is Keates,[1] he is a youth of promise too great for the sorry company he keeps. You perhaps have heard from Mr Monkhouse that my younger son is at the Central School, Baldwyns Gardens. I should like you to know what impression your picture makes upon him, and shall beg of Mr Monkhouse to take him to see it. Do you skate, we have charming diversion in that way about our lakes. I wish you were here to partake of it. The splendor of the snow-clad mountains, by moonlight in particular is most charming; and the softness of the shadows surpasses anything you can conceive; this when the moon is at a particular point of elevation. I never saw any thing so exquisite; though I believe Titian has; *and* so, therefore, perhaps may you.—Let me hear from you at your leisure, and particularly how far you are pleased with your own performance. If I could see your Picture, I think it would inspire me with a Sonnet; and indeed without seeing it I do not lack matter for so slight a tribute to your merit.—Mrs Wordsworth and Miss Hutchinson join me in most hearty congratulation, and sincerest regards; and believe me, my dear Haydon,

Your faithful friend
and sincere admirer
Wm Wordsworth

88. *To* the Earl of Lonsdale

Paris, October 7 [1820], 45 Rue Charlot,
Boulevards du Temple.

My Lord,

I had the honor of writing to your Lordship from Lucerne, 19th of August, giving an account of our movements. We have visited,

---

[1] W. W. had met John Keats (1795–1821) in London in Dec. 1817.

since, those parts of Switzerland usually deemed most worthy of notice, and the Italian Lakes; having stopped four days at Milan, and as many at Geneva. With the exception of a couple of days on the Lake of Geneva, the weather has been most favorable, though frequently, during the last fortnight, extremely cold. We have had no detention from illness, nor any bad accident, for which we feel more grateful, on account of some of our fellow-travellers, who accidentally joined us for a few days. Of these, one, an American gentleman, was drowned in the Lake of Zurich, by the upsetting of a boat in a storm, two or three days after he parted with us; and two others, near the summit of Mount Jura, and in the middle of a tempestuous night, were precipitated, they scarcely knew how far, along with one of those frightful and ponderous vehicles, a continental Diligence. We have been in Paris since Sunday last; and think of staying about a fortnight longer, as scarcely less will suffice for even a hasty view of the Town and neighbourhood. We took Fontainebleau in our way, and intend giving a day to Versailles. The day we entered Paris we passed a well-drest young man and woman dragging a harrow through a field, like cattle; nevertheless, working in the fields on the Sabbath Day does not appear to be general in France. On the same day, a wretched-looking Person begged of us, as the Carriage was climbing a Hill; nothing could exceed his transport in receiving a pair of old Pantaloons which were thrown him from the carriage. This poor mendicant, the Postilion told us, was an *ancien Curé*. The churches seem generally falling to decay in the country. We passed one which had been recently repaired. I have noticed, however, several young persons, men as well as women, earnestly employed in their devotions, in different churches, both in Paris and elsewhere.— Nothing which I have seen in this city has interested me at all like the *Jardin des Plantes*, with the living animals, and the Museum of Natural History which it includes. Scarcely could I refrain from tears of admiration at the sight of this apparently boundless exhibition of the wonders of the creation. The Statues and pictures of the Louvre affect me feebly in comparison. The exterior of Paris is much changed since I last visited it in 1792. I miss many antient Buildings, particularly the Temple, where the poor king and his family were so long confined. That memorable spot where the Jacobin Club was held, has also disappeared. Nor are the additional buildings always improvements; the *Pont des Arts*, in particular, injures the view from the *Pont Neuf* greatly; but in these things public convenience is the main point.

I say nothing of public affairs, for I have little opportunity of knowing anything about them. In respect to the business of our Queen,[1] we deem ourselves truly fortunate in having been out of the country, at a time when an inquiry at which all Europe seems scandalized, was going on.

I have purposely deferred congratulating your Lordship on the marriage of Lady Mary with Lord Frederick Bentinck, which I hear has been celebrated. My wishes for her happiness are most earnest.

With respectful compliments and congratulations to Lady Lonsdale, in which Mrs. Wordsworth begs leave to join, I have the honour to be, my Lord

Your Lordship's
obliged and faithful friend and servant,
Wm Wordsworth

PS

I am at a loss whither to direct, but I risk Lowther Castle, thinking that your late arrival there may detain you beyond your usual time.

89. *To* Sir George Beaumont

10th Jan ry, 1821.

My dear Sir George,

Yesterday I performed a great feat—wrote no less than 7 letters, reserving yours for to-day, that I might have more leisure, and you consequently less trouble in reading. I have been a good deal tossed about since our arrival here. Mrs W. and I were first called away by the sudden death of my near kinsman, Mr Myers. We went to College together, and were inseparables for many years. I saw him buried in Millom Church, by the side of his Wife. The churchyard is romantically situated; Duddon Sands on one side,

[1] The trial of Queen Caroline.

and a rocky Hill scattered over with antient trees on the other. Close by are the remains of the old Castle of the Huddlestones, part of which are converted into farm Houses, and the whole embowered in tall trees that tower up from the sides and bottom of the circular moat. The churchyard is in like manner girt round with trees.—The church is of striking architecture, and apparently of remote antiquity.—We entered with the funeral train, the day being too far advanced to allow the clergyman to see to read the service, and no light had been provided; so we sat some time, in solemn silence. At last one candle was brought, which served both for minister and clerk, casting a wan light on their faces. On my right hand were two stone figures in a recumbent Position (like those of the monument in Coleorton church)—Huddlestones of other years; and the voice of the minister was accompanied, and almost interrupted by the slender sobbing of a young person, an Indian by half blood, and by the father's side a niece of the deceased wife of the person whom we were interring. She hung over the coffin and continued this oriental lamentation till the service was over, everybody else, except one faithful servant, being apparently indifferent. Mrs W. I find has mentioned our return by Duddonside, and how much we were pleased with the winter appearance of my favourite River.

Since that expedition I have been called to Appleby, and detained there upon business. In returning, I was obliged to make a circuit which showed me for the [first] time several miles of the Course of that beautiful stream, the Eden, from the bridge near Temple Sowerby down to Kirkoswald. Part of this tract of country I had indeed seen before, but not from the same points of view. It is a charming region, particularly at the spot where the Eden and Emont join. The Rivers appeared exquisitely brilliant, gliding under Rocks and through green meadows, with woods and sloping cultivated grounds, and pensive russet moors interspersed, and along the circuit of the Horizon, lofty hills and mountains clothed, rather than concealed, in fleecy clouds and resplendent vapours.

My Road brought me suddenly and unexpectedly upon that ancient monument called by the Country People Long Meg and her Daughters.[1] Every body has heard of it, and so had I from very early childhood, but had never seen it before. Next to Stone Henge,

[1] A stone circle near Glassonby.

it is beyond dispute the most noble relick of the kind that this or probably any other country contains. Long Meg is a single block of unhewn stone, 18 feet high, at a small distance from a vast circle of other stones, some of them of huge size, though curtailed of their stature, by having sunk into the ground, by their own incessant pressure upon it. Did you ever see that part of the Eden? If not, you must contrive it. I was brought to Kirkoswald, but had not time to visit Nunnery,[1] which I purpose to do next summer. Indeed, we have a thought of taking the whole course of the Eden from Carlisle upwards, which will bring us near the source of the Lune, so that we may track that river to Lancaster, and so return home by Flookborough and Cartmel.

It is now high time to say a word about Coleorton. I often have the image before me of your pleasant Labours, and see the landscape growing under your patient hand. The large picture you were about must be finished long since. How are you satisfied with it? I am not a little proud that our scenery employs your pencil so sedulously after a visit to the Alps. It has lost little in my estimation by the comparison. At first I thought the coppice woods, and alas! we have little else, very shabby substitutes for the unshorn majesty of what I had lately seen. The rocks and crags also seem to want breadth and repose, their surfaces appearing too often crumbled and frittered. But, on the other hand, the comparison is often to our advantage. The lakes and streams not only are so much more pure and crystalline, but the surfaces of the one, and the courses of the other, present a far more attractive variety—a superiority which deserves to be set off at length, but which will strike your practised mind immediately.—It happened that Southey, who was so good as to come over to see us, mentioned to me Nichols' Book[2] with great commendation. I found also a vol. of it at Dr Satterthwaite's[3] who says that it is both instructive, exhaustive and entertaining. When you offered so kindly to present it to me I was unwilling that you should incur the expense, but now I confess I long to possess it, with the additional value of its coming from you.—Another obligation, but this at your perfect leisure, is the little oblong picture to match with the one I possess from the pencil of a friend

[1] An estate noted for its water-walks.
[2] *The History and Antiquities of the Town and County of Leicester*, 1795–1815.
[3] i.e. at Lowther rectory.

in Portugal. Its dimensions are marked at the foot of this sheet. A Pass on the banks of a rocky stream would please me much, or a *bit* of the Val d'enfer near Friburg, or a glade in a wood, or whatever you like.—My Sister reached home last Saturday; part of her journey was very perilous on account of a blinding fog. Two Coaches that preceded her had their four horses all down together in a pit.

Ever yours,
W. W.

90. *To* Walter Savage Landor

Rydal Mount, near Ambleside,
September 3^d, 1821.

My dear Sir,

After waiting several months in the hope that an irritation in my eyes which has disabled me both from reading and writing would abate, I am at last obliged to address you by means of the pen of Mrs Wordsworth, which however I should not have had courage to do, had not an opportunity occurred of forwarding my letter by a private hand, that of my esteemed Friend Mr Kenyon[1] who is not unknown to you. I felt myself much honoured by the present of your book of Latin Poems,[2] and it arrived at a time when I had the use of my eyes for reading; and with great pleasure did I employ them in the perusal of the dissertation annexed to your Poems, which I read several times—but the Poems themselves I have not been able to look into, for I was seized with a fit of composition at that time, and deferred the pleasure to which your Poems invited me, till I could give them an undivided attention; but alas the complaint in my eyes, to which I have been occasionally subject for several years past, suddenly returned and I have since suffered from it as already mentioned. I have also to thank you for a letter containing several miscellaneous observations in which I had the satisfaction of concurring.

We live here somewhat singularly circumstanced—in solitude during nearly nine months of the year, and for the rest in a round of

---

[1] See List of Correspondents.　　　[2] *Idyllia heroica decem*, 1820.

engagements. I have nobody near me who reads Latin, so that I can only speak of your Essay from recollection. You will not perhaps be surprized when I state that I differ from you in opinion as to the propriety of the Latin language being employed by Moderns for works of taste and imagination. Miserable would have been the lot of Dante, Ariosto, and Petrarch, if they had preferred the Latin to their Mother tongue (there is, by-the-by, a Latin translation of Dante which you do not seem to know), and what could Milton, who was surely no mean master of the Latin tongue, have made of his Paradise Lost, had that vehicle been employed instead of the language of the Thames and Severn! Should we even admit that all modern dialects are comparatively changeable, and therefore limited in their efficacy, may not the sentiment which Milton so pleasingly expresses when he says he is content to be read in his Native Isle only, be extended to durability, and is it not more desirable to be read with affection and pride, and familiarly for five hundred years, by all orders of mind, and all ranks of people, in your native tongue, than only by a few scattered Scholars for the space of three thousand? My own special infirmity moreover gives me an especial right to urge this argument—had your Idylliums been in English I should long ere this have been as well acquainted with them as with your Gebir,[1] and with your other Poems—and now I know not how long they may remain to me a sealed book.

I met with a hundred things in your Dissertation that fell in with my own sentiments and judgments; but there are many opinions which I should like to talk over with you. The ordonnance of your Essay might, I think, be improved, and several of the separate remarks, upon Virgil in particular, though perfectly just, would perhaps have been better placed in notes or an appendix; they are details that obstruct the view of the whole. Vincent Bourne[2] surely is not so great a favourite with you as he ought to be, though I acknowledge there is ground for your objection upon the score of ultra *concinnity* (a queer word for a female pen, Mrs W. has boggled at it) yet this applies only to a certain portion of his longs and shorts. Are you not also penurious in your praise of Gray? The fragment at the commencement of his fourth book,[3] in which he

---

[1] Publ. 1798.   [2] Vincent Bourne (1695–1747), poet in Latin.
[3] Of his *De Principiis Cogitandi*.

laments the death of West,[1] in cadence and sentiment, touches me in a manner for which I am grateful. The first book also of the same Poem appears to me as well executed as anything of the kind is likely to be. Is there not a speech of Solon to which the concluding couplet of Gray's sonnet bears a more pointed resemblance than to any of the passages you have quoted? He was told, not to grieve for the loss of his son, as tears would be of no avail; 'and for that very reason,' replied he, 'do I weep.' It is high time I should thank you for the honorable mention you have made of me. It could not but be grateful to me to be praised by a Poet who has written verses of which I would rather have been the Author than of any produced in our time. What I now write to you, I have frequently said to many. Were I able to recur to your book I should trespass further upon your time, which, however, might prove little to your advantage. I saw Mr Southey yesterday at his own house—he has not had his usual portion of relaxation this summer, and looked, I thought, a little pale in consequence—his little Boy is a stout and healthy Child and his other Children have in general good health, tho' at present a little relaxed by the few days of extreme heat. With best wishes for your health and happiness,

I remain, my dear sir, sincerely yours,

Wm Wordsworth

91. *To* James Losh

Rydal Mount, Dec[r] 4th 1821.

My dear Losh,

Your letter enclosing the Prescription ought to have been much earlier acknowledged, and would have been so, had I not been sure you would ascribe my silence to its true cause, viz procrastination, and not to indifference to your kind attention. There was another feeling which both urged and indisposed me to write to you,—I mean the allusion which in so friendly a manner you make to a supposed change in my Political opinions. To the Scribblers in

---

[1] A poet of promise, commemorated in Gray's sonnet *On the Death of Richard West*.

Pamphlets and Periodical publications who have heaped so much obloquy upon myself and my friends Coleridge and Southey, I have not condescended to reply, nor ever shall; but to you, my candid and enlightened Friend, I will say a few words on this Subject, which, if we have the good fortune to meet again, as I hope we may, will probably be further dwelt upon.

I should think that I had lived to little purpose if my notions on the subject of Government had undergone no modification—my youth must, in that case, have been without enthusiasm, and my manhood endued with small capability of profiting by reflexion. If I were addressing those who have dealt so liberally with the words Renegado, Apostate etc, I should retort the charge upon them, and say, *you* have been deluded by Places and Persons, while I have stuck to Principles—I abandoned France, and her Rulers, when they abandoned the struggle for Liberty, gave themselves up to Tyranny, and endeavoured to enslave the world. I disapproved of the war against France at its commencement, thinking, which was perhaps an error, that it might have been avoided—but after Buonaparte had violated the Independence of Switzerland, my heart turned against him, and the Nation that could submit to be the Instrument of such an outrage. Here it was that I parted, in feeling, from the Whigs, and to a certain degree united with their Adversaries, who were free from the delusion (such I must ever regard it) of Mr Fox and his Party, that a safe and honourable Peace was practicable with the French Nation, and that an ambitious Conqueror like B[uonaparte] could be softened down into a commercial Rival. In a determination, therefore, to aim at the overthrow of that inordinate Ambition by War, I sided with the Ministry, not from general approbation of their Conduct, but as men who thought right on this essential point. How deeply this question interested me will be plain to any one who will take the trouble of reading my political Sonnets, and the Tract occasioned by the Convention of Cintra, in which are sufficient evidences of my dissatisfaction with the mode of conducting the war, and a prophetic display of the course which it would take if carried on upon the principles of Justice, and with due respect for the feelings of the oppressed nations. This is enough for foreign politics, as influencing my attachments. There are three great domestic questions, viz. the liberty of the Press, Parliamentary reform, and

Roman Catholic concession, which, if I briefly advert to, no more need be said at present.

A free discussion of public measures thro' the Press I deem the *only* safeguard of liberty; without it I have neither confidence in Kings, Parliaments, Judges, or Divines—they have all in their turn betrayed their country. But the Press, so potent for good, is scarcely less so for evil; and unfortunately they who are misled and abused by its means are the Persons whom it can least benefit—it is the fatal characteristic of their disease to reject all remedies coming from the quarter that has caused or aggravated the malady. I am *therefore* for vigorous restrictions—but there is scarcely any abuse that I would not endure, rather than sacrifice, or even endanger this freedom.

When I was young, giving myself credit for qualities which I did not possess, and measuring mankind by that standard, I thought it derogatory to human nature to set up Property in preference to Person, as a title for legislative power. That notion has vanished. I now perceive many advantages in our present complex system of Representation, which formerly eluded my observation; this has tempered my ardour for Reform; but if any plan could be contrived for throwing the Representation fairly into the hands of the Property of the Country, and not leaving it so much in the hands of the large Proprietors as it now is, it should have my best support—tho', even in that event, there would be a sacrifice of Personal rights, independent of property, that are now frequently exercised for the benefit of the community.

Be not startled when I say that I am averse to further concessions to the Catholics. My reasons are, that such concessions will not produce harmony among the Catholics themselves— that they, among them who are most clamorous for the measure, care little about it but as a step, first, to the overthrow of the Protestant Est^nt in Ireland, as introductory to a Separation of the two Countries—their ultimate aim. That I cannot consent to take the character of a Religion from the declaration of powerful Professors of it disclaiming Doctrines imputed to that religion; that, taking its character from what it actually teaches to the great mass, I believe the Catholic religion to be unchanged in its doctrines and unsoftened in its spirit,—how can it be otherwise unless the doctrine of infallibility be given up? That such concessions would set all other Dissenters in motion—an issue which has never fairly been met by the Friends to concession; and deeming the Church Establishment not only a fundamental part of our Constitution, but one of the greatest Upholders and Propagators of civilization in our own Country, and, lastly, the most effectual and main Support of religious toleration, I cannot but look with jealousy upon Measures which must reduce her relative Influence, unless they be accompanied with arrangements more adequate than any yet adopted for the preservation and increase of that influence, to keep pace with the other Powers in the Community.

I do not apologize for this long letter, the substance of which you may report to any one worthy of a reply who, in your hearing, may animadvert upon my Political conduct. I ought to have added, perhaps, a word on *local politics*, but I have not space; but what I should have said may in a great measure be deduced from the above.

[Unsigned]

92. *To* John Kenyon

Lee Priory, May 16th [1823]

My dear Friend,

Your very welcome letter followed me to this place; the account it gave of your happiness and comfort was such as we wished to hear—may the like blessings be long, very long, continued to you—changing their character only according to the mildest influences of time! You gave me liberty to reply to your letter as might suit what you knew of my procrastinating disposition—I caught at this, but be assured you would have heard from me immediately if I could have held out any hopes, either to myself or you, that we should be able to accept of your kind invitation to visit you and Mrs K. (with whom we should be most happy to become acquainted) at Bath. We came hither 5 weeks ago, meaning after a fortnight's stay to cross the Channel for a little Tour in Flanders and Holland—but we had calculated, as the saying is, without our Host—the Spring was tardy and froward—when a day or two of fine weather came, they were followed by blustering, and even tempestuous, winds—these abated, and out came my own vernal enemy, the Inflammation in my eyes, which dashed our resolutions, and here I am, still obliged to employ Mrs W. as my amanuensis.

This day however being considerably better we shall go to Dover with a view to embark for Ostend to-morrow; unless detained by similar obstacles. From Ostend we mean to go to Ghent, to Antwerp, Breda, Utrecht, Amsterdam—to Rotterdam by Harlem, the Hague and Leyden—thence to Antwerp by another route, and perhaps shall return by Mechlin, Brussels, Lille and Ypres to Calais—or direct to Ostend as we came. We hope to be landed in England within a month. We shall hurry thro' London homewards, where we are naturally anxious already to be, having left Rydal Mount so far back as February.

Now for a word about yourself, my d[r] Friend. You had long been followed, somewhat blindly, by our good wishes; we had heard nothing of you, except thro' Mr Quillinan[1] and from Mr Monkhouse. If there was any fault in your not writing sooner, you make amends by entering so kindly into the particulars of what you had done and proposed to do; where you are living, and how you were as to estate, body and mind. It is among my hopes that, either in Westmoreland or West of England, I may at no very distant time be a witness of your happiness; and notwithstanding all my faults and waywardness, have an opportunity of recommending myself to the good graces of your Help-mate.

I have time for little more; as, in an hour and a half, we must leave our good friends here—this elegant Conventual Mansion,[2] with its pictures and its books, and bid a farewell to its groves and nightingales, which this morning have been singing divinely—by the bye it has been so cold that they are silent during the season of darkness. These delights we must surrender and take our way on foot three miles along the pleasant banks of Stour to fall in with the Dover coach. At this moment the S.W. wind is blustering abominably, and whirling the leaves and blossoms about in a way that reminds me of the tricks it is playing with the surf on the naked

---

[1] W. W.'s future son-in-law (see List of Correspondents).

[2] Lee Priory, Wyatt's Gothic mansion, formerly home of Sir Egerton Brydges, the bibliophile and poet, E. Q.'s father-in-law.

coast of Ostend—but courage! we depart with many good wishes, to which yours shall be added as no act of presumption on our part. God bless you and yours! and grant us a happy meeting if not in this world, in a better! to which my wife says Amen.

Every aff^{ly} yours,
Wm Wordsworth

If you should be in London about a month hence let us know by a letter to the Post Off. Dover, as we should be sorry to pass thro' without a glimpse of you.

John is at New Coll. Oxford. Should you pass enquire after him—he would be overjoyed to see you.

93. *To* Henry Taylor

Rydal Mount, Dec^{br} 26th [1823]

Dear Sir,

You perhaps are not aware that the infirmity in my eyes makes me afraid of touching a pen, and, tho' they are always much better in winter than in the Summer Season, I am obliged, mostly to employ an Amanuensis, as I do at present. I should not, however, have failed to answer your obliging letter immediately, if I could have been of any service to you in the point to which you directed my attention. I have not, nor ever had, a single poem of Lord Byron's by me, except the Lara, given me by Mr Rogers, and therefore could not quote any thing illustrative of his poetical obligations to me: as far as I am acquainted with his works, they are most apparent in the 3rd canto of Childe Harold; not so much in particular expressions, tho' there is no want of these, as in the tone (*assumed* rather than natural) of enthusiastic admiration of Nature, and a sensibility to her influences. Of my writings you need not read more than the blank verse poem on the river Wye[1] to be convinced of this. Mrs W. tells me that in reading one of Lord B.'s poems of which the story was offensive she was much disgusted with the plagiarisms from Mr Coleridge—at least she *thinks* it was in that poem, but as she read the Siege of Corinth in the same

---

[1] *Tintern Abbey.*

volume, it might possibly be in that. If I am not mistaken there was some acknowledgment to Mr C. which takes very much from the reprehensibility of literary trespasses of this kind. Nothing lowered my opinion of Byron's poetical integrity so much as to see 'pride of place' carefully noted as a quotation from Macbeth, in a work where contemporaries, from whom he had drawn by wholesale, were not adverted to. It is mainly on this account that he deserves the severe chastisement which you, or some one else, will undoubtedly one day give him: and may have done already, as I see by advertisement the Subject has been treated in the London Mag.

I remember one impudent instance of his thefts. In Raymond's translation of Coxe's travels in Switzerland,[1] with notes of the translator, is a note with these words, speaking of the fall of Schaffhausen: 'Lewy, descendant avec moi sur cet échaffaud, tomba à genoux en s'écriant: *Voilà un enfer d'eau!*' This expression is taken by Byron and beaten out unmercifully into two stanzas, which a critic in the Quarterly Review is foolish enough to praise. They are found in the 4th Can: of Childe Harold. Whether the obligation is acknowledged or not I do not know, having seen nothing of it, but in quotation.

Thank you for your parallels; I wished for them on Mr Rogers' account, who is making a collection of similar things relating to Gray. There are few of yours, I think, which one could swear to as conscious obligations—the subject has three branches— accidental coincidences without any communication of the subsequent Author; unconscious imitations; and deliberate conscious obligations. The cases are numerous in which it is impossible to distinguish these by any thing inherent in the resembling passage, but external aid may be called in with advantage where we happen to know the circumstances of an Author's life, and the direction of his Studies. Do not suffer my present remissness to prevent you favouring me with a letter if there is the least chance of my being of Service to you. I shall reply immediately if I have any thing to say worthy your attention. With best wishes from myself and family, I remain, dear sir,

very sincerely yours,
Wm Wordsworth

[1] Publ. 1781.

When you write to your Father, be so good as to make my respectful remembrances to him.

94. *To* Walter Savage Landor

Rydal Mount, Jan^ry 21, 1824

My dear Sir,

I am both tired and ashamed of waiting any longer: many months have I looked for your dialogues[1] and they never appear; the expectation of the book prevented my answering your former letter in which were mentioned some unpleasant topics relating to your own feelings;—as you do not advert to these in your second letter, rec^d about a fortnight ago, I trust the storm is blown over. I am truly sensible of your kindness, as testified by the agreeable, and allow me to say valuable present of Books from your hand, but you will be mortified to hear as I was bitterly vexed, that some of them have been entirely spoilt by the salt water; and scarcely one has escaped injury. The two Volumes of de Re rustica[2] in particular which I did not possess and had often wished to consult, are sorely damaged—the binding detached from the book, the leaves stained, and I fear rotted:—the venerable Bible is in the same state—indeed all to pieces. These are such unpleasant facts that I doubt whether I ought not to have suppressed them.

You promise me a beautiful Copy of Dante, but I ought to mention that I possess the Parma folio of 1795,—much the *grandest* book on my shelves,—presented to me by our common friend, Mr Kenyon (who, by the bye, is happily married since I last wrote to you and has taken up his residence at Bath.)

When at Mr Southey's last summer, my eyes being then in a very bad state, he read me part of that dialogue of yours, in which he is introduced as a speaker with Porson. It had appeared (something I must say to my regret) in a Magazine, and I should have had the pleasure to hear the whole, but we were interrupted. I made out part of the remainder myself. You have condescended to

---

[1] *Imaginary Conversations.*   [2] By the elder Varro.

minute criticism upon the Laodamia.[1] I concur with you in the first stanza, and had several times attempted to alter it upon your grounds. I cannot, however, accede to your objection to the 'second birth', merely because the expression has been degraded by Conventiclers. I certainly meant nothing more by it than the *eadem cura*, and the *largior æther*, etc., of Virgil's 6th Æneid. All religions owe their origin or acceptation to the wish of the human heart to supply in another state of existence the deficiencies of this, and to carry still nearer to perfection whatever we admire in our present condition; so that there must be many modes of expression, arising out of this coincidence, or rather identity of feeling, common to all Mythologies; and under this observation I should shelter the phrase from your censure; but I may be wrong in the particular case, though certainly not in the general principle. This leads to a remark in your last, 'that you are disgusted with all books that treat of religion.' I am afraid it is a bad sign in me, that I have little relish for any other—even in poetry it is the imaginative only, viz., that which is conversant [with], or turns upon infinity, that powerfully affects me,—perhaps I ought to explain: I mean to say that, unless in those passages where things are lost in each other, and limits vanish, and aspirations are raised, I read with something too much like indifference—but all great poets are in this view powerful Religionists, and therefore among many literary pleasures lost, I have not yet to lament over that of verse as departed. As to politics, what do you say to Buonaparte on the one side, and the Holy Alliance on the other, to the prostrate Tories, and to the contumelious and vacillating Whigs, who dislike or despise the Church, and seem to care for the State only so far as they are striving,—without hope, I honestly believe,—to get the management of it? As to the low-bred and headstrong Radicals, they are not worth a thought. Now my politics used always to impel me more or less to look out for co-operation, with a view to embody them in action—of this interest I feel myself utterly deprived, and the subject, as matter of reflection, languishes accordingly. Cool heads, no doubt, there are in the country, but moderation naturally keeps out of sight; and, wanting associates, I am less of an Englishman than I once was, or could wish to be.

[1] W. W.'s poem was discussed in Landor's 'Southey and Porson', published in the *London Magazine* in July 1823.

Show me that you excuse this egotism, if you can excuse it, by turning into the same path, when I have the pleasure again to hear from you.

It would probably be wasting paper to mention Southey, as no doubt you hear from him. I saw Mrs S. and 4 of his Children the other day; 2 of the girls most beautiful Creatures. The eldest Daughter is with her Father in town. S. preserves excellent health, and, except that his hair is gryzzled, a juvenile appearance, with more of youthful spirits than most men. He appears to be accumulating books in a way that, with my weak eyes, appalls me. A large box of them has just strayed into my house through a blunder in the conveyance.

Pray be so good as to let me know what you think of Dante—it has become lately—owing a good deal, I believe, to the example of Schlegel[1]—the fashion to extol him above measure. I have not read him for many years; his style I used to think admirable for conciseness and vigour, without abruptness; but I own that his fictions often struck me as offensively grotesque and fantastic, and I felt the Poem tedious from various causes.

I have a strong desire to become acquainted with the Mr Hare[2] whom you mention.—To the honour of Cambridge he is in the highest repute there, for his sound and extensive learning. I am happy to say that the Master of Trinity Coll. (my brother) was the occasion of his being restored to the Muses from the Temple. To Mr H's Br, Augustus, I am under great obligation for having *volunteered* the Tuition of my elder Son, who is at New Coll. Oxford, and who, though he is not a youth of quick parts, promises, from his assiduity and passionate love of Classical literature, to become an excellent Scholar. By the bye he seems very proud of your Idylls and the accompanying Elegy, as an honour to modern times. Farewell—be so kind as write soon, and believe me, ever sincerely and aff^{ly}. yours,

Wm Wordsworth

[1] A. W. von Schlegel (1767–1845), German critic.
[2] See List of Correspondents.

95. *To* the Earl of Lonsdale

Rydal Mount
23rd Jan^ry 1824

My Lord,

I am quite ashamed of being so long in fulfilling my engagement. But the promises of Poets are like the Perjuries of Lovers, things at which Jove laughs. At last, however, I have sent off the two first books of my Translations,[1] to be forwarded by Mr Beckett.[2] I hope they will be read by your Lordship with some pleasure, as having caused me a good deal of pains. Translation is just as to labour what the person who makes the attempt is inclined to. If he wishes to preserve as much of the original as possible, and *that* with as little addition of his own as may be, there is no species of composition that costs more pains. A literal Translation of an antient Poet in verse, and particularly in rhyme, is *impossible*; something must be left out and something added; I have done my best to avoid the one and the other fault. I ought to say a prefatory word about the versification, which will not be found much to the taste of those whose ear is exclusively accommodated to the regularity of Pope's Homer. I have run the couplets freely into each other, much more even than Dryden has done. This variety seems to me to be called for, if any thing of the movement of the Vergilian versification be transferable to our rhyme[d] Poetry; and independent of this consideration, long narratives in couplets with the sense closed at the end of each, are to me very wearisome. I should be grateful for any communication of your Lordship's feelings on these parts of my labour, or any other.

I have had a piece of good luck in the Stamp Off; the other day; particularly acceptable after the loss of the Custom House Stamps at Whitehaven. Mr Thompson Lord Egremont's Agent at Cockermouth paid into my offices upward of £4,000 duty upon the personal Estate of his late Uncle Mr Allan Pearson of Bridekirk; this large sum would have been paid directly to the office in London, without passing through my hands, if it had not been for strenuous exertions on my part. Mr Thompson seems heartily sick of his Whig Gentry connections about Cockermouth.

I have deferred to the conclusion my congratulations upon your

---

[1] Of Virgil's *Aeneid*.   [2] Lord Lonsdale's son-in-law.

Lordship's escape with no severe injury, bad as it was, from your late accident. These misadventures are nearer to my feelings than it would become me to express.

Since I last wrote to your Lordship, we received a second present of game from Lowther, for which though late, accept our best thanks; ever most sincerely and faithfully your Lordship's

W Wordsworth

96. *To* Jacob Fletcher

Rydal Mount Feb^{ry} 25th [1825]

My dear Sir

Many pressing engagements have prevented an earlier acknowledgment of your last letter, in the way I wished: since it reached me I have carefully perused the whole essay with much pleasure—but neither by the remarks, nor by the explanation in your letter, have I been able to gain a distinct understanding of your notion of the picturesque as something separate from what is suited to the pencil. But first let me correct an error respecting my own meaning, into which I have led you. When I observed that many objects were fitted for the pencil without being picturesque, I did not mean to allude, as you infer, to the Dutch School—but to the highest order of the Italian Artists, in whom beauty and grace are predominant; and I was censureably careless in not marking, that my eyes was less upon landscape than upon their mode of treating the human figure—in their Madonnas, Holy families, and all their pieces of still life. These materials as treated by them, we feel to be exquisitely fitted for the pencil—yet we never think of them as picturesque—but shall I say as something higher—something that realizes the idealisms of our nature, and assists us in the formation of new ones. Yet I concur with you that the Dutch School has made excellent use of Objects which in life and nature would not by a superficial Observer be deemed picturesque, nor would they with any propriety, in popular language, be termed so—this however I suspect is, because our sense of their picturesque qualities is overpowered by digust which some other properties about them create: I allude to their pictures of insides of

stables—dung carts—dunghills and foul and loathsome situations, which they not infrequently are pleased to exhibit. But strip
objects of these qualities—or rather take such as are found without
them, and if they produce a more agreeable effect upon canvas
than in reality, then I think it may be safely said, that the qualities
which constitute the picturesque, are eminently inherent in such
objects. I will dismiss this, I fear tedious, subject with one remark
which will be illustrated at large, if I execute my intention—viz—
that our business is not so much with objects as with the law under
which they are contemplated. The confusion incident to these
disquisitions has I think arisen principally from not attending to
this distinction. We hear people perpetually disputing whether
this or that thing be beautiful or not—sublime or otherwise,
without being aware that the same object may be both beautiful
and sublime, but it cannot be felt to be such at the same
moment—but I must stop—let me only add, that I have no doubt
the fault is in myself and not in you that I have not caught, as
clearly as I could wish, your meaning.

I do not relish the notion of interfering with any use you might be
disposed to make of your interesting MS.—my own plan is so
uncertain that you ought not to cede anything to it—my first view
was as I have said,[1] to analyze the regions of Snowdon and Cader
Idris, with a glance at some more remote river scenery in N.W.—I
have since taken up another thought, and feel inclined to make
Snowdon the scene of a Dialogue upon Nature, Poetry, and
Painting—to be illustrated by the surrounding imagery.

Notwithstanding the particulars which make you averse to send
your MS. on Scotland, I have a strong wish to be favoured with a
sight of it. If you think proper it might be sent by Coach—or if you
preferred, by some private hand to Kendal—'to the care of Mr
Cookson,[2] Kent Side—Kendal', who would be sure to forward it in
the safest way immediately.

I wish your Tragedies had been more successful, particularly if
you are likely to be discouraged from a second adventure—tho' I
am the last person to press publication upon any one, and I think it
for the most part very prejudicial to young writers. I have not
seen your Plays—from which no inference can be drawn to their
prejudice—very few Modern publications find their way to

[1] In a previous letter.   [2] A local friend.

me—we have no Book clubs in this neighbourhood—and when I am from home, in Spring and Summer, my eyes are so apt to be inflamed that I am able to profit little by any thing that falls in my way.

> With many thanks, and sincere respect
> Believe me to be truly your's
> Wm Wordsworth

97. *To* Sir George Beaumont

> May 28th [1825] Rydal Mount

My dear Sir George,

It delights me indeed to receive a Letter from you written in such a happy state of mind. Heaven grant that your best wishes may be realized; and surely the promises from this alliance[1] are of the fairest kind. What you say of George gives me great pleasure; I hope he will enter into your feelings and Lady Beaumont's in respect to Coleorton, with a becoming spirit; so that your views may not be frustrated. This I have much at heart. The Place is worthy of the pains you have taken with it, and one cannot breathe a better wish for him, as your Successor, than that his duties there should become his principal pleasure. How glad should we be to hear that Lady Beaumont is tranquillized; I wish we could transport her hither for a week at least under this quiet roof, in this bright and fragrant season of fresh green leaves and blossoms. Never, I think, have we had so beautiful a spring; sunshine and showers coming just as if they had been called for by the spirits of Hope, Love, and Beauty. This spot is at present a Paradise, if you will admit the term when I acknowledge that yesterday afternoon the mountains were whitened with a fall of snow.—But this only served to give the landscape, with all its verdure, blossoms, and leafy trees, a striking Swiss air, which reminded us of Unterseen and Interlaken.—

Most reluctantly do I give up the hope of our seeing Italy together; but I am prepared to submit to what you think best. My

[1] The marriage of his cousin and heir to the daughter of Dr Howley, Bishop of London.

own going with any part of my family must be deferred till John is nearer the conclusion of his University studies; so that for this summer it must not be thought of. I am truly sensible of your kind offer of assistance, and cannot be affronted at such testimonies of your esteem. We sacrifice our time, our ease, and often our health, for the sake of our Friends (and what is Friendship unless we are prepared to do so?). I will not then pay *money* such a Compliment, as to allow *it* to be too precious a thing to be added to the Catalogue, where Fortunes are unequal, and where the occasion is mutually deemed important. But at present this must sleep.

You say nothing of Painting. What was the fate of your Mont Blanc?—and what is the character of the present annual exhibitions? Leslie,[1] I hear, has not advanced. John Bull[2] is very bitter against poor Haydon who, it is to be apprehended, is not making progress in the art.—

I never had a higher relish for the beauties of Nature than during this spring, nor enjoyed myself more. What manifold reason, my dear Sir George, have you and I to be thankful to Providence! Theologians may puzzle their heads about dogmas as they will; the Religion of gratitude cannot mislead us. Of that we are sure; and Gratitude is the handmaid to Hope, and hope the harbinger of Faith. I look abroad upon Nature, I think of the best part of our species, I lean upon my Friends, and I meditate upon the Scriptures, especially the Gospel of St John; and my creed rises up of itself with the ease of an exhalation, yet a Fabric of adamant. God bless you, my ever dear friend! Kindest love to Lady B.

W. Wordsworth

98. *To* Allan Cunningham

Rydal Mount Novr. 23^d [1825]

My dear Sir,

On returning from Leicestershire a few days ago, I had the pleasure of finding in its destined place the Bust of Sir Walter Scott.[3] It is, as you say, a very fine one; and I doubt not you have been equally select in the one which you have sent *of* me to Sir

---

[1] C. R. Leslie, RA (1794–1859).   [2] The weekly paper.
[3] By Francis Chantrey, RA (1781–1842).

Walter. I will take care that my debt to you on this score shall be speedily discharged. And here I am reminded of an obligation of the same kind which I am afraid has not been met as it ought to be. Pray, has Mr E.^d Coleridge[1] paid for the Cast of my Bust which at his request was forwarded to him at Eton? Bear in mind that I am ultimately responsible for it. I am already in possession of a cast of Mr Southey—a striking likeness, as to feature, but so ill executed in point of character and expression, that I must defer placing a likeness of that honored friend in company with this fine one of Sir Walter, till I can procure one from the hand of Mr Chantrey, who I hope will one day undertake a work which would redound to the credit of both Parties. I am not without hope also that Mr Chantrey may be induced to transmit to posterity the magnificent forehead of one of the first Intellects that Great Britain has produced.—I mean that of Mr Coleridge, and proud should I be to place this triumvirate of my Friends in the most distinguished stations of my little mansion.

Many thanks for your letter. The interest which yourself and family take in my writings and Person is grateful to my feelings—testimonies of this kind are among the very pleasantest results of a literary life. The ground upon which I am disposed to meet your anticipation of the spread of my Poetry is, that I have endeavoured to dwell with truth upon those points of human nature in which all men resemble each other, rather than on those accidents of manners and character produced by times and circumstances; which are the favourite seasoning, and substance, too often, of imaginative writings. If therefore I have been successful in the execution of my attempt, it seems not improbable, that as education is extended, writings that are independent of an over—not to say vicious—refinement will find a proportionate increase of readers, provided there be found in them a genuine inspiration.

The selection you again advert to will no doubt be executed at some future time. Something of the kind is already in progress at Paris, in respect to my Poems in common with others. The value of such selections will depend entirely upon the judgement of the Editor. In this case Mr Washington Irvin,[2] whose taste I have no

---

[1] S. T. C.'s nephew.
[2] Washington Irving (1783–1859), the American writer.

great opinion of, if I may judge from his Sketch book, which, tho' a work of talent, is disfigured by abundance of affectation. In the mean while I am going to press (at last) with a re-publication of the whole of my Poetry,[1] including the Excursion, which will give me an opportunity of performing my promise to you, by sending you the whole, as soon as it is ready for delivery.

The collection of Songs[2] which you announce I had not heard of: your own poetry shews how fit you are for the office of editing native strains; and may not one hope that the taste of the public in these matters is much improved since the time when McPherson's frauds[3] met with such dangerous success, and Percy's Ballads[4] produced those hosts of legendary Tales that bear no more resemblance to their supposed models than Pope's Homer does to the work of the Blind Bard. Do not say I ought to have been a Scotchman. Tear me not from the Country of Chaucer, Spencer, Shakespeare and Milton; yet I own that since the days of childhood, when I became familiar with the phrase, 'They are killing geese in Scotland, and sending the feathers to England' which every one had ready when the snow began to fall, and I used to hear in the time of a high wind that

> Arthur's Bower has broken his band
> And he comes roaring up the land
> King of Scotts wi' a' his Power
> Cannot turn Arthur's Bower,

I have been indebted to the North for more than I shall ever be able to acknowledge. Thomson, Mickle, Armstrong, Leyden, yourself, Irving[5] (a poet in *spirit*), and I may add Sir Walter Scott were all Borderers. If they did not drink the water, they breathed at least the air of the two countries. The list of English Border poets is not so distinguished, but Langhorne was a native of West^d, and Brown, the author of the Estimate of Manners and Principles, etc., a Poet as his letter on the vale of Keswick, with the accompanying verses, shows—was born in Cumberland. So also was Skelton,[6] a

---

[1] The edn. of 1827.   [2] *The Songs of Scotland . . .*, 1825.

[3] The Ossianic poems.   [4] *Reliques of Ancient English Poetry*, 1765.

[5] Edward Irving, the preacher. W. W.'s list illustrates his wide knowledge of Scottish and Border literature in the eighteenth century.

[6] John Skelton (?1460–1529), the satirist.

Demon in point of genius; and Tickell in later times, whose style is superior in chastity to Pope's, his contemporary. Addison and Hogarth were both within a step of Cum^d and West^d, their several Fathers having been natives of those counties, which are still crowded with their name and relatives. It is enough for me to be ranked in this catalogue, and to know that I have touched the hearts of many by subjects suggested to me on Scottish ground; these pieces you will find classed together in the new Ed^n. Present my thanks to Mrs C. for her kind invitation. I need not add that if you, or any of yours, come this way we shall be most happy to see you.

Pray give my congratulations to Mr Chantrey on the improvement in Mrs C.'s health; they have both our best wishes; and believe me, my dear sir,

Very faithfully yours,
Wm Wordsworth

99. *To* Henry Crabb Robinson

Rydal Mount 6th April [1826]
I have not time to read this over—

My dear Friend,

My Sister had taken flight for Herefordshire when *your* Letter, for such we guessed it [to] be arrived—it was broken open—(pray forgive the offence) and all your charges of concealment and reserve frustrated—We are all, at all times, so glad to hear from you that we could not resist the temptation to purchase the pleasure at the expense of the peccaddillo for which we beg pardon with united voices.

—You are kind enough to mention my poems—let me touch first the business part of this question. In the publication I have had many disappointments. Rogers was kind enough to negotiate with Murray for the publication—three months elapsed before this personage could find leisure to settle the terms; and three months more without my being able to obtain any notice to a Letter I had addressed to him; upon which I took the thing out of his hands.

Some time after, through the kind offices of Mr Alaric Watts,[1] I effected a bargain, in my judgement, more favorable with Hurst and Robinson; but after a delay of many weeks the embarassments in their affairs prevented the fulfillment of it.—Mr Watts is now in London and has undertaken to ascertain whether they are likely to be able to proceed.—Now as I know that Mr Watts is very much occupied in his own affairs, it has struck me, that if you had a few spare moments, you might assist him in a negotiation in that quarter or some other. Mr Watts may be heard of at Robinson and Hursts, and this Letter would be a sufficient introduction. I have never had the pleasure of seeing Mr W. but he has given himself very much trouble about my affairs, and I cannot but think you would find him an amiable acquaintance, as he is undoubtedly a man of no common abilities—But pray attend to this suggestion or not, just as you find it agreeable—It is certainly to be regretted that the Poems have been and are likely to remain so long out of print.—Your valuable remarks about the arrangement I should not have acted upon had they reached me earlier—at present it is quite out of the question—as the 4 Vols have been carefully gone over and decided upon after the most mature consideration.—There is no material change in the classification—except that the Scotch Poems have been placed all together, under the Title of Memorials of Tours in Scotland; this has made a gap in the poems of Imagination which has been supplied by Laodamia, Ruth, and one or two more, from the close of Affections[2] etc—But I need not trouble you with these minutiae—Miscellaneous poems ought not to be jumbled together at *random*—were this done with mine the passage from one to another would often be insupportably offensive; but in my judgement the only thing of much importance in arrangement is that one poem should shade off happily into another—and the contrasts where they occur be clear of all harshness or abruptness—I differ from you and Lamb[3] as to the classification of Imagination etc—it is of slight importance as matter of Reflection, but of great as matter of *feeling* for the Reader by making one Poem smooth the way for another—if this be not

---

[1] See List of Correspondents.
[2] i.e. from *Poems founded on the Affections*.
[3] Lamb had advocated a chronological arrangement based on the order of composition.

attended to classification by subject, or by mould or form, is of no value, for nothing can compensate for the neglect of it.—When I have the pleasure of seeing you we will take this matter up, as a question of literary curiosity—I can write no more. T. Clarkson[1] is going.—Your supposed Biography[2] entertained me much. I could give you the other side.—farewell.

W. W.

T. Clarkson was to have been the Bearer of this to you—but I find he will not reach London for three weeks, he will therefore get it franked—pray excuse the miserable scrawl—written in extreme hurry.

100. *To* Robert Jones

Rydal Mount
May 18th [1826]

My dear Jones,

I have been very busy about the threatened contest for Westd,[3] that is no excuse for not writing to you earlier; in fact I have no hope of visiting Wales this spring or summer; we have received notice to quit Rydal Mount[4] and I am entangled in preparations for building a house in an adjoining field purchased at an extravagant fancy price. I enter upon this work with great reluctance and wd feign hope that some turn of fortune may yet prevent it going forward; if so I go into Ireland with a friend and perhaps my Sister, and if this be, we will have a peep at you going or returning—it is now time to express the regret of the whole family at not seeing you here this spring, we looked for you with no little confidence. How comes it to be so difficult to procure clerical substitutes in yr part of the world? we have plenty of them in this—do come and see us, we are growing old and ought to make

---

[1] Clarkson's son.

[2] H. C. R. had implied that W. W. had ceased to sympathise with the cause of liberty.

[3] Brougham was again standing against Lord Lowther and Col. Lowther.

[4] A false alarm, as it turned out.

the best of our time to keep up long tried affections. My Sister is still in Herefordshire wishing to avoid the bustle of our approaching election; when she went thither in Feby our plan was that I was to meet her in the Vale of Clwydd at the end of this month as you know—but this is impossible both on account of the possible building, and the election.

Dr Wordsworth, you will be sorry to hear, has been seriously ill—he takes too much out of himself—studies hard and applies as sedulously to business, and both together are more than he can bear. Remember the Cambridge election, what a pity there should be three anti-Catholic candidates. My Daughter is my amanuensis, an office she is pleased to perform as it brings her into the society of her old and much esteemed Friend. We often talk of you and your good nature at Barmouth[1]—and your calm and even temper so enviable compared with mine.

Mr Brougham's support of the Catholics has done him harm among the electors of W^std and the nation seems opening its eyes upon this question.

We have had here dry weather for many weeks—the middle of the day hot, the evenings sharp and frosty, which has made colds too plentiful in this house and elsewhere—I am the last sufferer but am getting better—my eyes have felt the bad effects. Grass of course here makes little progress—corn has not suffered—we have little but oats and we sow late.

My son John is still at Oxford, reading I hope industriously—he takes his degree December next or rather goes up for examination—if he comes away a good scholar I shall be satisfied. I think we could have succeeded in getting him made fellow of Merton but he is not eligible on account of his birth-place, so that he will be thrown for advancement and maintenance upon his own exertions—my younger Son still continues with me—his constitution has been so shatter'd by maladies the foundations of which were laid at the Charterhouse, that I do [   ] He is however pretty well at present.

With kindest regards [   ] joins with my Daughter [   ] Jones your faithful Friend

Wm Wordsworth

[1] During their Welsh tour of 1824.

101. *To* Alaric Watts

Lowther Castle,
June 18, 1826.

My dear Sir,

I was from home when your last obliging letter arrived. Truly am I grieved to hear of your losses through Hurst and Robinson, and thankful for the prudent care you took of my interests. I will with pleasure speak to Mr De Quincey of your wish to have him among the contributors to your *Souvenir*; but, whatever hopes he may hold out, do not be tempted to depend upon him. He is strangely irresolute. A son of Mr Coleridge[1] lives in the neighbourhood of Ambleside, and is a very able writer; but he also, like most men of genius, is little to be depended upon. Your having taken the *Souvenir* into your own hands makes me still more regret that the general rule I have laid down precludes my endeavouring to render you any service in that way.

The state of Miss Jewsbury's[2] health gives me and all her friends very great concern. She is a most interesting person, and would be a great loss should she not recover.

I remain, my dear sir,
Your much obliged friend,
Wm Wordsworth

102. *To* the Earl of Lonsdale

[Appleby]
Monday, 3 o'clock
26th June 1826

My Lord,

Nothing has occurred worthy of particular notice since my last, except a scuffle and Row in the streets, which terminated in breaking windows, on Saturday, in each of the principal Inns, Yellow and Blue.[3]

---

[1] Hartley, who had returned to the Lakes after the loss of his Oxford fellowship.
[2] Maria Jane Jewsbury, writer for the Annuals.
[3] Yellow was the Tory, and blue the Whig colour.

In the earlier part of this morning the Blues gained ground—but they are now losing it fast. Today they intended to make great push,—it has failed—and, for my own part, I cannot but think that they will give in earlier than was intended. I have conversed with a good number of intimate acquaintances of their party, and am convinced that not one of them entertain a hope of success—if the contest be protracted till the end of the week it must be merely to harrass the Candidates with expenses. The Defection tells heavily against the Blues and of new tendered Votes appearing in their favor, and the Votes not previously known to the Lowther Agents,—the number is small; if such exist it is high time *they* should make their appearance

Jeffrey Editor of the Edinburgh Review is here to vote for B.[1] with other Scotch advocates as is said; but Jeffrey is certainly here.

The Report in the Carlisle Patriot of what passed at the Nomination is very correct.

I write before the Poll is closed—the state of it will be sent your Lordship.

The weather is intensely hot—Brougham's health has nevertheless obviously improved—indeed he assured me on Saturday in the Assessor's Court that he was perfectly well at present, and that the heat agreed with him.

On the gross Poll the Col: is at this moment 91 ahead—half past three.

> Ever most faithfully your Lordship
> W. Wordsworth

103. *To* Jane Marshall

Keswick,
Friday [22 Sept. 1826]

Dear Mrs. Marshall,

Many thanks for your obliging letter. My visit here was to Mr. Southey, whom I had not seen before since the death of his child.[2] But Sir G. Beaumont and Mr Rogers are both here, and I am committed with them and Mr. Southey, to-day we go to

---

[1] Brougham.   [2] His youngest daughter Isabel.

Buttermere, and I could not get off an engagement to-morrow. I shall however call at Halsteads towards the latter part of next week, and then perhaps we may settle when I can have the pleasure of paying a visit in which I have been thus far disappointed. Dora, I am happy to learn, is considerably better, so that I hope she may be trusted over the mountain.

I am truly sorry for Mr. Marshall's accident particularly so in this most beautiful weather.

I promise myself a good deal of pleasure in [   ] the neighbourhood of Buttermere.

I remain dear Mrs. Marshall
faithfully your obliged
W. Wordsworth

My sister is at present at Sir G. Beaumont's.

104. *To* Samuel Rogers

[17 Apr. 1828]

My dear R—

To-night I set off for Cambridge, passing by Coleorton, where I shall stay a couple of days with the Rector.[1] My Son accompanies me; being about to undertake a Curacy in a Parish adjoining that of Coleorton, near Grace-Dieu, the birth-place of Beaumont the Dramatist. At Cambridge I purpose to stay till the 10th or 11th May, and then for a short, very short, visit to London, where I shall be sadly disappointed if I do not meet you. My main object is to look out for some situation, mercantile if it could be found, for my younger son. If you can serve me, pray do.

I have troubled you with this note to beg you would send any further sheets of your Poem,[2] up to the 8th or so of next month, to me at Trin: Lodge, Cambridge. Farewell. My Wife and Daughter are, I trust, already at Cambridge. My sister begs her kindest regards. Miss Hutchinson is here, who has also been much gratified by your Poem, and begs to be remembered to you.

Ever faithfully yours
Wm Wordsworth

---

[1] The Revd Francis Merewether.   [2] The second part of *Italy*.

105. *To* Sir Walter Scott

[Rydal Mount]
28th August [1828]

My dear Sir Walter,

Professor Norton[1] of Cambridge University, America, is the Bearer of this. His request for a Letter of introduction, his *desire* rather to have one (for a request he did not make) was expressed with such diffidence that I had a real pleasure in telling him that I could venture to meet his wishes. He is highly respected in his own Country, and came to me with a Letter from Professor Ticknor[2] of Boston, whom probably you remember. He is travelling in search of health and Mrs Norton and a female Friend accompany him.—

Perhaps you may have heard that I have been rambling on the Continent with my Daughter and Mr Coleridge since we met in London: Our principal objects were the Rhine and Holland, and Flanders, which countries were not new to me, but were revisited with great interest in such pleasant Company. You would have enjoyed floating down the Meuse and the Rhine with us, and I heartily wish you could have made a fourth to the Party, had it only been for one day.—

Short as was my stay in London, on my return, I called at Mr Lockart's,[3] but was not lucky enough to find either him, or Mr Charles, your Son, at home; pray express my regret, especially to the latter who left a Card for me a short while before we started for the Continent: when I was so hurried that I could not return his visit.—

We only reached home last night—Mrs Wordsworth and my Daughter after a year's absence—so that all is new and strange to them; and myself after so long an interval that I cannot encourage the hope of getting to Abbotsford this Summer, or rather Autumn—for alas the Summer is fled, if indeed we have seen her face this year.—This inability, for such it strikes me at present, is I assure you a great disappointment; another year I hope to be more fortunate.

Southey is wonderfully well—he had an operation performed

---

[1] Andrews Norton, Unitarian divine.
[2] Professor George Ticknor of Harvard.
[3] J. G. Lockhart (1794–1854), Scott's son-in-law and biographer.

when in Town, which has removed an infirmity he has suffered from for ten years. To-morrow he will be on the top of Saddleback with Sir Robert Inglis.[1] My Sister and I should have joined them if I had not been so freshly arrived—But I am tiring you—I could ask a hundred questions, about Mrs Lockart and her little Boy, but I have heard he is not better. Do not let Major Scott[2] or Mr Charles, or any body belonging to you, pass this way without calling here—farewell, a thousand kind wishes in which I am joined by Mrs W. my Sister and Daughter—ever most

faithfully yours
Wm Wordsworth

106. *To* Basil Montagu

Rydal Mount
29th July [1829]

My dear M—

The day after I wrote my last, arrived the Selections[3]—many of which I have read—they seem to me judicious.—How or where the Book had been detained I know not.

Hartley Coleridge has been staying some time with Professor Wilson on the Banks of Windermere, where he has been doing very well except for one disappearance, which lasted a few days. It is a thousand Pities that he should give way to these temptations, arising from a cause which is one [we] can guess at—[4]

What you Londoners may think of public affairs I know not; but I forebode the not very distant overthrow of the Institution under which this Country has so long prospered. The Liberals of our neighbourhood tell me that the mind of the Nation has outgrown its institutions; rather say, I reply, that it has shrunk and dwindled from them, as the body of a sick man does from his clothes.

We are on fire with zeal to educate the poor, which would all be very well if that zeal did not blind us to what we stand still more in need of, an improved education of the middle and upper classes;

---

[1] The Tory politician.   [2] Scott's elder son.
[3] *Selections from the works of Taylor, Hooker, Hall, and Lord Bacon*, 3rd edn., 1829.
[4] i.e. drunkenness.

which ought to begin in our great public schools, thence ascend to the Universities (from which the first suggestion should come), and descend to the very nursery.

If the Books from which your Selections are made were the favorite reading of men of rank and influence, I should dread little from the discontented in any class. But what hope is there of such a rally in our debilitated intellects? The soundest Heads I meet with are, with few exceptions, Americans. They seem to have a truer sense of the benefits of our government than we ourselves have. Farewell,

with many thanks
yours faithfully
W. W.

107. *To* Mary Wordsworth

Cork Wednesday 9th [Sept. 1829]

My dearest Mary,

We arrived here this day at eleven a.m. where I found your Letter. Tomorrow if we are not detained on the road for want of horses or other accident, we shall be at Killarney—and in something less than a month I expect to be at Rydal Mount, for in 3 weeks and 3 days we hope to have finished Ireland and in three more will be home I trust—I am truly sorry to learn that Wm's health continues so indifferent I would gladly write to him from Ireland but I am afraid I shall scarcely find opportunity, my eyes are so often in the state that makes writing or reading hurtful; though at present they are pretty well. My dear Sister, I hope, is by this time safe at home and well, and Dora continues well—I cannot say how anxious I am to hear of and still more to see you all.—I dispatched a letter for you just as I left Dublin this day week, hoping for an answer here but the allowance of time was too small, it will follow us—the day you receive this by all means write directing to Iniskilling where we hope to be in 10 days. You will naturally look for some account of what we have seen—but I must beg leave to be brief and dull hoping to make amends when we meet.—Upon the whole, but don't say so, I was rather disappointed with the scenery of Ireland—though by no means so with the general effect of the Tour, as far as concerns both country and people. On the day we left Dublin (last Wednesday) we slept, look at the great Map, at New Town Mount Kennedy, have crossed the Dublin Mountains through an over-celebrated pass called the Scalp and seen the beautiful valley of the Dargle and the too-famous waterfall of Powerscourt. In the morning I rose early and walked 3 miles out and as many back to see Dunran a wild glen, but we left unseen a spot still more famous the Devil's Glen, and proceeded from New Town M.K.—six miles where our Friends the Professor[1] and Mr Otway from Dublin met us and we breakfasted, thence to the 7 Churches with which and the wild romantic situation of three that I saw together with a huge Pillar near them we were highly gratified. About 4 o'clock we parted with our friends and slept at Rathdrum. Next day Friday down the Avon to the celebrated meeting of the waters and down the Ovoka to Arklow, all this through a charming country but by no means equal to Fascally and the Tummel and Garry and Tay. On Saturday night we reached Wexford, having passed through Enniskorthy and under Vinegar Hill where the Rebels were defeated in 98—At Wexford—a dull Town we stopped all Saturday, a day of heavy rain—On Sunday we went to Waterford—with which we were much pleased, and slept at Carrick-on-Suir, on Monday at Shanbally Castle (near Clogheen) the seat of Mr O-Callan's Brother.[2] We found the latter at Home—the next [day] to Lismore upon the Blackwater and up it to Fermoy where we slept last night and here we are—but I will not trouble you with these dull particulars in future—I have only a quarter of an hour to say that I have laid in much observation to muse upon and think of—and as to our future Tour I expect the same—But for splendor and beauty of scenery, what I have yet seen of Ireland is not to be compared to Scotland, the North of England or Wales.—The Wicklow Mountains make a charming tour for the people of Dublin and are well worth a stranger's holiday, but no Englishman, still more would I say no English-woman, should trouble herself to visit them till she has seen the best part of our own island; I therefore do [not] much regret that

---

[1] W. R. Hamilton (see List of Correspondents).
[2] Viscount Lismore.

neither of the Dorothys have yet taken the trouble and put themselves to the expense of the voyage and journey—I will describe everything as well as I can when we meet—the people are just what we supposed—I mean the poorest of them, nothing can be more wretched than their appearance and habitations; but the Country shows thus far great signs of improvement, in roads, in habitations, bridges etc—All these you shall hear of—Today we have had a charming drive along the justly celebrated waters of Cork down to a place called the Cove—ridges of land on both sides richly covered with groves and gentlemen's houses, etc.—but I must conclude—the post goes out—farewel Love and welcome to the 2 Dorothys, say how they like the house improvements[1] I hope to write you shortly.

ever faithfully yours—

W.

108. *To* G. Huntly Gordon

[Rydal Mount]
14th Novr 1829.

My dear Sir,

I am quite at a loss what to say about Ireland. Its political condition is not a little alarming as is obvious to every one from the late trials. In my own mind I have no doubt that the same disposition to conspire against Landlords, Magistrates, and the supporters of Protestantism are spread through much the greatest part of Ireland. Will the leading people who have been propitiated by the Relief-Bill[2] prove a compensation for that loss of strength which is unavoidable where intimidation is known to have been the cause of success? I fear not.—But my pen might for you be more agreeably employed in giving you some account of the impression which the scenery of Ireland and the face of the Country made upon my mind. This, except for the wretched state of swarms of the inhabitants was very favorable. We were five weeks travelling about and saw almost every thing. The County of Kerry far exceeds the rest; so much so it well deserves that a

---

[1] Alterations to Rydal Mount.   [2] The Emancipation Act of 1829.

leading artist, and a man of taste and general information should unite their powers to illustrate it. With the Coast of Antrim also, including the Giants Causeway, which is however far from being the most interesting object it presents, I was highly delighted.—

I could not resist the temptation to ascend the highest mountain in Ireland, higher than any of our's—Curran-thuil its name[1]— 3,410 feet above the level of the sea. The mountain is itself a magnificent object from many points of view—and the prospect from it very splendid; gulphs of awful depth below and sea and land, and inland waters, and bays spread around within a vast horizon. I was not disappointed with Killarney—and that is saying a great deal. In the County of Wicklow objects are upon a smaller scale—but very attractive, especially as scenes of recreation for the neighbouring Inhabitants of Dublin—Of the Rivers the Shannon struck me most—The Slaney, the Suir and the Blackwater have their several attractions—but upon the whole they disappointed me—even the celebrated meeting of the waters the two Avons is far inferior to that of the Garry and Tummel near Fascally; and in general the Irish Rivers fall short in interest of those in Scotland and Wales—I ought to add that we were much pleased with the neighbourhood of Sligo, which is mountainous though upon a much smaller scale than the County of Kerry.

We are all pretty well—W^m included, his last letter being very satisfactory in all respects. With kind regards from my family

I remain dear Sir
Your most obliged Wm W.[2]

109. *To* John Gardner

May 19th 1830
Whitehaven
(I return home in a few days.)

My dear Sir,

I feel that I ought to thank you for your judicious Letter, and for the pains you have taken towards settling the question of the

---

[1] i.e. Carrantual.   [2] M. W. adds a PS.

eligibility of low-priced Publications.[1] Messrs Longman talk strangely when they say that my annual Account will shew what is advisable. How can that shew anything but what number of Purchases I have had? it cannot tell me how many I have missed by the heavy price. Again, Messrs L. affirm that my Buyers are of that class who do not regard prices—but that class, never perhaps very large, is every day going smaller with the reduced incomes of the time—and besides, in this opinion I believe these Gentlemen to be altogether mis-taken. My Poetry, less than any other of the day, is adapted to the taste of the Luxurious, and of those who value themselves upon the priviledge of wealth and station. And though it be true that several passages are too abstruse for the ordinary Reader, yet the main body of it is as well fitted (if my aim be not altogether missed) to the bulk of the people both in sentiment and language, as that of any of my contemporaries.—I agree with you, (and for the same reason) that nothing can be inferred from the failure of cheap publication in Kirke White's[2] case. To the above considerations I would add the existence of the pirated editions, and above all an apprehension that there is a growing prejudice against high-priced books. Indeed I am inclined to think with my Friend Mr Southey that shortly few books will be published except low-priced ones, or those that are highly ornamented, for persons who delight in such luxuries. These considerations all seem in favor of the experiment which you recommend. Yet I am far from sure that it would answer. It is not to be questioned that the perpetually supplied stimulus of Novels stands much in the way of the purer interest which used to attach to Poetry. And although these poorer Narratives do but in very few instances retain more than the hold of part of a season upon public attention, yet a fresh crop springs up every hour. But to bring these tedious *pros* and *cons* to a close, I will say at once that if I could persuade myself that the Retail Bookseller you speak of is not mistaken in his notion that he could sell *ten* copies, (or less than half of that number,) when he now sells *one*, were the price something under a pound, I would venture upon such an edition. I ought to say to you, however, that I have changed my intention of making additions at present, and

---

[1] i.e. the commercial justification of cheaper editions.

[2] Henry Kirke White (1785–1806), whose popular *Remains* were published posthumously.

should confine myself to inter-mixing the few poems that were published in the Keep-sake[1] of year before last. I have already stated to you my notions as to the extreme injustice of the law of copy-right; if it has not been mis-represented to me, for I never saw the Act of Parliament. But I am told that, when an Author dies, such of his Works as have been twice fourteen years before the Public are public property, and that his heirs have no pecuniary interest in anything that he may leave behind, beyond the same period. My days are in course of nature drawing towards a close, and I think it would be best, in order to secure some especial value to any collection of my Works that might be printed after my decease, to reserve a certain number of new pieces to be intermixed with that collection. I am acquainted with a distinguished Author who means to hold back during his life-time all the Corrections and additions in his several works for the express purpose of benefiting his heirs by the superiority which those improvements will give to the pieces which may have become the property of the public. I do sincerely hope and trust that the Law in this point will one day or other be brought nearer to justice and reason. Take only my own comparatively insignificant case. Many of my Poems have been upwards of 30 years subject to criticism, and are disputed about as keenly as ever, and appear to be read much more. In fact thirty years are no adequate test for works of Imagination, even from second or third-rate writers, much less from those of the first order, as we see in the instances of Shakespeare and Milton. I am sorry that want of room prevented me from being favored with your account of the effect my attempts in verse had produced upon your mind. It would, I doubt not, have pleased me much and might have been of service to my future labours if I should write any more. With sincere thanks for the trouble you have taken, I remain dear Sir

faithfully yours
W. Wordsworth

---

[1] The Annual.

110. *To* Charles Wordsworth

Rydal Mount: Thursday
[? 17 June 1830]

My dear Nephew,

The pleasant news of your station in the first class[1] reached Rydal Mount yesterday—but I was from home and did not learn it till this morning, when I entered the house from Patterdale, and Dora who is always the first to report well of her Cousins, called out to me from the top of the Stairs, "Charles is in the first class". We all congratulate you most heartily; and I hope, notwithstanding some disappointments heretofore, that you feel yourself recompensed, as far as honour goes, for your Labours. But I trust that you value the honor infinitely less than the habits of industry and the knowledge which have enabled you to acquire it. You have hitherto been in study a busy Bee; let the "amor florum" and the "generandi *gloria* mellis",[2] continue to animate you, and be persuaded, my dear Charles, that you will be both the better and happier.

Your Aunts are both well; your aunt Dorothy has had no relapse for a long time, though She complies with our earnest request in retaining her invalid precautions. Dora, alas! had a severe attack of bilious fever three weeks ago—she is convalescent, but regains her strength slowly.—I have a piece of domestic news for you, which I will thank you not to repeat. Your Cousin John is to be married in September or October.[3] To whom, as a young man, you perhaps will little care, provided he is likely to be happy—I trust he is so, for the object of his choice is truly amiable, and her fortune such, as enables them to marry without imprudence. [*Dora W. writes in*: This is a twice told Tale, but my Father forgot when writing that you must now be in Cambridge.]

The other day I had the pleasure of being greeted in the road by your Bowness Tutor and Friend—Martin.[4] He was in excellent Spirits, and looked well: one of his Companions was a young Man, Fellow of Trinity, whose name, though they drank tea with us, I did not learn. He was guiding them through the country.

The weather has been with us very cold—but sometimes such as

---

[1] At Oxford.   [2] Virgil, *Georgics*, iv. 205.   [3] To Isabella Curwen.
[4] A Cambridge don who held a reading party at Bowness in 1827.

to make walking truly delightful. I found it so this morning, when with Mrs W. I crossed Kirkstone. She rode to the top of the mountain; but down hill we tripped it away side by side charmingly. Think of that, my dear Charles, for a Derby and Joan of sixty each!! Farewell; where are you going this summer—to Cambridge first no doubt, but whither afterwards? Could not you come hither with your father? I fear we could not *lodge* you both in the house, but at the foot of the hill we can procure a bed, with due notice beforehand. Ever your affectionate uncle,

W.W.

111. *To* Samuel Rogers

Rydal Mount
Friday [30 July 1830]

I cannot sufficiently thank you, my dear Rogers, for your kind and long Letter, knowing as I do how much you dislike writing. Yet I should not have written now but to say I was not aware that you had any such near connections in the Church;[1] I had presumed that your Relatives by both sides were Dissenters, or I should have been silent on the subject; being well assured that I and mine would always have your good word as long as we continued to deserve it.

Lord Lonsdale, to whom I mentioned my son's intended Marriage, naming (as I was at liberty to do in *that* case) the Lady, has written to me in answer with that feeling and delicacy which mark the movements of his mind and the actions of his life. He is one of the best and most amiable of men; and I should detest myself if I could fail in gratitude for his goodness to me upon all occasions.

I wish Lady Frederick's mind were at ease on the subject of the Epitaph.[2] Upon her own ideas, and using mainly her own language, I worked at it—but the production I sent was too long and somewhat too historical—yet assuredly it wanted neither discrimination nor feeling. Would Lady F. be content to lay it aside till she comes into the North this summer, as I hope she will do. We

---

[1] Rogers was seeking preferment for a nephew.
[2] For her recently deceased husband.

might then lay our judgements together in conversation, and with the benefit of your suggestions and those of other friends with which she is no doubt furnished, we might be satisfied at last. Pray name this to her, if you have an opportunity.—

Your Italy can no where, out of your own family, be more eagerly expected than in this House. The Poetry is excellent we know, and the Embellishments, as they are under the guidance of your own taste, must do honor to the Arts. My Daughter, alas, does not recover her strength; she has been thrown back several times by the exercise, whether of walking in the Garden or of riding, which she has with our approbation been tempted to take, from a hope of assisting nature.

We like Mrs Hemans[1] much—her conversation is what might be expected from her Poetry, full of sensibility—and she enjoys the Country greatly.

The Somnambulist is one of several Pieces, written at a heat, which I should have much pleasure in submitting to your judgement were the fates so favorable so that we might meet ere long. How shall I dare to tell you that the Muses and I have parted company—at least I fear so, for I have not written a verse these twelve months past, except a few stanzas[2] upon my return from Ireland, last autumn.

Dear Sir Walter! I love that Man, though I can scarcely be said to have lived with him at all; but I have known him for nearly 30 years. Your account of his seizure grieved us all much. Coleridge had a dangerous attack a few weeks ago; Davy[3] is gone. Surely these are men of power, not to be replaced should they disappear, as one has done.

Pray repeat our cordial remembrances to your Brother and Sister, and be assured, my dear Rogers, that you are thought of in this house, both by the well and the sick, with affectionate interest—ever faithfully yours

Wm Wordsworth

---

[1] The popular poetess.
[2] Additions to *On the Power of Sound*.
[3] Sir Humphry Davy.

112. *To* Edward Quillinan

Sept. 10 1830

My dear Mr Quillinan,

Dora has already by a short note thanked you for bearing us in mind while you were in Paris, and for your interesting Letter. My own notions of the late changes in France, you will be at no loss to form an opinion about. From what you have heard me say upon Politics and government, reform and revolution, etc, you will not doubt but that I must lament deeply that the Ex-King of France[1] should have fallen into such a desperate course of conduct, and given his enemies so much the advantage over him. He has done much harm to the cause of rational monarchy all over the world by placing himself in the wrong; to a degree that one would have thought impossible. As to the future, fair and smooth appearances are not to be trusted, though the French, having passed lately through so many commotions and disappointments, may be in some degree checked in this democratical career by their remembrance of those calamities.

For the last two or three months we have been in a continual crowd and bustle, and are likely to be so for five or six weeks more, when a portion of us will move off to Cambridge for rather a lengthy visit to Dr Wordsworth, who has been making us happy with his Company for the last fortnight. We had Professor Hamilton and his Sister for three weeks, and many other visitors. Miss Curwen and John are now both with us, and Dr W. does not depart till a week hence. Today we were to have gone to Patterdale to Mr Marshall's, but it rains most forbiddingly, and the visit must be put off. Orson the hairy, alias, Professor Airey,[2] dined with us yesterday, and his Derbyshire Bride, a pretty woman to whom he was married last spring. Her profile reminded Miss Stanley[3] and her cousin Miss Hughes also (who is staying at the Hall) of poor Margaret Stanley,[4] but she is far from being so handsome. We have had Mr and Mrs Sharpe, and the delightful Miss Kinnaird[5] with us; if ever you happen to meet with her beg that for my sake, if not for yours or any one else that might be present, she would say

---

[1] Charles X, deposed in the July revolution.
[2] The Cambridge mathematician.   [3] A relation of Isabella Curwen.
[4] Unidentified.   [5] Sharp's ward.

for you Auld Robin Grey; if you dont like, if you are not in raptures with her performance, set me down as a Creature not without ears (that is nothing for I have not a good pair) but without a soul.

The wedding takes place on the 11th of next month at Workington Hall—the more we see of Miss Curwen the more are we pleased with her, and the higher are our hopes. Another year, I hope, we may see you here—this I cannot wish it—for I am up to the neck in engagements, and have not seen the Lonsdales except for a couple of days at the close of the election, when I found them at the Castle without expecting it. My visit was to Lord Lowther—I took Professor Hamilton along with me, who was much pleased with both the Person and the place.

I leave the rest of the sheet to the Ladies; remaining, my dear Friend, very sincerely yours

Wm Wordsworth

I dined at Mrs Watson's and at Mr Bolton's[1] with the great Blackwoodite of Elleray,[2]—he came down for the Regatta, with his two sons and eldest daughter. Bp Mant[3] was also present at Mr B's—he was said to be the Author of a forgotten Poem called the Simpliciad—the principal butt of which was to ridicule me, so that I was somewhat drolly placed in such company.

113. *To* W. Rowan Hamilton

Trinity Lodge, Cambridge,
November 26, 1830.

My dear Mr Hamilton,

I reached this place nine days ago, where I should have found your letter of the 28th ult., but that it had been forwarded to Coleorton Hall, Leicestershire, where we stopped a week on our road. I am truly glad to find that your good spirits put you upon writing what you call nonsense, and so much of it, but I assure you it all passed with me for very agreeable sense, or something better, and continues to do so even in this learned spot; which you will not be surprised to hear, when I tell you that at a dinner-party the

[1] i.e. at Calgarth and Storrs, on Windermere.
[2] John Wilson.   [3] Richard Mant, Bishop of Down and Connor.

other day I heard a Head of a House, a clergyman also, gravely declare, that the rotten boroughs, as they are called, should instantly be abolished without compensation to their owners; that slavery should be destroyed with like disregard of the *claims* (for rights he would allow none) of the proprietors; and a multitude of extravagances of the same sort. Therefore say I, Vive la Bagatelle; motley is your only wear.

You tell me kindly that you have often asked yourself, Where is Mr Wordsworth? and the question has readily been solved for you. 'He is at Cambridge'—a great mistake! So late as the 5th of November, I will tell you where I was; a solitary equestrian entering the romantic little town of Ashford-in-the-Waters, on the edge of the wolds of Derbyshire, at the close of day, when guns were beginning to be let off and squibs to be fired on every side, so that I thought it prudent to dismount and lead my horse through the place, and so on to Bakewell, two miles farther. You must know how I happened to be riding through these wild regions. It was my wish that Dora should have the benefit of her pony while at Cambridge, and very valiantly and economically I determined, unused as I am to horsemanship, to ride the creature myself. I sent James[1] with it to Lancaster; there mounted; stopped a day at Manchester, a week at Coleorton, and so reached the end of my journey safe and sound—not, however, without encountering two days of tempestuous rain. Thirty-seven miles did I ride in one day through the worst of these storms. And what was my resource? guess again: writing verses to the memory of my departed friend Sir George Beaumont, whose house I had left the day before. While buffeting the other storm I composed a Sonnet upon the splendid domain at Chatsworth, which I had seen in the morning, as contrasted with the secluded habitations of the narrow Fells in the Peak; and as I passed through the tame and manufacture-disfigured country of Lancashire I was reminded by the faded leaves, of Spring, and threw off a few stanzas of an ode to May.

But too much of self and my own performances upon my steed—a descendant no doubt of Pegasus, though his owner and present rider knew nothing of it. Now for a word about Professor Airey; I have seen him twice, but I did not communicate your message; it was at dinner and at an evening party, and I thought it

[1] W. W.'s gardener.

best not to speak of it till I saw him, which I mean to do, upon a morning call. There is a great deal of intellectual activity within the walls of this College, and in the University at large; but conversation turns mainly upon the state of the country and the late change in the administration.[1] The fires have extended to within 8 miles of this place; from which I saw one of the worst, if not absolutely the worst, indicated by a redness in the sky, a few nights ago.

I am glad when I fall in with a member of Parliament, as it puts me upon writing to my friends, which I am always disposed to defer, without such a determining advantage. At present we have two members, Mr Cavendish, one of the representatives of the University, and Lord Morpeth, under the Master's roof. We have also here Lady Blanche, wife of Mr Cavendish, and sister of Lord Morpeth. She is a great admirer of Mrs Hemans' poetry. There is an interesting person in this University for a day or two, whom I have not yet seen—Kenelm Digby, author of the 'Broad Stone of Honor', a book of chivalry, which I think was put into your hands at Rydal Mount. We have also a respectable show of blossom in poetry. Two brothers of the name of Tennyson in particular, are not a little promising.[2] Of science I can give you no account; though perhaps I may pick up something for a future letter, which may be long in coming for reasons before mentioned. Mrs W. and my daughter, of whom you inquire, are both well; the latter rides as often as weather and regard for the age of her pony will allow. She has resumed her German labours, and is not easily drawn from what she takes to; therefore I hope Miss Hamilton will not find fault if she does not write for some time, as she will readily conceive that with this passion upon her, and many engagements, she will be rather averse to writing. In fact she owes a long letter to her brother[3] in Germany, who, by the bye, tells us that he will not cease to look out for the Book of Kant you wished for. Farewell, with a thousand kind remembrances to yourself and sister, and the rest of your amiable family, in which Mrs W. and Dora join.

Believe me most faithfully yours,
Wm Wordsworth

---

[1] Lord Grey now headed a ministry committed to parliamentary reform.

[2] Alfred Tennyson (1809–92) and his brother Charles (1808–79), authors of *Poems by Two Brothers* (anon. 1827).   [3] Willy W.

114. *To* B. R. Haydon

[*c.* 8 July 1831]

My dear Haydon.

I have to thank you for two Letters—I am glad you liked the Sonnet.[1] I have repeated it to one or two Judges whom it has pleased.—You ask my opinion about your daughter learning Music. If she had an independent fortune I should say no, unless she have a strong inclination to the Study. I am aware that such a natural bent is by no means necessary for the attainment of excellence both in playing and singing,—I know one striking instance to the contrary—still I am not friendly to the practice of forcing music upon females—because I think their time might be better employ'd; but if you look to the situation of a Teacher or Governess for any of your Daughters Music would serve them much in procuring such situation. I know several persons otherwise well qualified who are unemployed solely from their want of that accomplishment.

You ask my opinion about the Reform Bill.—I am averse (with that wisest of the Moderns Mr Burke[2]) to all *hot* Reformations; i.e. to every sudden change in political institutions upon a large scale. They who are forced to part with power are of course irritated, and they upon whom a large measure of it is at once conferred have their heads turned and know not how to use it. To the *principle* of this particular measure, I object as *unjust*; and by its injustice opening a way for spoliation and subversion to any extent which the rash and iniquitous may be set upon.—If it could have been shewn of such or such a Borough that it claimed the right to send Members to Parliament, upon usurpation, or that it had made a grossly corrupt use of a legal privilege—in both these cases I would disfranchise—and also with the consent of the owners of burgage Tenure, but beyond this I would not have gone a step. As to transferring the right of voting to large Towns; my conviction is that they will be little the better for it—if at all—but een let them have their humour in certain cases and try the result. In short the whole of my proceedings would have been *tentative*, and in no case would I have violated a principle of justice. This is the sum of what

---

[1] *To B. R. Haydon, on seeing his picture of Napoleon Bonaparte on the island of St. Helena.*
[2] Edmund Burke (1729–97), the statesman.

I have to say. My admirers, as you call them, must have been led (perhaps by myself) to overstate what I said to Lord John Russel.[1] I did not conceal from him my utter disapprobation of the Bill; and what I said principally alluded to its effect upon the Aristocracy. I remember particularly telling him that the middle and lower classes were naturally envious haters of the Aristocracy—unless when they were *proud* of being attached to them—that there was no *neutral* ground in these sentiments—the Mass must either be your zealous supporters, said I, or they will do all in their power to pull you down—that power, all at once, are you now giving them through your ten pound renters who to effect their purpose will soon call in the aid of others below them till you have the blessing of universal suffrage; and what will become (I might have said in that case, I did hint it) of Covent Garden[2] and Wooburn[3] etc etc. I am called off and you must accept the wretched Scrawl poor return as it is for your [   ] letters—

[*a line or two, and the signature, torn away*]

115. *To* Sir John Stoddart

[23 July 1831]

. . . I became acquainted with Sir Humphry Davy when he was a lecturer at the Royal Institution;[4] and have since seen him frequently at his own house in London, occasionally at mine in the country and at Lord Lonsdale's, at Lowther, where I have been under the same roof with him several days at a time. Of his scientific attainments I am altogether an incompetent judge; nor did he talk upon those subjects except with those who had made them their study. His conversation was very entertaining, for he had seen much, and he was naturally a very eloquent person. The most interesting day I ever passed with him was in this country.[5] We left Patterdale in the morning, he, Sir Walter Scott, and myself, and ascended to the top of Helvellyn together. Here Sir H. left us, and we all dined together at my little cottage in Grasmere, which you must remember so well. When I last saw him, which was for several days at Lowther (I forget the year), though he was

---

[1] Grey's Home Secretary. [2] Part of the Bedford estates.
[3] i.e. Woburn Abbey. [4] In 1801. [5] In 1805.

apparently as lively as ever in conversation, his constitution was clearly giving way; he shrank from his ordinary exercises of fishing and on the moors. I was much concerned to notice this, and feared some unlucky result. There were points of sympathy between us, but fewer than you might perhaps expect. His scientific pursuits had hurried his mind into a course where I could not follow him; and had diverted it in proportion from objects with which I was best acquainted . . .

116. *To* Sir Walter Scott

Carlisle, Friday Eve^ng Sept. 16th [1831]

My dear Sir Walter,

'There's a man wi' a veil, and a lass drivin',' exclaimed a little urchin, as we entered 'merrie Carlisle' a couple of hours ago, on our way to Abbotsford. From the words you will infer, and truly, that my eyes are in but a poor state—I was determined however to see you and yours, and to give my daughter the same pleasure at all hazards; accordingly I left home last Tuesday, but was detained two entire days at Halsteads on Ullswater by a serious increase of my complaint—this morning I felt so much better that we ventured to proceed, tomorrow we hope to sleep at Langholm, on Sunday at Hawick, and on Monday, if the distance be not greater than we suppose, under your roof.

In my former letter I mention a nephew of mine, a student of Christ Ch:,[1] and I may add, a distinguished one, to whom (so far did I presume upon your kindness) I could not but allow the pleasure of accompanying us—he has taken the Newcastle road into Scotland, hoping to join us at Abbotsford on Tuesday, and I mention him now from an apprehension of being again retarded by my eyes, and to beg that if he should arrive before us he may be no restraint upon you whatever.—Let him loose in your library, or on the Tweed with his fishing-rod, or in the Stubbles with his gun (he is but a novice of a shot, by-the-bye) and he will be no trouble to any part of your family.

With kindest regards to Miss Scott and to M^r and Mrs Lockhart

[1] Charles Wordsworth.

if still as we hope with you, in which my Daughter unites, and with the same for yourself and a thousand good wishes

> I remain my dear Sir Walter
> very affectionately yours
> Wm Wordsworth

117. *To* John Kenyon

Rydal Mount, 26th Jan^y, [1832]

My dear Mr Kenyon,

You have enriched my house by a very valuable present, an entire collection of all that it is desirable to possess among Hogarth's Prints—the Box also contained a quarto volume, 'Hogarth Illustrated,' and 3 Vols of a French work for Mr Southey, which shall be forwarded to him. I have been thus particular as because there was no Letter within the Box perhaps it was not made up under your own eye—and I am now at a loss where to direct to you.

We are great admirers of Hogarth, and there are perhaps few houses to which such a collection would be more welcome; and living so much in the Country, as we all do, it is both gratifying and instructive to have such scenes of London life to recur to as this great master has painted.

You are probably aware that he was of Westmorland extraction, his name is very common hereabouts, and it is amusing to speculate on what his genius might have produced if, instead of being born and bred in London, whither his Father went from West^d, he had been early impressed by the romantic scenery of this neighbourhood, and had watched the manners and employments of our rustics. It is remarkable that his pictures, differing in this from the Dutch and Flemish Masters, are almost exclusively confined to indoor scenes or city life. Is this to be regretted? I cannot but think it is, for he was a most admirable *painter*, as may be seen by his works in the British Gallery; and how pleasant would it have been to have had him occasionally show his knowledge of character, manners, and passion by groupes under the shade of Trees, and by the side of Waters in appropriate rural dresses. He reminds me both of Shakespeare and Chaucer; but these great Poets seem happy in softening and diversifying their views of life, as often as they can, by metaphors and images from rural nature; or by shifting the scene of action into the quiet of groves or forests. What an exquisite piece of relief of this kind occurs in The Merchant of Venice—where, after the agitating trial of Antonio, we have Lorenzo and Jessica sitting in the open air on the bank on which the moonlight is sleeping—but enough.

Since I last heard from you I have received, and carefully read with great pleasure, the poems of your friend Baillie.[1] The scenes among which they were written are mainly unknown to me, for I never was farther south in France than St. Valier on the Rhone, where I turned off to the Grand Chartreuse,[2] a glorious place—were you ever there? I think you told me you were.

Mr B. has, however, interested me very much in his sketches of those countries, and strengthend the desire I have had all my life to see them, particularly the Roman Antiquities there, which H. C. Robinson tells me are greatly superior to any in Italy, a few in Rome excepted. I do not know where Mr Baillie is now to be addressed, and beg, therefore, if you be in communication with him, or with any of his friends who are, you would be so kind as to have my thanks conveyed to him, both for his little volume and the accompanying letter.

It is now time to say a word or two about ourselves. We are all well, except my Sister, who, you will be sorry to hear, has been five weeks confined to her room by a return of the inflammatory complaint which shattered her constitution three years ago. She is, God be thanked, convalescent, and will be able to take her place at our fireside in a day or two, if she goes on as well as lately.

We long to know something about yourself, Mrs Kenyon, and your Brother. Pray write to us soon.

We have had a most charming winter for weather—Hastings[3] could scarcely be warmer, and as to beauty the situation of Rydal Mount at this season is matchless. I shall direct to your Brother-in-law's House, as the best chance for my letter reaching

---

[1] Archdeacon Benjamin Bailey, friend of Keats.
[2] In 1790.   [3] Where Kenyon was.

you. Mrs Wordsworth, sister, daughter and Miss Hutchinson join me in kindest remembrances to yourself and Mrs Kenyon.

Farewell, and believe me, with every good wish,

faithfully yours,

Wm Wordsworth

My son Wm is at Carlisle, as my Sub-Distributor, and pretty well. John quite well, and happy with his excellent and amiable wife—a better Living would not be amiss—but where is it to come from? We Conservators are out of date.

W. W.

118. *To* Alexander Dyce

[*c.* 22 Apr. 1833]

My dear Sir,

The dedication[1] which you propose I shall esteem as an honor; nor do I conceive upon what ground, but an over-scrupulous modesty, I could object to it.

Be assured that Mr Southey will not have the slightest unwillingness to your making any use you think proper of his Memoir of Bampfylde.[2] I shall not fail to mention the subject to him upon the first opportunity.

You propose to give specimens of the best *Sonnet-writers* in our language. May I ask if by this be meant a Selection of the *best Sonnets, best* both as to *kind* and *degree*? A Sonnet may be excellent in its kind, but that kind of very inferior interest to one of a higher order, though not perhaps in every minute particular quite so well executed, and from the pen of a writer of inferior Genius. It should seem that the best rule to follow, would be, first to pitch upon the Sonnets which are best *both* in kind and perfectness of execution, and, next, those which, although of a humbler quality, are admirable for the finish and happiness of the execution, taking care to exclude all those which have not one or other of these recommendations, however striking they might be as characteris-

[1] To Dyce's *Specimens of English Sonnets*, 1833.
[2] Author of *Sixteen Sonnets*, 1778.

tic of the age in which the author lived, or some peculiarity of his manner. The tenth sonnet of Donne, beginning 'Death, be not proud', is so eminently characteristic of his manner, and at the same time so weighty in thought, and vigorous in the expression, that I would entreat you to insert it, though to modern taste it may be repulsive, quaint, and laboured.

There are two sonnets of Russell,[1] which, in all probability, you may have noticed, 'Could then, the Babes', and the one upon Philoctetes, the last six lines of which are first-rate. Southey's Sonnet to Winter pleases me much; but, above all, among modern writers, that of Sir Egerton Brydges, upon Echo and Silence. Miss Williams's[2] Sonnet upon Twilight is pleasing; that upon Hope of great merit.

Do you mean to have a short preface upon the Construction of the Sonnet? Though I have written so many, I have scarcely made up my own mind upon the subject. It should seem that the Sonnet, like every other legitimate composition, ought to have a beginning, a middle, and an end—in other words, to consist of three parts, like the three propositions of a syllogism, if such an illustration may be used. But the frame of metre adopted by the Italians does not accord with this view, and, as adhered to by them, it seems to be, if not arbitrary, best fitted to a division of the sense into two parts, of eight and six lines each. Milton, however, has not submitted to this. In the better half of his sonnets the sense does not close with the rhyme at the eighth line, but overflows into the second portion of the metre. Now it has struck me, that this is not done merely to gratify the ear by variety and freedom of sound, but also to aid in giving that prevading sense of intense Unity in which the excellence of the Sonnet has always seemed to me mainly to consist. Instead of looking at this composition as a piece of architecture, making a whole out of three parts, I have been much in the habit of preferring the image of an orbicular body,—a sphere—or a dew-drop. All this will appear to you a little fanciful; and I am well aware that a Sonnet will often be found excellent, where the beginning, the middle, and the end are distinctly marked, and also where it is distinctly separated into *two* parts, to which, as I before observed, the strict Italian model, as they write it, is favorable. Of this last construction of Sonnet, Russell's upon

---

[1] Thomas Russell (1762–88).   [2] Helen Maria Williams (1761–1827).

Philoctetes is a fine specimen; the first eight lines give the hardship of the case, the six last the consolation, or the *per-contra*. Ever faithfully,

Your much obliged Friend and Ser^{nt},
W. Wordsworth

Do not pay the postage of your letter to me.

In the case of the Cumberland poet,[1] I overlooked a most pathetic circumstance. While he was lying under the tree, and his friends were saving what they could from the flames, he desired them to bring out the box that contained his papers if possible. A person went back for it, but the bottom dropped out and the papers fell into the flames and were consumed. Immediately upon hearing this the poor old Man expired.

119. *To* Charles Lamb

Rydal Mount
Friday May 17th [1833] or thereabouts

My dear Lamb,

I have to thank you and Moxon,[2] for a delightful vol.[3]—your last, I hope not, of *Elia*. I have read it all, except some of the popular fallacies which I reserve not to get through my Cake all at once. The Book has much pleased the whole of my family, viz my Wife, Daughter, Miss Hutchinson, and my poor dear Sister, on her sick bed; they all return their best thanks.—I am not sure but I like the Old China and The Wedding as well as any of the Essays.—I read Love me and love my Dog to my poor Sister this morning, while I was rubbing her legs at the same time.—She was much pleased, and what is rather remarkable, this morning also I fell upon an Anecdote in Madame D'Arblayes' life of her father,[4] where the other side of the question is agreeably illustrated. The heroes of the Tale are David Garrick and a favorite little Spaniel of King-Charles's Breed, which he left with the Burneys when he and Mrs Garrick went on their Travels. In your remarks upon

---

[1] Thomas Sanderson of Kirklinton, author of *Original Poems*, 1800.
[2] See List of Correspondents.   [3] *Last Essays of Elia*, 1833.
[4] i.e. Frances Burney's *Memoirs of Dr Burney*, 1832.

Martin's pictures,[1] I entirely concur.—May it not be a question whether your own Imagination has not done a good deal for Titian's Bacchus and Ariadne?

With all my admiration of that great artist I cannot but think, that neither Ariadne or Theseus look so well on his Canvas as they ought to do.—But you and your Sister will be anxious, if she be with you, to hear something of our poor Invalid.—She has had a long and sad illness—anxious to us above measure, and she is now very weak and poorly—though she has been out of doors in a chair three times since the warm weather came. In the winter we expected her dissolution daily for some little time.—She then recovered so as to quit her bed, but not her room, and to walk a few steps, but within these few days the thundery weather has brought on a bilious attack which has thrown her back a good deal and taken off the flesh which she was beginning to recover—Her Spirits however thank God are good, and whenever she is able to read she beguiles her time wonderfully.—But I am sorry to say that we cannot expect that whatever may become of her health, her strength will ever be restored.—

I have been thus particular, knowing how much you and your dear Sister value this excellent person, who in tenderness of heart I do not honestly believe was ever exceeded by any of God's Creatures. Her loving kindness has no bounds. God bless her for ever and ever!—Again thanking you for your excellent Book, and wishing to know how you and your dear Sister are, with best love to you both from us all

I remain my dear Lamb
Your faithful Friend
W Wordsworth

120. *To* William Whewell

Rydal Mount May 14ᵗʰ. [1834]

Dear Mr Whewell,

I have been a *long time* in your debt for the present of your valuable Bridgewater Treatise[2]—and a *few weeks also*, for an

---

[1] The spectacular canvases of John Martin (1789–1854).

[2] *Astronomy and general physics considered with reference to Natural Theology*, 1833.

excellent Discourse by Mr Birks[1] in your Chapel. Two or three words I must say upon the latter in expression of my admiration of it, and of the delight which I felt in the proof that such Strains of thinking are not unknown among your young Students. The first reflects great honor upon the course of Studies pursued in your University. As to your own Treatise I have been prevented from writing to you, first by successive inflammation in my eyes, which cut me off from reading—and latterly, and up to this hour, by a weakness consequent upon the remedies. Having only Females about me, you will not be surprized when I frankly tell you that I am not as well acquainted with your Book as I hope to be. What I have seen of it adds to the admiration which I have always felt of the power and versatility of your talents. Again let me thank you, for what I value very much.

The other evening the Spirit of John Bunyan brushed by me, with a sort of 'mysterious dream waving at his wings', which was 'laid upon my eyelids'—not quite so softly touched as Milton felt his to be, when he put on the character of a Penseroso. To drop this figure I had a vision that presented to me your neighbour Old Cam, raised by such a flood as I witnessed on his banks once when I was at Cambridge in the month of May. Furthermore the waters were lifted out of their bed, by a sort of earthquake and, taking their course right across Clare Hall Lawn, made an attack upon the base of King's Coll Chapel. Out came the Provost, Fellows and Students, and to my great astonishment, fell to work most manfully for the destruction of the buttresses: in the meanwhile a crowd gathered, some of whom assisted in the labour. I myself went up and asked what they were about, and why? Some of the most active said we dislike these old fashioned deformities, the building would look better without them, and instead of being of use they encumber and weaken it. Others cried out, 'down with them! we are pulling them down, that the flood may have free way.' I continued to look on, and sure enough they got rid of all the buttresses, but the roof and the walls of the Chapel fell in, and they who had been so busy were crushed in the ruins. Now dreams, as we learn from high authority, are from Jove; this vision of mine may perhaps be from the same quarter—if so, the day will come when you (one of the 62 Petitioners[2] if I have not been

[1] Fellow of Trinity.   [2] For the abolition of religious tests at Cambridge.

misinformed) will excuse me for having troubled you with the report of it.

Ever faithfully and thankfully yours
Wm Wordsworth

My Sister tells me (and I hope she is not mistaken) that your name was *not* among the sixty two.

121. *To* Sara Coleridge

[early summer 1834]

My very dear Sara,

Thirteen years ago before I stood Godfather for Rotha[1] I told her father when he asked me to take that office upon me that I was too old to allow of a hope of my being of service to the child: his answer was that as she grew up and became acquainted with my works and heard her friends speak of their author she would derive from that relation to him greater benefit than could reasonably be expected from any other Sponsor who might offer to stand for her, or he could select from among his friends. To this partial view I deferred and I have since undertaken the same office for other children being influenced chiefly by the same persuasions and if you will accept of me for your expected little one from like considerations I have only to say that it would give me great pleasure to connect myself with your family by that tie.

Your letter to Dora moved me much. With a thousand tender wishes for your perfect recovery and Kindest regards to your husband

I remain my dear Sara your affec^{te} and faithful friend—

Wm Wordsworth

122. *To* H. N. Coleridge

July 29, [1834]

My dear Sir,

Though the account which Miss Hutchinson had given of the State of our Friend's health had prepared us for the sad Tidings of

[1] E. Q.'s younger daughter by his first wife.

your Letter the announcement of his dissolution[1] was not the less a great shock to my self and all this family. We are much obliged to you for entering so far into the particulars of our ever-to-be-lamented Friend's Decease, and we sincerely congratulate you and his dear Daughter upon the calmness of mind and the firm faith in his Redeemer which supported him through his painful bodily and mental trials, and which we hope and trust have enrolled his Spirit among those of the blessed.—

Your letter was received on Sunday Morning, and would have been answered by return of Post, but I wished to see poor Hartley first, thinking it would be comfortable to yourself and his Sister to learn from a third Person how he appeared to bear his loss. Mrs Wordsworth called on him yesterday morning, he promised to go over to Rydal, but did not appear till after Post-time. He was calm, but much dejected; expressed strongly his regret that he had not seen his Father before his departure from this world, and also seemed to lament that he had been so little with him during the course of their lives. Mrs Wordsworth advised him to go over to Keswick, and there provide himself with fit mourning under the guidance of Miss Crosthwaite,[2] Ambleside being a bad place for procuring any kind of clothes. I mention this that you may name it to his Mother.—

I cannot give way to the expression of my feelings upon this mournful occasion; I have not strength of mind to do so—The last year has thinned off so many of my Friends, young and old, and brought with it so much anxiety, private and public, that it would be no kindness to you were I to yield to the solemn and sad thoughts and remembrances which press upon me. It is nearly 40 years since I first became acquainted with him whom we have just lost; and though with the exception of six weeks when we were on the continent together,[3] along with my Daughter, I have seen little of him for the last 20 years, his mind has been habitually present with me, with an accompanying feeling that he was still in the flesh. That frail tie is broken and I, and most of those who are nearest and dearest to me must prepare and endeavour to follow him. Give my affectionate love to Sara, and remember me tenderly to Mrs Coleridge; in these requests Mrs Wordsworth, my poor

[1] S. T. C. had died on 25 July at the Gillmans'.
[2] A local draper.   [3] In 1828.

Sister, Miss H—, and Dora unite, and also in very kind regards to yourself; and believe me, my dear sir,

Gratefully yours,
W. Wordsworth

Pray remember us kindly to Mr and Mrs Gillman when you see them. We shall be happy to hear from you again at your leisure.

123. *To* Sir Robert Peel

Rydal Mount, Kendal
Feb^{ry} 5th 1835

Sir,

I have the honor to acknowledge the receipt of your Letter of the 3^d Inst^{nt}. That, at a period of such national anxiety, with so heavy a pressure of public business as you must now be under, you should have made, I cannot say *found*, leisure to express yourself as you have done, concerning me and my writings, affords me a gratification inferior to none which during a pretty long literary life I have ever known. With these words inadequate as they are to my feelings, a consciousness of the value of your time, obliges me to content myself.

The best manner in which I can meet your kind request that I would tell you without reserve whether there be any thing which you can do to serve me, is to state explicitly the motives which induced me to apply for your Patronage thro' my honored Friend Lord Lonsdale, for the transfer to my Son[1] of the office[2] I have held for nearly twenty two years. He is now in his 25th year. I designed him for one of the English Universities; but, when a Boy, he lost his health through an error of judgement on my part; and consequently could not be put forward in that walk of life. He was afterwards placed in Germany under a private Tutor, and subsequently he passed a short time at the University of Heidelberg, whence he returned upon an opening occurring at Carlisle, where, by acting as my Subdistributer for three years, he has been able merely to

---

[1] Willy W.   [2] His Distributorship.

maintain himself. This is but a melancholy station in life for one of his years, and connections.

After consulting with my powerful Friends, and through my Brother the Master of Trinity, with the Home Sec^ry, I saw no prospect of effectually serving him, notwithstanding their zealous wishes, but by making, for his benefit, this, to me, important sacrifice of the place which I hold.—Under no other circumstances should I have desired the transfer. For the duties of this Off: I know him, from experience, to be fit; as I trust he may be for many others, where the confinement is not excessive, and the labor *severe*; as in that case I should fear for his health, which is now good.—He is a Youth of sound principles, and staid opinions, modest, though of lively and agreeable manners, prudent, assiduous, very active, and methodical. The duties of an employment rather ambulatory than sedentary, would suit him best. But I must check my pen, fearing that as a prime minister you may smile at the above, as a parental eulogy; it is nevertheless a report which every competent Judge in the City of Carlisle, however differing from him in politics, would readily confirm.—

Allow me to say in further explanation and justification of myself for having thus troubled my Friends, that the course of my life, though strictly economical, has not allowed me to lay up more than would be necessary for the comfortable maintenance, in the event of my decease, of my Widow and only Daughter. My elder Son who for the last twelve months has held the Living of Workington for his Brother in law will have to retire with his family in less than two years to a Benefice under £200 per ann: which he owes to the patronage of Lord Lonsdale. Such is the State of my small family. Had I followed Literature as a *Trade* it might, as to pecuniary circumstances, have been very different. In common with the worthier and nobler class of Authors, who write not with a view to instant profit, and immediate effect, but with a hope of being permanently beneficial to mankind, I have to complain of injury proceeding from the laws of my own Country and the practices of a neighbouring one. During more than thirty years many of my productions have been before the Public. No one will deny that they had gradually wrought their way into estimation; and now when the Sale of them might considerably benefit such part of my family as may survive, the short time of Copy-right allowed by law, would make these public property, some at my decease, and others soon after. In the meanwhile the Parisian Piracies, for *morally* such they are, inundate our Country, with Copies at a price under what can possibly be afforded, if the claim of the Author is to be regarded.—

Pray excuse this long Letter, which precludes me from giving vent to the expression of my heartfelt satisfaction in seeing one so distinguished for every Statesmanlike quality at the head of affairs. You and your Colleagues have the good wishes, I sincerely believe, of a vast majority of the educated portion of our Countrymen, and of the Friends to the Constitution. May the almighty disposer of events support and guide you through the trials that await you!

> I have the honor to be
> with sincere admiration, and grateful respect
> most faithfully your obliged Ser^{vnt}
> Wm Wordsworth

124. *To* Samuel Carter Hall

> Rydal Mount
> near Kendal
> 5th June [? 1835]

Dear Sir,

Your obliging Letter through Mr Johnstone has remained too long unanswered for which, sickness in my family and much consequent anxiety must be the cause.

I had always a strong aversion to have any thing to do with Annuals. Money tempted me into one, and if money were not to a Person in my situation a rational object, I should have been properly punished by the subsequent conduct of those Parties for being seduced by such a consideration.

I am pleased with your frankness, and your sagacity has anticipated my answer. Poets, whatever Painters may do, seldom succeed when they work to order. I am not under that necessity having several Pieces by me which were Voluntaries, but a word will suffice between us, the best terms you can offer are below what I can bring my self to accept—You are perhaps aware that the

Annuals with their ornaments, have destroyed the Sale of several Poems which—till that Invention of some evil Spirit (a German one I believe)[1] was transplanted to this Country—brought substantial profit to their Authors, [and] were regarded as Standard works. You will regret this, I know, as much as any one, and your liberality would prompt you, I am sure to do your utmost, for the less wealthy part of that community—but what avails it?—Competition, the Idol of the Political economists, in fact ruins every thing.—Adieu, present my Comp[ts] to Mrs Hall, and believe me sincerely yours

W[m] Wordsworth

125. *To* Isabella Fenwick

[*c.* 26 June 1835]

My dear Miss Fenwick,

Mrs W. would have written in a way more agreeable to my wish than I am able; but at present she has not courage to touch the Pen. Dear Miss Hutchinson, her beloved Sister, and let me say, mine also, was seized with Rheumatic fever five weeks ago—the fever was subdued by medicine, but she did not recover her strength—nevertheless (she had been in such fine health before the attack) we had little fear about her, but an alarming change took place on Monday, and she departed this life on Tuesday evening. This has been a grievous shock, little did we apprehend when her anxiety for my sister and daughter hastened us home, that she herself would be the first called away. Upon the beauty of her character I will not dwell—she is we humbly trust among the blessed. We are comforted by this faith, and bear up as well as human infirmity allow. My poor Sister *must* soon follow her, she is calm and said to me only yesterday 'my tears are all to shed', and to another of the family she said, 'I do not feel that I have lost her, I am brought nearer to her'. Dora does not yet seem to have suffered in her health to the degree that we feared—and my Wife is wonderfully supported. She had her Sister-in-law with her, from Herefordshire, nearly three weeks; otherwise she must have sunk

---

[1] Ackermann, the fine-art publisher.

with anxiety and care and watching, for in addition to what you know, I must mention, that one of our two maid-servants who has lived with us twelve years has also been severely ill with something of the same complaint that carried off the one of our small household that we have lost.

It would have seemed unjust to our friendship for you, dear Miss Fenwick, if I had witheld these melancholy details—they will distress you, but the distress may do your spirit good. Pray for us, and do not forget how feelingly we love you. Farewell. May the Almighty bless you—

ever faithfully yours,
Wm Wordsworth

126. *To* Edward Moxon

Rydal Mount Novr. 20 1835

My dear Sir,

In a few days I hope to have an opportunity of sending through a private channel such a selection of Lamb's letters, to myself and this family, as appear to us not unfit for immediate publication. There are however in these, some parts which had better be kept back, but being fearful of using the pencil marks too freely we have left the decision to your discretion and that of our common friends—especially Mr Talfourd[1] and Mr Robinson—I need scarcely add, Mrs M.[2] and poor dear Miss L., if she be in a state of mind that allows of her attending to such a matter. I have kept back several letters—some because they relate merely to personal and domestic concerns, others, because they touch upon the character and manners of individuals who are now living, or too recently deceased to be brought under the public eye, without indelicacy.—I have also thought proper to suppress every word of criticism upon my own Poems—though the strictures are merely such, as might prove generally interesting—and occasionally lead to pleasing strains of sentiment, and descriptions which he has himself felt or observed. The suppressed letters shall not be

---

[1] See List of Correspondents.
[2] Mrs Moxon, Lamb's adopted daughter.

destroyed.—Those relating to my works are withheld, partly because I shrink from the thought of assisting in any way to spread my own praises and still more, as being convinced that the opinions or judgements of friends given in this way are mostly of little value. On this point I have no more to say, than that I trust to your care for preventing the possibility of any suppressed portion of the letters sent, being copied by any one, from any motive whatever—and that the originals may be returned to me through safe hands after you have done with them.

On the other page you have the requested Epitaph,[1] it was composed yesterday—and, by sending it immediately, I have prepared the way, I believe, for a speedy repentance—as I dont know that I ever wrote so many lines without some retouching being afterwards necessary. If these verses should be wholly unsuitable to the end Miss L. had in view, I shall find no difficulty in reconciling myself to the thought of their not being made use of, tho' it would have given me great, *very* great pleasure to fulfil, in all points, her wishes.

The first objection that will strike you, and every one, is its extreme length, especially compared with epitaphs as they are now written—but this objection might in part be obviated by engraving the lines in double column, and not in capitals.

Chiabrera[2] has been here my model—tho' I am aware that Italian Churches, both on account of their size and the climate of Italy, are more favourable to long inscriptions than ours—His Epitaphs are characteristic and circumstantial—so have I endeavoured to make this of mine—but I have not ventured to touch upon the most striking feature of our departed friend's character and the most affecting circumstance of his life, viz, his faithful and intense love of his Sister. Had I been pouring out an Elegy or Monody, this would and must have been done. But for seeing and feeling the sanctity of that relation as it ought to be seen and felt, lights are required which could scarcely be furnished by an Epitaph, unless it were to touch on little or nothing else.—The omission, therefore, in my view of the case was unavoidable: and I regret it the less, you yourself having already treated in verse the subject with genuine tenderness and beauty.

[1] The first part of *Written after the death of Charles Lamb*.
[2] Gabriello Chiabrera (1552–1638).

Now for a few words of business. What is doing with the engraving of my Portrait?[1] of which I hear nothing. If I told you that my Yarrow[2] was out of print, I said more than was true. Mess[rs] L only told me that it was so nearly out that it would be well to go to press with another Ed: which accordingly they set about—but what progress has been made I do not know, never hearing from them. If you see Mr Talfourd tell him that we are all delighted with his drama[3]—and which may seem odd—*that* is the very reason why I have put off writing to him—as I wished to do more than merely let him know, with thanks, how much he has pleased us. If you should be in communication with Mr Trench[4]—say I beg, a few words for me to him which may be done with the utmost sincerity to the same effect. I had a sprain in my right arm, 3 months ago, and I am yet unable to write with my own hand. You know how much the only pen I can command must be occupied—but I will express my gratitude and admiration to both the Gentlemen as soon as I shall be able. I cannot conclude without adding that the Ep: if used at all, can only be placed *in* the church. It is much too long for an out-door stone, among our rains, damps, etc.

Dora is much better and my poor Sister easier in body tho' her mind has of late faded sadly.

Kindest regards to y[r]self and every one about you in which Mrs. W. unites.

I remain faithfully yours
W. W.

After an absence of 3 weeks I only returned home last Wednesday, else you should have heard from me sooner. Kindest remembrances to Mr Rogers if he be returned from Ramsgate.

127. *To* James Stanger

Apr 16[th] [1836]

My Dear Sir,

Your obliging letter transmitted by Miss Southey, did not reach me, through an unusual neglect of the Carrier, till this morning—

---

[1] As frontispiece for the proposed new edition. Moxon had now taken over from Longmans as W. W.'s publisher. [2] *Yarrow Revisited, and Other Poems.*
[3] *Ion.* [4] R. C. Trench, later Archbishop of Dublin.

The obstacle arising out of conflicting opinions in regard to the Patronage,[1] one must be prepared for in every project of this kind. Mutual giving way is indispensable, and I hope it will not ultimately be wanting in this case.

The point *immediately* to be attended to is the raising a sufficient sum to ensure from the Church Building Society a portion of the surplus fund which they have at command, and which I know, on account of claims from many places, they are anxious to apply as speedily as possible. If time now be lost, that sum will be lost to Cockermouth.

In the question of the Patronage as between the people and the Bishop, I entirely concur with you in preferring the latter. Such is now the force of public opinion, that Bps are not likely to present upon merely selfish considerations, and if the judgment of one be not good, that of his Successor may make amends, and probably will. But elections of this sort, when vested in the people, have, as far as my experience goes, given rise to so many cabals and manœuvres, and caused such enmities and heart-burnings, that Christian charity has been driven out of sight by them. And how often and how soon have the successful party been seen to repent of their own choice!

The course of public affairs being what it is in respect to the Church, I cannot reconcile myself to delay from a hope of succeeding at another time.—If we can get a new church erected at Cockermouth, great will be the benefit, with the blessing of God, to that place; and our success cannot, I trust, but excite some neighbouring places to follow the example.

The little that I can do in my own Sphere shall be attempted immediately with especial view to ensure the coöperation of the societies. Happy should I be if you and other Gentlemen would immediately concur in this endeavour.

I remain my dear Sir,

with great respect sincerely yours

Wm Wordsworth

---

[1] Of the proposed new church at Cockermouth.

128. *To* his Family

[London]
Tuesday morning 9 0 clock [14 June 1836]
Mr Horace Twiss's.[1]

My dearest Friends,

I am come here to Breakfast: Last night dearest Mary returning from Windsor, I received your anxiously-expected Letter, which pleased me with the prospect of Dora having the benefit of change of scene.—How I wished you could have added that she was in the way of recovering flesh instead of losing it. God grant I may [have] such news, before I quit England if that is to be.—Last night I found also Mr Graves's[2] parcel, if possible I will call upon his Mother to day; but I have been sadly tired of late, partly in consequence of some cold caught in my face and limbs at that weary flower-show, whither I went to gratify the Miss Marshalls. Tell dearest Sister, that we went all through Windsor Castle, with the exception of the Library and St Georges Chapel. It is very greatly altered since the Renewal,[3] scarcely to be recognized, the Round Tower by being raised and I think spoiled, but the whole greatly improved and the appearance of the Courts from the living Rooms is most magnificent. Upon the whole the day was agreeably spent except for fatigue, went down to Eton, and saw Edward Coleridge and his wife both looking marvellously well and prospering abundantly; went also under the guidance of the provost through the Lodge. I forgot to mention that we passed the Queen and some ladies in the long Corridor; I rather think they had heard of us and came out on purpose. From Windsor we went to Mr Jesse's,[4] Hampton Court, a beautiful ride along the Thames. He lives in a wren's nest of [a] cottage, small as the smallest Lodging house in Ambleside, beautifully situated with a Grand Park behind and a beautiful village green in front. Mrs Fraser[5] was there, I liked her much—I think she has sound sense. Her little Boy is a fine child, but when I kissed him he made an ugly face, a trick, his mother said, taught

---

[1] The lawyer and MP.   [2] Curate of Windermere.
[3] i.e. the reconstruction in the later 1820s.
[4] Edward Jesse (1780–1868), the naturalist.
[5] W. W. probably means Jesse's daughter, Mrs Houstoun.

him by his Grandfather who spoils him a little. Mrs Jess is a fine looking woman for her years. Hallam[1] tells me that he has made upwards of 700£ by his books since he told me himself that he is going to publish another. This one will pay for the enlargement of his House which he is going to undertake. Mrs Fraser expressed much interest in you dearest Dora, she talks of going to the North in August. Judge how my time is spent when I tell you that at 8 this Monday I received a Card with the name of Mr Conolly upon it. He was waiting below, he had heard of my being in Town from the newspapers and called thus early to pay his respects. He took a high tone of admiration. He is an American, a converted Catholic, having been a protestant minister in America. His wife and family are at Rome, where he *himself* lives a good deal with Lord Shrewsbury.[2] He returns to Rome in September. Having to be here at 9 I walked him down with me to the end of the street.—I am sorry you were disappointed in not having a Letter from me when you expected it but I assure you I have written as much and as often as the state of my eyes and engagements will allow. I have no pleasure equal or comparable in the slightest degree to writing to you.—When I get to Moxons I will make up a parcel to send you, though I fear it will contain little that will much interest you.—My engagements are as follows: today, dine at Home, evening a Levée. Tomorrow breakfast with Lord Northampton,[3] dine at home. Thursday dine with Mr Courtenay;[4] friday with Lord Liverpool,[5] Saturday Sir Robert Inglis. Mr Twiss is coming and I must conclude—

W. W.

129. *To* T. N. Talfourd

Rydal Novr 16th [1836]

My dear Friend,

It would have given me great pleasure to have signed the paper you have sent me, but for two reasons, which will appear to you I

---

[1] The historian, who (with Rogers) accompanied W. W.
[2] The 16th Earl, a leading figure in the Roman Catholic revival.
[3] Politician and patron of the arts.   [4] W. W.'s financial adviser.
[5] The 3rd Earl, half-brother of the 2nd Earl, the Prime Minister.

think sufficient. First, I cannot speak of my own knowledge to the very important fact of English books being garbled by American Publishers at all, much less for any sordid purpose. The only two books printed in America which I have had an opportunity of looking into—are Tacitus' Works in Latin, and my own Poems in 4 Vols—given me by an American Friend—which are certainly not altered in the least from the original text. Therefore I feel it would be wrong in me, upon hear-say evidence merely (tho', of course not doubting the fact) to join in so grave a censure of American Publishers.

Secondly, I submit whether it would be politic to condemn those Publishers in such strong language; if the Agent for the American Publishers who communicated with Mr Moxon last Summer be trust-worthy, they as well as the American Authors are anxious to have English-Copyright established in America, and have for this purpose drawn up a petition, either jointly or severally, which is to be introduced by Mr Clay[1] to Congress, next Session.

Now if this be so, I must repeat my doubt whether it be politic to put forth, from English Authors in a body, such an accusation, so strongly expressed, as it might irritate the American Publishers, and in consequence their tempers might stand in the way of their interest.

Sometime ago I wrote rather a long letter to Sir R. Inglis upon Copy-right—tho' being then, and still continuing to be, unpossessed of accurate historical knowledge of the Subject. I am not aware that there was any thing important to you in that letter, but still I should like you to see it; and if you know Sir R. I. it might not perhaps be disagreeable to you to express to him my wish.

If I were Master of the facts historically, and had access to the arguments which have been used on both sides, when the question has been brought before the courts of law, or Parliament, I would readily give my best judgment to the consideration of the whole case. As it is, I feel incompetent to treat it in a manner to be of use to you.

Am I mistaken in supposing that I mentioned to you the name of Mr Stewart Mackenzie,[2] as a Member of Parliament who would support the side of justice in this matter?

---

[1] Henry Clay (1777–1852), formerly Secretary of State.
[2] MP for Ross and Cromarty.

Looking at it practically it is a mere question of degree—the Statute by assigning a term,[1] has relinquished the abstract ground of denying Copyright in the productions of Mind altogether: and by the same restriction, it has refused to admit the doctrine of independent perpetuity of Copyright in literature. So that we have, in the existing law, or any law upon the subject, a compromise between two principles. The practical question then is, does the existing law allow a *sufficient* recompence—to which, along with every thinking and unprejudiced Man, I should say no—without going further than my own case I feel the grievous injustice of the law as it now exists—but with this point you are fully acquainted. Nevertheless I would not appear as a Petitioner, but in the last extremity.

I am sorry that I have not time to add more. Believe me, with kindest regards to Mrs T. in which Mrs W. and my Daughter joins

Ever faithfully Yours
Wm Wordsworth

At your leisure will you be so good as direct, and forward the enclosed.

130. *To* Samuel Carter Hall

Rydal Mount
Jan^ry 15th 1837

My dear Sir

Accept my thanks for your elegant present of the two volumes of the Book of Gems, which I received two days ago, and also for the very friendly letter that accompanied them. You speak feelingly of the pleasure which you and Mrs Hall had in seeing me some years ago—be assured that it was reciprocal, and nothing but overwhelming engagements, more than at my years I ought to have exposed myself to, could have prevented me seeking you out when I was in Town last Spring.

Being much engaged in a monthly race with the Press—in which a new Edition of my Poems has involved me, I have not had time

---

[1] Of twenty-eight years.

for more than a glance at your part of the Volumes—but I must say how much I was pleased with your notice of our Westmorland Poet, Langhorne—The Critique is very judicious, both as to his merits and his faults—I do not wonder that you are struck with his Poem of the Country Justice—You praise it, and with discrimination—but you might have said still more in its favour; as far as I know, it is the first Poem, unless perhaps Shenstone's Schoolmistress[1] be excepted, that fairly brought the Muse into the Company of common life, to which it comes nearer than Goldsmith, and upon which it looks with a tender and enlightened humanity—and with a charitable, (and being so) philosophical and poetical construction that is too rarely found in the works of Crabbe. It is not without many faults in style from which Crabbe's more austere judgment preserved him—but these are to me trifles in a work so original and touching.

You ask me to furnish you with a few notices of my life—an application to the same effect was lately made to me by a french Gentleman[2] who had been engaged upon what he calls a 'long labor upon my works'—a translation I believe of many parts of them, accompanied with a commentary. My answer was, that my course of life had been altogether private, and that nothing could be more bare of entertainment or interest than a biographical notice of me must prove, if true. I referred him to Gagliani's Ed:[3] which, as to the date and place of my birth, and the places of my Education is correct—the date of my publications is easily procured—and beyond these I really see nothing that the world has to do with, in my life which has been so retired and uniform. Since the beginning of the year 1800 I have had a home either at my present residence or within two miles of it—tho', as appears from my writings, I have made excursions both on the Continent and on our own Island—and also that I have sometimes sojourned in Leicestershire.

With my cordial regards to Mrs Hall and every good wish to both of you whom I have often thought of with sincere esteem believe me to be truly yours

Wm Wordsworth

[1] Publ. (anon.), 1742.
[2] Probably Hippolyte de la Morvonnais, the Breton poet.
[3] i.e. Galignani's Paris edn. (1828).

131. *To* Dorothy Wordsworth

Saturday Paris 25th March [1837]

My dearest Sister,

It is now near twelve at night and my eyes are worn out. I have only to say I have written at length to Miss Fenwick, to be forwarded to Mary and then to you, or perhaps first to Dora as nearest. We[1] set off tomorrow for Fontainbleau on our way to Italy; how I wish your strength had been equal to the journey. I have seen the Baudouins all well, a thousand kind inquiries after you. We reached Paris on Wednesday evening, and I have rambled about every where. God bless you and dear Joanna and kind remembrances to all the servants. And pray tell Mr Carter[2] that I shall be greatly obliged to him, if he will correct the misprints of the Stereotype of the Yarrow and send the corrections up to Mr Moxon, who is desirous to strike off from the Stereotype thus corrected a new edition with the additional Poems of the last, for the purpose of accommodating the purchasers of the Edition of 1832.

farewell again farewell my dear Friends.

[*Unsigned*]

132. *To* Mary and Dora Wordsworth

[Rome]
[6 May 1837]
—This will be in London in eleven days.—
Saturday

My dearest Mary,

Yesterday put an end to my anxieties and depression of mind by bringing me your most welcome Letter of the 17th April with a postscript from Dora of the 19th. Mr Stephen[3] had kindly sent it to the English ambassador which perhaps occasioned delay of a day or two but I believe I had been unreasonable in calculating so confidently upon an answer to my Toulon letter upon my arrival at

---

[1] i.e. W. W. and H. C. R.   [2] W. W.'s clerk.
[3] James, later Sir James, Stephen, of the Colonial Office.

Rome. I have therefore to beg your pardon for writing in such bad spirits as I did. Dearest Dora your mother speaks of a letter from yourself to me but I have not received it. How glad I was to have so good an account of your health, and most thankful to Drs Holland and Brodie and to all your kind friends for their goodness to you. I rejoice that you are in Town, thank Mrs Harrison[1] in my name with my best love and give the same to one and all of the family with whom you are. I cannot feel sufficiently grateful to God for the good account of you all except your poor dear Cousin at Brinsop,[2] for whom there appears to be no hope. Of Sister and Joanna also the accounts are good to my heart's delight.—Your Letter took off such a weight from me as I cannot describe, for I feared I should have no news till your answer came to mine from Rome, which would have had to follow us to Florence, for there is not the least chance of our being able to include Naples in our tour, on account of the Quarantine. In the course of next week we shall go to Tivoli etc etc and 3 or 4 days after our return will suffice for Rome. You will naturally wish for details, but what can I select out of such a wilderness of sights antient and modern, though I have not seen a 100th part of the indoor attractions, not yet even the Vatican, to which we go on Monday under the guidance of Mr Gibson[3] the Sculptor. Several times however I have been at St Peter's, have heard Mass before the Pope in the Sistine Chapel, and after that seen him pronounce the benediction upon the people from a balcony in front of St Peter's and seen his Holiness scatter bits of paper from aloft upon the multitude, indulgences I suppose. Of the outside of Rome, and the ruins and the modern town, antient walls etc I have seen a great [? deal] both on foot, and in a carriage, for which latter accommodation we are indebted to the kindness of Miss Mackenzie an old Friend of Mr R. and Sister-in-law to Mr Mackenzie[4] who with his son was at Rydal last summer. She is an amiable person and nothing can exceed her attentions. Mr Collier also, an acquaintance of Lord Lowther, has accompanied me on two excursions in the neighbourhood, one to the Monte Mario which commands the most magnificent view of modern Rome the

[1] Probably Mrs Benson Harrison, W. W.'s cousin.
[2] In Herefordshire, now the residence of the Hutchinsons.
[3] John Gibson, RA (1790–1866), pupil of Canova.
[4] The MP mentioned in Letter 129.

Tiber and the surrounding country. Upon this elevation I stood under the pine redeemed by Sir G. Beaumont, of which I spoke in my former Letter. I touched the bark of the magnificent tree and could almost have kissed it out of love for his memory. One of the most agreeable excursions we have made was with Miss Mackenzie and Mr Collier to the Tomb of Cecilia Metella and the other antiquities in its neighbourhood. This was on the first of May. The air was clear and bright, and the distant hills were beautifully clothed in air and the meadows sparkling with rich wild flowers. In our ramble after alighting from the carriage we came to the spot which bears the name of the fountain of Egeria; but this is all a fiction, nevertheless the grotto and its trickling water and pendent ivy and vivid moss, have enough of Poetry and painting about them to make the spot very interesting independent of all adjuncts whether of fact or fiction. Dearest Dora say to the Miss Marshalls that I hope they will one day see most of what I have seen, particularly the Cornice Road and Rome and its neighbourhood; as to yourself, notwithstanding your own and your Doctor's good report I fear you will never feel strong enough to adventure so far. I do not think dearest Dora that you could stand it, and after all it is very trying at this season of the year, and through all the summer and in winter the weather appears to be often very rainy and what may be called bad. This morning we have been with Mr Severn[1] the Painter a friend of Keats the Poet. He has excellent health in Rome summer and winter, but his House stands clear of Malaria and how does he live in Summer? Why he is out in the open air at five in the morning with his Wife and children when she is well enough, returns at 7, paints all day and does not stir out again till an hour or so after sunset. But this sort of life you see ill suits anyone but a person with occupations like his. Upon the whole the weather since we came, or rather the state of the atmosphere, has not except upon the first evening of our arrival been favorable to landscape beauty. We have several times been out as early as six in the morning, but then the sun has too much power for beauty, and the evenings have all, since that one, been without fine nights. Of Villas and their gardens I have seen I can scarce tell you how many, some from the views they command of the city, old and new, very impressive. But of churches and

[1] Joseph Severn (1793–1879).

pictures and statues in them I am fairly tired—in fact I am too old in head, limbs and eyesight for such hard work, such toiling and such straining and so many disappointments either in finding the most celebrated picture covered up with curtains, a service going on so that one cannot ask to have a sight, or the church closed when one arrives at the door. All this will however be forgotten long before I get back to dear England and nothing but the pleasure, I hope, survive. The only very celebrated object which has fairly disappointed me on account of my ignorance I suppose is the Pantheon. But after all it is not particular objects with the exception perhaps of the inside of St Peter's that make the glory of this City; but it is the boun[d]less variety of combinations of old and new caught in ever varying connection with the surrounding country, when you look down from some one or other of the seven hills, or from neighbouring eminences not included in the famous seven. Tomorrow we are going into the Campagna to see a sheep-shearing upon the farm of a wealthy Peasant who lives in that *sad* and *solemn district*, as I believe it is around his abode, which lies about four miles along the Appian Way. And there this hospitable Man dwells among his herds and flocks with a vast household, like one of the Patriarchs of old.—

I write with watering eyes; caused I think by the glare of the sun, but some tell me it is a slight touch of influenza. I wish it may and then it will go off. The influenza has been travelling with me or rather I with it since I left Rydal. I found it in London in Paris every where in the south of France and even greatly prevalent in Rome though abating. I should not have mentioned my eyes, but to account for this penmanship even more wretched than usual—nor should I have written today but to beg you to direct to Florence, 'poste restante', and remove your regret at my not having heard from you before. Your Letter, Dearest Dora may be forwarded instantly through Mr Stephen to the Minister at Florence, so I should suppose, but that you can ascertain through Mr Taylor or himself and if there be any doubt of the elegibility of that mode of conveyance, notwithstanding the postage, pray write instantly by post, à la Poste Restante or as you may learn to do best, for I believe in some parts of the continent the post off: will not charge itself with Letters so directed. This however is not the case at Rome. If you can send through the Minister so much the better, pray write instantly without waiting for Mother's reply to this and even if you cannot send through her write by the Post. Say if the Master of Harrow[1] undertook the off:[2] and tell me all the news you can of our Friends. I fear the legacy story is too good to be true. We live for nothing almost here, but travelling Post is for one cause or another more expensive than we were led to expect. Here comes Mr Robinson to whom I resign the Pen.

With love and blessings to all. W. W.

133. *To* Henry Reed

London, August 19, 1837.

My dear Sir,

Upon returning from a tour of several months upon the Continent I find two letters from you awaiting my arrival, along with the edition of my poems you have done me the honour of editing. To begin with the former Letter April 25, 1836. It gives me concern that you should have thought it necessary not to apologize for that you have not done, but to explain at length why you addressed me in the language of affectionate regard.—It must surely be gratifying to one whose aim as an author has been to reach the hearts of his fellow-creatures of all ranks and in all stations to find that he has succeeded in any quarter, and still more must he be grateful to learn that he has pleased in a distant country men of simple habits and cultivated taste, who are at the same time widely acquainted with literature. Your second letter, accompanying the edition of the poems, I have read, but unluckily, have not before me. It was lent to Sergeant Talfourd on account of the passage in it that alludes to the possible and desirable establishment of English Copyright in America.

I shall now hasten to notice the Edition which you have superintended of the poems. This I can do with much pleasure, as the Book which has been shewn to several persons of taste, Mr Rogers in particular, is allowed to be far the handsomest specimen of print in double Column which they have seen. Allow me to thank you for the pains you have bestowed upon the work. Do not

---

[1] C. W. jnr. (see List of Correspondents).   [2] A trusteeship.

apprehend that any difference in our several arrangements of the poems can be of much importance; you appear to understand me far too well for that to be possible. I have only to regret, in respect to this Volume, that it should have been published before my last Edition in the correction of which I took great pains as my last labour in that way, and which moreover contains several additional pieces. It may be allowed me also to express a hope that such a law will be passed ere long by the American legislature as will place English Authors in general upon a better footing in America than at present they have obtained, and that the protection of Copyright between the two countries will be reciprocal.

The vast circulation of English works in America offers a temptation for hasty and incorrect printing; and that same vast circulation would, without adding to the price of each copy of an English Work in a degree that could be grudged or thought injurious by any purchaser, allow an American remuneration which might add considerably to the comforts of English Authors who may be in narrow circumstances, yet who at the same time may have written solely from honorable motives.—Besides, justice is the foundation on which both law and practice ought to rest.

Having many letters to write on returning to England after so long an absence I regret that I must be so brief upon the present occasion. I cannot conclude, however, without assuring you, that the acknowledgements which I receive from the vast continent of America are among the most grateful that reach me. What a vast field is there open to the English Mind, acting through our noble language! Let us hope that our Authors of true Genius will not be unconscious of that thought or inattentive to the duty which it imposes upon them of doing their utmost to instruct, to purify and to elevate their readers. That such may be my own endeavour through the short time I shall have to remain in this world, is a prayer in which I am sure you and your life's partner will join me.

Believe me gratefully

Your much obliged friend

Wm Wordsworth

134. *To* Edward Quillinan

Brinsop Court, Wednesday Sept. 20th [1837]

My dear Mr Quillinan,

(I[1] hold the pen for Father)

We are heartily glad to learn from your letter just received that in all probability by this time you must have left the unhappy country in w^h you have been so long residing. I should not have been sorry if you had entered a little more into Peninsular politics, for what is going on there is shocking to humanity, and one would be glad to see anything like an opening for the termination of these unnatural troubles—the position of the Miguelites[2] relatively to the confliction of so-called liberal parties is just what I apprehended and expressed very lately to Mr Robinson, who would not hear of it; very inconsiderately, I think, setting down that body as all but extinguished. He came down with us to Hereford with a view to a short tour on the banks of the Wye w^h has been prevented by an unexpected attack of my old complaint of inflammation in the eye; and in consequence of this Dora will accompany me home with a promise on her part of returning to London before the month of Oct^{br} is out. Our places are taken in to-morrow's coach for Liverpool, so that since we must be disappointed at not seeing you and Jemima[3] here, we trust that you will come to Rydal from Leeds. This very day Dora had read to me your Poem again; it convinces me along with your other writings that it is in your power to attain a permanent place among the poets of England, your thoughts, feelings, knowledge, and judgement in style, and skill in metre entitle you to it; if you have not yet succeeded in gaining it the cause appears to me mainly to lie in the subjects w^h you have chosen. It is worthy of note how much of Gray's popularity is owing to the happiness with which his subject is selected in three pieces—his Hymn to Adversity, his ode on the distant prospect of Eton College, and his Elegy. I ought however in justice to add that one cause of your failure appears to have been thinking too humbly of yourself, so that you have not reckoned it worth while to look sufficiently round you for the best

---

[1] i.e. Dora W.   [2] The absolutists in the Spanish civil war.
[3] E. Q.'s elder daughter by his first marriage.

subjects or to employ as much time in reflecting, condensing bringing out and placing your thoughts and feelings in the best point of view, as is necessary. I will conclude this matter of poetry, my part of the letter, with requesting that as an act of friendship at your convenience you would take the trouble, a considerable one I own, of comparing the corrections in my last edition with the text in the preceding one. You know my principles of style better I think than any one else, and I should be glad to learn if anything strikes you as being altered for the worse. You will find the principal changes in The White Doe, in w^h I had too little of the benefit of your help and judgement: there are several also in the sonnets both miscellaneous and political—in the other poems they are nothing like so numerous, but here also I should be glad if you w^d take the like trouble. Jemima, I am sure, will be pleased to assist you in the comparison by reading new or old as you may think fit. With love to her I remain my dear Mr Quillinan, faithfully yours,

Wm Wordsworth

135. *To* Sir William Rowan Hamilton

Rydal Mount Decr 21st [1837]

My dear Sir W^m,

The Papers had informed me of the honor[1] lately conferred upon you, and I was intending to congratulate you on the occasion, when your letter arrived. The Electors have done great credit to themselves by appointing you, and not a little by rejecting the Ultra-liberal Archbishop,[2] and that by so decided a majority. We are much pleased that your Sister, who we conclude is well, has sent her Poems to press, and wish they may obtain the attention we are sure they will merit. Your own two sonnets, for which I thank you, we read, that is Mrs W. and myself (Dora is in the South), with interest—But to the main purport of your letter. You pay me an undeserved compliment in requesting my opinion, how you could best promote some of the benefits which the Society, at whose head you are placed, aims at; as to patronage, you are right

---

[1] Presidency of the Royal Irish Academy.
[2] Richard Whateley (1787–1863).

in supposing that I hold it in little esteem for helping genius forward in the fine arts, especially those whose medium is words. Sculpture and painting *may* be helped by it; but even in these departments there is much to be dreaded. The french have established an Academy at Rome upon an extensive scale, and so far from doing good, I was told by every one that it had done much harm. The Plan is this: they select the most distinguished Students from the School or academy at Paris and send them to Rome, with handsome stipends, by which they are tempted into idleness and of course into vice: so that it looks like a contrivance for preventing the french nation, and the world at large, profitting by the genius which nature may have bestowed, and which left to itself would in some cases, perhaps, have prospered. The principal, I was indeed told the *only*, condition imposed upon these Students is, that each of them send annually some work of his hands to Paris. When at Rome I saw a good deal of English artists. They seemed to be living happily and doing well—tho' as you are aware, the public patronage any of them receive is trifling.

Genius in Poetry, or any department of what is called the Belles Lettres, is much more likely to be cramped than fostered by public Support; better wait to reward those who have done their work, tho' even here national rewards are not necessary, unless the Labourers be, if not in poverty, at least in narrow circumstances. Let the laws be but just to them, and they will be sure of attaining a competence, if they have not misjudged their own talents, or misapplied them. The cases of Chatterton, Burns and others, might, it should seem, be urged against the conclusion that help beforehand is not required—but I do think that in the temperament of the two I have mentioned there was something which however favourable had been their circumstances, however much they had been encouraged and supported, would have brought on their ruin. As to what Patronage can do in Science, discoveries in Physics, mechanic arts, etc. you know far better than I can pretend to do.

As to 'better canons of criticism, and general improvement of Scholars', I really, speaking without affectation, am so little of a Critic or Scholar that it would be presumptuous in me to write upon the Subject to you. If we were together, and you should honor me by asking my opnion upon particular points, that would be a very different thing, and I might have something to say, not wholly without value. But where could I begin with so comprehensive an argument, and how could I put into the compass of a letter my thoughts, such as they may be, with any thing like order. It is somewhat mortifying to me to disappoint you—You must upon reflection I trust perceive, that in attempting to comply with your wish I should only lose myself in a wilderness. I have been applied to to give lectures upon Poetry in a public Institution in London, but I was conscious that I was neither competent to the Office, nor the public prepared to receive what I should have felt it my duty to say, however in[adequately].

I have [had] a very pleasant and not profitless tour on the Continent, tho' with one great drawback, the being obliged on account of the cholera to return without seeing Naples and its neighbourhood. Had it not been for the State of my eyes which became inflamed after I got back to England, I should have been able to take Liverpool in my way home, at the time you were there. The attack continued for a long time, and has left a weakness in the organ, which does not yet allow me either to read or write; but with care I hope to come about.

My Sister continues in the same enfeebled State of mind and body. Mrs W. is well—but your Godson[1] we hear is suffering from derangement of the Stomach, so that at present he is not a thriving child, but his elder brother is now remarkably so, and he about the same age was subject to the same trials. We trust that your little family are all flourishing, and with our united affectionate regards believe me, faithfully

Dear Sir W. yours
Wm Wordsworth

I am sorry that I cannot send this thro' Lord Northampton, because he tells me he is coming northward.

[1] W. W.'s grandson William.

136. *To* T. N. Talfourd

Rydal Mt
Jan 8th [1838]

My Dear Sir,

As the time draws near when your bill[1] is to be brought in to Par[2] would you be so kind as to name the day, for the 2d reading—that I may apprize the few personal friends whom I may have in the house—and urge them to attend. Mr Southey tells me that he knows not one to whom he could apply beyond those whom he is sure will attend without such application. We are reading the 6th Vol. of Lockhart's life of Scott—what a deplorable picture of distress and humiliation all to be traced up to one mis[take]—an undervaluing of the dignity and importance of literature in comparison with what is called *rising in the* world, and those indulgences, and that sort of distinction which the acquiring money with rapidity, and spending it with profusion, afford.

Wishing you and yours a happy new year in which Mrs W cordially joins with a request that you will send the enclosed to the twopenny post, I remain

dear Sir, ever faithfully yours
Wm Wordsworth

137. *To* J. C. Hare

Rydal Mount, May 28 [1838]

My dear Mr Hare,

Books are mostly long in reaching me, and so it was with your's,[3] but I might have thanked you sooner both for the Volume and the honor you have done me by the Dedication. That I have not sent you my acknowledgments sooner I am in fact to blame, but only for some want of resolution; I have been anxious to write but felt that I would not do justice to my feelings, especially in regard to your

---

[1] A Copyright Bill. The measure was not finally passed until 1842.
[2] Parliament.
[3] The enlarged edn. of *Guesses at Truth, By Two Brothers*.

lamented Brother.[1]—I cannot exactly recall the time when I received his sermons, but it was not long before I went abroad, and Mrs Wordsworth tells me she fears I never returned thanks for them. If so, I have to request your indulgence, the reason must have been that I had not read them all, and the cause of that, the frequent irritations and inflammations to which my eyes are subject, an infirmity which has brought my knowledge of new books into very narrow compass and also taken from my familiarity with old ones. Nor have I any one near me who can read *much* aloud, so that we are a disabled Household even when my Daughter, who has long been about, is at home [*M. W. adds in the margin*: This is not quite the fact—Mrs W *can* read but listening sends her husband to sleep. M W] Your excellent Brother's death was much lamented by me and mine, and what a loss he was to the world and to his sacred calling his sermons prove. The Copy you were so kind as to send me, I have lent to my Son, as my Daughter possesses another. He much values the work for its own sake, and as a memorial of one to whom he was so greatly obliged. My own judgement is perhaps not entitled to high respect, for I do not profess to be much of a Theologian or Divine, but there can be no presumption in stating that the sermons appeared to me models of simplicity in laying down the truths, and of unbounded earnestness in enforcing it. Some of the illustrations however though quite suited, I have no doubt, to a congregation so illiterate as your brother's, would be found a little too homely for the taste of our Yeomanry, who have all more or less of a school education. They would think that their attainments were rated too low, and that they were treated a little too much like Children, or at least more as inferiors in Culture and exercise of mind, than they ought to be.

I have contrived to read a great part of the Guesses of Truth, and with great pleasure and profit; though I have not yet compared the present edition with the former.—I know little of Hazlitt's writings, but judging from my recollections of his conversation, I should be inclined to say you treat him with more respect than for any originality of mind that was in him [which] he could lay claim to. He was an acute analyst, but he had little imagination, and no wholesome or well regulated feeling. But for what he learned from

---

[1] Augustus Hare (1792–1834), John W.'s tutor at Oxford: author of *Sermons to a Country Congregation*, 2 vols., 1836.

Coleridge and Lamb, he never would have been listened to as a critic. Something also, he learned from myself, but I never took to him, and therefore that perhaps was not much. As you most justly observe, the wreck of his morals was the ruin of him, as it must be of every one else—

I am anxious to hear of your Brother Francis; he was very kind to us at Rome, and we saw him again at Florence, where he was seized with an illness which I did not hear of, till between nine and ten at night, our horses being ordered for Bologna early next morning. I wrote to Mrs Hare from Bologna to make inquiries and learned from her that he was convalescent, though she was still somewhat anxious about him.—Pray give me a line, were it only to let me know how he and his family are going on. I am really anxious about this for before that seizure, I had an apprehension that his liveliness of nature was wearing him out before his time. Give my best regards to him and Mrs Hare when you write and believe me dear Sir faithfully your much obliged Friend W. Wordsworth

My Continental Tour was very agreeable but too fatiguing and taken too late in life to turn in much profit. My allowance of time was too short for the work I had to do.[1]

138. *To* B. R. Haydon

Rydal Mount July 28 [1838]

My dear Haydon

I received your 2nd Letter more than a month ago when I was upon the point of setting off for Northumberland and Durham where I have been detained till yesterday. In the course of this tour I wrote to you at some length; but upon consulting your Letter when I had written my own I find no date but the general one of London and though you are a distinguished Person I thought that the Post office might neverthless be ignorant of your habitat. I therefore did not send my Letter. Since it was written I have had an opportunity of reading your Essay in the Encyclopaedia, and neither in that, nor in your Letter, do I find any thing said

[1] M. W. adds a PS.

concerning Michael Angelo, to which I object. I acknowle[d]ged him to be liable to all the charges you bring against him; it would only be a question between us of the *degree* in which he is so. Therefore do not take the trouble of sending your essay for my inspection before hand. I need only add, that through Messrs Whitaker Booksellers Ave Mary Lane, I can receive any parcel addressed to me under cover to Messrs Hudson and Nicholson, Booksellers, Kendal, to be forwarded by Mr W. in his first Parcel to Messrs Hudson and Nicholson, with an under cover for me—

There are some opinions in your essay about which I should like to talk with you; as for example when you say that Raphael learned *nothing* from Perugino but what he had to unlearn. Surely this is far from the truth; undoubtedly there is in him, as in all the elder Masters, a hardness and a stiffness, and a want of skill in composition, but in simplicity, and in depth of expression he deserved to be looked up to by Raphael to the last of [his] days. The transfiguration[1] would have been a much finer picture than it is if Raphael had not at the period of his life lost sight of Perugino and others of his predecessors more than he ought to have done.—Whoever goes into Italy, if Pictures be much of an object with him, ought to begin where I ended, at Venice. Not as I did, with the pure and admirable productions of Fra Bartolomeo at Lucca and with Raphael at Rome, so on to Florence, Bologna and Parma and Milan: and Venice by way of conclusion. Italian Pictures ought to be taken in the following order or as nearly as may be so, Milan, Padua, Venice, Bologna, Parma, Florence, Rome.—Your essay does you *great credit*; and your practise, I trust still more. I had a sad account of the French Academy at Rome; the students appear to be doing little or nothing and spend their time in dissipation.—Believe me with kind regards to Mrs Haydon

ever faithfully yours

W Wordsworth

[1] In the Vatican.

139. *To* Henry Crabb Robinson

[*c.* 5 Dec. 1838]

My dear Friend

It was very good in you to write so long a letter from abroad—we found it not a little interesting, and it was the more so to me, because even with those parts of your tour which I had not seen I was previously pretty well acquainted by drawings, prints, books and conversation. You hint at the possibility of my taking some such a Tour, but I have no inclination that way; my *wishes* even, are bounded to getting to Chalons-sur-Soane and floating down that river to Lyons, and downward by the Rhone, to take the Steam boat from Marseilles to Naples; and thus complete our tour in Italy, so unfortunately cut short. If money were no object, and circumstances allowed, I would endeavour to do this; tho' I could not offer myself as a Companion to any one so vigorous and animated as you are. Rogers is a wonderful Man—his life is worthy of being written with care, and *copiously*—but I fear so valuable a work as that would be, will never be produced—

Nothing has happened that gave me so much pleasure, joy I might say, as Mr Clarkson's triumph over his enemies—to which you, my good friend, have not a little contributed. Your part of the pamphlet,[1] exclusive of the extracts from the minutes which are so important, does you in every respect much honour. Mr Clarkson's performance, for a man of his years and infirmities, is scarcely less than wonderful; and the candour with which he admits the imperfections and deficiencies of his book, must endear him still more to his friends, and to the sound-hearted portion of the community who have taken an interest in the great cause.

We had learnt the intended marriage of Southey[2] from his daughters, who were upon a visit to Miss Fenwick at Ambleside, when their Father announced his intentions to them. It was naturally a great shock to them both—and nothing could have been more fortunate than that the tidings reached them when they were here; as we all contributed greatly to reconcile them to the

---

[1] *The Life of William Wilberforce* by his sons had depreciated Clarkson's part in the abolition movement. Clarkson had replied in a pamphlet, to which H. C. R. contributed.

[2] His second marriage, to Caroline Bowles, divided the family.

step, much sooner and with less pain, than they could have effected a thing so difficult, of themselves. For our parts, we were all of one mind, that Mr S. had acted wisely, provided he has taken the pains dispassionately to ascertain as far as he could, whether the state of Miss Bowles' health is such as to give him just ground to hope that he will find in her a helpmate, and a comforter, rather than a source of perpetual anxiety. Sorry am I to say, that from what I know, I cannot get rid of the fear that for this cause, things may not turn out satisfactorily—to his friends at least. Mr Kenyon's information to you, that *both* the girls are about to be married is not correct—it is true of Bertha,[1] but not of Kate—tho' so amiable a Person is not likely long to remain single.

As to my employments, I have from my unfortunate attacks, in succession, been wholly without any thing of the kind—till within this last fortnight, when my eye, tho' still alas weak, was so far improved as to authorize my putting my brain to some little work—Accordingly timid as I was I undertook to write a few Sonnets,[2] upon taking leave of Italy—these gave rise to some more; and the whole amount to 9 which I shall read to you when you come, as you kindly promised before you went away, that you would do, soon after your return. If however you prefer it, the 4 upon Italy shall be sent you, upon the one condition that you do not read them to *verse-writers*. We are all in spite of ourselves a parcel of thieves. I had a droll instance of it this morning—for while Mary was writing down for me one of these Sonnets, on coming to a certain line, she cried out somewhat uncourteously 'that's a plagiarism'—from whom? 'from yourself' was the answer. I believe she is right tho' she could not point out the passage, neither can I.

Pray remember me aff^{ly} to Sergeant Talfourd—I fear he will have a hard battle to fight for us in Feb^{ry} and it will be still proved that the Legislature of Britain prefer Stealing to buying—for themselves and the People.

Say all that is kind from me to Kenyon Moxon and other enquiring friends—Tell us something about dear Mary Lamb—and give her our love if she is in a state to receive it.

Have you heard that a proposal was made to me from a

---

[1] She married Herbert Hill, a master at Rugby.
[2] Included in *Memorials of a Tour in Italy, 1837*.

Committee in the University of Glasgow—to consent to become a Candidate for the Lord Rectorship on a late occasion, which I declined—I think you must be aware that the University of Durham conferred upon [me] the Degree of DC.L—last summer—it was the first time that the honor had been received there by anyone in Person. These things are not worth adverting to, but as signs that imaginative Literature notwithstanding the homage now paid to Science is not wholly without esteem. But it is time to release my Wife, this being the second long letter she has written for me this mor^g

With best love from all ever faithfully

Yours

Wm Wordsworth

I have said nothing about public affairs—I am sick of them—for we are deluged with newspapers—tho' we do not pay for one.—Ld Durham[1] as I have had recent proof from a private source is a miserably weak Man.

140. *To* Edward Quillinan

[Bath]

Sat: 13th April [1839]

My dear Mr Quillinan,

By yesterday's post I rec^d a letter from Dora, containing a long extract from one of yours to her. Upon the subject of this extract I cannot enter without premising, that calling upon her in so peremptory a manner to act on so important an occasion *during the absence of her parents*, is, to say the least of it, an ill-judged proceeding. And this I must, notwithstanding my present knowledge that the proposal you have made to her, and thro' her to me, was agitated between you when you were at Rydal; and notwithstanding any thing that appears in your letter, in justification of its being made now.—As sincerity required this declaration from me, I make no apology for it, nor do I, dear Sir, think you will require one.—I will now come to the point at once.

---

[1] Governor-General of Canada, and author of the far-reaching *Report on the Affairs of British North America*.

Your Letter contains these sentences, which are the only ones I shall touch upon.

'If hereafter I should have an opportunity of making a provision for you, I certainly will do so, and I could not ask you to run the risk if I thought it possible that my death would leave you destitute of resources as from *my* side, I have not any fear as to that. The thing is will you *dare* to run the rough chance?'—Before I enter upon the former sentence, I must direct your attention to the fact, that you must have overlooked the state of health in which Dora has long been, or you cannot have been fully aware of it; or you could not have called upon her Parents, thro' her, circumstanced as they are, as to age, to give their Daughter up to '*a rough chance*'.

But from the former part of what I have copied, I must infer, that, tho' you can settle nothing upon her at present, you are not without hope of being able to do so etc etc. Now it is *my duty* to request of you, my dear Sir, to state as specifically as you can, upon what the hopes and expectations implied or expressed in the above Quotation from your Letter, rest. I mean in respect of a provision in case of your death.

There is no call for my saying more till I have received your answer upon this point, which I beg may be, on all our accounts, as definite and explicit as possible.

Wm is here and in a state of health that causes us much anxiety—the Bath waters do not seem to agree with him, and his stomach and bowels are much deranged. Miss F.[1] owing, we hope, solely to the severity of the weather, is not quite so well as she was at Ambleside. We all unite in affectionate remembrances to yourself and Children, and believe me, my dear Mr Q., faithfully yours,

Wm Wordsworth

141. *To* Dora Wordsworth

[Bath]
[*c*. 24 Apr. 1839]

My dear Daughter

The Letter which you must have received from Wm has placed before you my judgement and feelings; how far you are reconciled

---
[1] Fenwick.

to them I am unable to divine; I have only to add, that I believe Mr Q. to be a most honorable and upright man, and further that he is most strongly and faithfully attached to you—this I must solemnly declare in justice to you both; and to this I add *my blessing upon you and him*; more I cannot do and if this does not content you with what your Br has said, we must all abide by God's decision upon our respective fates. Mr Q. is, I trust, aware how slender my means are; the state of W's health will undoubtedly entail upon us considerable expense, and how John is to get on without our aid I cannot foresee. No more at present, my time is out; I am going to join Miss Fenwick at Miss Pollard's.[1]

ever your most tender hearted and affectionate Father
Wm Wordsworth

In a beautiful churchyard near Bath I saw the other day this inscription:

> Thomas Carrol Esq[r]
> Barrister at Law
> Born—so—died, so—
> Rest in peace, dear Father—

There was not another word.[2]

142. *To* Dora Wordsworth

[London]
Sunday morning, nine o'clock [9 June 1839]

My dearest Dora,

I am looking for Mr Quillinan, every moment. I hope to revive the conversation of yesterday. The sum is: I make no opposition to this marriage. I have no resentment connected with it toward any one: you know how much friendship I have always felt towards Mr Q, and how much I respect him. I do not doubt the strength of his love and affection towards you; this, as far as I am concerned, is the fair side of the case. On the other hand, I cannot think of parting with you with that complacency, that satisfaction, that hopeful-

[1] Jane Marshall's sister.   [2] M. W. adds a PS.

ness which I could wish to feel; there is too much of necessity in the case for my wishes. But I must submit, and do submit; and God Almighty bless you, my dear child, and him who is the object of your long and long-tried preference and choice.

                                    Ever your affectionate father,
                                            Wm Wordsworth

I have said little above of your dear mother, the best of women. O how my heart is yearning towards her, and you, and my poor dear Sister.—

My ancle is rather worse this morning than yesterday at this time. Would that the next week were fairly over.[1]—I enjoyed the Ballet and the Opera last night.

143. *To* Thomas Powell

                                            [Rydal Mount]
                                            [late 1839]

My dear Mr Powell

Excuse my not writing earlier as I wished to do—From a letter of mine to D[r] Smith,[2] which I enclose you will learn every thing respecting the Sanatorium to which your last letter referred,—so that I need not here dwell upon the subject.—I am glad that you enter so warmly into the Chaucerian project,[3] and that Mr L. Hunt is disposed to give his valuable aid to it. For myself I cannot do more than I offered, to place at your disposal the Prioresses Tale, already published, the Cuckoo and the Nightingale,[4] the Manciples Tale, and I rather think, but I cannot just now find it, a small portion of the Troilus and Cressida—You ask my opinion about the Poem—Speaking from a recollection only of many years past, I should say that it would be found too long—and probably

---

[1] W. W. was to receive an honorary degree at Oxford.

[2] Thomas Southwood Smith (1788–1861), sanitary reformer, was planning a new hospital in London.

[3] *Chaucer's Poems Modernized*, 1841, to which Leigh Hunt and W. W. contributed.

[4] Then attributed to Chaucer.

tedious. The Knights Tale is also very long, but tho' Dryden[1] has executed it, in his own way observe, with great spirit and harmony, he has suffered so much of the simplicity, and with that of the beauty, and occasional pathos of the original to escape, that I should be pleased to hear that a new version should be attempted upon my principle by some competent Person. It would delight me to read every part of Chaucer over again, for I reverence and admire him above measure, with a view to your work, but my eyes will not permit me to do so—who will undertake the Prologue, to the C. Tales? For your publication that is indispensible, and I fear it will prove very difficult. It is written, as you know, in the couplet measure, and therefore I have nothing to say upon its metre—but in respect to the Poems in stanza, neither in the Prioresses Tale, nor in the Cuckoo and Nightingale have I kept to the rule of the original as to the form and number and position of the *rhymes*, thinking it enough if I kept the same number of lines in each stanza, and this I think is all that is necessary—and all that can be done without sacrificing the substance of sense, too often, to the mere form of sound.

I feel much obliged by yr offer of the Ist Ed: of the Paradise Lost, and I apprehend from what you say that you are already aware of my possessing a Copy—otherwise I should not have felt justified in accepting the one you so kindly intend for me—The copy I possess was given me by Mr Rogers—and your's shall take its place on my shelves by its side, Mr Moxon is about to send down a parcel of books in which your valuable present might be included, with a certainty that it would arrive safe.

It is thought by every one that Mrs W.'s Portrait[2] (who appears, as now engaged writing for me) is an excellent likeness—The chalk drawing has yet a good deal to do at it. Dora has been *attempted*, but not yet, as we think, with much success. I think you will be delighted, with a profile Picture on ivory of me, with which Miss G. is at this moment engaged, Mrs W. seems to prefer it as a likeness to any thing she has yet done. We all rejoice as you and Mrs P. will in her general success in this neighbourhood.

Thanks for your kind enquiries after Mrs W's health—She is I am glad to say quite well again, and joins with Miss G., my

---

[1] In his *Fables*, 1700.   [2] By Margaret Gillies.

Daughter, and myself in affec regards to you and Mrs P.—and
believe me

ever faithfully and aff^ly yours
Wm Wordsworth

144. *To* Barron Field

Rydal Mount, January 16, 1840.

My dear Mr Field,

I have at last brought myself to write to you. After maturely
considering the subject, however painful it may be to me, I must
regret that I am decidedly against the publication of your Critical
Memoir;[1] your wish is, I know, to serve me, and I am grateful for
the strength of this feeling in your excellent heart. I am also truly
proud of the pains of which you have thought my writings worthy;
but I am sure that your intention to benefit me in this way would
not be fulfilled. The hostility which you combat so ably is in a great
measure passed away, but might in some degree be revived by your
recurrence to it, so that in this respect your work would, if
published, be either superfluous or injurious, so far as concerns the
main portion of it. I shall endeavour, during the short remainder of
my life, to profit by it, both as an author and a man, in a private
way; but the notices of me by many others which you have thought
it worth while to insert are full of gross mistakes, both as to facts
and opinions, and the sooner they are forgotten the better. Old as I
am, I live in the hope of seeing you, and should in that event have
no difficulty in reconciling you to the suppression of a great part of
this work entirely, and of the whole of it in its present shape. . . .
One last word in matter of authorship: it is far better not to admit
people so much behind the scenes, as it has been lately fashionable
to do. . . . Believe me to be,

Most faithfully, your much obliged
Wm Wordsworth

[1] This work had remained in manuscript in the British Library.

145. *To* Henry Alford

[*c.* 20 Feb. 1840]

My dear Sir,

Pray excuse my having been some little time in your debt. I could plead many things in extenuation, the chief, that old one of the state of my eyes, which never leaves me at liberty either to read or write a tenth part as much as I could wish, and as otherwise I ought to do.

It cannot but be highly gratifying to me to learn that my writings are prized so highly by a Poet and Critic of your powers. The essay upon them which you have so kindly sent me, seems well qualified to promote your views in writing it. I was particularly pleased with your distinction between religion in Poetry and versified Religion. For my own part, I have been averse to frequent mention of the mysteries of Christian faith, not from a want of a due sense of their momentous nature; but the contrary. I felt it far too deeply to venture on handling the subject as familiarly as many scruple not to do. I am far from blaming them, but let them not blame me, nor turn from my companionship on that account. Besides general reasons for diffidence in treating subjects of holy writ I have some especial ones. I might err in points of faith; and I should not deem my mistakes less to be deprecated because they were expressed in metre. Even Milton, in my humble judgement, has erred and grievously; and what Poet could hope to atone for his apprehensions in the way in which that mighty mind has done?

I am not at all desirous that any one should write an elaborate critique on my Poetry—there is no call for it—if they be from above they will do their own work in course of time, if not, they will perish as they ought. But scarcely a week passes in which I do not receive grateful acknowledgments of the good they have done to the minds of the several writers. They speak of the relief they have received from them under affliction and in grief, and of the calmness and elevation of Spirit which the Poems either give, or assist them in attaining. As these benefits are not without a traceable bearing upon the good of the immortal soul, the sooner perhaps they are pointed out and illustrated in a work like yours the better.

Pray excuse my talking so much about myself; your Letter and critique called me to the subject, but I assure you it would have been more grateful to me to acknowledge the debt we owe you in this House, where we have read your poems with no common pleasure. Your Abbot of Muchelnaye[1] also makes me curious to hear more of him.

But I must conclude, dinner being on the Table. I was truly sorry to have missed you when you and Mrs Alford called at Rydal.

Mrs W. unites with me in kind regards to you both, and believe me

my dear sir

Faithfully your much obliged,

Wm Wordsworth

146. *To* Henry Reed

Rydal Mount
Ambleside
August 16th 41

My dear Mr Reed,

I have just received your last very obliging letter, and not to lose the Pacquet which leaves Liverpool in a day or two I write to thank you for it at once. It is already on its way to my Friend.[2] Mrs W. and I rejoice in the good news more than she will. She is so charitable and benevolent a creature that every one who knows her would grieve at her means being curtailed. Notwithstanding the resumption of payment I much wish that she had her money on this side the Atlantic; for it appears to me next to impossible that peace can long be preserved in your Country. Your government I fear is too feeble; nor will your tumultuous democracy, I apprehend, be reconciled to subordination, till war either foreign or civil or perhaps both has taught them the necessity of it—God grant it may be otherwise, but such are my fears.

I have lately had the pleasure of seeing both in London and at my own Home the B of New Jersey.[3] He is a man of no ordinary powers of mind and attainments, of warm feeling, and sincere piety. Indeed I never saw a person of your Country, which is remarkable for cordiality, whose manner was so thoroughly cordial. He had been greatly delighted with his reception in

---

[1] Publ. 1841.   [2] I. F.   [3] G. W. Doane, Bishop of New Jersey.

England and what he had seen of it both in Art and Nature. By the bye, I heard him preach an excellent sermon in London, I believe this privilege is of modern date. The B'p has furnished me with his funeral sermon upon Bp White,[1] to assist me in fulfilling a request which you first made to me, viz, that I would add a Sonnet to my ecclesiastical series, upon the union of the two episcopal churches of England and America.[2] I will endeavour to do so, when I have more leisure than at present, this being the season when our beautiful region attracts many strangers, who take up much of my time.—

Do you know Miss Peabody[3] of Boston? She has just sent me with the highest eulogy certain Essays of Mr Emerson. Our Carlyle and he appear to be what the French used to call Esprits forts, though the French Idols shewed their spirit after a somewhat different Fashion. Our two present Philosophers, who have taken a language which they suppose to be English for their vehicle, are verily "Par nobile Fratrum," and it is a pity that the weakness of our age has not left them exclusively to the appropriate reward, mutual admiration. Where is the thing which now passes for philosophy[4] at Boston to stop?

I shall be very glad to hear from you at any time, being truly grateful for all your kindness, and sensible I trust of the claims you have upon my sincere esteem.

Ever faithfully yours
W Wordsworth

147. *To* Adam Sedgwick

[late Mar. 1842]

My dear Sir,

You have much obliged me by the promptitude with which you have met the request made through an Acquaintance or Friend of my Publishers;[5] and I should be very happy to be the Medium of conveying to the public your view of the Geology of this interesting

---

[1] William White, first Bishop of Pennsylvania.
[2] W. W. added three sonnets on 'Aspects of Christianity in America'.
[3] The American educationalist.
[4] i.e. New England transcendentalism.
[5] To provide letters on local geology for a new edn. of W. W.'s *Guide to the Lakes*.

District, however concisely given. First, however, I must tell you exactly how the matter stands between me and the Publishers. The last edition of my little work being nearly out I undertook about a twelvemonth since to furnish some new Matter in the way of a more minute Guide for the *Body* of the Tourist, as I found that the Guide Books which attended mainly to this were preferred much, by the generality of Tourists, to mine, which, though in fact containing as much of this sort of matter as could be of any real use, appeared to be wanting in this respect. The employment to which I had by a sort of promise committed myself I found upon further consideration to be very troublesome and *infra dig.*; and as I was still desirous that my Book should be circulated, not for any pecuniary emolument, for that was quite trifling, but for the principles of Taste which it recommended, I turned all that I had written over to Mr Hudson the Publisher, stipulating only that all that related to *mind*, should in my book be printed entire and separated from other matter, and so it now stands. Every thing of mine will be reprinted, but the *guide matter* of mine will be interwoven with what Mr Hudson has undertaken to write or compile, the whole however before struck off to be submitted to my approbation. Mr Gough of Kendal, a Son of the celebrated blind man[1] of that place, will, Mr Hudson expects, promote the Botany, and if you would condescend to act upon your promise made to me long ago under somewhat different circumstances, I think a Book would be produced answering every purpose that could be desired.

I am truly sorry, my dear Sir, to hear that your health is so much deranged. I believe that the bottom of it all is, your intense ardour of mind, and activity both of mind and body. In fact you have been living too fast; pray slacken your pace, and depend upon it you will not only, in a little time, be more comfortable in yourself, but the world will in the end get more out of the very great deal that you have to give it. We are pretty well and unite in kindest remembrances and good wishes.

Ever faithfully, My dear Mr Sedgwick,
Your much obliged,
W. Wordsworth

Pray give me a letter, however short.

[1] John Gough, the mathematician.

148. *To* Dora Quillinan

April 7, 1842.

My dear Daughter,

I cannot suffer the morning of my Birth-day to pass without telling you that my heart is full of you and all that concerns you. Yesterday was lovely, and this morning is not less so. God grant that we may all have like sunshine in our hearts so long as we remain in this transient world.

It is about half-past nine; two hours hence we go to pay a condoling visit to poor Fanny.[1] Mr Carter, James, and I all attended the funeral on Monday,—it was a beautiful afternoon, the light of the declining sun glowing upon Fairfield, as described in the *Excursion*, at Dawson's funeral. The Psalm sung before raising the Coffin from its Station before the door, and afterwards as the procession moved between the trees, was most touching. Mr Greenwood[2] was there and told me the name (which I forget) of the Composer, who lived 200 years ago. The music was worthy of the occasion and admirably given, the Schoolmaster, a very respectable man, leading the four or five voices; upon these occasions the Women do not sing, and I think that is well judged, the sound being more grand and solemn, whatever it may lose in sweetness by the want of female tones. After the funeral we walked to Mrs Fletchers[3]—the place very tempting—they are expected on Saturday.

I am pretty well, but far from having recovered the strength which I lost through several sleepless nights, the consequence of over and ill-timed exertion, to get the Volume[4] out before Easter in which attempt I failed. I am glad you like the tragedy.[5] I was myself surprized to find the interest so kept up in the 4th and fifth Acts. Of the third I never doubted, and quite agree with you that Herbert's speech is much the finest thing in the drama; I mean the most moving, or rather, the most in that style of the pathetic which one loves to dwell upon; though I acknowledge it is not so intensely dramatic as some parts of the 5th act especially. As to the first, my only fear was that the *action* was too *far* advanced in it. I think the

---

[1] Apparently a neighbour.
[2] A Grasmere acquaintance.   [3] i.e. Lancrigg, in Easedale.
[4] *Poems, Chiefly of Early and Late Years*, 1842.   [5] *The Borderers*.

scene where the Vagrant tells her false story has great merit—it is thoroughly natural and yet not commonplace nature. Some of the sentiments which the development of Oswald's character required will, I fear, be complained of as too depraved for anything but biographical writing.

With affectionate remembrances to your Husband and the Girls

ever yours

W. W.

149. *To* Aubrey de Vere

Rydal Mount, Nov. 16, 1842

My dear Mr de Vere,—Every day since I received your kind letter, I wished to write to you, and most days have resolved to do so; but in vain, so inveterate is the habit of procrastination with me in these matters. I have only, therefore, to throw myself upon your indulgence, as I am so often obliged to do with all my other friends. First, let me express my pleasure in learning that I had been misinformed concerning the article in 'The Quarterly'.[1] The thing I have not read, nor probably ever shall read; but it grieved me to think, from what I heard of it, that it should be written by any friend of mine, for whom I have so much regard, and whom I esteem as highly as yourself. And I was the more concerned upon these occasions because the only disparaging notices which I have ever cared the least for, unfortunately have ever come from persons with whom I have lived in close intimacy. And this occurred in several remarkable instances. Now, though I am far from supposing that everyone who likes me shall think well of my poetry, yet I do think that openness of dealing is necessary before a friend undertakes to decry one's writings to the world at large. But too much of this. Not till a couple of days ago did I hear of the volume of your poems which you designed for myself, lying at Mr Taylor's for several months. But Mr Quillinan will be down here in a week or ten days, to join his wife, who is here with us, and will

---

[1] A review of Tennyson, which praised Byron at the expense of W. W. It was by John Sterling.

bring the book with him. Miss Fenwick, who is now under our roof for the winter, has read the volume with much pleasure, especially the Hymns. Upon her coming here she lent it to Mr Faber,[1] as we have all been paying visits up and down as far as Halsteads and Carlisle. But then we are settling down in quiet for the winter, and your poems will be among the first I shall peruse. But, alas, the state of my eyes curtails my reading hours very much in these short days. Your father's 'Sonnets', and Mr Taylor's 'Tragedy',[2] are the only verse I have read for many months. If the expression, especially in point of truthfulness, were equal in your father's poems to the sanctity and weight of the thoughts, they would be all that one could desire in that style of writing. But in respect to your father's poems, your own, and all other new productions in verse, whether of my friends or of strangers, I ought frankly to avow that the time is past with me for bestowing that sympathy to which they are entitled. For many reasons connected with advanced life, I read but little of new works either in prose or verse. Rogers says of me, partly in joke and partly in earnest, as he says of himself and others as frankly, and has avowed in one of his letters written when he was an old man, 'I read no poetry now but my own'. In respect to myself, my good old friend ought to have added that if I do read my own, it is mainly, if not entirely, to make it better. But certain it is that old men's literary pleasures lie chiefly among the books they were familiar with in their youth; and this is still more pointedly true of men who have practised composition themselves. They have fixed notions of style and of versification and their thoughts have moved on in a settled train so long that novelty in each or all of these, so far from being a recommendation, is distasteful to them, even though, if hard put to it, they might be brought to confess that the novelty was all improvement. You must be perfectly aware of all that I have said, as characteristic of human nature to a degree which scarcely allows of exceptions, though rigidity or obtuseness will prevail more in some minds than in others. For myself, however, I have many times, when called upon to give an opinion on works sent, felt obliged to recommend younger critics as more to be relied upon, and that for the reason I have mentioned. It is in vain to regret these changes which Time

[1] Frederick Faber, poet, Tractarian, and (later) Oratorian priest.
[2] *Edwin the Fair.*

brings with it; one might as well sigh over one's grey hairs. Let me, with Mason, the poet, say:

> 'As my winter, like the year's, is mild,
> Give thanks to Him from whom all blessings flow. [1]

You enquire after my MS. poem on my own life.[2] It is lying, and in all probability will lie, where my 'Tragedy', and other 'Poems' lay ambushed for more than a generation of years. Publication was ever to me most irksome; so that if I had been rich, I question whether I should ever have published at all, though I believe I should have written. I am pleased that you find some things to like in my last volume. It has called out a good deal of sorry criticism, as in truth happens to all my publications in succession and will do so as long as anything of mine comes forth. With respect to my last volume I feel no interest but that those who deem it worth while to *study* anything I write would read the contents of that volume, as the prelude hints, in connection with its predecessors.

Throwing myself upon your kind indulgence for having deferred this letter so long, I remain, with high regard,

Faithfully yours,
William Wordsworth

150. *To* Unknown Correspondent

Rydal Mount
Ambleside
13 Jan^ry—44

Dear Sir,

I have put off replying to your Letter partly from pressure of engagements; but still more from the embarrassment in which I found myself placed by it. There is no species of composition upon which I should be so unwilling to pass judgement as an Epitaph; for diverse reasons, and chiefly because it is impossible to condemn without wounding personal feelings in the tenderest point. The lamented Individual possessed, I doubt not, the valuable qualities

[1] The last lines of William Mason's seventh sonnet *Anniversary* (misquoted).
[2] *The Prelude.*

ascribed to her and many more akin to them; but she would not, when alive have been pleased to be told so; and it is reasonable that this truth should be kept constantly in mind, amid the composition of the monumental inscription, regulated and governed by it, more than, as seems to me, has been done upon this occasion. Praise of the departed should be brief; all human beings who deserve it are in exact proportion to their desert, conscious of their own simplicity and frailty, and would shrink accordingly from posthumous encomium, especially when exposed to public view, and in the House of God. Am I then to be understood as forbidding enumeration of the virtues of a beloved Friend or Relative who is no more seen upon earth? I do not go that length—but I deeply feel the exceeding difficulty of publicly recording the truth without some offense to modesty, and I should therefore prefer that instead of a formal proclamation of excellent qualities, the excellence should rather be left to be inferred from the language of gratitude to the Almighty by whom the deceased had been so endowed, or of sorrow for the premature removal of goodness from this world, and from those to whom the person was peculiarly endeared—

I beg pardon for having written so much in which I feel that my notions must have been very imperfectly explained. I have taken the liberty of underlining a few expressions which I think are not suitable in style to an epitaph. I recommend that the whole should be shortened and that one passage should be read thus, "the assurance of a blessed immortality"; an *enduring* immortality is faulty, as endless duration is implied in the word 'immortality'. Here also the epitaph ought to end both for brevity's sake and because the text must be presumed to be known to all readers. In an epitaph I think that the birth-name should be mentioned as well as that of the Husband; which might easily be done without lengthening the Inscription, by leaving the age to be calculated, as the time of birth and death are both recorded.

Excuse this long Letter written without that command of time which a subject so delicate required.

I remain, dear Sir, with regard

faithfully yours

Wm Wordsworth

151. *To* W. E. Gladstone

Rydal Mount, Mar. 21st, 1844.

My dear Mr Gladstone,

Pray accept my thanks for your State and Prospects of the Church,[1] which I have carefully read; I lent it immediately to a neighbouring Clergyman. You have approached the subject in a most becoming spirit, and treated it with admirable ability. From scarcely anything that you have said did I dissent; only felt some little dissatisfaction as to the limits of your Catholicity; for some limits it must have; but probably you acted wisely in not being more precise upon this point. You advert to the formal and open Schism of Methodism, but was not that of Disney,[2] and of others to which Cowper adverts, in some respects of more importance? not as relates to the two or three conspicuous Individuals, who seceded and became preachers in London; but from its leading the way to the transit of so great a number of Presbyterian Clergy, with no small portion of their several congregations, into Unitarianism. This occurred all over England, and was, I believe, especially remarkable in the city of Norwich, though many there took refuge in the Church of England. Happily there is both in the written Word of God, and in the constitution of his Creature Man, an adequate preservative from that lifeless form of Religion; nevertheless, as it influenced in no small degree what in the Presbyterian and other congregations was called the better educated part of the Community, the result was to be lamented, in some respects more than the Schism of the Wesleyans, which turned mainly, if not exclusively, at first, upon the rejection of episcopal juridiction, leaving the great points of Catholic doctrine untouched.

To what you have so justly said upon Tractarianism much in the same spirit might be added. It was a grievous mistake that these Tracts issued from the same place were *numbered*, and at the same time anonymous. Upon the mischief that unavoidably attaches to publications without name, especially, you might have added,

---

[1] An article which discussed the progress of the Oxford, or Tractarian, Movement since 1833, and the strength of the Romeward tendency in the Church of England.

[2] John Disney (1746–1816), Unitarian divine.

corporate publications, you have written with much truth and feeling. But the whole proceeding was wrong, and has led to errors, doubts, and uncertainties, shiftings and ambiguities, not to say absolute double-dealing, injurious to Readers and perilous to those in whom they originated. First, it has caused the great and pernicious error of the Movement being called the *Oxford* Movement, as if it *originated* there, and had sprung up in a moment. But this opinion, which is false in fact, detracts greatly from its dignity, and tends much to narrow and obstruct its range of operation. There is one snare into which it was impossible that Writers so combined should not fall, that of the Individual claiming support for his opinion from the body when it suited him so to do, and rejecting it and resting upon his individuality when that answered his purpose better.

As to Romanism, having lived much in countries where it is dominant, and being not unacquainted with much of its history, my horror of it, I will not use a milder term, notwithstanding all that I love and admire in that Church, is great indeed. I trust with you that there is small reason for believing that it will ever supplant our Church in this Country, but we must never lose sight of its manifold attractions for the two extremes of our artificial society, the opulent and luxurious, never trained to vigorous thinking, and who have outlived the power of indulging in their excesses, these on the one hand; and on the other, the extreme poor, who are greatly in danger of falling under the influence of its doctrines, pressed upon them by a priesthood so constituted.

But as my departed Friend Southey said long ago,

> Onward in *faith*, and leave the rest to Heaven.[1]

With a thousand thanks for your valuable tract, and the best of good wishes for your health and welfare, I remain, with sincere respect and regard, my dear Mr Gladstone,

Faithfully yours,
Wm Wordsworth

[1] The last line of *The Retrospect*, 1794.

152. *To* W. L. Bowles

Rydal Mount
Ambleside
May 17th 1844

My dear M[r] Bowles,

The newspapers informed me of your mournful bereavement,[1] and deeply did I sympathize with your sorrows, but I could not bring myself to write to you immediately, being persuaded that my condolence had better be deferred till you had time to feel what through your own heart and mind the goodness of God would effect for your Support and Consolation. It is indeed a sad thing to be left alone, as it were, after having been so long blessed as you have been with a faithful companion; no one can judge of this but they who have been so happily placed, and either have been doomed to a like loss, or, if the tie still be unbroken, are compelled daily to think how soon it certainly must, by one or other being called away. Under this consciousness, I venture to break in upon you, and to offer my heartfelt sympathy. The separation cannot be long between you, nor would I advert to so obvious a reflection were it not that from the advanced age which my wife and I have, through God's blessing, attained together, I feel the power of it to soothe and mitigate and sustain, far beyond what is possible for your young friends to do.—

It is more than half a century since, through your poetry, I became acquainted with your mind and feelings, and felt myself greatly your debtor for the truth and beauty with which you expressed the emotions of a mourner. My Remembrance is thrown back upon those days with a Sadness which is deep, yet far from painful. A beloved Brother with whom I first read your Sonnets (it was in a recess from London Bridge) perished by Shipwreck long ago, and my most valued friends are gone to their graves. 'But not without hope we sorrow and we mourn.' So I wrote when I lost that dear brother. So have I felt ever since, and so I am sure in my [? heart], you do now. God bless you through time and through eternity. Believe me

faithfully yours
W[m] Wordsworth

[1] The death of his wife.

153. *To* Henry Crabb Robinson

Rydal
14th July
1844

My dear Friend,

I wrote to you at some length immediately on the receipt of your last to M^{rs} W—but as my Letter turned mainly on the subject of yours, the Dissenters chapel Bill[1] I could not muster resolution to send it, for I felt it was reviving a matter of which you had had too much.

I was averse to the Bill, and my opinion is not changed. I do not consider the authorities you appeal to as the best judges in a matter of this kind, which it is absurd to treat as mere question of property or any gross material, right or priviledge, say a right of road, or any other thing of the kind for which usage may be pleaded. But the same considerations that prevented my sending the Letter in which the subject was treated at length forbid me to enter again upon it; so let it rest till we have the pleasure of meeting and then, if it be thought worth while we may revert to it.—

Your Correspondent who declined writing to you in answer to a Letter turning upon things which she had not considered, and in which she took no interest begged that I would be her substitute. I have consented though well aware what a dull creature I am at work of this kind. You will be but little concerned to hear that we are now beginning to be overrun with Tourists and summer Visits—a few of whom, I am happy to say will be very welcome. Among others we expect my Brother, and Mr Rogers along with Moxon. I am also looking daily for Mr Salvin[2] the Architect, who is likely to pass through this country on his way to Naworth Castle on the Borders which has been burned down, and which he is employed to rebuild. He is a Relative of Miss Fenwick; and we hope that he will be so kind as to furnish us with a plan for a Cottage which we mean to build for her to occupy, who has been so long looking out in vain for An Abode of her own in this neighbourhood. The Site of the Intended Building will be some part of the field, near our garden, at the top of which runs the green

---

[1] A Bill to legalise the Dissenters' right to hold property.
[2] Anthony Salvin (1799–1881). The cottage for I. F. was never built.

terrace. The views as you remember are very fine; and the approach to the house, as we mean to place it low in the field, will be easy. Among other visitors whom I have reason to expect, is an American Artist, who is just arrived, I believe in London, and purposes at the earnest request of my valued Friend Mr Reed of Philadelphia to take for him my Portrait. Mr Reed speaks highly of this Gentlemans talents, both for portrait and Landscape. His name is Henry Inman Esq which I mention as you may, perhaps fall in with him—his address care of Messrs Wiley and Puttenham No 6 Waterloo place Regent street. To day Mr Julius Hare is expected at Mrs Arnolds,[1] and I am to dine with him there in the course of the week.

Sergeant Talfourd and his family we expect about the middle of August, he has taken Mr Harden's Cottage on the Banks of the Rotha, for ten weeks; I hope they will enjoy themselves. The House is now occupied by Mr Price[2] second Master of Rugby now, as he was in Dr Arnold's time for many years. In the D^{rs} life by Mr Stanley[3] is inserted a paper of his which no doubt you have read. These pending engagements will prevent my attending the fête about to be given on the Banks of the Dune in honour of the Poet Burns and his Sons. I had an invitation from the Committee seconded by a most urgent one from my old Friend Professor Wilson, who will act as Vicepresident upon the occasion——The Scotch are fond of ceremonials and solemnities and commemorations, partly owing to their nationality, and partly perhaps in opposition to the spirit of the Kirk which is austere and forbidding. Then there is to recommend them the intoxication of speechifying: Was it lucky or unlucky for me that I was born and bred before the age of oratory; a qualification which since the reform bill especially no Town-council man is without, as the provincial Newspapers give abundant proof.

Dr Arnold's life M^rs W has read diligently. the 1st Vol she read aloud to me, and I have more than skimmed the 2nd. He was a truly good man; of too ardent a mind however to be always judicious on the great points of secular and ecclesiastical politics that occupied his mind and upon which he often wrote and acted under strong

---

[1] i.e. Fox How, home of the widow of Thomas Arnold, late headmaster of Rugby.
[2] Bonamy Price, later Professor of Political Economy at Oxford.
[3] Arthur Penrhyn Stanley, later Dean of Westminster.

prejudices, and with hazardous confidence. But the Book, notwithstanding these objections, must do good, and *great* good.

His benevolence was so earnest, his life so industrious, his affections domestic and social so intense, his faith so warm and firm, and his endeavour to regulate his life by it so constant, that his example cannot but be beneficial even in quarters where his opinions may be most disliked. How he hated sin and loved and thirsted after holiness; O that on this path he were universally followed! Mrs Arnold and all the family are well, Susan recovered from the severe illness which she fell into last winter. The Fletchers[1] and Davies[2] and Harrisons[3] are well. And now let me ask how you have borne with this gossiping Letter. If it has annoyed you, I won't beg pardon, for I cannot write any other kind of Letter to my satisfaction, having scarcely any *thoughts* to which I can do justice either in prose or verse. Pray remember me kindly to all common Friends, especially the Rogers's and Coleridges[4] if you happen to see them, Kenyon also and many more whom I have not space to name; besides my pens are intolerable and I have tried in vain to mend them

[*Unsigned*]

154. *To* Edward Moxon

Friday 18th April [1845]

My dear Moxon,

An invitation from the Lord Chamberlain to attend the Queen's Ball on Friday the 25th left me without a choice as to visiting London, and in consequence I purpose to start on Wednesday next with Mr and Mrs Quillinan who are going to Oporto, he to attend his Brother's marriage, and she accompanying him in the hope of benefiting her health which as you know has been declining for several years. I should prefer arriving at your house rather than

---

[1] Of Lancrigg.
[2] The family of Dr John Davy, Sir Humphry's brother, and son-in-law of Mrs Fletcher.
[3] The Benson Harrisons of Green Bank.
[4] Sara and Henry Nelson Coleridge.

Mr Robinson's if I could be received there early on Thursday
Morning, your maid-servant having provided me a bed to lie down
upon for two or three hours, as I am but a poor Traveller in the
night Season. If it be in your power to accomodate me pray let me
know by return of Post. I have another favor to ask, which is that
you would mention my errand to Mr Rogers, and perhaps he could
put me in the way of being properly introduced, and instructed
how to behave in a situation, I am not sorry to say, altogether new
to me. My stay in London for several cogent reasons will be very
short. Hoping that my proposal of coming first to you may not
prove inconvenient to Mrs Moxon, and your Household,

I remain my dear Mr Moxon
faithfully yours
Wm Wordsworth

155. *To* Christopher Wordsworth, jnr.

[Aug. 1845]

My dear Christopher,

I have not yet heard of your Books[1] sent to Ambleside but I shall
inquire after them immediately.

One Copy I have myself, and have read with very great interest
and much instruction, so that I wish it were read by every person of
station or consideration in the Country. I hope it has been noticed
in periodical Publications, though I myself have seen no *other*
notice of it than in two numbers of the *Morning Post*. Mr Johnston,
an Irishman who writes the Leading Articles in that Journal is an
old and intimate Acquaintance of mine and spent last Sunday with
us. Your Book has greatly interested him; and the more so because
he knows his native Country so well.

Charles[2] and W^m went yesterday by Coniston and down the
Vale of Duddon, and by Broughton to Dalton where they would
sleep. It was a beautiful grey day, and this is a splendid sunshining
one, most favorable to the continuance of their Tour. Their first

[1] Three pamphlets on the Maynooth controversy.
[2] C. W. jnr.'s brother.

object this morning would be Furness Abbey. They return this Evening. What do you think of a Railway being driven as it now is, close to the magnificent memorial of the piety of our ancestors? Many of the trees which embowered the ruin have been felled to make way for this pestilential nuisance. We have also surveyors at work with our beautiful Valley the line meditated to pass through Rydal Park and immediately behind Rydal Mount.[1]

We are sorry that we are not likely to see our dear Brother. At our age one cannot but be strongly desirous of making the most of opportunities of intercourse whenever they present themselves. Emmie Fisher[2] is still with us and will remain another week or so, when she will go to Keswick with Miss Fenwick; and her brother who has been residing at Grasmere, will come here for a few days, and follow her to Keswick; whence they both will proceed to Newbiggin[3] on their way homeward—we like them both very much.

You say nothing about your health, I hope it has been benefited by your Residence at Leamington; pray mention it, when you write again.

Your Aunt Dorothy often complains but on the whole I am persuaded she is no worse than she has been for many years. Pray when do you think of going into Italy, and how, and by what route do you mean to travel? You cannot be an acceptable visitor to the authorities of Rome; you may be pretty sure that they are not ignorant of the character and tendency of your writings, and I should not at all wonder if you were to receive a hint that you would do well to quit the Country. But I may be in error on this point; and you are likely to know much better than I how things would stand with you. If we do not hear more satisfactory accounts than we have done lately—old as we are, it is not improbable that Mary and I may go to Pisa to visit Isabella.[4] I earnestly hope however that such a long journey may not be necessary for us. An Edition of my Poems in double column is passing through the Press, the Book will not I hope extend beyond 400 pages. Southey's I see contains 1000.

---

[1] This extension to the Kendal and Windermere railway was never built.
[2] A cousin of W. W.'s who wrote poetry.
[3] Seat of W. W.'s Crackanthorpe relatives.
[4] John W.'s wife was convalescing in Italy.

Best love to Susan[1] in which Mary and Aunt unite with me ever
Your affectionate Uncle

W Wordsworth—

156. *To* H. S. Tremenheere

16th Dec[r] 1845.

My dear Sir,

I have been long in your debt; but, as I believe you are aware, I
was from home during six weeks of autumn, and on my return I
found numerous engagements pressing upon me in consequence.
Besides as I scarcely am able to read or write by candlelight my
allowance of time for the pen is but scanty during these short days.
The acknowledgment of y[r] Kindness was not among the least
important of those engagements, but I felt that I could not make it
with much satisfaction till I had read y[r] second Report and the
Volumes which thro' y[r] suggestion were transmitted to me from
the Committee of the Council on Education. These I shall have an
opport[y] of returning in the course of a fortnight. Y[r] own Report and
every one in the two Vols. which you pointed out to me, I have
carefully perused; and had I an opport[y] of conversing with you
upon the subject I might perhaps be able to make upon the details,
some remarks not wholly unworthy of attention, but I could say
little by Letter which could be satisfactory either to you or myself. I
must therefore be confined to a general observation or two. First
however let me express my gratitude to all the Reporters, yourself
especially, for the information and instruction I have gained from
their labours, and also my admiration of the perseverance and
judgment with which their important work has been carried on.
The prospect surely is upon the whole full as promising as could
have been expected. Generation after Generation will I trust start
from a higher point than the preceding one, and the improvement
be progressive accordingly. Encouraged by this belief the
Inspectors, to whom we already owe so much, will not relax their
efforts, in which all good and wise men will concur.—Having given
vent to these feelings, let me ask you, dear Sir, whether throughout
the Minutes too little value is not set upon the occupations of

[1] C. W. jnr.'s wife.

Children out of doors, under the direction, or by permission, of their Parents, comparatively with what they do or acquire in school? Is not the Knowledge inculcated by the Teacher, or derived under his managem¹, from books, too exclusively dwelt upon, so as almost to put out of sight that which comes, without being sought for, from intercourse with nature and from experience in the actual employments and duties which a child's situation in the Country, however unfavorable, will lead him to or impose upon him? How much of what is precious comes into our minds, in all ranks of society, not as Knowledge entering formally in the shape of Knowledge, but as infused thro' the constitution of things and by the grace of God. There is no condition of life, however unpromising, that does not daily exhibit something of this truth. I do not relish the words of one of the Reporters (Mr Allen I believe whose notices are generally very valuable) in which he would reconcile the Parents to the expence of having their Children educated in school by remarking that the wear and tear of clothes will be less; and an equivalent thus saved in shoe-leather.— Excuse this disagreement in opinion, as coming from one who spent half of his boyhood in running wild among the Mountains.

It struck me also that, from the same cause, too little attention is paid to books of imagination which are eminently useful in calling forth intellectual power. We must not only have Knowledge but the means of wielding it, and that is done infinitely more thro' the imaginative faculty assisting both in the collection and application of facts than is generally believed. But I must conclude.

> Believe me, My dear Sir,
> with many thanks,
> Sincerely yʳ much obliged
> Wᵐ Wordsworth

157. *To* Charles Wordsworth

Rydal—12ᵗʰ March 1846

My dear Charles,

Many thanks for your Farewell Sermon¹ which your Aunt has read to me. It is well suited to the occasion and very touching, and

---

¹ On resigning his post at Winchester.

cannot but be remembered by your Pupils who heard it, to their future benefit. In every part I went along with you, except when you speak in praise of emulation; on that subject I was not entirely in accord with you. I know well that you have St Paul in your favour in one or two passages. Homer also, and other wise and good men among the heathen: I am aware too that you have had greater experience among Boys, and the way of usefully influencing their minds, than has been my lot, yet still I cannot help being afraid of encouraging emulation—it proves too often closely akin to envy, in spite of the christian spirit you recommend. My own case is, I am aware, a peculiar one in many respects, but I can sincerely affirm, that I am not indebted to emulation for my attainments whatever they be. I have from my Youth down to this late day cultivated the habit of valuing knowledge for its own sake and for the good that may and ought to come out of it, the unmixed pure good. I used often to press this view of the subject upon the late Dᴿ Bell, in whose system of Tuition this was a master-spring.— Pray my dear Charles let us hear of you from time to time—above all don't omit telling us immediately, when any plan of life, or course of employment, may open upon you. We hear of Chris: and his Family from Wm who is now for a few days in London.

I am truly glad to see your Winchester Discourses advertized.

Notwithstanding our anxieties and distresses, we are pretty well, though your Aunt has been a good deal shattered lately.

ever my dear Charles your affectionate Uncle
W. Wordsworth

158. *To* William Boxall

[21 May 1846]

My dear Mr. Boxall,

I shall be well pleased to receive Mr. Ruskin's second volume[1] both for its own sake and as a token of your kind remembrance. In your letter, for which accept my sincere thanks, I wish you had been able to mention that you found for your pencil more interesting

[1] Of *Modern Painters.*

employment than mere portraits, but I am afraid that little else is suitable to English demand.

Turner is undoubtedly a man of extraordinary genius, but like many others he has not forborne abusing his gift. It pleases me to learn that Mr. Ruskin has modified some of his extreme opinions concerning this artist, because, as I believe you know, I think very highly of Mr. R's talents and that he has given abundant proof how closely he has observed and how deeply he has reflected. I shall have the pleasure of receiving your present of the volume in ten days or a fortnight at the latest through the hands of some Ambleside friends now in London.

I don't know whether you are acquainted with the works of Luca Giordano—he is a clever painter. My son picked up at Lucca three large pictures of his which now hang in my staircase, which they exactly fill. One is Vulcan presenting to Venus the armour he has forged for her Aneas, the other Diana hanging over Endymion on Mount Latmos, and the third, a scene from Ariosto or Tasso, of a lady bending over her dead lover, who has been slain. These pictures cost John but little on the spot and I shall take care that he does not lose the purchase. They have cost me a good deal putting into order.

Mrs. W. is glad to be remembered by you and joins me in kind regards. Believe me, dear Mr. Boxall, faithfully your much obliged
Wm Wordsworth

Rydal Mount—1846.
21st May—a glorious day for beauty. I wish you could see how lovely our country is at this fine season.

159. *To* Isabella Fenwick[1]

Rydal Mount Monday Morning [July 1847]

We are much comforted beloved Friend by learning from your letter to Mr Quillinan that you are able to come to us. To no other quarter could we look for support so precious as we shall have in and from you.—Wm is here and will be able to stay till the end of

[1] On the death of Dora Q.

the week—I enter into no particulars as you will soon hear every thing from our own mouths. Pray make all the arrangements you can to facilitate your remaining with us as long as possible—

God almighty bless you!—ever your most affectionate Friends
William and Mary Wordsworth

You say nothing about your Brother—does he still think of coming to England? or rather is he able to encounter the journey?—

160. *To* J. P. Nichol

Rydal Mount
near Ambleside
Augst 1846.

Mr Wordsworth is much obliged by Professor Nichol's kindness in transmitting to him Mr Longfellow's Poem, Evangeline.[1] Mr W— is sorry for the mistake which occasioned Mr Nichol some additional trouble—

Mr Longfellow's Poem is obviously in metre and in manner and matter, after the model of Voss' Louisie[2] a Poem which used to be as popular in Germany as the *Metre* would allow, which does not suit modern Languages. In our own we have no spondees, and are therefor obliged to substitute trochaics, or to make spondees out of the end of one word and the beginning of the next.

What Mr Nichol says of the attention paid to Mr W's Poems in America accords with what Mr W has had the pleasure of hearing from several other quarters. What a momentous obligation does the spread of the English Language impose upon the Persons who write in it. It has already taken the lead of the French, and will I must hope keep the precedence

[1] Longfellow's narrative poem on the Acadians of Canada, publ. 1847.
[2] *Luise*, by Johann Heinrich Voss (1751–1826), which S. T. C. had planned to translate into English hexameters.

161. *To* John Peace

Brigham[1] [*c.* 17 Nov. 1848]

My dear Friend,

Mrs Wordsworth has deputed to me the acceptable office of answering your friendly letter, which has followed us to Brigham, upon the banks of the river Derwent, near Cockermouth, the birthplace of four brothers and their sister. Of these four I, the second, am now the only one left. Am I wrong in supposing that you have been here? The house was driven out of its place by a railway, and stands now not nearly so advantageously for a prospect of this beautiful country, though at only a small distance from its former situation.

We are expecting Cuthbert Southey[2] to-day from his curacy seven or eight miles distant. He is busy in carrying through the press the first volume of his father's letters, or rather collecting and preparing them for it. Do you happen to have any in your possession? If so, be so kind as to let me or his son know what they are, if you think they contain anything which would interest the public. . . .

Mrs W. and I are, thank God, both in good health, and possessing a degree of strength beyond what is usual at our age, being both in our seventy-ninth year. The beloved daughter whom it has pleased God to remove from this anxious and sorrowful world I have not mentioned; but I can judge of the depth of your fellow-feeling for us. Many thanks to you for referring to the text in Scripture which I quoted to you so long ago. 'Thy kingdom come. Thy will be done.' He who does not find support and consolation there will find it nowhere. God grant that it may be continued to me and mine, and to all sufferers! Believe me, with Mrs W.'s very kind remembrance,

Faithfully yours,
Wm Wordsworth

[1] John W.'s parish.   [2] Southey's younger son.

162. *To* David Leitch

Friday—8 Dec^br 1848—

My dear Sir,

You have obliged me much by the attention which you have so readily paid to the little Property at Applethwaite, which as you know is interesting to me far beyond its pecuniary value.

My wishes are that encroachments should be prevented upon what is now Common, and that the Larches in the Plantation should give way to the Oaks wherever the latter are likely to thrive;—and that reasonable repairs when wanted should be made in the Dwelling House or Houses.[1] This, with the repetition of my sincere thanks, is all that I have to say at present.

Early in spring if our lives are spared and our health continues Mary and I will profit by your hospitality again.

We have no news from this neighbourhood.

Kind love to Mary[2] and yourself in which my Wife joins—

ever faithfully
your *much* obliged
Wm Wordsworth

[1] W. W. never lived at Applethwaite himself, but his son William did, at a later date.

[2] Leitch's daughter.

Suggestions for Further Reading

*

Where possible, the latest available edition is cited.

LETTERS, PROSE, AND JOURNALS

The Letters of William and Dorothy Wordsworth, ed. Ernest de Selincourt, 2nd enlarged edition: *The Early Years*, ed. Chester L. Shaver (Oxford, 1967). *The Middle Years*, Part 1, ed. Mary Moorman (Oxford, 1969). *The Middle Years*, Part 2, ed. Mary Moorman and Alan G. Hill (Oxford, 1970). *The Later Years*, Parts 1, 2, and 3, ed. Alan G. Hill (Oxford, 1978–9, 1982); Part 4, and Supplement to *The Middle Years*, ed. Alan G. Hill, forthcoming.

Letters of Dorothy Wordsworth, A selection ed. Alan G. Hill (Oxford Paperbacks, 1981).

The Prose Works of William Wordsworth, ed. W. J. B. Owen and Jane Worthington Smyser (3 vols., Oxford, 1974).

The Illustrated Wordsworth's Guide to the Lakes, ed. Peter Bicknell (Exeter, 1984).

Journals of Dorothy Wordsworth, ed. Mary Moorman (Oxford Paperbacks, 1971).

POEMS

The Poetical Works of William Wordsworth, ed. T. Hutchinson, rev. Ernest de Selincourt (Oxford Paperbacks, 1978).

The Prelude, ed. Ernest de Selincourt, A new edition rev. Stephen Gill (Oxford Paperbacks, 1970).

MEMOIRS AND BIOGRAPHY

THOMAS DE QUINCEY, *Recollections of the Lakes and the Lake Poets*, ed. David Wright (Penguin English Library, 1972).

JOHN E. JORDAN, *De Quincey to Wordsworth, A Biography of a Relationship* (Berkeley, Calif., 1962).

H. M. MARGOLIOUTH, *Wordsworth and Coleridge, 1795–1834* (Oxford, 1953).

MARY MOORMAN, *William Wordsworth, A Biography:* I, *The Early Years*, II, *The Later Years* (Oxford Paperbacks, 1968).

For critical studies, consult J. V. Logan, *Wordsworthian Criticism: A Guide and Bibliography* (Columbus, Ohio, 1947), and E. F. Henley and D. H. Stam, *Wordsworthian Criticism, 1945–1964* (New York, 1965).

Subject Index

*

ON HIS OWN LIFE:

on his own talents, 8; intends to take Orders, 10; plans periodical, 16–20; his future prospects, 20; at Racedown, 22–5; at Alfoxden, 25–8; settles at Dove Cottage, 33–5, 82, 89; skating, 34, 207; autobiographical sketch, 44, 277; as letter-writer, 50, 55, 61, 63, 68; settles affairs with Lord Lowther, 57–9, 169; the Applethwaite estate, 63, 64–5, 323; sets up Grasmere Volunteers, 65; moves to Allan Bank, 107; his love for M. W., 129, 131; seeks situation from Lord Lonsdale, 149–51, 155; moves to Rydal Mount, 164; on his portrait, 189; engraved portrait, 271; Miss Gillies's portrait, 298; on his neighbours, 197; on his eye trouble, 206, 212, 218–19, 227, 255, 262, 281, 287, 289, 300; attends funeral, 210, 304; on his Distributorship, 224; on Rydal, 227; buys Dora's field, 233; plans cottage, 312; on his visitors, 249–50, 313; as godfather to Rotha Quillinan, 263; tries to transfer Distributorship to W. W., jnr., 265–6; receives honorary degree at Durham, 294, at Oxford, 297; sends condolences to Bowles, 311; attends Queen's Ball, 314

FAMILY:

on M. W., 129, 131, portrait, 298; on D. W., her Italian studies, 25, keeps house for John W. at Whitwick, 237, illness, 246, 257, 261, 268, 316; on C. W., 21, 130, 234, Priscilla's death, 183–4; on the death of his brother John, 76–82, 311; his relations with Richard W., 128, 169, R. W.'s second marriage, 170, his death, 189–90; on Annette Vallon and Caroline, 40, M. Baudouin, 197, 278; on his own children, 133, 147–8, 171; on John, 69, 219, 223, 234, 237, 250, marriage, 246; death of Catharine, 161; death of Thomas, 161–3; on W. W., jnr., 207, 234; on Dora, 246, 252, her marriage to E. Q., 295–7, her ill health, 314, death, 322; on his nephew Charles, 246, 255, 319; death of S. H., 268

FRIENDS:

on Raisley Calvert, 17, 20, 21; on S. T. C., 26, 70, 75, 78, 82, 88, 90, 118–19, 125–6, 136, quarrel, 151–2, 156, 158, 160, 177, 199, death, 264; on Godwin, 35–6; on Southey, 67, 223, 239, remarriage, 292, his letters, 322; on Sir George Beaumont, 93; on Basil Montagu, 106–7; on Bowles, 157; on Hartley and Sara Coleridge, 176–7; on De Quincey, 196, 235; on J. C. Hare, 223, on Hartley C., 235, 239; on Lord Lonsdale, 247; on Scott, 248; on Humphry Davy, 255; selects Lamb's letters for publication, 269–70; *Guesses at Truth*, 288; on Bishop Doane, 301; on Dr Arnold, 313–14; on Isabella Fenwick, 321

INTERESTS AND OPINIONS:

on his admiration of Nature, 4; on the Swiss, the French, and the Italians, 5; on his political opinions, 12–13, 14–15, 222, change, 214–17; on learning languages, 31; on friendship, 61, 86, 228; on Oxford and Cambridge universities, 71; on landscape

*More Oxford
Paperbacks*

Details of other Oxford Paperbacks are given on the following pages. A complete list of Oxford Paperbacks, including the World's Classics, Past Masters, OPUS, and Twentieth-Century Classics series, can be obtained from the General Publicity Department, Oxford University Press, Walton Street, Oxford OX2 6DP.

JOURNALS OF
DOROTHY WORDSWORTH

Edited by Mary Moorman
Introduction by Helen Darbishire

Dorothy Wordsworth was not only the cherished companion of two great poets but herself a poet in prose. The journals she kept at Alfoxden in 1789, when her brother and Coleridge were composing the *Lyrical Ballads*, and at Grasmere from 1800 to 1803, when she and Wordsworth were living at Dove Cottage, are more than a valuable record of their day-to-day life, for Dorothy combined an intense and minute observation of nature with a genuine poetic imagination, whose influence can be seen in many of Wordsworth's poems of the period, printed in an appendix to this volume.

LETTERS OF
DOROTHY WORDSWORTH

A Selection

Edited by Alan G. Hill

In this selection of Dorothy Wordsworth's letters, a
companion to Dorothy's *Journals*, Alan G. Hill presents
seventy complete letters drawn from the new and enlarged
edition of *The Letters of William and Dorothy Wordsworth* (of
which he is General Editor). They have been chosen to
provide a portrait of the writer and her milieu, and can be
read as a continuous narrative, following the course of her
life from youth until the onset of her last tragic illness.

THE PRELUDE

William Wordsworth

Edited by Ernest de Selincourt
A new edition, corrected by Stephen Gill

The Prelude, Wordsworth's great autobiographical poem, is crucial to our understanding of his life and poetry. It was written between 1798 and 1805, when it was read to Coleridge, but the text first published in 1850, after the poet's death, had been subjected to intensive revision in his later years. This volume, first published in the Oxford Standard Authors series, contains the original version of 1805, edited from manuscripts and with an Introduction and Notes by Ernest de Selincourt.

WORDSWORTH: POETICAL WORKS

Revised by Ernest de Selincourt

This edition of Wordsworth's poems contains every piece
of verse known to have been published by the poet himself,
or of which he authorized the posthumous publication.
The text, which Thomas Hutchinson based largely upon
the 1849–50 standard edition—the last issued during the
poet's lifetime—was revised in 1936 for the Oxford
Standard Authors series by Ernest de Selincourt.

GUIDE TO THE LAKES

William Wordsworth

Complete with illustrations, notes, and a map, this is the best-selling guide to the part of England that inspired one of its greatest poets.

'the archetypal book for the Lake District connoisseur . . . a classic of committed prose about a passionately loved landscape' *Melvyn Bragg*

COLERIDGE: POETICAL WORKS

Edited by Ernest Hartley Coleridge

This edition by Ernest Hartley Coleridge, grandson of the poet, contains a complete and authoritative text of Coleridge's poems. Here are his earliest extant teenage poems, his masterly meditative pieces, and the extraordinary supernatural poems—'The Rime of the Ancient Mariner', 'Kubla Khan', and 'Christabel'.

The text follows that of the 1834 edition, the last published in the author's lifetime. The poems are printed, so far as is possible, in chronological order, with Coleridge's own notes as well as textual and bibliographical notes by the editor.

ROMANTICS, REBELS AND REACTIONARIES

English Literature and its Background 1760–1830

Marilyn Butler

This book takes a fresh look at one of the most fertile periods in English literature, an age which produced writers of the stature of Blake, Keats, Coleridge, Byron, Scott and Jane Austen. In following the cross-currents of culture and history Dr Butler provides a new insight into Romanticism itself.

'Dr Butler is brilliantly acute . . . at restoring to literary works the subdued political ticks and rumblings which the alarmed ears of their first readers would have picked up.' John Carey, *Sunday Times*

'Why has it not been done before?, one asks of Marilyn Butler's excellent new book, which analyses the diverse writers of the Romantic period exclusively—but also exhaustively and subtly—in political and ideological terms.' *Listener*

An OPUS book